Norwegian Newspapers in America

Norwegian Newspapers *in America*

Connecting Norway and the New Land

ODD S. LOVOLL

Minnesota Historical Society Press

The publication of this book was supported though a generous grant from The Bean Family Fund for Business History

 For information, write to the Minnesota Historical Society Press, 345 Kellogg Blvd. W., St. Paul, MN 55102-1906.

www.mhspress.org

The Minnesota Historical Society Press is a member of the Association of American University Presses.

Manufactured in the United States of America

10 9 8 7 6 5 4 3 2 1

∞ The paper used in this publication meets the minimum requirements of the American National Standard for Information Sciences—Permanence for Printed Library Materials, ANSI Z39.48-1984.

International Standard Book Number
ISBN: 978-0-87351-772-0 (paper)
ISBN: 978-0-87351-796-6 (e-book)

Library of Congress Cataloging-in-Publication Data
Lovoll, Odd Sverre.
Norwegian newspapers in America : connecting Norway and the new land / Odd S. Lovoll.
p. cm.
Includes bibliographical references and index.
ISBN 978-0-87351-772-0 (pbk. : alk. paper) — ISBN 978-0-87351-796-6 (e-book)
1. Norwegian American newspapers—History.
2. Ethnic press—United States—History. I. Title.
PN4885.N6L68 2010
071'.30893982073—dc22

2009053296

FRONT COVER: Laurits Stavnheim studio portrait, Institute for Regional Studies, NDSU, Fargo (Mss 325.10.1)
BACK COVER: Carl Søyland and Sigurd Daasvand reading *Nordisk Tidende,* courtesy the newspaper

For the men and women who founded
and through the years sustained
a Norwegian press in America

Contents

Preface and Acknowledgments

"We hereby have the true pleasure of presenting the first number of *Nordlyset,*" the newspaper's publishers announced on July 29, 1847. The weekly organ would give those who could not read English-language newspapers "an opportunity to acquire knowledge especially about this country's government. . . . In addition to general information, history, farming, and religious news—[and] contributions from private individuals and everything else that may be suitable and useful for enlightenment and entertainment for our readers." This, the first Norwegian-language newspaper in the Midwest, was a precursor to an institution that would flourish and inform the immigrant community over generations.

Some 280 Norwegian American secular periodicals have been recorded between 1847 and 2010, published weekly, semiweekly, or daily; they were, as their mastheads occasionally noted, *American* newspapers printed in the Norwegian language. The role of the foreign-language press in general and the Norwegian-language press in particular has held a special scholarly fascination for me since the late 1960s, when I wrote my master's thesis on the Norwegian immigrant press in North Dakota based on the extensive holdings of the Chester Fritz Library at the University of North Dakota in Grand Forks. The newspapers' yellowing pages printed in Gothic script and an archaic Dano-Norwegian linguistic form were intriguing and engrossing sources to an understanding of the immigrant world of bygone days. Their perusal became an engaging and stimulating experience.

The Norwegian ethnic press, whether published in a country town or in a bustling urban center, provided a link with the old country and access to the new land. It pursued several roles, functioning not only as a bridge to the homeland but also as both a preserver of Norwegian culture and an Americanizer. The hypothesis of the present study holds that these separate roles did not conflict but were played out simultaneously, and even complemented each other.

A chronological approach shows how the Norwegian press adjusted to changing circumstances and contingencies and responded to specific issues of the day during the century and a half of its existence. Geographically, Norwegian-language periodicals advanced from their start in the Upper Midwest to other regions of Norwegian settlement from coast to coast, becoming a national press and creating a sense of a Norwegian America. The growth and maintenance of Norwegian American newspapers related to the volume of Norwegian immigration and preservation of the Norwegian language. The Norwegian immigrant press began modestly under pioneer conditions on the American frontier; it reached its height in the decades before the Great War, serving a large and self-confident Norwegian American community. Beginning in the 1920s, the Norwegian press experienced a troubling decline; many of the major periodicals ceased publication in the 1930s. In the post–World War II years, the viability of a Norwegian press was very much an issue; to most observers its days were numbered. A diminishing population attuned to the Norwegian language and consequently a loss of subscribers led many newspapers to close up shop. The surviving journals were published for the few and increasingly appealed to an English-speaking readership.

Files of Norwegian American newspapers now exist mainly on microfilm, which aids preservation and is more efficient but deprives students of the press the opportunity to physically touch the original newsprint. Through the magic of interlibrary loan, microfilms from various repositories made their appearance in the St. Olaf College Library, Northfield, Minnesota. The library staff maintained a warm and welcoming environment in which to conduct the major portion of my research. I would most especially like to thank Brian Conlan, interlibrary loan associate, currently reference and instruction librarian, who engaged himself in the project far beyond his library responsibilities and became an enthusiastic co-researcher and attentive assistant in a variety of capacities, such as locating newspaper repositories, identifying library resources, and producing facsimiles of selected newspaper fronts. Inga Velde, library circulation, cheerfully welcomed me when I arrived in the early morning hours and was consistently helpful; Dawn Moder arranged interlibrary loans toward the end of the research. I also wish to express my appreciation to the library staff in general and to the many student workers who took an interest in the research.

Repositories of Norwegian American newspapers exist in state and local historical societies, in college and university libraries, and in special collections throughout the United States. Files of major periodicals may be located in more than one repository.

The Luther College Library, Decorah, Iowa, has the largest collection of files of Norwegian American periodicals. A compilation by Oivind M. Hovde and Martha E. Henzler from 1975 titled *Norwegian-American Newspapers in Luther College Library* identifies the library's holdings. I wish to thank Jane Kemp, professor of library and information studies at Luther College, for generously allowing me to retain library materials beyond posted deadlines. The St. Olaf College Library has a significant holding of newspaper files, both national and regional. I also received microfilms from the following repositories: Minnesota Historical Society; Wisconsin Library Services; State Historical Society of Wisconsin; South Dakota State Archives; University of North Dakota Library; University of Utah Library; Washington State Library; University of Washington Libraries; Swedish-American Archives of Greater Chicago at North Park University; New York State Library. I thank them all most sincerely.

I enjoyed full access to the archival collections of St. Olaf College and the Norwegian-American Historical Association (NAHA), encouraged and assisted by Professor Gary DeKrey, college and NAHA archivist, and by Jeff Sauve, associate archivist. At the Minnesota Historical Society, Deborah Miller, reference specialist, as in earlier projects was a knowledgeable and enthusiastic guide in the research process. Longtime friend and frequent well-wisher Chuck Haga, currently senior writer for the *Grand Forks Herald* and for twenty years staff writer for the *Minneapolis Star Tribune,* deserves a word of gratitude for his generous reporting on my research and my published works. I should also like to thank Kim Nesselquist, honorary Norwegian consul, executive director and CEO of the Norwegian American Foundation, for his invitation to share the story of the Norwegian American press with an interested audience in Seattle, Washington, and for his warm hospitality during my visit, and Terje I. Leiren, Sverre Arestad Endowed Professor in Norwegian Studies, University of Washington, for his friendship and support of the press study.

My greatest benefactor in Norway was the Freedom of Expression Foundation/*Institusjonen Fritt Ord.* A generous grant from the foundation facilitated research and enabled me to give full time to the project's completion. For some months during the fall of 2007, Vidar Bjørnsen from Tromsø, Norway, joined me as a research assistant, supported by the *Fritt Ord* grant; he conscientiously read newspaper files and engaged in well-grounded discussions. I am greatly indebted to Dina Tolfsby, curator of the Norwegian-American Collection at the National Library of Norway, Oslo, who tirelessly and with imagination identified sources and images and communicated these to me on a regular basis. Jostein Molde, editorial associate, *Lokalhistorisk magasin* (Magazine of Local History), and Harry T. Cleven, editor, *The Norseman,* introduced the project in articles in their respective magazines. I thank Lis Byberg, University College in Oslo, for information on literacy. The research benefited from my association with the Norwegian Association for Media History and its distinguished members in journalism, with Knut Sprauten, director of the Norwegian Institute of Local History, and with Einar Niemi, professor of history, University of Tromsø. I thank Martin Nag for his gift of two booklets of letters printed in *Visergutten* and Jørn-Kr. Jørgensen for securing for me the two-volume history of *Nordisk Tidende.*

I am indebted to Professor J. R. Christianson, Luther College, who served as external reviewer, for his careful reading of the manuscript and for his reassuring and helpful commentary, to Julie Odland for her meticulous editing of the text, and to Shannon Pennefeather for her expert partnering in preparing the manuscript for publication. Mary R. Hove, longtime assistant when I served as

NAHA's editor, prepared the index. I thank all those who aided in selecting appropriate illustrative images and the many repositories that granted free permission to reproduce the images. My wife, Else Lovoll, has been my most patient and encouraging supporter during the years given over to research and writing, for which I thank her with much affection and gratitude.

This history is dedicated to the men and women who founded and sustained Norwegian newspapers in America. The contributions of these servants of the press to the life and adjustment of an immigrant people can never be adequately gauged or appreciated, even taking into account the many individual motives—both self-serving and more noble—that encouraged their entry into the uncertain world of ethnic newspaper publishing. Regardless of the cause they advanced or personal incentives, the men and women who engaged in Norwegian journalism in America steadfastly offered an invaluable service to the Norwegian American community, to American society, and to the Norwegian homeland.

Norwegian Newspapers in America

CHAPTER 1

Pioneer Years

The press has become a power
in all languages in this country.

WITH THIS PITHY STATEMENT, the Chicago journal *Skandinaven* (The Scandinavian)—destined to become the largest Norwegian-language newspaper in the United States and, indeed, for some time the entire world—in January 1888 assessed the influence of the press in America. Newspapers were a part of American life and exhibited a basic community-building function. The press made its way into villages and country towns and flourished in large urban centers. The history of American journalism extends back to the early eighteenth century with the establishment in 1704 of the first successful continuous newspaper in the colonies, the *Boston News-Letter.* In their multitude of visages and objectives in the ensuing centuries, newspapers shaped and challenged the new nation. The press became a powerful cultural, social, and political institution through shifting historical and social circumstances. The pioneer Norwegian newspaperman Knud Langeland was clearly correct when he described America as “the Land of Newspapers.”[1]

The non-English-language press represents a notable manifestation of American journalism; immigrant journals printed in foreign languages became nearly as commonplace as the mainstream American press. They bore witness to America as a land of immigration. The first issue of the German-language newspaper *Philadelphische Zeitung* (Philadelphia Times) appeared among German settlers in Pennsylvania the spring of 1732. Though ultimately unsuccessful, the *Zeitung* heralded establishment of a separate German-language press. The German American press was not only the earliest foreign-language press in America but throughout its history the largest. However, as Carl Wittke explains, not until German immigration picked up in the 1830s after a hiatus of over thirty years and then greatly increased in the decade before the Civil War did the German-language press expand significantly. Large numbers of new German immigrants, particularly hundreds of political refugees of the 1848 revolution, arrived, and many of the Forty-Eighters became active in journalism and spread their reform message in the German-language press.

Immigration from Norway, Denmark, and Sweden inspired journals published in Dano-Norwegian and Swedish to appear in that same decade; in the postbellum years, immigrants from many other parts of the world created increased diversity at a rapid pace; newspapers appeared in Yiddish, Russian, Slovak, Czech, Greek, Italian, Polish, Finnish, and many other mother tongues foreign to most Americans. Thus, the foreign-language press in the United States has endured since colonial days, not in competition with but as a special expression of American journalism alongside the much larger English-language press. Robert E. Park in *The Immigrant Press and Its Control* determined that in 1919 there were "forty-three or forty-four languages and dialects spoken by immigrant peoples in the United States." He continued, "Each one of these little communities is certain to have some sort of co-operative or mutual aid society, very likely a church, a school, possibly a theater, but almost invariably a press." In *The German-language Press in America,* Wittke concurs, stating, "There is scarcely a nationality or language group in the United States, however small, that has not at some time or other supported its own press." He is obviously right in his claim, as suggested by the success of *Skandinaven,* that "there have been more foreign-language papers and periodicals published and read in America, in proportion to population, than in the home countries from which their readers came."[2]

"The mother tongue is the natural basis of human association and organization," Park states; its literary forms assumed added significance. Only through the written language could immigrant populations of the same nationality living in many parts of the United States be united. The newspapers published in the homeland's language created a sense of national ethnic communities; one may define a Norwegian America, if you will, but also a Swedish America, a German America, a Greek America, and a great number of other "imagined communities" grounded in national roots and consciousness.

The Norwegian American press was thus not unique but part of a general phenomenon among the many immigrant groups as well as in American society more broadly. In its initial issue, dated June 1, 1866, *Skandinaven* explained how for several years "a strong general wish among Norwegians in Chicago [was] to have a newspaper in the ancestral language published here." *Skandinaven*'s publishers continued, "Many were completely convinced that Chicago was the place . . . the large central point for the prosperous Northwest, where Scandinavians for the most part had settled; here the Norwegian news reports from all regions of the country were most available; from here the many railroad lines branched out across the states of Illinois, Wisconsin, Iowa, Minnesota, Missouri, Kansas etc., whereby the newspaper very quickly could reach most places where the Norwegians and Danes live."[3]

It was an optimistic beginning, and one that in this case succeeded. Many immigrant journals failed after a brief existence. Nevertheless, the immigrant press's vitality is one of the most remarkable dimensions of Norwegian American history, enjoying as it did a loyal and enthusiastic constituency. Until World War I the foreign-language press was allowed to develop with few, if any, government restrictions and regulations, free to respond to the novelty and news in the new country. For its readers, the Norwegian American press, as with other foreign-language presses, eased adjustment to the new society while retaining ties to the one left behind, all in a familiar and treasured language. Indeed, its close relationship to newspapers in Norway makes it possible to view the Norwegian American press as an extension of the homeland's press. The press was an international cultural bridge, as historian Theodore Blegen describes its function: it furnished immigrants with news about the old country, a special purpose it held, but also provided the people of Norway with news about the immigrants. The homeland's newspapers regularly reprinted articles and news items taken from the columns of Norwegian American publications.

A selection of mastheads of Norwegian American newspapers and periodicals suggests the vitality of the immigrant press.

Norwegian American newspapers powered the creation of immigrant religious and secular organizations and institutions while enabling the immigrants to retain the sacred and profane cultural traditions of the homeland. These traditions were, however, reinterpreted and reinvented in the new setting as American-born generations fashioned a positive ethnic identity. The group's place in American society and how Norwegians were viewed by competing immigrant populations and by the host society were all important considerations. The Norwegian-language press became engaged in a broader strategy of adjustment driven by these concerns.

Historians have generally based their analyses of the immigrant press on its function, a major consideration in this study, too. The foreign-language press obviously played the dual role suggested above. The question has frequently been asked whether the press, as well as other immigrant institutions, retarded assimilation or represented the first step toward it. The present treatment, concurring with Marion Marzolf in her study of the Danish American press, holds that these two functions—as a preserver of ethnic cultures and as Americanizer—did not conflict; both roles were played out simultaneously. In a broader sense, as demonstrated by Jon Gjerde in *The Minds of the West,* it was a complementary identity "that pledged allegiance to both American citizenship and ethnic adherence"—a hypothesis proposed in the present study as well. The Norwegian American press did not encourage a clannish segregation nor a passive surrender to Americanization but instead a dynamic interplay with the larger society based on ethnic social and cultural resources. Paraphrasing what this author writes elsewhere, the Norwegian immigrant press became a primary expression of the resilience of Norwegian American culture, its interaction rather than assimilation with American society, and its influence on the cultural, social, and political fabric of the American social order.[4]

A Tenuous Foundation

The Norwegian immigrant press had humble beginnings. The inception and development of Norwegian American journalism is related, to state the obvious, to early Norwegian immigration and settlement, which must be considered before moving on to a discussion of pioneer newspapers. The Kingdom of Norway was reestablished toward the end of the Napoleonic Wars in 1814 after a four-hundred-year union with Denmark; the constitution adopted at Eidsvoll on May 17 became the symbol and foundation of an independent Norway. Later that year, however, the great powers of Europe forced Norway into a union with Sweden under a common monarch, each country retaining its own national government. This union was dissolved in 1905.

Movement to the United States from Norway began with the small sloop *Restauration,* which landed in the port of New York on October 9, 1825; it had departed from the town of Stavanger on the southwest coast of Norway on July 4. This first boatload of Norwegian immigrants numbered fifty-two, passengers and crew; the birth of a baby girl during the fourteen-week voyage added one to their number.

Most of the "Sloopers" hailed from rural areas in the county of Rogaland, mainly from the community of Tysvær, and a few from Stavanger. Rather uniquely in the history of Norwegian emigration, a strong religious motivation alongside hope for a better material future encouraged them to leave the homeland. They were members or sympathizers of the Society of Friends and Haugeans, followers of the lay Lutheran religious leader Hans Nielsen Hauge. Hauge's evangelical message left a deep imprint on Norwegian Christianity; his preaching in violation of church law resulted in repeated imprisonment. Persecution by the powerful, monopolistic Norwegian Lutheran State Church's clergy united the Quakers and Haugeans. Quakerism had been brought to Norway by prisoners of war held in England between 1807 and 1814, and the Friends formed societies in Stavanger and Oslo. Together with the Haugeans, they sought religious freedom and the right of lay people to preach the word of God. The pietistic lay movement that came out of the Haugean revival would play a significant role in religious life in Norway as well as among Norwegians in America.

Land had been bought for them on the shores of Lake Ontario in Kendall Township by their agent, the enigmatic Cleng Peerson, who had gone to America in 1821 to explore conditions. After their arrival, nearly all, with the assistance of American Quakers, moved to their new location in northern New York State.

They had come to a nation on the move. News of better opportunities in the west inspired most of the Kendall colonists to move to the Fox River region southwest of Chicago during the years 1834 and 1835. This settlement, standing ready to receive newcomers, became an important mother colony. Annual emigration commenced in 1836 with about two hundred Norwegians joining their compatriots in America. That same year a Norwegian colony was formed in Chicago, which by then had a population of nearly four thousand people. By 1850, Norwegians in Illinois numbered 2,067 immigrants with an additional 422 of the second generation; the largest number resided in the Fox River settlement in LaSalle County and thereafter in Chicago in Cook County.

In the 1840s, Wisconsin became the main region of settlement for the rising tide of Norwegian immigrants. At midcentury, the state's total Norwegian population was 9,467; of these, 1,456 were born in America; Norwegians numbered 3 percent of the total population of the state, which on May 29, 1848, had joined the union as the thirtieth state. Articles in *Billed-Magazin* (Picture Magazine), edited in 1868–70 by Svein Nilsson, are a major source on early Norwegian settlement in Wisconsin. Based on personal interviews and inspired by Nilsson's interest in historical background, these articles made him "the father of Norwegian American historical writing." In a sensitive portrayal of his compatriots in America, Nilsson gives an insightful account of the founding phase of immigration and settlement in Wisconsin.

"One of the most remarkable phenomena of this century," he wrote in the magazine's first issue, October 3, 1868, "is the emigration that has taken place from Europe to the New World which Columbus discovered." Considering the later debate over discovery, Nilsson's final statement might seem somewhat surprising. He interviewed the founder of the Jefferson Prairie settlement in Rock County, Ole Nattestad, who reported that "for a whole year I did not see any countryman of mine, but lived secluded without friends, family, or companions." In 1838, Nattestad was the first Norwegian to settle in Wisconsin; pioneering was a lonely enterprise. The following year, when his brother Ansten returned from

Billed-Magazin.

No. 6.] Madison, Wisconsin den 5te Februar. [1870.

Gartnerboligen i Christiania.

Christiania Slotspark hører nu til de smukkeste Anlæg i Christiania, medens denne Del af Byen en Menneskealder tilbage i Tiden var en Udkant, en slet opdyrket Mark og kun undtagelsesvis en Del af en Løkke. Kunst og Natur have i Forening omdannet det Hele, og især er Haven paa Syd- og Vestsiden af Slottet det vakreste offentlige Anlæg, der staar aabent for Almenheden. Vort Billede viser Gartnerboligen med nærliggende Drivhus; rundt omkring ere mange Blomsterpartier, der fremvise ligesaa sjeldne som vakre Planter, medens et almindeligt velordnet Haveanlæg giver det Hele et venligt, hyggeligt Præg, saa at man med Glæde dvæler under de høie, skyggefulde Træer. Baade Formiddag og Eftermiddag er denne Del af Slotsparken meget besøgt; de mange Spadserende nyde her Synet og Vellugten fra de talrige Blomsterbed eller gjør sig en liden Tur

Gartnerboligen i Christiania.

rundtomkring og betragter Svanerne, der svømme om i Dammen, og som opfange de Hvedebrødsmuler, der tilkastes dem. Publikum paaskjønner ogsaa, hvad Parkanlægget yder dem af Hygge og som forfriskende Ophold[illegible] nogetsteds ser man i eller udenfor [illegible] efter et uhindret Besøg af en [illegible]ker: Publikum er her selv [illegible] Blomster, Buske og Træer [illegible]lorden begaaes. Saa[illegible] fentlige Anlæg burde [illegible] overtage et almin-

De skandinaviske Setlementer i Amerika.

(Fortsættelse fra No. 5).

Pleasant Spring.

Men saa fik jeg efter to Ugers Forløb Besøg af Nykommerens farligste Fiende, Klimatfeberen, der i hine Dage sjelden gik nogen forbi, og her, blandt lutter Fremmede og ubekjendt med Sproget, blev jeg for nogen Tid fængslet til Sygeleiet. Til Forladthedens Kvaler sluttede sig Længsler efter Venner og Hjemland, idet Minderne fra Ungdommens glade Dage i vexlende Skikkelser fremmanedes for mit aandelige Blik og op-

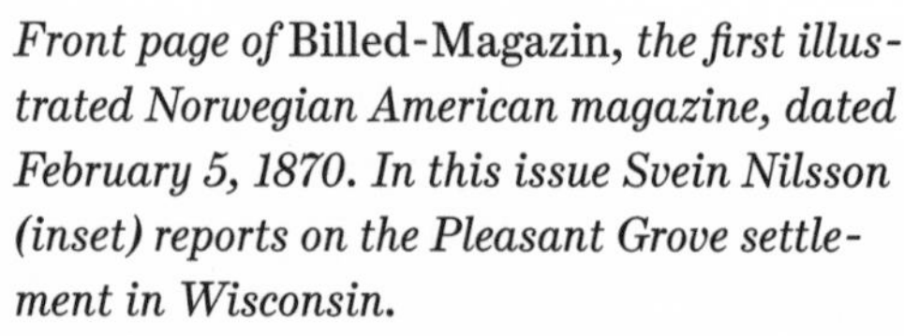

Front page of Billed-Magazin, *the first illustrated Norwegian American magazine, dated February 5, 1870. In this issue Svein Nilsson (inset) reports on the Pleasant Grove settlement in Wisconsin.*

Norway with a large group of people, the Rock Prairie settlement, or Luther Valley settlement, farther west became a second Norwegian enclave in the state.

While the Rock Prairie settlement was being established, the Muskego settlement was founded near Lake Muskego in Waukesha County southwest of Milwaukee; it became one of America's most noteworthy pioneer Norwegian settlements. In Dane County, on the prairies surrounding the capital city of Madison, a circle of communities came into being. The Koshkonong settlement, founded in 1840, was perhaps the most important of the early ones in Wisconsin; it grew large by beautiful Lake Koshkonong, comprising the four townships of Dunkirk, Albion, Christiana, and Pleasant Springs in eastern Dane and western Jefferson counties. It prospered so that in 1870 Nilsson could state, "It seems as if here our countrymen first found the America of which they had heard such wonderful stories in their homeland."

Settlement in western Wisconsin began toward the end of the 1840s. The pioneers were from Muskego and Koshkonong; much of the desirable land in southeastern Wisconsin had by then been taken. The pioneer period in western Wisconsin belongs mainly to the decades of the 1850s through the '70s. The coulee country along the Mississippi River, from Crawford to Barron counties, in time became solidly settled by Norwegian pioneers; the famous Coon Valley and Coon Prairie settlements in Vernon County were established in 1848. Wisconsin remained the center of Norwegian American activity until the Civil War. By then, the state was home to 29,557 Norwegians; of these, 9,598 were born in Wisconsin. In their main regions of settlement, Norwegian pioneers exhibited a strong and influential presence.[5]

The First Norwegian Newspaper in the Midwest

The desire for a separate Norwegian newspaper arose among "the more enlightened emigrated Norwegian peasants," Knud Langeland wrote in 1888. It was an idea whose time had come. In 1846, several Norwegians, among these Gudmund Haugaas, a passenger on the *Restauration* and a convert to the Church of Jesus Christ of Latter-day Saints, attempted to establish a newspaper in Chicago titled *De Norskes Opmærksomhed* (The Norwegians' Observer). This early impulse was followed by the weekly *Nordlyset* (Northern Lights), a small four-page publication whose first issue is dated July 29, 1847, with a postal address at Norway, Racine County, Wisconsin. It was "printed by Bache, Heg, and Reymert, and edited by J. D. Reymert"—some of the enlightened men to whom Langeland referred. The newspaper was actually printed in Even Heg's log cabin in Muskego, a "mother colony" with an exceptional group of leaders. Heg, the son of a prosperous farmer from Lier, Norway, was influenced by the Haugean religious conviction and became a pragmatic leader of the Muskego settlement, having arrived there in 1840. Søren Bache, the son of Tollef Bache, a well-to-do lumber merchant in Drammen, came to the Fox River settlement from Norway in 1839 and moved to Muskego the following year. Before returning to Norway in 1847, he recorded the life of the settlement in a unique diary, published as *A Chronicle of Old Muskego*. James Denoon Reymert, a lawyer by training from Farsund, Norway, was a prominent member of the settlement; his association with *Nordlyset* became a springboard into American politics.[6]

A Scandinavian joint organ, *Skandinavia,* published by the Scandinavian colony in New York with entries in Dano-Norwegian and Swedish, preceded *Nordlyset* by some months and may arguably be seen as "the first Norwegian-Danish newspaper in America," as Juul Dieserud stated in an article published in 1929. An organized Scandinavian society was responsible for launching the newspaper in January 1847. Adopting a pan-Scandinavian tone, it carried news from the three countries. It is of interest to note that eighty-three of the 220 subscribers in May 1847 were Norwegian settlers in Wisconsin. It was edited by the Dane Hans Peter Christian Hansen, the son of a Copenhagen instrument maker; he was educated as a scientist and had been employed in Copenhagen and Oslo (Christiania) before emigrating in 1846. This pioneer newspaper enterprise did not succeed; Dieserud identifies only eight semimonthly issues. A notice in number five may have added interest: "In Rochester in Wisconsin according to a correspondence from the same place, 'a Scandinavian weekly' will shortly be published. Its purpose will be to give our countrymen in Wisconsin, Illinois, and Iowa news from home as well as from America. . . .

Nordlyset

"Vi ere vort Pligt, til nyttig Lærdoms Lys, Før med fornyet Kraft, at øve hen paany."

No. 1. Norway, Racine County, Wisconsin. — Tirsdagen den 29de Juli 1847. 1ste Aargang.

The front page of the first issue of Nordlyset, *dated July 29, 1847, with postal address in Norway, Racine County, Wisconsin.*

It will please us if this venture, which we by no means consider a rival, will succeed."[7]

A significant point is that *Nordlyset* was launched by lay leaders rather than the Lutheran clergy, especially when considering religion's dominance in the Norwegian immigrant community in general, including the pioneer press. The three men listed in the initial issue, Bache, Heg, and Reymert, entered into a contractual agreement on March 22, 1847, to in equal shares purchase a printing press and other requisites to carry on a printing business in Muskego. Entries in Søren Bache's diary describe preparations for publishing a newspaper; the June 8, 1847, entry records the establishment of a post office "in our newly created township, with Even Heg duly appointed and sworn in as postmaster." Bache believed the postal business would prosper once a newspaper was started. A printing press was ordered from Philadelphia. Eric Anderson was hired as compositor and set the type of the initial issue. Anderson immigrated with his family to Chicago from Voss in 1839 at the age of twelve and early on entered the printing trade, working as a pressman on the *Chicago Democrat,* the city's first newspaper, launched in late 1833.[8]

Editorial responsibility remained in Reymert's hands until the February 1, 1849, issue, when he left to pursue a political career; *Nordlyset*'s press had by then been moved to the neighboring village of Rochester. In late fall, Knud Langeland wrote, "I committed the folly of purchasing the press from Heg and Reymert and with O. J. Hatlestad as co-owner we moved it to Racine and in 1850 began publishing *Nordlyset* anew." The final ten issues edited by Langeland appeared from March 9 to May 18, 1850. With the next issue, June 8, the name had been changed to *Democraten,* first published in Racine and later in Janesville; this paper, to quote Langeland, "did not get the necessary support and for that reason was discontinued after one and a half years." The last issue is dated October 29, 1851.

Langeland's *Nordmændene i Amerika* (The Norwegians in America) contains what he described as an "Old Subscription List" for *Nordlyset* and *Democraten;* analysis of the list illustrates the newspapers' distribution. The names of 278 subscribers are included, 70 percent in Wisconsin, 26 percent in Illinois, and the remaining

4 percent in Iowa, Indiana, Missouri, New York, and Rhode Island. Chicago alone had twenty-five subscribers. "It is a list," Langeland insisted, "of enlightened and broadminded progressive men, whose memory deserves to be preserved as long as their descendants live in the American West." *Nordlyset* and *Democraten* were read by many in addition to subscribers. Ole Huset informed *Nordlyset*'s editor that he had not signed on because "My closest neighbor Thor Kittelsen has subscribed to *Nordlyset* and I have the opportunity to read it by paying half the subscription price and half the postage." Such arrangements, likely not uncommon, gained readers but not additional income.

As political organs, Langeland surmised, *Nordlyset* and *Democraten* were premature, and one might add that Norwegian immigrants were likely not yet ready to sustain a separate Norwegian-language press. Of peasant background, they were not accustomed to subscribing to newspapers, which were costly and not necessary to their simple way of life. According to Arlow W. Andersen, "Before the turbulent 1880s, the press in Norway directed itself mainly toward the social and intellectual elite." The contrast between the Old World and the New was striking in this regard, but not immediately; poverty and to some extent lack of schooling were additional barriers. Another hardship was the cholera epidemic in 1849–52, which affected most Norwegian pioneer settlements, taking many lives. Muskego, with its unhealthy marshy landscape, was especially afflicted, draining people of resources.

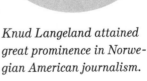

Knud Langeland.

Knud Langeland attained great prominence in Norwegian American journalism.

Literacy was commonplace among Norwegian immigrants, although illiteracy was by no means unknown, especially in the pioneer migration. A literacy survey in Wisconsin in 1870 determined that 48 percent of the parents of Norwegian children attending school could not read or write any language; the percentage seems high and is at odds with studies made in Norway. The findings might, as even suggested by the study itself, be a result of Norwegian immigrants having thought the question was in regard to literacy in English and not in their native language, though Norwegian census takers were employed in some districts.

In assessing literacy rates, the cultural divide that existed between the Dano-Norwegian language employed by the government, the clergy, and the press on the one hand and the multitude of dialectal variations spoken throughout the country on the other must be borne in mind. In the American setting, the consecrated usage of the formal Dano-Norwegian literary forms—a legacy of the centuries-long union with Denmark—in religious services gave comfort and a sense of continuity; it was, however, for the ordinary immigrant a book language, different from their local vernaculars transplanted from farming communities in Norway's valleys and along its fjords. An examination of the so-called "America letters"—correspondence back home to friends and kin—suggests that immigrants did indeed learn to write Dano-Norwegian or, perhaps more to the point, an approximation of it.

Norway's Department of Church and Education in 1840 published "Statistics concerning the educational system in Norway," based on carefully assembled and analyzed information from 1837 and providing a compelling and insightful portrait of Norwegian society at the start of the transatlantic exodus. These statistics may clarify the challenges faced by pioneer newspaper publishers among Norwegian compatriots in America. In 1837, there were 175,000 school-age children in rural communities in Norway; compulsory school attendance began at age seven; most children who enrolled left school at age twelve in order to "be of help to parents at home." Children numbering 1,624 and mainly from the class of government officials were privately tutored; 8,200 children did not attend school, due mainly to poverty, lack of clothing, or illness and in some cases because of parental "ill will." More than 90 percent—160,000 children—were taught by ambulatory teachers in homes; only 10 percent—15,500—attended permanent schools. Reading and religious knowledge, i.e., Lutheran, exemplified by Luther's Small Catechism, were the main subjects; only 35,000—22 percent—instructed by ambulatory teachers learned to write; the permanent schools did better, with 42 percent mastering this skill.

In Norway's small urban centers, public schools were operated in connection with economic assistance; some of the schools were even officially designated as "poor relief schools" *(Fattigskoler)*. Of school-age children, 4,200 were privately tutored while 3,600 did not attend school, 2,000 because of lack of space, 1,000 due to poverty, and the remainder due to "ill will." Of the 12,000 children distributed among eighty-nine schools, as many as 8,500—71 percent—learned to write. The fact remains, then, that the vast majority of all Norwegian children, in spite of the many deficiencies in the educational system, received some schooling. The economic situation for Norwegian pioneers on the American frontier, more so than meager schooling and cultural roots, explains the difficulty in founding a Norwegian immigrant press.

This departmental report was an early link in the reforms that produced significant improvements in Norway's educational system, including an 1848 law establishing permanent public schools *(Almugeskole)* in the cities followed twelve years later by a law that did the same in rural communities; the latter replaced the ambulatory school *(Omgangsskole)* common in rural areas. The law liberated students from the old authoritarian rule of the Lutheran clergy and offered a definitive departure from the one-sided religious school to a civil one where subjects such as history, geography, and science could be taught. The literacy rate—the ability to read and write Norwegian—among peasants in Norway increased rapidly; those emigrating later in the century came educationally better prepared.[9]

What the Pioneer Press Offered

It is quite obvious that editors favored an American emphasis in their selection of materials for their readers. *Nordlyset*'s stated purpose in its initial issue was to enlighten Norwegian immigrants and provide those whose ability to read American newspapers was not adequate "with an opportunity to acquire knowledge especially about this country's government. . . . In addition to general information, history, farming, and religious news—[it promised] contributions from private individuals and everything else that may be suitable and useful for enlightenment and entertainment." American loyalty was evidenced in Norwegian translation of part of the Declaration of Independence and from time to time in later issues by stories of well-known Americans. When the state of Wisconsin in 1848 required that its newly adopted constitution appear in every newspaper in the state, *Nordlyset* devoted an entire issue to a Norwegian translation of the document.

Nordlyset announced its intent "to obtain the best Scandinavian newspapers regularly so that we then can at all times report the most important accounts in these, so that we always can be informed about what is happening in our fatherland." In the age of sailing ships—before the transatlantic telegraph cable crossed the ocean shortly after the Civil War had ended—current news was not easily communicated. In the February 24, 1848, issue, *Nordlyset*'s editor thanked the Swedish-Norwegian consul general in New York, Adam Løvenskjold, for "a pack of *Morgenbladet* to the end of August 1847." This example might not be the norm; more usual perhaps was *Democraten*'s complaint October 12, 1850, that "The newspapers from Norway arrive very irregularly, and now for some time nothing has arrived." Reports culled from the Norwegian newspapers were printed in *Nordlyset*'s February issue cited above, including information about the 1847 election to the Norwegian parliament, the *Storting*. Suggesting contact across the Atlantic, *Nordlyset* reprinted from *Morgenbladet* for August 19, 1847, news of its own appearance in July; the Norwegian journal got its information from the *Milwaukee Gazette,* which reported that there were "20 [Norwegian] colonies in Wisconsin, Illinois, and Iowa, whereof 16 in the first-mentioned territory." The newspaper then opined, "These have a population of 15 to 20,000 humble, diligent, honest, and law-abiding citizens."[10]

Nordlyset engaged in the promotion of Norwegian settlement and spurred the westward movement by printing letters by Hans Christian Heg, son of Even Heg and later a hero of the American Civil War, reporting on his and his fellow Argonauts' trek to the California gold fields in the far West. The November 4, 1847, issue carried a letter by Thore Spaanem, a pioneer settler in Blue Mounds from Valdres, Norway, "about," to quote Hjalmar Rued Holand, "the land area by Blue Mounds, and it was this piece that influenced the migration of people from Valdres [to the settlement]." Such letters foreshadowed the profusion of those carried by the immigrant press from Norwegian enclaves as well as the organized promotion of settlement seen in their columns by railroad and land companies as well as by land speculators and state agencies.

Advertising became another regular feature given much space in later publications. In his informal travel letters written in 1847 and 1848, Ole Munch Ræder, a Norwegian scholar sent by his government to make a study of the American jury system, gave his impression of the paper: "*Nordlyset* from Wisconsin indicates that the Norwegians there are learning American methods of advertising." They were, in other words, adjusting to a new commercial reality. Munch Ræder cited several advertisements for drug stores, including, "If you care about your health at all, go to H. M. Hansen's Drug-Store in Kilbourntown, Milwaukee, at the sign of the red mortar, near the upper bridge." He presented examples of advertising by merchants, a tailor, a painter, physicians, a real estate agent—all taken from a single issue of *Nordlyset*. "Just one glance at a few columns of such advertising," Munch Ræder wrote, "is probably sufficient to dispel the notion that Wisconsin is still a lonely wilderness far out there in the West."[11]

Entering American Politics

Public affairs attracted participation by the Norwegian community's leading members. Their motives, as reflected in the competing political voices of the journals they launched, related to personal ambition as well as to educating their compatriots on the variety of social and political issues debated in American society. In February 1848 *Nordlyset* adopted as its motto the slogan of the Free Soil Party: "Free land, free speech, free labor, and free men" *(Fri Jordbund, Fri Tale, Frit Arbeide og Frie Mœnd)*, replacing the earlier motto "Freedom and Equality" *(Frihed og Liighed)*. Both indicated an affiliation with the ideals of the Free Soil Party's intense antislavery stance, notwithstanding the publishers' initial professed political neutrality. The Free Soil Party at its national convention in August 1848 adopted a platform that prohibited the extension of slavery and provided for free homesteads. *Nordlyset* for September 7, 1848, and subsequent issues until the November election printed the names of Martin Van Buren and Charles F. Adams, the party candidates for president and vice president, on its masthead. Van Buren failed to carry a single state in the November 7 election. *Nordlyset*'s advocacy for the Free Soil Party never gained wide support among Norwegian immigrants, and the party itself was in decline.

The Democratic Party, on the other hand, could claim a considerable following among Norwegian immigrants in the early years. The Jacksonian tradition of celebrating the common man remained an appealing attraction for immigrants, and the Democrats consistently expressed a friendly attitude toward them. Wisconsin had a liberal constitution that gave the vote to all male immigrants of age, as well as the right to be elected to public office, upon taking a simple oath of allegiance. James Reymert realized his greater opportunity within that party and cultivated its support. In spring 1848, while continuing his editorship of *Nordlyset,* he began publishing a second newspaper, *Democraten,* as a temporary campaign organ. Only one number is preserved. Before emigrating in 1842 at the age of twenty-one, Reymert spent some years in Scotland, his mother's native land, and arrived in America with facility in English. He built a distinguished political career as a member of the Wisconsin constitutional convention in 1847 and later of the state's house and senate. Reymert is thought to be the first Norwegian to hold an American state office.[12]

Knud Langeland attained great prominence in Norwegian American journalism; his leadership role was widely recognized by his contemporaries. As it did for Reymert, journalism led to politics. In 1860 he served in the Wisconsin legislature. His editorship of the Chicago newspaper *Skandinaven* from its establishment in 1866 nearly continuously until 1881 gained him his greatest fame. In *Nordmændene i Amerika,* published the year of his death in 1888, he reflected on his memories from life in Norway and in America, offering a striking social and political portrait of the time in which he lived. From his youth he had a strong sense of the social injustice he witnessed, making him a champion of the "social class that carried the burden . . . of a daily struggle for the most basic essentials to maintain life." He was born in 1813 in Samnanger, a community east of Bergen, received the customary education under the Lutheran state church's authority, and was employed as an itinerant schoolteacher *(Omgangsskolelærer)* and sexton in his home district before emigrating to America in 1843. Three years later, he settled on a farm in Racine, Wisconsin.

Renaming *Nordlyset* to *Democraten* in June 1850 did not, as Langeland saw it, indicate a new partisan affiliation but simply "Free Soil Democrat," a democratic organ *(Folkestyrets Organ)*. Democratic newspapers in the state had satirized the newspaper's original name; it would therefore, Langeland wrote, be better to have a name Americans would readily understand. His son-in-law and co-owner O. J. Hatlestad possessed a greater sense of changing political realities. *Democraten* soon espoused the principles of the Democratic Party. Hatlestad left the newspaper in May 1851, and with the June 18 issue it moved to Janesville; Langeland was then sole owner and editor. *Democraten*—analogous to *Nordlyset*'s view—was strongly antislavery and advocated the Free Soil policy of free public lands. "The slavery question is not one between Democrats and Whigs," Langeland accurately stated in November 1850, "but between North and South."[13]

Pioneer Newspapers of the 1850s

Langeland's comments on slavery appeared in an editorial assailing the short-lived weekly *De Norskes Ven* (The Norwegians' Friend), started summer 1850 in Madison, Wisconsin, and lasting only about half a year. *Democraten* saw itself as the Norwegian standard-bearer of the Democratic Party in Wisconsin and accused *De Norskes Ven* of being financed by the aristocratic Whig Party; its publisher and editor was Ole Torgersen (Hyllestad), an immigrant from Sogn, Norway, in 1845; he learned the printing trade in Madison. Torgersen denied the charge of publishing a Whig organ and engaged in a heated controversy with *Democraten*. However, in 1853, *Emigranten,* which began publication in Inmansville, Wisconsin, in 1852, observed that *De Norskes Ven* "was a completely unsuccessful attempt to establish a Whig press among Norwegians." The writer continued, "It had to fail because the attempt was made by a man who was completely lacking in talent and totally unable to keep up with his Democratic opponent in Racine." The Whig Party found little support among Norwegian immigrants, and the party itself suffered disunity and decline at a time when the Norwegian American press was ascendant.

Controversy and debate on personal, political, and religious issues characterized the Norwegian American press in the nineteenth century, reflecting the divisions and competing interests in an immigrant population rapidly coming to terms with life in America. The basic function of communication through the media, it may be argued, consists primarily in determining the agenda for public discussion and in forming the values and opinions of society. By engaging Norwegian immigrants in public debate, the Norwegian-language press not only assisted in their adjustment to the new society but made them a force in shaping it.[14]

Wisconsin remained the center of immigrant publications throughout the 1850s, but pioneering ventures in newspaper publishing occurred in Chicago and New York as well. These metropolises became hubs of Norwegian American journalism in the postbellum decades. The weekly *Skandinaven* was launched in New York in 1851 and issued somewhat irregularly, according to O. M. Norlie, until 1853; it was edited by the Swede Anders G. Öbom and like the earlier *Skandinavia* was pan-Scandinavian, employing Dano-Norwegian, Swedish, and English in its columns. In an article in 1938, Oliver Linder, earlier editor of *Svenska Amerikanaren* (The Swedish American) in Chicago, claimed *Skandinaven* as "the *very* first newspaper in the Swedish language" and described its editor as "a very erratic person . . . [who] certainly did not exert himself much on behalf of his countrymen." Linder's comments echoed earlier criticism of this pioneer publication.

The anonymous contemporary observer in *Emigranten* characterized *Skandinaven* as follows: "*Skandinaven* began its dispersion among us, if correctly recalled, at the end of 1851, published in New York, as it was said, by three Scandinavian republicans. . . . This newspaper was edited in a genuine partisan saloon manner; its greatest joy seemed to be to relate all kinds of scandalous stories from all corners of the world, though preferably from Sweden, whether they were true or not. Its politics, if not communistic–red republicanism, then they were only very foolish incoherent nonsense." The commentator objected in particular to *Skandinaven*'s hostility toward Swedish royalty and officials.

Friheds-Banneret (The Banner of Freedom) of Chicago appeared with its first weekly issue October 4, 1852, and closed with its final May 7, 1853. *Skandinaven* and *Friheds-Banneret* both gained reputations for being politically radical and were negatively branded as "red republican," which neither denied but instead embraced. *Friheds-Banneret* brandished its opposition to royal institutions and its loyalty to republican ideals in its very title and in its editorial columns, explaining, "We are of the so-called red republicans who want everything that does not smell or taste as genuine republicanism to be made red, that is burned." These views were, not surprisingly, negatively judged by conservative partisan voices; controversy in domestic issues of the day, most especially the divisive slavery question, intensified the war of words. When *Friheds-Banneret* ended in May 1853, Charles Reese (Carl Riise), editor of *Emigranten,* remarked, according to Carl G. O. Hansen, "with evident malicious pleasure that *Friheds-Banneret* died of a disease, which, according to Reese's diagnosis, consisted of 'inflammation of the brain *[Hjernebetændelse]* with periodic attacks of insanity.'"[15]

In its first number, *Friheds-Banneret* declared on its masthead that it was "A Free Democratic Newspaper, edited and published by Two Norwegians" *(Et Frie-Demokratisk Blad),* or, in other words, like *Nordlyset,* a Free Soil advocate, and thus at odds with the Norwegian Democratic Party media. From January 8, 1853, *Friheds-Banneret* was published by the Norwegian Press Association in Chicago *(Den norske Presseforening i Chicago),* organized as a stock company for that purpose. It listed four hundred subscribers. John Mauritzon edited the newspaper from the start; beginning April 9 he was joined by George P. Hansen. Hansen had earlier in the columns of the Democratic *Emigranten* severely criticized *Friheds-Banneret* and its editor "at the request of several Scandinavians," accusing Mauritzon of "assaulting Scandinavians who do not agree with [his] high-flown red republican ideas in sordid articles." Mauritzon was dismissed as "a political Don Quixote." Understandably, then, the new editorial alliance made *Friheds-Banneret*'s commentary less strident during its final month of existence.

Friheds-Banneret was, as a Free Soiler or Free Democrat, vocally antislavery and illustrative of the pioneer press's bitter editorial partisanship, defending its political stance against vitriolic attacks. In its opening greeting to readers in October 1852, it criticized existing Scandinavian newspapers, since *Skandinaven* in New York was the only genuine republican newspaper among them. "We know the editors personally," Mauritzon editorialized, "and know that they wholeheartedly are genuine republican, which their newspaper gives evidence of." The best in the newspaper—here defending editor Öbom—appeared, however, in the Swedish language, which "very few of our countrymen understand." *Friheds-Banneret* would be published "in the same free Democratic spirit," but "only for our countrymen, the Norwegians in this country." Its defense of "freedom's holy cause" as a Free Soil organ—the newspaper's claimed purpose—was destined to fail. The presidential election in 1852 was likely a major motive for establishing *Friheds-Banneret*. However, the weakened Free Soilers, after defections from the party to the Democrats, nominated John P. Hale of New Hampshire as their presidential candidate. The Democrats, united and revitalized, made Franklin Pierce their nominee and won a great victory over the Free Soilers and Whigs in the fall election; the Free Soil vote was reduced by half from its political success in 1848, when the thirteen elected Free Soil representatives held the balance of power in the House of Representatives.[16]

The Lutheran Matrix

"*Democraten,* like its predecessor *Nordlyset,*" Arlow Andersen wrote, "counted upon the support of faithful Norwegian Lutheran pioneers." The same could be said for most immigrant journals, given the central position of the Lutheran church in Norwegian American society. Frequent column themes were discussions of moral uplift and church news. Muskego played a significant role not only in immigrant journalism, but also in establishing the homeland's church on American soil. The Muskego church, started the winter of 1843–44 and dedicated in March 1845, has been recognized as the first Norwegian Lutheran church in America. Søren Bache described in some detail the dedication of the church

March 13; the two pastors J. W. C. Dietrichson and Claus Lauritz Clausen officiated at the solemn ceremony. Dietrichson arrived in 1844 nearly thirty years old; he was the first representative in America of the university-trained Norwegian pastors. As Bache's diary noted, "He gave as his reason for coming to America that the Word, the Holy Biblical Word, spurred him on to visit his countrymen in the Far West in order to maintain among them the Lutheran faith which they had taken with them from their homes." Clausen welcomed Dietrichson at Muskego August 7, 1844. Dietrichson made his headquarters in the Koshkonong settlement and returned to Norway in 1850. Clausen was born on the island of Ærö, Denmark, 1820, and as a young man studied theology and developed an interest in foreign missions. On a visit to Norway he met Tollef Bache, Søren Bache's father, who became instrumental in having him accept a call to come to Muskego as a teacher.

Clausen came to the settlement in August 1843. He soon realized that he could serve more effectively as a pastor. The Muskego settlers themselves felt a need for an ordained ministry; and Clausen consequently let himself be ordained by a German minister, L. F. E. Krause, on October 18 that year. Despite his strong sympathy for the Haugean pietism evident in the Muskego settlement, Clausen, on December 14, 1843, organized the first Norwegian Lutheran congregation that came out of the high-church arrangement of the Church of Norway. He became the first pastor for two hundred members whose edifice was dedicated in 1845. Clausen became a significant leader in Norwegian American Lutheranism; he engaged himself with great sensitivity in his many duties as pastor and missionary, publisher and settlement organizer. March 15, 1849, Clausen wrote in *Nordlyset* as a defender of the faith against "the sects which have gained proselytes." An emerging Lutheran leadership faced great challenges, as well as dissent in regard to doctrine and polity, in their endeavors to transfer the homeland's faith to the voluntary free-church environment of America with its religious marketplace of competing creeds.[17]

A brief outline of organized religious life among Norwegian Americans is essential in order to give an interpretive narrative of the individual Lutheran synods—or ecclesiastical communions—and their involvement in immigrant journalism. A fractious Lutheran clergy fueled the fires of discord in the columns of the Norwegian-language press as well as in separate synodical publications. Norwegian American Lutheranism's pronounced denominationalism became evident in heated polemics on the true teachings of the faith; these exchanges were frequently reduced to personal denunciations and censures. As historians of the Norwegian American Lutheran church have suggested, however, intense controversies may simply represent the religious diversity of the Norwegian state church, which found independent expression in Norwegian American church life.

Uncompromising traditionalists like J. W. C. Dietrichson transferred the Church of Norway's prohibition against lay preaching to America, a subject of controversy in Norway during much of the nineteenth century; in this same high-church mode the pious C. L. Clausen approved of the traditional ecclesiastical vestments and liturgy of the state church. Before the arrival and ordination of Clausen, however, the Haugean leaders in Muskego, men like Even Heg, had from necessity performed lay ministries, led prayer meetings, and even baptized children, since no ordained pastor had been available.

The evangelist Elling Eielsen (Sundve), a pietistic, anti-clerical Haugean lay preacher, became a third trailblazer in the organized religious life among Norwegian Americans. Eielsen was born in Voss, Norway, 1804, the year of Hans Nielsen Hauge's final arrest and imprisonment for violating the ordinance against lay preaching. He emigrated in 1839 to the Fox River settlement in Illinois. Clausen initially sought to cooperate with Eielsen, but a definitive break occurred the year Clausen came to Muskego; in Dietrichson's eyes lay activity was anarchy. Eielsen had been a familiar figure in Muskego; his extreme form of anti-clericalism found support in Fox River, as those settlers reflected the low-church currents from Rogaland, from which most hailed, while in Muskego, "he was thwarted by men who had a revulsion for his extreme attitude toward pastors." In Norway lay preachers had functioned as an adjunct to the state church; ordained ministers administered the sacraments. Even Eielsen and his friends began to feel the need for an ordained ministry and a formal church organization. In October 1843 Elling Eielsen let himself be ordained by a Lutheran

German pastor, F. A. Hoffman. The Evangelical Lutheran Church in America, commonly known as Eielsen's Synod, emphasizing Haugeanism and a low-church practice, was formed at a meeting at Jefferson Prairie in April 1846.

The liturgical high church, after earlier failed attempts, agreed on doctrinal and organizational issues at a meeting at Rock Prairie in October 1853 and established the second American Norwegian Lutheran church body, the Synod of the Norwegian-Evangelical Lutheran Church in America. Generally referred to as the Norwegian Synod, or merely the Synod, it embodied Dietrichson's ultra-conservative principles in Norwegian American Lutheranism. Dietrichson had by then returned to Norway, but other university-trained ministers arrived to serve their compatriots in America. They, like Clausen, became forceful actors in Norwegian American religious and secular journalism. Dietrichson was succeeded in the Koshkonong pastorate by A. C. Preus, the Synod's president, born in 1814 and trained at the theological faculty in Oslo; H. A. Stub, born 1822, also a Norwegian-trained pioneer pastor, arrived at Muskego in 1848; Clausen had earlier moved to serve the congregation at Luther Valley. These three pastors in March 1851 edited and published *Maanedstidende* (Monthly Times); it was printed at first in Racine on the press of *Democraten.*

Before the end of 1851, three new theological graduates arrived in the West; G. F. Dietrichson, born 1813, Nils Brandt, born 1824, and H. A. Preus, born 1825. They were all young men, Dietrichson the oldest yet not forty. Preus served for forty years as pastor in Spring Grove, Wisconsin; joined by other churchmen of the aristocratic classes of the homeland, he became a dynamic and forceful leader in the Norwegian Synod. His dominance in churchly and doctrinal issues is evidenced by his regular and frequently combative letters and other contributions printed in the columns of *Emigranten* and *Maanedstidende.*

A second religious periodical appeared in 1851, yet more evidence of differing points of view in Lutheranism. As Knud Langeland relates, he and O. J. Hatlestad printed *Maanedstidende* on *Democraten*'s press, but when Hatlestad also wished to publish a church magazine, they as co-owners decided to divide the press equipment. Hatlestad was born in Skjold, Norway, in 1823, and emigrated in 1846. In Norway, like Langeland, he had been an itinerant rural school teacher; in America he was a lay preacher in the Eielsen tradition with deep low-church convictions. In 1854 he was ordained as a Lutheran minister in Northern Illinois Synod, a communion organized in 1851 by dissenters from Eielsen Synod who joined English, Norwegian, and Swedish Lutherans to form the new church body. Hatlestad's rival to *Maanedstidende* was published as an independent monthly titled *Kirketidende* (Church Times). Hatlestad defended lay preaching and attacked both the ministers who supported *Maanedstidende* and the state church tradition. *Maanedstidende* and *Kirketidende,* Theodore Blegen posited, were "instruments for the deepening of a controversial tradition destined to absorb much of the intellectual energy and fertility of the Norwegian Americans in the next two generations."[18]

Reverend Herman Amberg Preus, who served for forty years as pastor in Spring Grove, Wisconsin, was a dominant force in the Norwegian Synod.

Elias Stangeland and the Democratic Party

The newspaper *Friheds-Bannneret* noted, belatedly, November 27, 1852, that "a young Norwegian by the name of Elias Stangeland from Wisconsin is now on his way to Norway in order to initiate his proposed emigration plan from the fatherland in general, and, as we have been told, on very favorable conditions." Stangeland was born at Avaldsnes on the island of Karmøy, Norway, and was a pioneer settler at Muskego in 1848. He was a respected member of the settlement. In April 1852 *Emigranten* printed an announcement "To Our Countrymen" signed by Synod pastors, among others C. L. Clausen, at that time listed as *Emigranten*'s editor, G. F. Dietrichson, A. C. Preus, and H. A. Preus, with the news that "We believe it will please our countrymen to learn that at our request, two reliable, honest, and Christian-minded men, namely Aslak Olnæs from Koshkonong and Elias Stangeland from Muskego, have taken upon themselves to go to New York this summer to assist arriving Norwegian immigrants secure contracts with reliable companies for transportation inland and to serve as interpreters." Stangeland went to Norway in the fall of 1852 as agent for the American forwarding company of Maxwell and Patten; he was active in Norway in 1853, and in spring published an America guide "Some Guiding Suggestions for Norwegian Emigrants to America" *(Nogle veiledende Vink for norske Udvandrere til Amerika).*

At meetings in several parts of Norway, Stangeland recommended the Northwest as a place of settlement, especially Wisconsin. A December 26, 1852, article in *Emigranten,* reprinted in newspapers in Norway, attacked Stangeland, warning emigrants to stay away from such agents if they did not wish to be cheated. Complaints against Stangeland multiplied. The Synod pastors, who just a few months earlier had strongly endorsed Stangeland, thought it wise to make it known in *Emigranten* that they "have nothing to do with Stangeland." Accusations and counteraccusations took up space in the columns of *Emigranten* and Stangeland's own newspapers for several years. The criticism became known as the "Stangeland Affair" or the "Crusade against Stangeland" by himself and his friends.

This "affair" led directly to Stangeland's newspaper activity. The first number of *Den Norske Amerikaner* (The Norwegian American) appeared in Madison, Wisconsin, January 1, 1855, published as "A Newspaper for the People" *(Et Blad for Folket),* with the motto, "Whoever Wishes to Promote Truth and Enlightenment, Must Not Be Frightened by Lies and Darkness." The initial motive behind the launching of *Den Norske Amerikaner* might have been to create an organ to defend against personal accusations made by the Synod pastors' secular organ *Emigranten;* it allowed Stangeland to make counter accusations and became a platform to express general animosity against the Synod pastors. Historian J. Magnus Rhone explained that the staff of *Den Norske Amerikaner,* from Stangeland himself to Charles M. Reese, ex-editor of *Emigranten,* and others who entered its service, until the newspaper was discontinued May 27, 1857, "all cordially hated the Synod pastors for one reason or another." As party positions on the many important political issues facing the nation in the mid-1850s were clarified, *Emigranten* and *Den Norske Amerikaner* engaged in mutual denouncements and heated debates.

Reese succeeded Stangeland as editor December 27, 1856; as editor of *Emigranten* he had made war on the rival publications, *Kirketidende* and *Friheds-Banneret;* at the helm of *Den Norske Amerikaner* he attacked *Emigranten* as a church organ and destroyer of reputations. Reese's failure to gain control of *Emigranten* due to lack of resources had in 1854 led to his resignation and cooperation with Stangeland. Charles Reese was born in Denmark in 1823 and came to Wisconsin at a young age. In his debut issue of *Den Norske Amerikaner,* Reese complained about how poorly he had been treated by *Emigranten,* which "it pleased to call" his departure from *Emigranten* "running away." He came to the defense of Stangeland, suggesting that the assault against him, totally unfounded, was that his journey to Norway "had been a fly in the ointment for other people's business affairs who until now have made a living off Norwegian emigrants, and the false tongues of such people convinced others that Stangeland really was the black soul he was made out to be." Reese had looked into the entire matter and found nothing wrong in Stangeland's activities; all emigrants, as long as they heeded his advice, had arrived safely at their destination. Accusations of wrongdoings were, in other words, "nothing more than professional jealousy" *(Brødnid).*[19]

Den Norske Amerikaner and *Emigranten* originated as Democratic organs, though *Emigranten* by 1854 espoused Republican political principles and gave its support to that party's candidates; in 1855 *Emigranten* printed the Republican state ticket at the head of its editorial column. In the decisive national election the following year it supported John C. Frémont, the Republican Party's first presidential candidate, whose platform called for congressional prohibition of slavery in the territories. As a fiercely Democratic organ, *Den Norske Amerikaner* found much at fault with *Emigranten.* After Frémont's loss in the fall election to the Democratic candidate James Buchanan, who supported "popular sovereignty" on the slavery controversy, as passed by the Kansas Nebraska Act in 1854, the latter newspaper deemed *Den Norske Amerikaner* "not to be so much a Democratic or anti-Republican newspaper as an anti-*Emigranten* newspaper."

The Republican Party was, in *Den Norske Amerikaner*'s strong opinion, infested with Whigs, abolitionists, disgruntled Democrats, and Know-Nothings. The newspaper even combined the names as the Republican Know-Nothing Party, claiming the two "were one and the same party" since they both in the 1856 election gave their support to Frémont. After the election, the Republican Party did indeed draw strength from the anti-Catholic and anti-immigrant American, or Know-Nothing, Party, which *Den Norske Amerikaner* even earlier had claimed "wished to remove the chains from the Negroes and put them on white Europeans."

Its celebration of Democratic victory at the national level asserted, "The Union is preserved! Buchanan is elected president! Down with the fanatics!!" The Democratic organ all the same had to admit that "Here in Wisconsin, it is true, the Republicans have gained the upper hand, but we are convinced it will be a brief source of joy, as the Democratic Party like the Bird Phoenix will rise from the ashes, rejuvenated and more brilliant than before." It was more difficult for *Den Norske Amerikaner* to make sense of why the heavily Norwegian Dane County had voted with the Republican Party. "What is it," editor Stangeland asked, "that has moved the Norwegians, who consistently have been good, faithful Democrats, this year in such large numbers to run over to the enemy?" "*Emigranten* cannot be blamed," the editorial continued,

Emigranten.

8de Aargang. No. 2.

Et uafhængig demokratisk Blad.

Løbende No. 344.

Madison, Dane Co., Wisconsin, Onsdagen den 12te Januar 1859.

Spnnove Solbakken

February 12, 1859, front page of the weekly Emigranten, *published in Madison, Dane County, Wisconsin, and edited by Carl Fredrik Solberg. The first issue of* Emigranten, *published at Inmansville, Rock County, Wisconsin, was dated January 23, 1852.*

"since it has not shown sufficient common sense to be able to turn the heads of two-thirds of the Norwegian population." "It pains us," Stangeland concluded, "to have to lay the blame for this turnabout on men who rightly should not even be involved in politics, but yet have taken an active part in it—we have in mind the Norwegian pastors." "These 'messengers of peace' . . . by stressing the abominable aspects of slavery, and using only this one point [have] scared the honest and credulous [congregational members] away from the Democratic Party."

Regardless of what explanations *Den Norske Amerikaner* put forward, the movement of a Norwegian electorate toward the Republican Party—the new party of freedom—and its leading issues was inevitable as the nation drifted toward disunion. In April 1857, Elias Stangeland announced that he had sold *Den Norske Amerikaner* to the newly organized Scandinavian Democratic Press Association, which issued its first number April 18 as "A National Democratic Newspaper" *(Et Nationalt Demokratisk Blad);* Charles Reese continued as editor. In its May 27 issue, *Den Norske Amerikaner* bid its readers farewell. The newspaper would, however, "arise in a glorified form from its own ashes . . . under the name *Nordstjernen* [The North Star] and in a substantially larger format."[20]

Nordstjernen appeared with its first number June 10, 1857, as volume 1, number 1, published by the Scandinavian Democratic Press Association and edited by Charles Reese. It greeted its readers in English as well as Norwegian, a practice that by then had some standing, and a special message "To Our American Brethren of the Democratic Creed," signed "A Scandinavian," elucidating the true principles of Democracy as they applied to the issue of slavery in the new territories "of popular sovereignty and the rights of man to self-government" and avowing "to tear the mask from Black Republicanism."

Nordstjernen continued *Den Norske Amerikaner*'s attacks on *Emigranten.* These exchanges disclosed *Nordstjernen*'s political philosophy. A discussion of giving the franchise to black Americans should many move to Wisconsin made *Nordstjernen* conclude that since the Supreme Court had ruled that they cannot become citizens, they could not be accorded equal rights with white men: "It would be the greatest misfortune for our state if the Negro suddenly should be placed on an equal footing with the white here." The debate was sparked by the legislative adoption in 1856 that "The franchise shall be extended to men of African blood, who have attained the age of 21 or above." Suggesting that *Emigranten* hid its true opinions behind Republican hypocrisy, evidenced by its motto "No Slavery for Black or White," *Nordstjernen* requested an equally honest declaration. The Democratic organ declared its support for the fugitive slave law and criticized *Emigranten*'s hostile attitude toward the enforcement of that act.

The political winds of change, as reflected in the American mainstream press, did not favor *Nordstjernen*'s political agitation, and its days were numbered. By this time, only a political movement that took a firm anti-slavery, not simply anti-extension, stand would find general support in the Norwegian electorate. Indeed, a radical alteration in the nation's attitude toward slavery was taking place. The many intense appeals to its subscribers and shareholders to help with production costs, as well as an irregular publication schedule, suggest its financial woes. It was not published at all between October 28 and December 19, 1857. Publication by the Scandinavian Democratic Press Society did not improve its prospects by much. The last issue edited by Charles Reese is dated March 20, 1858; its next number dated May 27 was edited by "A Committee." When *Nordstjernen* "again appears on newspaper literatures firmament," September 7, 1858, Hans Borchsenius is listed as editor and publisher.

Hans Borchsenius, born 1832 on the Danish island of Zealand, emigrated in 1856; he purchased *Nordstjernen* from the Scandinavian press society. He later pursued a successful career in public service, entered the legal profession, and was both elected and appointed to positions in state government. Borchsenius edited *Nordstjernen* in its established Democratic form, optimistically discovering minor uplifts for the Democratic ticket, finding comfort in the fact that in the November 1858 election the results showed "Great Democratic victory in Dane County." In the 1859 November election, Borchsenius reported with sadness that "the entire Republican state ticket was elected and that the Republicans had a small majority in both houses in the legislature." In an editorial he consoled the subscribers with the fact that the Republican majority was "insignificant." Borchsenius was, however, not able to build a circulation that would make *Nordstjernen* viable; at its height, he complained, the newspaper had fewer than nine hundred paying subscribers. Therefore in October 1860 he sold *Nordstjernen* to Carl Fredrik Solberg, the publisher and editor of *Emigranten,* in spite of the existing divisive political antagonism between the two; the final issue of *Nordstjernen* is dated October 10. The sale gave clear evidence, as Borchsenius also lamented, that "the political conflict is over, the Republican Party has triumphed."[21]

The Norwegian American pioneer press was strongly given to political controversy; it was found on all sides of issues confronted in the new environment. Efforts to mold public opinion among Norwegian compatriots confronted many obstacles; these dissuasions did not prevent politically ambitious individuals from endeavoring to do so as a Norwegian presence was established in new regions of settlement. A spectacular growth in the Norwegian population occurred in Minnesota, which attained statehood in 1858, from only nine Norwegians officially recorded in 1850, to 6,769 in 1857, and to 11,893 in 1860.

Republican and Democratic strength was about equal in Minnesota. According to Theodore Blegen, the Democratic *Folkets Røst* (Voice of the People) first appeared in St. Paul, Minnesota, on October 1, 1857, in order to defeat the swing of Norwegian voters toward the Republican Party. It was edited and published by O. Nelson, who, as stated in a letter to *Emigranten* from a correspondent in Minnesota, was employed by the Democrats. *Folkets Røst* was a campaign sheet launched shortly before the important election at the end of the territorial period in an attempt to win the Scandinavian vote for the Democrats. The Democrats obtained majorities in both houses, gaining the votes of people in the small commercial and industrial centers of St. Paul, Stillwater, and St. Anthony, while newcomers on the land tended to favor the new party and its advocacy against slavery and for free land to settlers. *Emigranten* had subscription agents and subscribers in Minnesota and had considerable influence among Norwegian settlers; *Folkets Røst* was thus a rival voice to the Wisconsin Republican newspaper. Nelson tried to diminish *Emigranten*'s sway in the Norwegian settlements through disrespectful observations about it as a church organ edited by priests, deacons, and other questionable individuals.

This first Norwegian American newspaper in Minnesota resurfaced July 10, 1858. Ignoring its single example in October of the previous year, *Folkets Røst* began volume numbering from the 1858 issue. O. Nelson continued as its editor; Nelson & Co. published it semimonthly. The final issue is dated November 20, 1858. It persisted as a strong Democratic advocate. *Folkets Røst*—the voice of the people, the publishers maintained, "is in our opinion the most appropriate name for a newspaper in this country" because "We live here under a government and in a land where the will of the people is the law and where the voice of the people is sovereign and final in all political issues." In the following issue, *Folkets Røst* addressed "Our American Friends," assuring them that the newspaper "aims to elevate and ennoble our foreign population, and enhance the best interests of our young State," and thus "we commend it to your favorable consideration." It took another decade or more, however, before the Norwegian-language press would be firmly rooted in Minnesota.[22]

The Newspaper Emigranten

Emigranten was clearly the most important and best edited of the pioneer newspapers. Hans Borchsenius, when in 1860 sending *Nordstjernen*'s subscription list to Carl Solberg, praised *Emigranten,* stating "irrespective of its political tendency it is the best Norwegian newspaper we have had in America." He wished to support *Emigranten* and increase its circulation by the addition of *Nordstjernen*'s subscribers. Experience during the past decade had convinced Borchsenius that the Norwegian immigrants could sustain only one newspaper; that being the case, "then it is obvious . . . that it is in our own common interest to support it with all our might so that it can become as good and complete as possible." For the next half a dozen years *Emigranten* would indeed be in sole possession of the Norwegian field.

The Norwegian American press, especially during its early decades, Albert Barton maintained, was "particularly inclined toward religious and theological disputation, to a much greater degree proportionately than in Norway." He found this situation natural, since "the leading men of the settlements were the ministers, and the newspapers were largely dependent upon them for their subscription lists." *Emigranten*'s founding represented the actions of prominent members of the Norwegian Synod clergy. Their dominance in its affairs might, however, by some accounts have been overstated, though their voices were quite audible during *Emigranten*'s early years.

The initial issue of *Emigranten* is dated January 23, 1852, at Inmansville, Rock County, Wisconsin, published by the Scandinavian Press Association *(Den Skandinaviske Presse-Forening)*. Its antecedents relate to the appearance of the Synod monthly *Maanedstidende* in March 1851 and the demise of Langeland's *Democraten* in October. C. L. Clausen initiated plans to purchase Langeland's press, then located in Janesville, and organize a Scandinavian press association; it was formed at a meeting held at the Rock Prairie Lutheran Church on November 15, 1851. The Scandinavian Press Association would publish not only *Maanedstidende*, but also a secular newspaper and religious books and pamphlets for use in schools and homes. Publishing a secular journal would give the Synod pastors a political voice; *Maanedstidende* was to be a strictly religious magazine. Though laymen held the majority of the Association's shares, the Synod pastors were in control. Three of the drafters of the constitution were Lutheran pastors—Clausen, A. C. Preus, and G. F. Dietrichson.

Despite *Emigranten*'s proposed status as a secular newspaper, the Association selected Clausen as editor at its meeting December 4, 1851; he is listed as editor in the newspaper's first number. Albert Barton maintained that Charles Reese did the majority of the editorial work. The printing press had been transferred from Janesville, to cite Barton, "to Gunder Springen's double log cabin on Rock Prairie, in section four, town of Newark, Rock County." Inmansville, listed as place of publication, was simply a post office at a farmer's house in the town of Plymouth north of the Springen cabin.[23]

Clausen declared in *Emigranten*'s initial number that it would be "An Independent Democratic Newspaper" and chose the motto: "Unity, Courage, Endurance" *(Enighed, Mod, Udholdenhed)*. In English he addressed "Our American Friends" with a clear Americanization message and revealed a sense of immigrant inferiority, humbly stating:

> We came here strangers and friendless, ignorant of Your institutions, Your language and your customs, but You cheered our hearts with a friendly welcome. . . . we look to You for help and assistance in our endeavors to emancipate ourselves from the degrading bondage of ignorance, regarding Your institutions and customs, regarding the privileges and duties devolving upon us with the rights of citizenship extended to us.

The first issue printed, again in English, the newspaper's platform, which reflected the fact that both Democratic and Whig opinions were represented in the press association, assuring *Emigranten*'s readers:

> We have without hesitation declared ourselves for the DEMOCRATIC PRINCIPLES, knowing that the Majority of our people coincide with us in our strong predilection for those principles. But we must here beg to let it be well understood, that although we in general join and make common cause with the democratic party, we by no means pledge ourselves to follow it through 'Thick and Thin.'

Under the heading "The Large American Political Parties: Whigs and Democrats" *(De store Amerikanske politiske Partier: Whigger og Democrater), Emigranten* endeavored to educate its readers about the principles of the two political entities as well as about America's naturalization laws and path to citizenship. Only by becoming one with Americans, Clausen stated, could Norwegian immigrants "contribute their part to the final development of this Great Nation." Already in its fifth number, February 20, 1852, the newspapers printed the first of eighty chapters of a serialized history of the United States in Norwegian translation, from colonial days to the presidency of Andrew Jackson, titled "The United States or the American Republic's History *(De Forenede Staters eller Den Amerikanske Republiks Historie)*. It was indeed an ambitious undertaking, but one that underscored *Emigranten*'s sense of mission to familiarize Norwegian immigrants with the nation's historical experience. Beginning in the summer of 1853, it was augmented by the history of the state of Wisconsin.

With *Friheds-Banneret*'s demise in May 1853, *Emigranten* declared in its June 10, 1853, number that it was then the only political newspaper in the United States printed in the Norwegian language; it would, of course, shortly have new political rivals. By the end of the year *Emigranten* reported a subscription list that numbered between five and six hundred. The files of *Emigranten* show that the Synod pastors failed in the original intent not to make *Emigranten* an addendum to *Maanedstidende.* It in fact gave much space to religious controversy, which frequently involved personal attacks, with mutual accusations between the warring parties. The pastors H. A. Preus and A. C. Preus, both members of the board of the Scandinavian Press Association, were forceful defenders of the faith in the columns of *Emigranten,* supporting what they judged to be "the pure doctrine" and attacking what was thought to be "false teachings" by Lutheran clergy brethren. The debate and bitter exchanges about church doctrine and polity, interspersed with invidious remarks against persons, rose and fell as controversial issues came to the fore.

Emigranten experienced difficulties in its management. Its January 27, 1854, issue announced that Charles Reese's connection "has entirely ceased with the present number." A committee was given editorial responsibility, though Knud J. Fleischer, treasurer for the Scandinavian Press Association, functioned as acting editor after Reese's departure. Fleischer was a recently arrived immigrant from Norway. In time he was appointed Swedish-Norwegian consul in Madison; he possessed strong literary and musical interests and became, according to Carl G. O. Hansen, "a natural leader in the culturally enlightened circle." *Emigranten* was at this time housed in a stone building north of the Luther Valley church. July 24, 1854, the printing office was struck by a cyclone, which blew the roof off the building and destroyed printing equipment. Albert Barton related that the destruction in a sense signaled a definitive change in political course: "As the Norwegians soon deserted the Democratic Party en masse it became a byword of the settlements that the cyclone of 1854 blew the Democracy out of the Norwegians." *Emigranten,* after a brief accommodation with the decadent Whig Party in response to the views of some members of the press association, moved firmly into the newly organized Republican camp.

In his capacity as editor and manager of the book printing operation Knud Fleischer earned the displeasure of A. C. Preus, who accused him of "defiling the Word of God" as well as of other unchristian acts. The bitter exchanges in *Emigranten* the spring of 1858, reviewing a lengthy conflict, suggest a strong mutual distrust and animosity between the two men with expressed differences of opinion on political involvement, the operation of the printing press, and the Synod clergy's influence on *Emigranten*'s content. The antagonism does not disclose what actually occurred behind the scenes to cause the conflict. It was, however, sufficiently severe to make A. C. Preus, G. F. Dietrichson, and likely a number of other clergymen who sat on the Scandinavian Press Association's board sever their connection with it. Preus suggested that one reason for his severance was "*Emigranten*'s extreme partisan politics." H. A. Preus remained a part of the Association's administration until it was dissolved in 1860. These events led Fleischer to issue a declaration stating that "the clergy dominion *[Prestevældet]* of *Emigranten*" had been broken. Fleischer had by then left the editorship but continued until March 1859 as manager and treasurer of the Association's book printing.

In *Emigranten*'s April 25, 1857, number, in a communiqué written by Fleischer, he and the committee that assumed editorial responsibility had bid their public adieu. In his farewell letter, Fleischer alluded to the difficult working conditions and accusations that he "used shabby means" *(lumpne Midler)* to promote his interests, in this case moving *Emigranten* and the printing press to Madison. The same issue announced, "the newspaper's editorship has as of April 17 been delegated to Mr. C. Fr. Solberg."[24]

Carl Fredrik Solberg

April 3, 1857, was the last *Emigranten* number dated in Inmansville; the April 20 number gave Madison, Dane County, Wisconsin, as place of publication. The Scandinavian Press Association stood as publisher under the motto "Forward to Truth and Enlightenment" *(Fremad til Sandhed og Oplysning);* "a Committee" allegedly still edited *Emigranten*. The April 25, 1857, issue acknowledged Carl Fredrik Solberg as editor.

Carl Fredrik Solberg was at his death in 1924 the last of the Norwegian pioneer editors. In a 1919 interview he gave his life story and his experience as an immigrant newspaperman, offering a unique perspective on the influence of the foreign-language press. He was born in Oslo 1833 but spent his youth in Sorö, Denmark, where his father took the family to operate a bakery. The business did not prosper, and in 1853 the family moved to America. While in Sorö, Carl Fredrik had attended the elite Sorö Academy. Solberg related that "in addition to book studies, we were taught every accomplishment then necessary to be a gentleman. . . . We were also taught English, German, and French, and as I thus knew English before coming to America I had an advantage over many other immigrants."

Solberg's father had been invited by the famed violinist-turned-colonizer Ole Bull himself to manage the Ole Bull colony, Oleana,

Carl Fredrik Solberg, about 1871. As publisher and editor of Emigranten, *he gained considerable influence in the pioneer decades of the Norwegian immigrant press.*

in Potter County, Pennsylvania. As emigrant agent, Elias Stangeland had vigorously campaigned against Bull's colony. Most settlers had at the time of the Solbergs' arrival in 1853 left; Bull's lofty and unrealistic plans could not be realized. After three years the Solberg family took their leave from the failed enterprise and moved to Madison, Wisconsin. The folly of Oleana did not diminish Bull's popularity among his compatriots in America. His visits and concert tours were everywhere met with enthusiasm. His statue, dedicated in Loring Park, Minneapolis, Minnesota, May 17, 1897, became "a shrine at which singers and others gathered . . . the Seventeenth of May . . . to pay tribute to the old homeland and to the memory of the artist."

One of Ole Bull's secretaries at Oleana was Bertol W. Suckow, who later became a prominent bookbinder in Madison and publisher of *Billed-Magazin,* edited by Svein Nilsson. By 1856 Suckow had left Oleana and was operating a bookbindery and bookstore in Beloit, Wisconsin, binding books for the Scandinavian Press Association, *Emigranten*'s publishers, who at that time were looking for a new editor for the newspaper. On the recommendation of Suckow, who knew, as Solberg stated, "I had some education," they offered Solberg the position. In early 1856 he came to Inmansville, where, he tells, he stayed at the home of Knud Fleischer; "there was nothing thrilling about life [in Inmansville]," he continued, "but I had good intellectual company." Solberg began work on his twenty-third birthday, June 8, 1856, and he explained: "We also got out the church paper *Maanedstidende,* of which I was practically the editor for some time." In spring 1857 *Emigranten* was moved to Madison, "and the lively times began," Solberg concluded.

Carl Fredrik Solberg had a keen intellect and exhibited broad cultural interests. *Emigranten*'s political influence and reputation as a cultural organ increased greatly during his competent editorship. As he himself explained: "Although I was a comparatively young man while I was an editor in Madison, I had considerable influence. I had practically free entree to the governor's office in the capitol." He increased the newspaper in size and news coverage by seeking information from Scandinavian settlements throughout the Northwest and continued earlier reporting of "Foreign News. According to Norwegian Newspapers" *(Udenlandske Efterretninger.*

Efter norske Aviser). Early on in its history, *Emigranten*'s publishers decided that it would be important to educate people in Norway on how their countrymen had fared in America by making the newspaper available through subscription. In the 1850s this became a complicated process. Norwegian post offices could arrange subscription through "the newspaper agent" in Hamburg; newspapers would be shipped via New York, "across England, Hamburg to Copenhagen and from there to Norway."

In a precursor to a common practice by Norwegian American newspaper publishers, Solberg made *Emigranten* into a literary magazine. In January 1859 he began a serialized publication on the front page of Bjørnstjerne Bjørnson's popular peasant tale *Synnøve Solbakken* (Synnøve of Sunny Hill), published in 1857; it was a breakthrough for the young Norwegian writer, as well as a promoter of Norwegian national pride and consciousness. In January 1861, *Emigranten* printed the first installment of another romanticized tale by Bjørnson of Norwegian peasant life, *En glad Gut* (A Happy Boy). It was a practice Solberg continued even during the Civil War. The Norwegian peasant *(bonde)* was viewed as the bearer of the true Norwegian national values; the peasant tales gained great favor with Norwegian immigrants. They were a part of creating a glorious past, as were the historical narratives from the Age of the Vikings. The spring and summer of 1858, *Emigranten* published extractions from the Norwegian historian P. A. Munch's history of the Norwegian people until 1397, the year that marked the start of national decline with the onset of unions with other Nordic nations lasting until Norway's national rebirth in 1814. Viking heroes symbolized the strength embodied in the Norwegian people and their expansive powers—their forays into new lands, including the discovery of America around the year 1000. Norwegian immigration to America occurred during a period of growing national pride with cultivation of the nation's heroic past and the writing of nationalistic and romantic literature. Historian Munch, as he stated, wished to show "the influence of the Norwegian nationality in Old Norse times and its Nordic genuineness at present."[25]

Emigranten, later joined by a flourishing Norwegian American press, embraced the symbols of Norwegian nationality. The pioneer press initially focused on American material, to acquaint the immigrants with the new land. *Emigranten* and the Norwegian American press later emphasized the cultural ties with the Norwegian homeland and the other Scandinavian lands. And, indeed, none of the pioneer newspapers had been entirely limited to political and church controversy but contained news of Norway, reports from pioneer settlements, and advice on practical matters of adjusting to American society. During the troubling times of the late 1850s, *Emigranten* naturally also gave ample space to the looming conflict, evidenced in political polemics with the few existing Democratic Norwegian-language organs and in strong editorial opinions. The prevailing conflict within Norwegian American Lutheranism and prejudice against non-Lutheran faiths were voiced as well in *Emigranten*'s columns during Solberg's editorship.

Solberg himself on occasion expressed his disagreement with the Lutheran clergy; though as he noted in his memoirs, he had good relations with most ministers, visited H. A. Preus at his parsonage at Spring Grove regularly, and "was instrumental in getting the Lutheran congregation in Madison organized." One well-known instance of discord relates to the issue of breaking the Sabbath: The *Wisconsin Argus* in Madison reported on a group of Scandinavians who arranged a picnic on a July Sunday afternoon and evening in 1857 after attending church service—eating, probably drinking, singing, and engaging in some country dances. *Argus* accused them of being unpatriotic and of lacking respect for the laws of "their adopted fatherland." In the debate that followed, recorded in *Emigranten* and *Maanedstidende,* Solberg as editor of the former was severely criticized by A. C. Preus for defending the revelers and for describing the event as "an innocent amusement" *(uskyldig Moro)* and a common custom in Norway. Preus in his criticism cited Wisconsin Sabbath statutes, prohibiting "public amusement on the Sabbath," as well as God's law. He strongly encouraged Solberg not to try to give him instruction in how to conduct his pastoral duties. Historian Marcus Lee Hansen interpreted the event as "spontaneous immigrant Puritanism," an adjustment to the practices of mainline American Protestant denominations. It might thus not have been as much an issue of right or wrong for A. C. Preus as a concern that such conduct would bring the church into disrepute and weaken it.

As Solberg saw the situation, however, and stated in *Emigranten,* Preus's personal criticism of Solberg and *Emigranten* were used as an excuse for renewed attacks by the Democratic newspaper *Argus.* Attempts to defeat the swing of the Norwegian electorate toward the Republican Party had, however, obviously failed; in 1859 Hans Christian Heg, in Racine County, enthusiastically endorsed by *Emigranten,* was elected prison commissioner for Wisconsin on the Republican ticket, outpolling his Democratic opponent Henry C. Fleck, a Norwegian farmer in Dodge County. Solberg had helped bring about Heg's nomination at the state convention. The very fact that Norwegian candidates were running for state office, in this case compatriots vying for the same elected position, represented a significant progression in the greater political maturity of the Norwegian American community; it also signaled solicitation for Norwegian support by the American political establishment. In an editorial to "Our Countrymen in Minnesota and Iowa," on September 12, 1859, *Emigranten* warned Norwegians against voting for Democratic state candidates, unless they wished "to give the Democrats a push toward victory in next year's [presidential] election." "The United States must have a president who has the non-slaveholding states in mind," Solberg's editorial continued, "and that only the Republican Party can give."

Knud Langeland, claiming to be the first "antislavery man among the Norwegians," revisiting the 1856 election, reminded *Emigranten*'s reader in its October 24, 1859, issue, that if "We poor immigrant working people had earlier understood our situation correctly, we could under [John] Frémont now have had the pleasure of every poor immigrant family being in possession of 160 acres free land." Listing the names of free states and slave states in its November 21, 1859, number, *Emigranten*'s editorial, following Republican victory at the state level, was optimistic about the possibility of electing a Republican president in the 1860 election, given the reality that the free states controlled a majority of the electoral votes. The Republican national convention would meet in Chicago May 16–18, 1860, to nominate a presidential candidate.

Emigranten's ownership changed at this time. Carl Fredrik Solberg purchased the newspaper and the property of the Scandinavian Press Association in January 1860, as announced January 23, and became both proprietor and editor. It gave him greater independence and influence; after he purchased the rival, Democratic *Nordstjernen,* in October, his was the sole Norwegian-language newspaper.

Solberg attended the Republican convention in Chicago. His May 21 editorial in *Emigranten* reported glowingly on the nomination process. "Yesterday afternoon [May 18] at 1:00 o'clock one hundred cannon shots . . . announced that the Chicago convention had nominated the Republican Party's candidate for president," Abraham Lincoln of Illinois and for vice president Hannibal Hamlin of Maine. Solberg declared in June that "*Emigranten* will actively engage in the election campaign and be 'in the thickest of the fight' for Lincoln and Hamlin, for the liberation of the territories, for the passage of the homestead bill . . . for the protection of the interests of Northern and Western states." *Emigranten*'s political advocacy increased the number of subscribers to four thousand. Even Charles Reese, the editor of three earlier Democratic newspapers, in September 1860 launched a Republican campaign sheet titled *Folkebladet* (People's Newspaper) in Chicago, strongly in support of Lincoln's election. It suggested the change in political allegiance of Scandinavians in general. Lincoln's election in November created great exultation, celebrated, to cite *Emigranten,* "with festive processions, illuminations, and cannon salutes in most cities in the free states." The foreboding signs of "Insurrection in the South," as *Emigranten* reported, would be countered another day.[26]

The First Decade

In evaluating the pioneer years of the Norwegian immigrant press, it is easy to concur with Albert Barton that "Petty jealousies and rivalries were among the directing influences in the starting of the various early Norwegian papers in Wisconsin and in their subsequent fortunes and vicissitudes." On the eve of the Civil War the Norwegian American press could look back on a stormy history of a decade and a half; the controversies themselves had offered Norwegian immigrants instruction in the diversity of opinions in American political life and had invited them to become active participants in public affairs. Financial hardships and shifting political loyalties cut the life of most of the publications short.

The leaders in the Norwegian American community, in the religious as well as the secular spheres, were mainly young men; the new society rewarded talent and dedication. Some of these gifted leaders, men like C. L. Clausen and Charles Reese, were Danish-born; the literary languages of Denmark and Norway were nearly identical, allowing for full entry into the Norwegian immigrant community. Because Danish mass migration began later than the Norwegian, a separate Danish American press did not appear until the 1870s. Religious dissent moved beyond church publications and became a visible aspect of secular journals; the Lutheran clergy were natural leaders. An immigrant society was taking shape in which the written Norwegian language assumed increased importance. Only through the written word could Norwegians no longer residing in the tight linguistic neighborhoods of the homeland promote a sense of ethnic unity; wherever Norwegians resided in the Northwest, away from compatriots or in settlements of fellow Norwegians, magazines and newspapers conveyed the idea of living in a Norwegian world, the latter carrying local news from a wide area; these same publications guided readers' adjustment to the challenges of the new society.

To meet the expectations of a growing readership, the pioneer publications expressed characteristics that came to define the Norwegian-language press in America. They carried news from the Scandinavian homelands and served as magazines; they entertained their readers with serialized literary works; and they addressed problems facing the immigrants. Queries and correspondence to the editor became commonplace, denoting an obvious intimate relationship between the newspapers and their public. Second only to the Lutheran church, the pioneer Norwegian newspapers represented a basic social and cultural institution in an emerging Norwegian American community.

Colonel Hans Christian Heg at Chickamauga, Georgia, in September 1863. As leader of the Norwegian Fifteenth Wisconsin Regiment, Colonel Heg became a symbol of Norwegian Americans' patriotism.

Emigranten.

Et uafhængig demokratisk Blad.

CHAPTER 2

Building a Norwegian American Community

The authorities in this our new fatherland have called on the citizens to take to arms in defense of the Union and its Constitution.[1]

THE CONFLAGRATION BETWEEN North and South was a watershed experience for the Norwegian immigrant community; the era of the Civil War—1861 to 1865—marked a decisive phase in the process of adjustment to the "new fatherland." Norwegian immigrants, newcomers and pioneer settlers, responded to President Lincoln's call for volunteers in exceptional numbers after the outbreak of hostilities; their bonds to the Republican Party were strengthened, solidifying the political loyalties that were created leading up to the war, and not challenged for several decades to come. The enormous conflict created a new sense of patriotism, of becoming an integral part of American society and history. Indeed, to cite Theodore Blegen, "the Civil War, to the accompaniment of death and suffering and stern trial, made a contribution to the larger immigrant transition to American life."

Emigranten, published and edited by Carl Fredrik Solberg, became a recorder of events. The immigrant press constitutes an irreplaceable source of historical information, of attitudes, opinions, and the daily experience of Norwegian Americans. The drama associated with the War between the States, its diverse events, tribulations, defeats, and successes may be gleaned from the pages of *Emigranten.* Solberg himself moved beyond his editorial charge and became a correspondent for his own publication; he contributed observant and informative reports. *Emigranten* enjoyed the singular responsibility, as it proudly advertised, of being "the only newspaper of general content published in the Norwegian language in America." This unique monopoly lasted until the appearance of the newspaper *Fædrelandet* (The Fatherland) in La Crosse, Wisconsin, in January 1864.

The South regarded Lincoln's election as forecasting an attack on their system of slave labor; *Emigranten* covered the consequent secessions of southern states, beginning with South Carolina in December 1860 and followed by all other states of the lower South during the next couple of months. Under the heading "The Insurrection in the South," *Emigranten* reported on the formation of the Confederacy and the installation of President Jefferson Davis on February 18, 1861, in Montgomery, Alabama, and the inauguration of Lincoln on March 4. *Emigranten* presented "a careful translation of the President's message"; the Norwegian translation of the inaugural address was accompanied by Solberg's editorial commentary. Its conciliatory tone, Solberg opined, and "Its early revelation that the new government, contrary to what the masses in the South were led to believe, will not interfere in the slavery in individual states . . . coming as it does from the Republican President's mouth will contribute much to calm down the misled masses in the slave states." However, it was not to be; the failure of congressional compromise, Lincoln's decision to use force, and the Confederate attack on Fort Sumter, Charleston, South Carolina, April 12, 1861, unleashed the Civil War.[2]

"To Arms! Countrymen!" was *Emigranten*'s April 22 response to Wisconsin Governor Alexander Randall's April 20 proclamation to take up arms in defense of the Union. Lieutenant T. J. Widvey, journalist and lawyer, and in 1860 president of the Scandinavian Press Association as ownership of *Emigranten* was being transferred to Solberg, summoned "those of [his] enlisted men" to a meeting in Madison. Widvey's infantry company, the Dane County Guards, consisted "to a great extent of Norwegians." It offered its services to Governor Randall, as requested by President Lincoln, for three months; sixty-five men had enlisted as of May 1861. Later, in the course of the hostilities, Widvey was made captain of Company K in the Third Wisconsin Infantry Regiment, a regiment joined by many Norwegian recruits.

The Norwegian Fifteenth Wisconsin Regiment under the leadership of Colonel Hans Christian Heg became a symbol of the patriotism of Norwegian Americans. Young Norwegian men served in many other military units as well, and other immigrant groups also expressed their loyalty by forming military units of their nationalities. The Fifteenth Wisconsin, organized the fall of 1861, thus was one representative of what historian William Burton refers to as "Melting Pot Soldiers," its organization clearly stimulated by interethnic rivalry. Solberg, as he related, "opened the columns of *Emigranten* and helped Heg to organize his regiment." "When the regiment went south [March 2, 1862]," Solberg continued, "I went with it to St. Louis and spent a while in the camp and field, sending home letters to my paper concerning the regiment and military matters generally."[3]

Heg served as the main recruiting officer while tending to his duties at the state prison. He enlisted men, preponderantly Norwegian, but also a few Danish, Swedish, and American recruits, from settlements in Illinois, Wisconsin, Iowa, and Minnesota. In its regular "War News" *(Krigsefterretninger)* column, *Emigranten* took the reader on a detailed journey from battle to battle, gave information on the political decisions made in Washington, D.C., and evaluated the strength and actions of what it disparagingly referred to as "the rebel troops." *Emigranten* highlighted the Fifteenth Wisconsin—generally referred to as the Scandinavian, or increasingly Norwegian—Regiment's movements and military encounters and printed letters written by soldiers in its ranks. *Emigranten* also gave space to letters from Norwegians serving in other Wisconsin regiments. These correspondences from the military front showed the human face of a conflict, where deficient logistics in delivering arms and provisions, lack of medical services, and military inexperience caused suffering and a great loss of life. Death rates were horrifying; cholera, pneumonia, typhoid, and other diseases caused the vast majority of casualties. Before the end of the war, about one third of the original Norwegian Regiment, 299 men in all, became casualties of war; of these 217 were taken by disease and 82 died from wounds or were killed in battle.

A letter in *Emigranten* in January 1862 from Dr. S. O. Himoe, the regiment's surgeon, requested "the Scandinavian Women" to come to the aid of hospitalized members of the Norwegian Regiment at Camp Randall in Madison and in health facilities spread throughout the theater of operations for the regiment. The newspaper later carried additional requests and acknowledgements of monetary gifts and even of refreshments *(Forfriskninger)*; such appeals evidence the reality of inadequate government supplies.

In May 1863, as reported in *Emigranten,* Colonel Heg was named brigadier general and put in charge of the Third Brigade, home to the Norwegian Regiment and one of nine brigades of the federal army's right wing. Heg stayed constantly with his regiment and brigade, from the departure from Madison to the South in spring 1862 until his death, September 20, 1863, the day after he was mortally wounded as he bravely led his brigade into battle at Chickamauga in northern Georgia.

Colonel Heg became the war hero of the Norwegians. His memory was celebrated in heroic statues raised by the capitol in Madison, in Muskego, and at Lier, Norway, where the Heg family had its roots; another monument marks the place where Colonel Heg fell. Lieutenant Colonel Ole C. Johnson (Skibnæs) became commander of the Fifteenth Wisconsin Regiment on Heg's promotion in May; Johnson was captured at Chickamauga and sent to the Libby Prison in Richmond, Virginia, the capital of the Confederacy. He escaped and joined the remnant of his regiment and resumed his command of it. While imprisoned he wrote a letter to his brother, the later industrialist John A. Johnson, dated November 3, 1863, where he related the events of the battle: "Col. Heg, with his great goodness and gallant behavior was always present where there was danger. He was something of an idol among us and his memory will always be held in high esteem by every man in the regiment."[4]

Emigranten circulated among Norwegians in the armed services to the extent possible; according to Waldemar Ager, "a great number of the soldiers had poor knowledge of English," so the Madison journal was consequently a welcome visitor. September 8, 1861, Lieutenant Widvey sent a letter to the newspaper from the military camp at Darnestown, Maryland, where he explained that he that very day had received "an armful [of] newspapers, among which there were a half score examples of *Emigranten* of August 19 and 26." "As soon as *Emigranten* arrives," Widvey further noted, "there are many hands reaching for it, everyone wishes to see it, and a few wish to see it first; the terms, however, are that one person in each tent has to read it aloud for his companions, in order for everyone as far as possible to absorb it at the same time." Widvey later entered directly into the publishing business; from 1881 to 1883 he edited and published the weekly *Varden* (The Beacon) in La Crosse, Wisconsin.

A Norwegian volunteer in the Second Wisconsin Regiment, John Jacobsen, wrote to *Emigranten* in August 1861 to describe the 1,060-man-strong regiment's experience since leaving Madison June 10. On their way to Washington, D.C., by train, they had been welcomed at each stop by the local people; in Cleveland "a wonderful meal had been prepared by the ladies." "They had been arranged in two lines, and the ladies had walked between the lines and not only filled their stomachs, but also filled their bread pouches with all sorts of delicious goodies." The regiment received weapons and ammunition in Harrisburg, Pennsylvania, before continuing on to the federal capital, where Lincoln greeted them personally; they then moved on to their camp outside Washington. From then on, the letter writer painted a much less positive picture of their existence; the warm patriotic outpouring they had experienced no longer obtained. Jacobsen dwelled on the poor supply of provisions: He "daily lost weight." On the regiment's march southward with thirty-six thousand troops, Jacobsen related reprovingly that the soldiers set fire to abandoned houses, broke furniture left behind, and butchered farm animals, "whether or not they needed food."

"Then came the big day, July 21, the Battle of Bull Run." The goal had been to attack the Confederate capital of Richmond, but the smaller Confederate force decisively defeated the much larger, but improperly trained, Union army. Jacobsen described the battle in detail. "I was under fire four hours, and the bullets whizzed by my ears without any hitting me." He continued, "I fired about thirty shots and had the honor of one of my shots laying an enemy standard-bearer dead on the spot." The casualties were great on both sides. "Our regiment had 150 killed, wounded, and missing, and the company to which I belong, nine killed and eight wounded, among these our premier lieutenant A. S. Hill," reported Jacobsen. "At five o'clock in the afternoon we retreated in disorder." "The cause of this disorder," he explained to *Emigranten*'s readers, "was essentially that our generals and colonels had abandoned us." "Greatly exhausted," Jacobsen concluded, "we arrived in Washington the following morning at eight o'clock."[5]

The letter cited above typifies personal accounts from later battles printed in *Emigranten;* many of the letter writers described life in their camps and the mundane travails of military service. Johan Nordal Brun, compositor in *Emigranten*'s print shop, then serving as sergeant in Company K in the Third Wisconsin Volunteer Regiment, wrote from Frederick, Maryland, in January 1862: "Mr. Editor. I should have written earlier to you, but the time I have been in service has been filled with drills, being on guard duty, marching from one place to another, and keeping my rifle and clothes in order, not to speak of how long it takes to keep the buttons on my frock and the brass on my belt and my cartridge pouch brightly polished, and having to do so many other things a man like me has to do for the company." In August 1864, *Fædrelandet* gave Brun's obituary, extolling him as one of the many young men who had died "directly or indirectly from disease" in the nation's service.

Embracing the canon of the North did not diminish an attachment to an Old World cultural heritage and love for the ancestral home; indeed, in the manner of other ethnic groups, retention of national traditions and symbols became a vital resource in adjusting to the demands of life in America. Immigrants saw no conflict of loyalty, for instance, in observing May 17, Norway's Constitution Day, and simultaneously supporting the Union cause. In 1862, the Fifteenth Wisconsin Regiment, as noted in *Emigranten,* marked the day at Island No. 10, in the Mississippi River, Tennessee. Sergeant Nils J. Gilbert of Company F, the Valdris Company, described the observance in a letter to his brother: "I also want to tell you that we had a 17th of May celebration here in honor of Norway's liberation; a very gay affair it was. We sent to Cairo, Ill. for beer. Our company got one and a half barrels, and the other companies also got some. The first thing in the morning, just as the sun came up, we fired a salute of 13 cannon shots in honor of the day. Later, we had a parade; and on our return we drank both much and freely."

Sergeant Henry Syvertson of Company A, St. Olaf's Rifles, known as the Chicago Company, composed a song for the day; in praise of freedom, the final verse, here in literal translation, expressed longing for the old homeland as well as loyalty to the new:

Vel er vi fjernt fra Hjemmet	Indeed, we are far from home
Og kjæmpe under fremmed Flag,	And fight under a foreign flag
Men sende dog vor Hilsning	But yet we send our greeting
Til Norges Frihedsdag.	To Norway's freedom's day.
"Gud skjærme Norges Folk og Land!	"God protect Norway's people and land!
For Frihed staae og det hver Mand	For freedom stands every man
Der, hvor vor Vugge stod!"	There, where our cradle stood!"

Norwegians were thus, in the words of the song, the true defenders of liberty and freedom, in America as in Norway. More than sixty-five hundred Union soldiers were born in Norway.[6]

The Norwegian Regiment participated in a total of twenty-six battles. Regular reports from its movements—victories and defeats—appeared on the pages of *Emigranten,* communicating the grim reality of the conflict to its readers. The siege of Island No. 10 was the first major military action of the Fifteenth Wisconsin Regiment; it began March 15, 1862; the Confederate forces evacuated the island April 7. *Emigranten* April 14 and May 19 published letters describing the hardships of the men of the regiment. Jerry Rosholt summarized that only one man in the regiment died of his wounds and one from an accident, "but 162 men fell sick and were unable to fight. . . . Of those 162, 42 died on the island; 46 became disabled and were given discharge; and 74, who were in hospitals, had to be left behind when the regiment moved on." Eight of the ten companies left Island No. 10 on June 12; two remained until October to garrison the island. Hardships were repeated on many subsequent confrontations with the Confederate forces.

April 6, 1865, Anthon Odin Oyen, then safe at Camp Fisk near Vicksburg, exchanged for rebel prisoners in the North, wrote to *Emigranten*'s editor about the plight of prisoners of war in the South. Oyen was a pharmacist in Bodø, Norway, and came to America at age twenty in 1861. He served as a hospital pharmacist. "Mr. Editor," he began his letter, "There are perhaps still a few readers of

Emigranten who are interested in hearing a few words from surviving soldiers of the Fifteenth Wisconsin who were so unfortunate as having been taken prisoner in the different battles and skirmishes, from Chickamauga to Atlanta, Georgia." Oyen spent eighteen months in southern prisons, including the infamous Andersonville prison in Georgia. He lists the names of members of the Norwegian Regiment who perished in Andersonville and in Danville, Virginia. "Of about seventy-five men who were taken prisoners since September 19, 1863, there are many who will be grieved by kin and friends—the majority found their grave in Virginia and Georgia, but these brave soldiers died for their adopted fatherland and to uphold freedom."

Emigranten provided realistic accounts from the war theater, though, to be sure, a message of heroism and pride was embedded in its columns. Hans Christian Heg was the best known and

Painting by Carl L. Boeckman, about 1915, of the historic Battle of Chickamauga in northern Georgia in September 1863, where Colonel Hans Christian Heg led his men of the Fifteenth Wisconsin Regiment into combat on the smoke-filled battlefield.

most celebrated of the war heroes, but he was not alone; returning veterans of the conflict gained high status in the immigrant community and beyond. *Emigranten* articulated a heroic narrative; it enhanced the status of Norwegians in the new land, making them contributors to its welfare and growth. A new and vibrant Norwegian American community began to claim its rightful place in the nation. In its April 10, 1865, number, *Emigranten* carried news of the fall of the Confederate capital of Richmond, claiming "the rebellion has virtually ended." The meeting at Appomattox Court House between the Union general Ulysses S. Grant and general Robert E. Lee of the Confederacy on April 9, 1865, finalized the surrender of the South. The Civil War was over; but the exultation it generated was short-lived. Only five days later an assassin fatally wounded President Lincoln at Ford's Theater; Lincoln died on April 15, 1865. In his memoirs Carl Solberg stated his strong support of Lincoln's candidacy, and, as he related, "when Lincoln was assassinated I was among the thousands who went to Chicago to see his funeral train and to pay our respects to his memory."[7]

The Norwegian Synod and Slavery

Throughout most of its history *Emigranten*'s editorship was in the hands of laymen; it was thus less of a newspaper controlled by pastors than has been assumed. The clergy of the Norwegian Synod, however, had great access to its columns. Their dominance and strife on doctrine permeated an emerging Norwegian American community and, one may claim, weakened its political engagement. In 1864 *Emigranten* was joined by *Fædrelandet,* regularly described as a second "Synod newspaper" and strongly Republican. Its main founder, Frederick Fleischer, was born in Våler, Norway, in 1821, the son of a parish pastor; he was a lawyer by training but active in various business enterprises; bad economic times, however, in 1852 convinced him to give up his commercial ventures and immigrate to the gold fields of California, where he sought his fortune for eight years before moving to Wisconsin. He there made a living as a sailor on Lake Michigan and as a teacher in Lafayette County, Wisconsin, and, according to Johannes Wist, also assisted his cousin Knud Fleischer in editing *Emigranten* in Madison.

Frederick Fleischer moved to La Crosse in 1863; the city sheltered a growing Norwegian population and served as a center for surrounding Norwegian settlements. It would in time become a major Norwegian American hub. On January 14, 1864, Fleischer launched *Fædrelandet,* listing Johan Schrøder as copublisher until summer 1865. Schrøder was forty years old when in 1863 he decided to visit North America; he changed his mind about returning to Norway. Schrøder's experience as an agricultural journalist in Norway allowed for easy entry into the world of immigrant journalism; in 1867 he published an exposition on Scandinavians in the United States and Canada. *Fædrelandet,* Blegen observed, "marked a natural step northwestward in the development of the Norwegian American press." Schrøder exemplified the emergence of a class of immigrant newsmen who advanced its progress. *Fædrelandet*'s initial editorial explained that the newspaper was intended as "a bond among people of kindred blood and a means of uniting with our American brethren." It assured "the American people" that "We do not intend to establish a Norway in America, but to unite with our American fellow citizens, so long as what is true and right governs your principles." The last statement referred to *Fædrelandet*'s motto "Right and True" and its Republican affiliation as "an independent Union newspaper"; in Norwegian it promised its regular readers that it would not engage in "discussions of questions of a religious nature," but leave that to "the special organs of the church."[8]

Neither *Fædrelandet* nor *Emigranten* succeeded in distancing themselves from theological controversy; in fact, for some time both papers featured strong conflicting views on biblical teachings in regard to chattel slavery. Leading Synod pastors, convinced by their belief in the doctrine of verbal inspiration of the holy scripture and its literal inerrancy, held that the Bible justified human servitude. They had, according to Arlow Andersen, "caught the spirit of the German Missouri Synod, domiciled in the slave state Missouri." The controversy started when Concordia Seminary in St. Louis closed at the start of the Civil War. From the late 1850s, Norwegian Synod ministerial candidates had been educated at Concordia; Pastor Laur. Larsen, longtime president of Luther College, Decorah, Iowa, was stationed there as advisor and professor for the Norwegian theological students. *Emigranten,* responding editorially in May 1861 to an announcement by Pastor Larsen in the same number on the closing of the seminary and return of the Norwegian theological students to the North, asked him kindly "to inform the Norwegian public of the position taken by the teachers at this College in regard to the insurrection in the South." *Emigranten* wished reassurance that those who trained future Norwegian ministers did not, like almost all other "churches' clerics in the slave states openly support the rebels." In spite of several letters printed in *Emigranten* requesting a response, Pastor Larsen kept his silence.

Not until June 17, 1861, did a response from Laur. Larsen appear in print in *Emigranten,* titled "Concordia College and the Insurrection" *(Concordia College og Oprøret).* Larsen, in consultation with the pastors A. C. Preus, the Synod's president, and Jakob Aall Ottesen, "a tenacious controversialist and grimly purposeful leader," as Blegen characterized him, concluded based on scripture that slavery was not sin; however, rebellion was invariably a sin in Larsen's opinion, but he was uncertain as to whether or not secession constituted rebellion. Unlike the laity, many members of the Synod clergy were Democrats and supported states' rights. It was the latter assumption Solberg most objected to in his rejoinder; preservation of the Union and loyalty to the national government were of paramount importance; the Concordia faculty held, he insisted, as reflected in Larsen's statement, an unacceptable position.

The issue reached its height at the annual deliberations as the Synod convened in the Luther Valley Church at Rock Prairie from June 26 to July 3, 1861; pastors and lay representatives of the congregations attended. As the discussion moved toward the Synod's teaching on slavery, the clergy and the laity became clearly divided. Toward the end of the meeting H. A. Preus and Ottesen drafted a ministerial declaration, signed by all ministers, but when put before the lay delegates, only twenty-eight out of sixty-six approved. The declaration stated:

> Although, according to God's Word, it is not in and by itself a sin *[ikke Synd i og for sig]* to own slaves, yet slavery in itself is an evil and a punishment from God, and we condemn all the abuses and sins which are connected with it, just as we, when our official duties demand it, and when Christian love and wisdom require it, will work for its abolition.[9]

The Synod clergy's declaration, given full coverage by editor Solberg in *Emigranten,* was intended as a compromise. Instead of gaining broad acceptance, however, the abstract theological interpretation of slavery, based on both the Old and the New Testaments, only served to generate more controversy. Their naïve confidence in clerical authority in making the declaration clearly backfired; the lay opposition did not, as anticipated, melt away. Knud Langeland wrote from his home in Racine an article titled "Is Human Slavery a Sin?" *(Er Menneskeslaveri Synd?).* Solberg printed it on the front page of *Emigranten* in October 1861. Langeland reviewed critically the ministerial declaration and dismissed the logic used by the pastors as being flawed. He stated his conclusion firmly, referencing the Declaration of Independence: "All human beings are created free and have certain rights which they themselves cannot voluntarily cede, among these are counted life, liberty, and happiness." "Slavery," Langeland held, "does violence to nature—nature's law is God's law." "Slavery," he argued, "annihilates mankind's innate natural right." Langeland spoke for the laity. His views reflected as well the early antislavery resolutions by the low-church Eielsen Synod.

The most major incident of the debate was Pastor C. L. Clausen's formal retraction of his initial approval of the ministerial declaration, printed in *Emigranten,* December 2, 1861; it was a sensational development from within the Synod itself that escalated the public debate among ministers and laymen. Clausen was a humanitarian and a democrat, greatly opposed to slavery, and close to the laity. His service for six months as chaplain for the Fifteenth Wisconsin Regiment gave him renewed faith in the cause of the North. In the ensuing heated debate, as emphasized by Blegen, Clausen found himself at a disadvantage, since "His antagonists were men of learning, university-trained for the most part, skilled in dialectics . . . and considerably less responsive than he to popular currents."

Clausen gained the strong support of Solberg in *Emigranten,* of Langeland, who in 1866 became editor of *Skandinaven,* and even of the freethinking Marcus Thrane of *Dagslyset* (The Light of Day); the Norwegian American newspapers were unified in their antislavery stance. In an age of personal, rather than commercial, journalism individual support mattered. As the heated controversy continued to fill the pages of the existing journals, editors and readers were increasingly impatient with a repetitious exchange of arguments. In February 1867 Frederick Fleischer complained editorially in *Fædrelandet* under the title "Pro- and Anti-Slavery Men" that "the last four days we have received no fewer than 17—repeat seventeen—long articles about the slavery question . . . we declare that it is high time for this controversy, which has turned into personal insults and is waged about circumstances which by civic law no longer exist among us, and must now come to an end if our church is not to be more split than it already is."

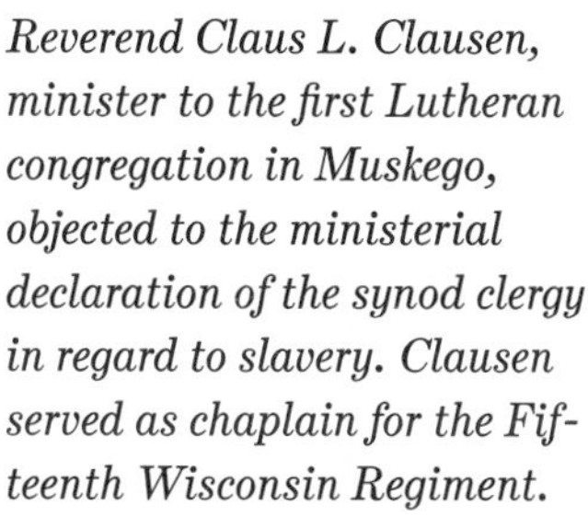

Reverend Claus L. Clausen, minister to the first Lutheran congregation in Muskego, objected to the ministerial declaration of the synod clergy in regard to slavery. Clausen served as chaplain for the Fifteenth Wisconsin Regiment.

Fleischer's reference was to the Thirteenth Amendment ratified in 1865, abolishing slavery in the United States. Even though the issue was settled, the newspaper polemics persisted. In early 1868, the Synod arranged a conference in Chicago, at which Clausen was present, where it reaffirmed its position; Clausen's only recourse was to resign from the Synod, which he did in a letter dated June 28, 1868. The following year he published his defense, titled *Gjenmæle* (Rejoinder), against accusations leveled at him by the Synod's church council. A unique chapter in the early history of Norwegians in America came to an end, although, quoting from one of the ten theses presented at the Chicago conference, "the doctrine of slavery as a divine institution protected by God's Law, and giving the owner the right of inheritance and sale of slaves," might on occasion resurface for debate in the Norwegian American press. Given the aversion of the vast majority of Norwegian immigrants to slavery, historians can only speculate on what Andersen summarized as, "A combination of factors—social, religious, and psychological—that contributed to the slavery argument of the contentious theologians."[10]

The Westward Movement

Norwegian immigration to the United States continued, though greatly reduced, during the Civil War years. After the end of hostilities, Norwegians took part in large numbers in the great westward advance of the American people; Norwegian settlement spread throughout the states of the Upper Midwest. The first great wave commenced in 1866 when Norwegian migration to America jumped from four thousand the year before to 15,455. A calmer period in transatlantic migration followed the major exodus in the late 1860s; it declined after 1873 when a postwar economic boom ended, lasting until the rate of economic growth picked up toward the end of the decade. According to Norwegian statistics, Norway lost a total of 110,896 citizens to emigration during the eight years of large-scale expatriation: 1866–73.

The states of Illinois, Wisconsin, Iowa, and Minnesota plus the Dakota Territory had a combined Norwegian population in 1870 of 149,004; of these 66 percent were Norwegian-born. The second generation had clearly made its entry into the Norwegian American community. There were smaller Norwegian settlements in Utah, Nebraska, Michigan, and Texas; in 1870 the Norwegian settlers in these parts of the United States were only 2,819 strong; 71 percent had been born in Norway, as one would expect in these less-established settlements with a younger and more recently immigrated population. No large Norwegian settlement resulted from the gold diggings in California, even though Norwegian immigrants, coming from older settlements or from Norway directly, joined the "forty-niners." Norwegians had not yet arrived in substantial numbers in the Pacific Northwest; the westward and northwestward movement of Norwegians would, however, in the following decades greatly expand their presence.

The Upper Midwest persisted as the major area of Norwegian settlement. A watchful Norwegian American press took notice of an expanding population of compatriots. Regular newspaper advertising offered land under the Homestead Act of 1862 and railroad land; various speculators and real estate agents also advertised. Many of those moving west were Civil War veterans, encouraged by a special homestead bonus that required only one year's residence, as compared to the regular five. Settlement promoters encouraged the formation of Norwegian settlements; men in the employ of the immigrant press engaged in land sales. In 1868, Hans Borchsenius, the earlier editor of *Nordstjernen,* advertised in *Emigranten* his intention, "provided it proved practical for the future, to open a land agency" in Madison. The prominent Swedish immigrant Colonel Hans Mattson of Civil War fame and a pioneer farmer was employed as land agent for the St. Paul and Pacific Railroad from 1868; this railroad adopted a special Scandinavian immigration policy. In October 1868 Mattson advertised in *Fædrelandet og Emigranten* three hundred thousand acres "of the best prairie, field, and forested" railroad land along its line being built westward through Wright, Meeker, Kandiyohi, Swift, Stevens, Grant, and Wilkin counties, Minnesota, and explained in the same advertisement that his goal was to "have the land as far as possible fall into Scandinavian hands." Wisconsin continued to trump the other states with 59,819 first- and second-generation Norwegians, but Minnesota was only some ten thousand behind, for a total of 49,569, Iowa 25,251, Illinois 13,281, and Dakota Territory, then at the start of Norwegian settlement, with only 1,284 Norwegian pioneer settlers.

Emigranten and *Fædrelandet* sought subscribers and carried news and correspondence from these same settlements, and on occasion from Norwegians who had settled beyond the core settlement area. It was of course the role of the frontier press to attract new settlers while it promoted specific party loyalty. Solberg recounted how he in 1868 sold *Emigranten* to Fleischer, "and I went to La Crosse for a while to assist in the consolidation of the two papers." The merged newspapers were published in La Crosse as *Fædrelandet og Emigranten,* the first issue dated September 3, 1868. Under the title "The United Newspapers," Fleischer explained that each of the two journals had three thousand to four thousand subscribers, which combined would make the enterprise more profitable, better able to serve the Norwegian American community, and a stronger advocate for civil rights and for enlightenment. La Crosse remained the place of publication because, "its railroad and steamship connections are now so advanced that the newspaper in the course of only one day can reach all main points, east, west, north, and south, in Wisconsin, as well as the railroads in Minnesota and northern Iowa, and likewise to Chicago and other northern points in Illinois."[11]

The stream of letters from the many able pioneer writers printed in the immigrant press constitutes a major historical source; the correspondents, regularly with great pride, related not only the mundane and the celebratory achievements of their new home in America, but also the triumph of the human spirit in overcoming homesickness and adversity, in making the wilderness prosper for the benefit of coming generations as they actively engaged in building new communities.

The settlement letters that saw print in various Norwegian American newspapers helped to create a social network and a sense of a larger Norwegian American fellowship. One of a multitude of examples is the December 1860 letter John Olsen Oian wrote to *Emigranten*'s editor from the town of Carlton, Kewaunee County, Wisconsin. Oian described the Norwegian settlement there, which then was five and a half years old and consisted of about fifty families. "Agriculture has progressed slowly," Oian wrote, "in this densely forested area, where the axe first had to fell the large trees. Only a hope of a free home and a better future could make the pioneer endure the burdens of pioneer life and keep his spirits alive." He further related that their pastor, Jacob Aall Ottesen, had moved to Koshkonong and would visit only rarely; "Last summer we laid the cornerstone for a small brick church," he continued, "which I think will be under roof this winter." He hoped that there soon would be a pastor in Manitowoc, who, "according to an agreement would to begin with come here four times annually."

As the agricultural frontier moved westward letters from greater distance were common. From a pioneer Norwegian settlement along the Sheyenne River in Dakota Territory, A. M. Anderson in September 1871 reassured the editor of *Fædrelandet og Emigranten* that the newspaper "has found its way to here, and wherever I go

I see this journal, and if you would give me some space for a few comments, which I will briefly make about the land here, it would be good." Anderson went on to describe the Sheyenne River, which "is a small river that runs 25 miles west of Fort Abercrombie and empties into the Red River 45 miles north of the fort"; the banks of the Sheyenne were covered with woods. The land had not yet been surveyed "but will be surveyed this fall, and on the market next summer." The prairie land was well suited for farming, Anderson informed potential settlers, and "there is grass in abundance for cattle breeding." And, when the Northern Pacific Railroad would cross the Red River a town and marketplace "will be established three miles from where I live."

Norwegian immigrants took up farming in exceptional numbers; they in fact did so in larger percentages than any other major immigrant group in the nineteenth century. This circumstance influenced the content of the immigrant press. In its opening issue in January 1864, *Fædrelandet* addressed this group of potential subscribers directly. "The mass of our readers operate farms. It would therefore be a great defect with this paper if we did not have articles on farming. That will happen and these articles will be of so much greater value since their author is himself a farmer." And articles appeared in succession, about fall planting, how to select dairy cows, care of farm animals, meat production, prospects for the harvest, and marketing and market prices of farm products. Similar contributions were printed in *Emigranten* as well and continued in *Fædrelandet og Emigranten*. Manufacturers of farm machinery thought it advantageous to advertise in the same journals; John H. Manny's "Reaper and Mower" was offered for sale, in 1862 made lighter by "one horsepower" since 1857 and much improved; Mendota Agricultural Works and Machine in Madison praised its Brockford's improved harvester as the best on the market; and Pitt's Agricultural Works in Buffalo, New York, made a similar claim for its threshing machine. These American producers of farm machines advertised them in lengthy announcements in Norwegian, frequently identifying their agents in Norwegian farm districts.[12]

The View toward Norway

Personal letters exchanged across the Atlantic and the news dispatches of a distant homeland carried by Norwegian American periodicals reinforced pre-emigration memories and maintained contact with Norway. Through these same means, Norwegian immigrants invited kin and friends to join them in America. Prepaid tickets purchased in America fueled an increasing portion of the immigration to the United States from Norway. "It has of late become more and more common," *Fædrelandet* explained in 1868, "for countrymen living here to send passage money to their relatives who are planning to come here." The advantages were tallied: "Those who have a greater opportunity have then generally bought steamship tickets and thus spared themselves the expense involved in purchasing bank notes here and selling them at home. Likewise the emigrant has avoided being exposed to the many swindles he is likely to experience when he without knowing the language tries to have his luggage transported from the ship to the railroad station and purchase a railroad ticket in this country." "Those who have not had the same good means," the newspaper further related, "and consequently have had to let their relatives travel by sailing ships, have sent them money as bank notes, whereby a loss is incurred, and likewise these have landed in Quebeck and have not had anyone to help them with their luggage and purchase of railroad ticket."

The great number of notices in *Emigranten, Fædrelandet,* and *Fædrelandet og Emigranten* advertising transatlantic transportation shows the prevailing competition for the emigrant trade; they were of course an advertising boon to newspapers. The practice of sending prepaid tickets to Norway broadened the social composition of the immigrant body as they enabled people without personal means to emigrate. In many instances, when it did not involve spouse and children, the passage money was considered a loan to be repaid in America. Quebec, Canada, was, as quoted from *Fædrelandet* above, the destination for Norwegian sailing ships; between 1854 and 1865, 90 percent of all Norwegian emigrants took this route. The average crossing was in excess of forty-four days, as compared to the much shorter voyage by steam, by the 1880s, of eight or nine days between Liverpool and New York. Norwegian emigrants continued to make the crossing on Norwegian sailing ships; as late as 1871 a third of them chose sail and two-thirds steam. The passenger sailing ship era ended shortly thereafter. Agents sold tickets in all major regions of Norwegian settlement; Knud J. Fleischer, the earlier editor of *Emigranten,* as a general agent for Norwegian shipping firms in Madison, advertised regularly in the press, offering tickets on Norwegian sailing ships from Norway to Quebec. Competing with many agents for other lines, Fleischer was also an agent for the British steamship line Guion with service from Liverpool to New York, as well as for the short-lived Norwegian-American Steamship Company *(Det Norsk-Amerikanske Dampskibsselskab),* established in 1871, with direct sailings between Bergen and New York.

Many of the immigrants, especially those who landed in Quebec, arrived penniless and in dire need. Whenever tragedy or need among fellow Norwegians became known, Norwegian-language newspapers invariably encouraged assistance, often spearheading collection drives. Scandinavian emigration aid societies appeared early in Chicago, Milwaukee, Madison, and La Crosse. The first, the Scandinavian Emigrant Aid Society *(Den skandinaviske Emigrant-Hjælpe-Forening)* in Chicago, was organized the summer of 1866; *Emigranten* joined the Chicago newspaper *Skandinaven* in making appeals for contributions and reporting on how the collected funds were used. There was pride in giving aid. *Fædrelandet* classified as false a report in the Minneapolis newspaper *Nordisk Folkeblad* (Nordic People's Newspaper) in July 1868, "that 25 Swedish emigrants had arrived in Minneapolis in a condition close to death, and that four of them later died from hunger and heat." *Fædrelandet* expressed disbelief, since such things did not even occur when little or nothing was done to relieve need among the emigrants, "and not to say at present when there are organized aid societies in all places where the emigrants pass." "In order to reach Minneapolis," the newspaper argued, "they have to pass through Chicago or Milwaukee or La Crosse, and at these three places they would without a doubt have been cared for so that they did not suffer any need."[13]

The mass arrival of newcomers directly from Norway was a constant reinforcement of the Norwegian impulse; even the organized aid became a unifying means to reflect on a sacred duty to come to the aid of fellow Norwegians. The immigrant press was the driving force in the process, facilitating an open discourse among Norwegian Americans, wherever they resided across the Upper Midwest, as well as with the homeland. An idealized past and shared rituals created a sense of commonality that extended across the ocean. Celebrations of May 17—*Syttende Mai*—commemorating the constitution adopted at Eidsvoll on May 17, 1814, which signaled the homeland's national rebirth more than any other single event, satisfied the need for a gloried history and symbolic order; by the 1860s observances of the day were rapidly becoming the most prominent of all ethnic festivals. As interpreted by a newspaper like *Emigranten,* these public displays, which invariably included an emotional oratory in honor of the day and the flying of Norway's national flag—tricolor red, white, and blue—promoted pride in the historic achievements of the homeland but were also compatible with the historical journey of their new "fatherland." "July 4th is at hand," *Emigranten* began its editorial June 26, 1865, "this day so rich in memories and blessings for the American people." "For us [Norwegians] July 4th and May 17th stand forth hand in hand and freedom's splendor surrounds them like a halo." The editorial reminded readers, however that "even though both are days of joy, America is now our fatherland by our own free choice," and thus "July 4th deserves our participation even more so than May 17th."[14]

May 17 and July 4 observances may both be seen as celebrating the freedom of America as well as a national identity. *Skandinaven* noted in 1866 that Nora Lodge in Chicago took the initiative to celebrate July 4 by arranging a "Norwegian basket picnic" by the Calumet River. Correspondents from the widely spread Norwegian settlements reported on their local celebrations of Norway's Constitution Day as well as of American Independence Day; in the church-centered scattered farming communities both days might be marked by a church outing. In urban colonies secular activities might be on display. The May 17 festivities in Chicago in 1868, as reported in *Skandinaven,* were arranged by the Norwegian Dramatic Society *(Den norske dramatiske Forening)* in the German Hall: a one-act comedy, a national tableau of "May 17 among Norway's Mountains, which made a good impression on all friends of freedom and the [Norwegian] fatherland," an epilogue "for the day of freedom," concluding with "an elegant ball."

An urban pan-Scandinavianism existed in American cities from midcentury; it failed toward the end of the 1800s. Norwegians, Swedes, and Danes gathered to present a unified cultural front in common organizations; as a minority—even when combining resources—they jointly met the challenges of a complex urban environment. In La Crosse May 17 observances in 1868 were under the auspices of the local Scandinavian Society *(Det skandinaviske Selskab)* organized in April 1866. *Fædrelandet* reported that "Norway's Constitution Day was not forgotten this year either by the

*May 17 (*Syttende Mai*) celebration in the mid-1870s, Winequaw (near Madison), Wisconsin. The Norwegian flag, analogous to the Swedish national banner, marks the union between Sweden and Norway in the upper left-hand quarter.*

Scandinavian Society." Out of respect for Wisconsin's Sabbath laws, since May 17 was that year on a Sunday, the festivities were moved to Monday, May 18. In the afternoon the members gathered "at the German Gardens outside the city . . . where one according to Norwegian fashion spent the day with merry games and song, the Norwegian choir entertained with national melodies from the balcony decorated with the Scandinavian and the American flags. When darkness fell, one took refuge in the large hall and took a lively dance. Speeches and toasts were given to Norway with its many precious memories, to America which admits the immigrants into its wide embrace and gives them the same rights as its own children, and to those who adorn and brighten the festival 'the ladies.'" May 17 celebrations were becoming a part of Norwegian American folkways, expressing their ethnic self-perception. Norwegians in America, in their interpretation of the significance of the day, constructed their own traditions, symbols, and rituals.[15]

The observance of May 17 in America was influenced by its rise as a national celebration in Norway. An enlightened social elite marked the day shortly after 1814 in private meetings where they toasted a free and independent Norway. Public markings of the day began in the 1820s; the first grand massive observances took place in Trondheim in 1826 and 1827. A national outpouring took place in 1864 in connection with the fiftieth anniversary of the May 17 constitution, highlighted by the first presentation of Bjørnstjerne Bjørnson's mighty national anthem, *"Ja vi elsker dette landet"* (Yes, we love this land). The anthem recounts the high points in Norway's history; the first verse extols love for the native land. Historical memory greatly influenced the formation of Norwegian nationalism; it was established through an appeal to a common past and common identity.

In its June 22, 1868, number, *Emigranten* devoted an entire page to "Seventeenth of May in Christiania" *(17de Mai i Christiania),* an outdoor event that attracted large crowds of people; the article included patriotic songs, detailed descriptions of banners and ceremonies as well as excerpts of May 17 orations. Anton Martin Schweigaard, prominent economics professor and politician, emphasized in his speech the collective historical journey of the Norwegian people. The men of Eidsvoll in forming the constitution, he expounded, incorporated the provincial laws from Old Norse times in a single law, the law codes adopted by the four assemblies *(ting)*, the west Norwegian *Gulating*, the *Frostating* in Trøndelag, and the *Eidsivating* and *Borgarting*, both in east Norway; the Eidsvoll Constitution of 1814 thus reflected the centuries-long traditions of a nation of laws, though, as Schweigaard noted, the constitution "was more in keeping with present expectations, but without breaking with ancient traditions." These were indeed breathtaking historical vistas, and Schweigaard expanded on them by reminding the audience of the adventurous spirit of their Viking forebears; "if the Norseman felt restricted in regard to available land, there were other possibilities open to him, the large, common, and jointly owned world oceans." "We are all descendants of the Norsemen of old," he persisted, "who in olden days crossed the ocean to America."[16]

News from Norway was read with great interest, the above illustrating the importance of glorifying the homeland. A flow of information crossed the ocean and appeared in the columns of Norwegian-language newspapers; providing news from the homeland represented a major function of the immigrant press. The individual journals regularly had columns titled "News from Norway" *(Nyt fra Norge)*, or *Fra Norge*, or even simply *Norge*, as *Emigranten* called its Norwegian column, as well as similar inserts of news from Sweden and Denmark. The Norwegian American journals had many Danish subscribers and were read as well by Swedish neighbors.

Coverage of news from Norway and the other Nordic countries relied on correspondence, subscription to newspapers, and telegrams. The challenges faced by ethnic newspaper publishers were highlighted in *Emigranten* in April 1864:

> Last Tuesday we received at one time Norwegian correspondence and large packages of Scandinavian newspapers, including *Morgenbladet* [The Morning Newspaper] and *Aftenbladet* [The Evening Newspaper] from March 1 to 18 and several numbers of [the Danish] *Dagbladet* [The Daily Newspaper]. Mail from Norway and Denmark must be very unreliable when so much has been sent in a single mailing. From these newspapers this issue of *Emigranten* prints several selections, among these the report of the opening of Norway's *Storting*, which we already last week announced in a short telegram.

The main coverage in the three newspapers listed above dealt with the severity of the second German-Danish conflict over Slesvig-Holstein and potential assistance by Norway and Sweden to Denmark in this uneven conflict; it was reported in later issues too, as was the ultimate failure when both the Swedish and the Norwegian governments declined military assistance. In October 1864, Denmark lost the two duchies, which represented a third of the Danish kingdom's territory. For the most part, Norwegian American press coverage of the homeland was much less dramatic; it reported from all regions of Norway, though, as one might assume—especially in the pioneer years—happenings in the Norwegian capital took precedence. Still, Norwegian American readers were informed about the fisheries in the Lofoten Islands, extreme weather conditions in the northern city of Tromsø, and news about the Sami people in Finnmark. *Fædrelandet* in March 1867 reprinted the report to the Norwegian government by the Russian consul general in Norway following his visit to Finnmark: "[he] says that he marvels at the progress in the fisheries and growth in Norway while in northern Russia there is little or no fishing."

Fædrelandet og Emigranten in September 1868 reported on "the grain harvest in the outer coastal districts" south of Bergen, haying in "Romsdalen Amt" on the northwest coast, the drought that threatened the harvest in "Buskerud Amt" in the East, and the depressing heat in Trøndelag; the same issue carried a news item about the departure from Oslo, "last Friday, as usual," of the steamship "with a large group of emigrants who over Liverpool would set out for America." "Among these," the Norwegian source noted, "There were three farmer families from Trysil who in their possession had quite considerable amounts of money, and who thus did not because of need have to leave the country." They left, they claimed, because "the poor relief burdens increased, while there were only a few in the community who were able to pay pauper tax, and consequently the burdens on the rich were too great." The three families had purchased the tickets for forty-four emigrants, including accompanying servants and impoverished families. It was a situation familiar to many of *Fædrelandet og Emigranten*'s readers. Optimism prevailed, however, even during "these hard times," evidenced in private share capital being raised in the affected districts to complete the railroad line between Oslo and Trondheim, a project finished in 1877.

Articles in *Aftenbladet* instilled homeland pride, informing readers that the Norwegian merchant fleet had prospered greatly since the repeal of the British Navigation Act in 1849; world trade increased by 50 percent every decade between 1840 and 1870; and Norwegian ships, which also served the needs of other nations—especially Great Britain—carried goods on all the oceans of the world. It was a golden age in Norwegian shipping. The immigrant press habitually painted the homeland's advances with a broad stroke.

Norwegian American newspapers closely watched the political life of the homeland: the sessions of the *Storting,* local and national elections, and Swedish Union relations. They also featured visits by the Union king to his Norwegian capital. Based on the assessments in contemporary Swedish and Norwegian school textbooks, one may claim that during these years both kingdoms held a positive view of the Union. *Emigranten* in October 1865 told of the baptism of the fourth son of Crown Prince Oscar, becoming King Oscar II of the Twin Kingdoms in 1872, adopting the motto "For the Well of the Sister Nations" *(Broderfolkenes Vel).* As the brotherly union in subsequent years waned in a crisis that eventually terminated the common monarchy, the Norwegian American press spoke with one voice for the rights of the homeland. The Union crisis also laid to rest the pan-Scandinavian movement in American urban centers.

The meetings of the Christiania Labor Society *(Christiania Arbeidersamfund)* were also of interest; in 1867 the press told of the increased use by members of its one-thousand-volume library. The press noted the Norwegian Bible Society's *(Det norske Bibelselskab)* fiftieth anniversary celebration in 1866 as well as church anniversaries, appointments of bishops in the Church of Norway, and the deaths of prominent Norwegian church leaders, politicians, artists, and scholars. An extensive coverage in the Norwegian American press of the world the immigrants had left behind, at a time when return visits were rare—for most immigrants even inconceivable—retained a sense of an ethnic consciousness in the Norwegian American community and maintained the contact with a changing homeland.[17]

Chicago as a Center of Newspaper Activity

Chicago as a major urban destination for Norwegian immigration was foreordained to become a hub for Norwegian-language publication, but it only achieved that status in the post–Civil War decades. The liberal Free Soil weekly *Friheds-Banneret* (The Banner of Freedom), 1852–53—save for Charles Reese's campaign sheet *Folkebladet,* fall 1860—was the only representative of Norwegian American journalism to make an appearance in Chicago until after the end of the Civil War. The pioneer immigrant press in general represented rural interests, though individual newspapers gained subscribers in the growing metropolis. Even the pioneer newspaper *Nordlyset* found readers and sought advertising there. *Emigranten* as well circulated among Norwegians in Chicago, and like the Lutheran church—formed in a rural setting and whose presence in Chicago initially represented a missionary venture—moved into the city with a rural perspective.

A Norwegian American press was established in Chicago during the second half of the 1860s. The opportunities and the diversity in an urban environment attracted an increasing number of Norwegian immigrants; they adjusted to an urban economy and many of the arrivals met with success in business and the professions. Chicago was a fertile ground for newspaper publishing. By 1870 8,325 Norwegians lived in Chicago; three-quarters of them had been born in Norway. About 68 percent of the Norwegians, immigrants and American-born, lived on Chicago's northwest side; the original community centered on Milwaukee Avenue and Kinzie Street; Milwaukee Avenue was the main route whereby Norwegians continued their trek northwestward. In the 1870s Grand Avenue (then Indiana Street), a few blocks farther north, became the center of the Norwegian enclave, and the fashionable Wicker Park neighborhood was developing. This tight-knit urban community required people with many skills. It gave opportunity for artistic development; more so than the countryside, it harbored a nonreligious and liberal concept of life in America. The Norwegian colony was clearly maturing.

The foreign-language press in Chicago, as in other urban settings, brought together the immigrants in churches, clubs, and societies and fostered a sense of community. The German-language *Chicago Volksfreund* (People's Friend) in 1845 was the first representative of the ethnic press, followed by the more influential *Illinois Staatszeitung* (State Times). These, in the manner of newspapers published by Norwegians, Swedes, and Danes in Chicago, had as political organs a basic civic educational role in the immigrant community and gave opportunity for individuals harboring political ambitions to be elected to public office. In April 1868 Just M. Kahn, a Danish Jew, announced in *Emigranten* that he sought subscribers to *Fremad* (Forward), "a newspaper the undersigned intends to publish in Milwaukee, Wisconsin, for the Scandinavian people in the United States of America from the month of April." Despite Kahn's Danish nationality, *Fremad* mainly addressed itself to a Norwegian audience. Established by a party of Democratic politicians in connection with the presidential campaign that year, *Fremad* campaigned aggressively for Democrat Horatio Seymour. As expected, Seymour's rival, Republican Ulysses S. Grant, was victorious by a large margin. Even so, a greatly diminished Norwegian Democratic vote was still being solicited.

Nordisk Folkeblad (Nordic People's Newspaper), then published in Minneapolis, in April 1869 informed its readers that *Fremad* had been sold to Sophus Beder, also a Dane and the journal's business manager, who moved it from Milwaukee to Chicago. The prominent Danish American banker Ferdinand S. Winslow financed *Fremad*'s publication; it switched its political affiliation to the Republican camp (sudden shifts in editorial policy were not uncommon in the early years of the immigrant press).

Fremad was discontinued 1871, a consequence of hard economic times for Winslow, as well as the great fire in October of that year, which destroyed its offices and bankrupted the companies it had bought insurance from, making it a total loss. The Republican *Nordisk Folkeblad* had concluded in its 1869 report that "the last of the Scandinavian newspapers established by Democrats has ceased, but, it must at the same time be said," the report concluded, "that of all Democratic newspapers, *Fremad* was our most worthy opponent, and it almost hurts us to see it gone."[18]

The Republican *Fremad* and the men associated with it competed with the Republican newspaper *Skandinaven* for political influence. Most of these men were of Danish birth, like the editor in chief Gustav Mueller, who was a knighted veteran of the Danish-German War of 1864; he arrived in Chicago in 1868, became popular in elite social circles, and exhibited talent as a poet and author. Also among *Fremad*'s writers were Norwegian Hjalmar Hjorth Boyesen, who later produced novels of immigrant life, and Swedish-born Norwegian John W. Arctander, who later gained prominence in Minnesota as a lawyer. Marion Tuttle Marzolf concluded that *Fremad*'s staff, consisting as it did of university-educated immigrants, typified many of the early Scandinavian American newspapers. They were frequently written by and for the elite.

Skandinaven parted company with *Fremad* in regard to elitism. Johannes Wist described *Skandinaven*'s founder, John Anderson, in glowing terms, as "a man of the people who felt himself in tune with his immigrated countrymen," since "he as so many of them had received as a gift from infancy quite a hatred of everything that was considered to be fashionable and aristocratic." This basic view, Wist thought, had to a great degree characterized *Skandinaven* as an organ for the ordinary person and explained "its powerful position among Norwegians in America." Its history, he insisted "is in its main features that of the fortunate Norwegian pioneer's history in this country" and "experienced an identical struggle as [the pioneers] in order to reach its goal to become a large and influential newspaper."

John Anderson, born in Voss, Norway, 1836, came to Chicago with his parents in June 1845; the death of his father Andrew during the cholera epidemic of 1849 left him at age thirteen with the responsibility of supporting his mother Laura and a baby sister. His youthful experiences as a family provider—working in a butcher shop, selling apples, and carrying newspapers—moved him after six months into the newspaper publishing business as a "printer's devil." From 1852, he, like Eric Anderson, who in 1847 set the type for the first issue of *Nordlyset,* gained initial knowledge of the trade as a printer on the *Chicago Democrat;* he continued as a journeyman printer, and in 1866, when he launched *Skandinaven,* he was head of the composing room of the *Chicago Tribune.* The Norwegian community gained access to a public medium before a separate Norwegian-language press existed through compatriots in the employ of American newspapers.[19]

The first regular issue of *Skandinaven* was dated June 1, 1866, though weekly sample copies were distributed from May 2, which in some later press releases was given as its date of founding. Anderson established the newspaper and the pioneer editor Knud Langeland assumed editorial responsibility. Iver Lawson (Ivar Larson Bøe) was one of the co-owners; as an early immigrant from Voss, Norway, he realized wealth and gained civic influence in the expanding Chicago environment. A large and prospering community of immigrants from Voss, referred to as "The Voss Circle" *(Vosseringen),* began in 1836 with the arrival in Chicago of Niels Knutson Røthe, his wife, Torbjørg, and their three children; they are held to be the first immigrants from Voss. Through the years many more Vossings

John Anderson, founder and publisher of Skandinaven, *in 1883 moved into an imposing building on Peoria Avenue. The sign on the horse-drawn wagon in front of* Skandinaven*'s new offices advertises the firm to be "printers in all languages."*

followed them. Solidarity along the lines of the Norwegian home community considerably impacted migration patterns to the United States. Many of the original leaders in the Norwegian colony came from the Vossing ranks, which reflected not only the early emigration, but also a close-knit community that allowed a leadership to emerge. October 23, 1856, Chicago Vossings, led by fellow Vossings Andrew Nelson (Brekke) and Iver Lawson, organized the Vossing Emigration Society *(Det vossiske Emigrationsselskab)* with the purpose of collecting funds to aid "needy and worthy families" who wished to emigrate to America. The activities of this group led to the founding of the unique newspaper *Wossingen* in Leland, Illinois, in December 1857. The following year more than one hundred copies were mailed to Norway; it was an early instance of how immigrant newspapers functioned as expanded America letters. *Wossingen* was discontinued in March 1860, in large part due to difficulties leading up to the Civil War.

Members of the Voss Circle, men like Iver Lawson, were significant players in the founding of *Skandinaven.* A passage from Knud Langeland's *Nordmændene i Amerika* (The Norwegians in America) sheds light on how the newspaper came into being and the role played by personal contact.

> It had long been a subject of discussion among my friends in Chicago that I ought to come there and make a new attempt with a Norwegian newspaper; but since I had had painful experiences myself and also seen the misfortune of others, I could not give them an encouraging response. Finally in summer 1865, Mr. John Anderson came out to my farm in Racine County while on a visit to his wife's parents in Racine. . . . That time nothing was settled because I still harbored reservations about entering into this risky enterprise. Early spring the next year he again came out here and brought a letter from Iver Lawson which held forth the idea of some financial support, should that be required, together with assurances that he considered Mr. Anderson to be a competent printer and businessman. With that my scruples were overcome, and the result was that the first issue of *Skandinaven* came out June 1, 1866.

In its initial regular issue the newspaper described its editorial policy as radical in the sense that "poor and rich, black and white should be punished or rewarded in equal measure according to the law." *Skandinaven* adopted an anticlerical position, expressed through criticism of the hierarchy in the Norwegian Synod. *Skandinaven* was by no means anti-religious; the low-church followers of the Norwegian lay Lutheran religious leader Hans Nielsen Hauge in fact regarded the newspaper as their organ. In its June 1 editorial *Skandinaven* assailed religious dissent as the main hindrance to newspaper publishing, as it splintered the immigrants into warring groups. As, to quote Johannes Wist, "the political newspaper par excellence" and Republican focused, *Skandinaven* asserted that the divisions among Norwegians in America could not be blamed on political differences because "the Scandinavians in Chicago are numerous and concordant in political conviction."[20]

A backdrop to *Skandinaven*'s attack on religious dissent may explain why the criticism surfaced in the newspaper's first appearance. In the annals of Norwegian church life in Chicago a religious dispute known as the "Vossing War" was raging at the time. It will only be possible to give a brief outline of a controversy that eventually made its way to the Illinois Supreme Court. It had its beginnings in spring 1861 when C. J. P. Petersen, an ordained minister of the Norwegian state church, succeeded to the pastorate of Paul Andersen of the First Norwegian Evangelical Lutheran Congregation, commonly known as Andersen's church, established on the North Side of Chicago in 1848. In 1860 ethnic feelings and the high confessionalism of Scandinavian Lutherans moved the Norwegian and Swedish congregations in the Northern Illinois Synod to depart and form the Scandinavian Augustana Synod; it saw itself as an heir of Haugeanism. Andersen's church joined the new ecclesiastical body, which represented a Lutheran direction that encouraged lay preaching and was broadly in opposition to the principles of church practices—the clericalism and dogmatism—in the Norwegian Synod.

Contrary to his promises, Petersen immediately introduced the Synod's liturgical ritual and donned ministerial vestments. A fight well documented in the Norwegian American press ensued; the congregation split in two warring factions. Leaders in opposition were the established Vossings, men like Iver Lawson, which gave the conflict its name. It eventually became a contest between the Norwegian Synod and Augustana. In March 1866 the Augustanians formally charged and tried Petersen for faithlessness, violations of its constitution, offensive preaching, and unchristian conduct. *Skandinaven* described him as "Preusian subject," in reference to the published correspondence by A. C. Preus, then serving Our Savior's Lutheran Church on Chicago's West Side, and H. A. Preus, the Synod's president, in his defense. Under the heading "The Petersenian War against *Skandinaven*" *(Den Petersenske Krig mod "Skandinaven"),* the newspaper in May 1867 accused its Synod-friendly competitors *Emigranten* and *Fædrelandet* of trying to destroy *Skandinaven* in weekly bitter, malicious, and untrue characterizations of its convictions and coverage of the charges against Pastor Petersen. This same editorial article reviewed "the well-known case of how Petersen [in his ministry] had gathered members and given them the right to vote *per fas et nefas* in order to gain a majority against the old congregation, while he denied membership to people whose sentiments he did not trust." By such nefarious well-documented means Petersen gained the support of the majority. The very year *Skandinaven* was founded Petersen asked President H. A. Preus to give him a call so that he could bring the congregation into the Synod; by these actions the Synod gained a second congregation in the city served by Pastor Petersen until his return to Norway 1873. The minority party, however, subsequently filed a civil suit in regard to possession of the church property, since, they argued, it belonged to the Augustana Synod. When the case finally reached the state's high court, the decision handed down favored the majority. Those in the minority left the congregation. In *Skandianven*'s opinion, fortified by the excesses of the Petersen discord, Lutheran theological differences would only lead to further strife and preclude any hope of unity among Norwegians in America.[21]

During Langeland's editorship a second major controversy was revived, namely differing attitudes toward the public or common school. The Norwegian Synod showed great organizational strength in the prebellum years and an added emphasis on the Norwegian heritage, powered by the many Norwegian-trained pastors as well as the growth fueled by the widening arrival of immigrants to Norwegian-speaking urban neighborhoods and agricultural communities. In 1866 the high-church Synod ministers reaffirmed their earlier position on the American public school system, which they saw as an inherent threat to Lutheranism and the Norwegian language. It was a concern of long standing and unique in the sense that Norwegians were the sole Scandinavians to question the American common school. It was the Norwegian Synod's cooperation with the German Missouri Synod in the late 1850s that convinced the leaders of the Synod that it might be possible to substitute separate Lutheran schools for the common school; a public debate ensued in the columns of *Emigranten,* then the only representative of immigrant journalism. Preoccupation with the Civil War postponed debate until after 1865, when it resumed with renewed zeal.

Langeland, a strong defender of the public school, editorially challenged the Synod clergy in *Skandinaven,* emphasizing that the common school encouraged democracy, indirectly taught religious tolerance, and promoted patriotism and love of freedom. In defining his editorial duties, Langeland asserted, "My defense of the common school constituted, aside from political activity, perhaps the main part of my editorial work and led to the unexpected distinction of having one of Chicago's elementary schools named after me."

In general Norwegian immigrants accepted the common school, lauded the opportunity it gave to learn English, and sent their children there in large numbers even before the enactment of compulsory school attendance, which in Wisconsin did not occur until 1879. According to Wist, Langeland's "ingrained ill will toward Norwegian authority figures made him give special attention to Norwegian theologians in this country, who in his eyes represented the same mindset as the government officials in [his birthplace] Samnanger." Reading his criticism of the Synod position leaves an impression that his passionate support of the American public school as well as his dislike of the Synod clergy on occasion made him overstate and even misrepresent their opposition to the common school; the Synod leaders quite obviously realized that creating a separate school system was beyond the Synod's resources; their distrust of the secular institution and the fear that it would distance coming generations from the true Lutheran faith was, however, evident. The discussion about the common school, interspersed with the persistent heated exchanges about the Synod's teachings on the biblical justification of slavery, according to Langeland, attracted attention and, to quote, "served greatly to increase the circulation of the newspaper where the Norwegians resided." Only toward the end of the 1870s did the newspaper debate quiet down.[22]

Disaster struck. Along with the newspaper *Fremad,* three other Norwegian-language publications and six Swedish-language newspaper establishments became a victim of the great fire that broke out the evening of October 8, 1871. *Skandinaven*'s offices on the southwest corner of Clark and South Water streets burned down, but the subscription lists were saved. John Anderson, in his customary untiring way, purchased printing equipment in Madison on credit, which made it possible for him to publish a small four-page edition of *Skandinaven* on October 14 in a basement on West Erie Street. "With God's help," he assured his readers, "it will not be long before *Skandinaven* will pay its regular visit in its usual form."

Six Scandinavian churches were swept away by the fire; one of these was the Norwegian church served by C. J. P. Petersen. In its second weekly issue after the great fire, dated October 19, *Skandinaven,* with its close ties to the opposing minority party, announced caustically that "The Norwegian Church on Erie Street, which so long has concerned the courts, exists no longer." *Skandinaven* recovered from the destructive forces of the conflagration; its triweekly issue, begun in 1870 for the local Chicago market, appeared on October 18. Anderson's professional background and capable leadership assured the newspaper's success.[23]

In 1872 Langeland parted company with *Skandinaven* to join John A. Johnson (Skibsnæs) and Iver Lawson in publishing the newspaper *Amerika;* its first number was dated in Chicago April 13, 1872. Johnson, civic leader and later founder of the Gisholt Machine Company, had emigrated from Telemark, Norway, with his family at age twelve in 1844; they settled in Wisconsin, where Johnson at age twenty-two established himself as a farmer in Pleasant Springs Township close to Madison and entered local and state politics. Johnson and Langeland both gave steady support to the common school. In 1872 Johnson entered the contest for the Wisconsin state senate on the Republican ticket and was elected. *Amerika,* published in Chicago in daily and weekly editions, in its political editorials complained in articles in Norwegian as well as English that the Republican Party, while seeking the Scandinavian vote, did not in return allocate Scandinavians their fair share of candidates and political appointments in Illinois, Wisconsin, or Minnesota. Such complaints were commonplace in the immigrant press; party leadership heeded them. *Amerika* clearly aided Johnson's candidacy.

Amerika's final issue was dated December 31, 1872. Iver Lawson's death that fall encouraged negotiations with Anderson by Johnson and Langeland, who were joined by Lawson's son Victor Fremont Lawson, to consolidate the two newspapers. The merged journals appeared as *Skandinaven og Amerika* from January 3 to December 30, 1873, when *Amerika* was dropped from the title, published by Johnson, Anderson, and Lawson. The young and wealthy Lawson purchased the struggling *Chicago Daily News,* then printed on *Skandinaven*'s press located in a building owned by the Lawson estate at 123 Fifth Avenue, and in time gained great fame as its successful publisher. *Skandinaven* benefited greatly from Johnson's personal and financial assistance, which likely secured the newspaper's survival. Both men sold their interests to Anderson, making him sole proprietor from May 1878. In 1890 the firm was incorporated as the John Anderson Publishing Company. In 1883 Anderson moved into his own large brick building—sixty feet wide and 118 feet deep, three stories high with a basement—located in the Scandinavian business district on Peoria Street close to Milwaukee Avenue.[24]

When Langeland left *Skandinaven* to begin publishing *Amerika,* Svein Nilsson, who had served as associate editor from 1870, was promoted to editor in chief. With the merger of the two journals, Langeland returned to the editorial office; he and Nilsson jointly edited *Skandinaven* until Langeland's departure in 1881; Nilsson then had sole editorial responsibility until 1886. Nilsson has been styled "the father of Norwegian immigrant history" for his articles in *Billed-Magazin,* published 1868–70, on pioneer Norwegian settlement in the Midwest. He was born in the parish of Overhalla in Namdalen, Norway, in 1826, the son of a long line of freeholders; he was one of the first graduates of the teachers' seminary, or normal school, established at Klæbu, a secluded parish east of Trondheim. The main educational opportunity for gifted rural youth in nineteenth-century Norway was in teachers' training institutions;

many graduates emigrated and in America contributed greatly to the intellectual and religious life of Norwegian immigrants.

Following graduation, Nilsson returned to his home community as a teacher and community leader; he became a progressive champion of enlightenment. He had larger plans, however, and from 1856 to 1867 he worked and studied in Oslo; he immigrated in 1867 to Dane County, Wisconsin, his first home in America. His apprenticeship with the Norwegian newspaper *Morgenbladet* and its legendary and controversial editor Christian Friele, serving as his "political detective and colleague," as Wist described, prepared him for his journalistic career in America; he was shrewdly able to ferret out political actions that took place behind the scenes and present unexpected scoops in the next morning's issue. The politically conservative *Morgenbladet,* founded in 1819, was at the time Norway's largest and credibly most influential news organ. It was, as suggested earlier, in correspondence with the Norwegian immigrant press and a major source of news from the homeland.

Nilsson's editorial work for *Skandinaven* was marked by strong individuality and by loyalty to its established policies. "Nilsson was personally a highly unassuming, modest, and friendly man, easy to get along with. As editor of *Skandinaven* he was not always quite so unpretentious and amenable, as his readers during some of the older newspaper feuds bear witness to. In accordance with his entire disposition he was in excellent accord with *Skandinaven*'s program, which he endeavored faithfully to carry through to the letter."

Skandinaven did not become financially successful until the years following the great fire; earlier investments, such as publishing a local edition, triweekly from 1870 and daily from the following year, with its own volume numbering from January 1, 1873, were consequent attempts to attract advertising and subscribers in its Chicago market. In 1877 *Skandinaven*'s weekly edition had a subscription of about ten thousand and the daily only a circulation of approximately five hundred; by 1880 the weekly was printed in sixteen thousand copies, according to Ayer's American newspaper annual, and the daily 2,800. Revenue from advertising, which sustained and made urban newspapers profitable, eventually secured *Skandinaven*'s success, but other factors played a significant role in its growth as well. Professional and careful leadership was naturally a basic condition for success; the newspaper's popular tone and discussions of burning issues, combined with a direct appeal to the ordinary person, increased circulation. It promoted Norwegian American activities and cultural interests and it informed about and nurtured kinship with the Norwegian homeland. *Skandinaven* was hawked by newspaper boys and given free to Norwegian newcomers at railroad stations. An earlier assessment by the author expressed the idea that *Skandinaven*'s "influence and its message of urban values and way of life intruded into remote immigrant communities, into farming settlements and small towns and villages, and announced Chicago as a major Norwegian American center." Its message was heard until it ceased publication in 1941.[25]

Dissenting Voices

Various interests and dissenting voices manifested themselves in heated newspaper polemics. The Scandinavian community was treated to an unremitting warfare between two Republican Swedish newspapers, the clerically dominated *Hemlandet* (The Homeland), founded in Galesburg, Illinois, in 1855 and relocated to Chicago in 1859, and its rival *Svenska Amerikanaren* (The Swedish American), launched on September 8, 1866 (the same year as *Skandinaven*). *Svenska Amerikanaren*'s attacks on the Swedish American clergy gained it the favor of the anti-religious element among Swedes in Chicago. Economic hardship in the early 1870s forced a merger between *Svenska-Amerikanaren* and *Nya Verlden* (The New World) in 1877 under the name *Svenska Tribunen* (The Swedish Tribune). "The new organ," stated historian Ulf Beijbom, "became the leading Swedish-American voice for middle-class liberalism and suspicion of rural hyper-evangelism." Swedish, Danish, and Norwegian newspaper publishers and editors had much in common; they knew each other personally and might on occasion socialize in spite of conflicting political and religious convictions.[26]

Chicago became a center of immigrant radicalism. In the German and Scandinavian neighborhoods anarchists, socialists, and freethinkers found many followers; Scandinavian Socialists cooperated extensively. Efforts from the mid-1860s by such radicals as Norwegian Marcus Thrane and the Dane Louis Pio are well known.

Thrane received support from Norwegian middle-class intellectuals and businessmen, individuals like the freethinking political activist and Norwegian-educated doctor Gerhard S. C. H. Paoli, very likely also from Iver Lawson, who in addition supported John Anderson and *Skandinaven,* and most certainly from the successful Chicago tailor G. Roberg. In late winter 1866, these men, joined by several others of like social status and tenet, convinced Thrane to move from New York to Chicago to start a Norwegian American newspaper there. They were inspired, as Roberg claimed, by their dissatisfaction with *Emigranten* and *Fædrelandet;* as opponents of religious orthodoxy they wanted an organ more in tune with radical thought.

Marcus Thrane landed in New York from Norway in February 1864; he was Norway's first important Socialist leader. In 1849 he established the first newspaper in Norway to champion the cause of the lower classes; by radical agitation and travels he established a popular protest movement known as the Thrane movement. At its height his national labor organization had 414 local workers associations with more than thirty thousand members. His remarkable success alarmed Norwegian authorities, who saw his actions as an attack on the social and political structure of society. He and his fellow agitators were arrested. Thrane was imprisoned from July 1851 until July 1858—seven long years; he eventually followed the pattern of many other persecuted European dissidents by seeking refuge in the more tolerant environment of the New World.

Many of Thrane's followers found their way to Chicago. May 25, 1866, he began publishing *Marcus Thrane's Norske Amerikaner.* Thrane's backers likely provided his capital; his name, it might be assumed, would draw moral and financial support and rouse his emigrated former followers. Johan Schrøder, earlier associated with *Fædrelandet,* became Thrane's subscription agent. *Fædrelandet* and *Emigranten* both—even as they regularly engaged in criticism of each other—distanced themselves from Thrane's publication either directly or by accepting critical correspondence and articles. Thrane's new publication—like these two rival journals as well as *Skandinaven*—celebrated the liberation of slavery. Bearing in mind Lincoln's martyrdom, *Marcus Thrane's Norske Amerikaner* (Norwegian American) aligned itself with the Repub-

Marcus Thrane's

Norske Amerikaner.

No. 1. Chicago, Illinois, Fredagen 25de Mai, 1866. 1ste Aargang.

Dagslyset.

Filosofisk-religiöst Maanedsblad,

udgivet af Marc. Thrane.

Motto: „Løgneren skyer Sandheden, hvo som elsker Sandheden søger den."

1. Aargang. Chicago, April 1869. No. 1.

Subskriptionsvilkaar:

For et Aar $1.20
For et halvt Aar 0.60
For et enkelt Nummer .... 0,15.

Subskribentsamlere erholde paa fire Numre det femte frit.

Breve til Udgiveren adresseres P. O. Box 972, Chicago, Illinois.

Bladets Office er: Dole's Building, north-west corner South Water and South Clark Street.

Indhold:

Vor Platform! — Er det tilladt at tænke frit? — Bibelens Modsigelser om Gud. — Er Treenighedslæren bibelsk? — Vær paa Post imod Præsten Palmgreen. — Pastor A. C. Preus's Retirade. — Pastor H. A. Preus og Folkeoplysningen. — En skinhellig Bedrager i New York. — Bekjendtgjørelser.

Vor Platform!

Historien lærer os, at fra de ældste Tider have Kongemagt og Præstemagt gaaet Haand i Haand for at undertrykke og forslave Menneskene. Alle Statssamfunds Historie har ikke været Andet end Beretninger om, hvordan Folkenes Masser ere blevne brugte til Fordeel for enkelte egennyttige og ærgjerrige Mennesker. Vel have de fortrykte Masser ofte søgt at frigjøre sig, og det har stundom lykkets dem at afskaffe Kongemagten og indføre den demokratisk-republikanske Forfatning; men aldrig have disse Republikker kunnet bestaa i Længden: Folkene have atter maattet bøie sig under Kongemagten! — og hvorfor?

Jo! fordi de ikke tillige have afskaffet Præstemagten!

Lidet kan det nytte, at frigjøre sig for det materielle Aag, saalænge man villig bøier Nakken under det aandelige Aag. Aanden er mere end Legemet. Den aandelige Frihed er Grunden for den materielle. En Republik, hvori Folkets Masser ere aandelige Slaver, er ingen virkelig Republik, og kan ikke bestaa. Sent eller tidligt vil den snedige Præstemagt forstaa at føre Alt tilbage til det Gamle.

Det er derfor enhver brav Republikaners Pligt at arbeide for Præstemagtens Afskaffelse. Dette er ikke at arbeide for Religionens Afskaffelse; thi Præstedom og Kristendom ere saa forskjellige som Mørket er forskjelligt fra Lyset.

I vor Stræben efter at afskaffe Præstemagten er det ikke nok at vise Folket, hvad Præstemagten gjennem alle Tider har været, og hvad den er endnu den Dag idag; men det er nødvendigt at give Folket en filosofisk-religiøs Oplysning.

Vi maa give Folkets uvidende Masse Oplysning:

1. Om Forskjellen imellem de mangfoldige Religioner,
2. Om hvad Religion egentlig er eller bør være,
3. Om hvad den kristne Religion var i sin Oprindelse, om hvorledes den i Tidernes Løb er udartet til en Fabel- og Eventyrlære, passende for Børn, men ikke for voxne Folk.
4. Om hvorledes den kristelige Religion, saaledes som den almindeligvis fremstilles, kun er en plump, afgudisk Institution, der hindrer Civilisationens Udbredelse og gjør Jorden til en værre Jammerdal end den virkelig er.

Først naar Menneskene have Oplysning herom ere de saadanne frie Væsener, som Gud har skabt dem til at være. Vi braute af, at vi leve i Civilisationens Aarhundrede og dog ligger Folkenes Masser nedsunkne i omtrent samme aandelige Mørke som Ægypterne mange tusinde Aar før „Verdens Skabelse".

Vi braute af, at vi have den eneste sande Religion, og dog dele disse kjærlige, fredelige Kristne sig i utallige Partier, der med infamt Had bagtale, nedrive, fordømme og forfølge hverandre, og ligesom fryde sig, jo mere Uenighed der er, og jo flere Partier de kunne dele sig i.

Engang maa alt dette Uvæsen faa en Ende; engang maa Menneskene faa Øinene op for, hvem de have at takke for Krigens Rædsler og for al den uhyggelige Splid; engang maa Lyset tændes og Mørket forjages!

At tænde Lyset er vort Maal. At Lyset ikke atter skal

Marcus Thrane, Norway's first important Socialist leader, after moving to Chicago in 1866 published the weekly Marcus Thrane's Norske Amerikaner *and the monthly* Dagslyset. *Chicago was the center of immigrant radicalism.*

lican Party, though without becoming a party organ. The United States had, after all, attained many of the freedoms Thrane had championed in Norway: voting rights (for men), complete freedom of religion and the press, opportunity for everyone who wished to work, and free land in the West. The newspaper also covered Thrane's radical views. *Emigranten* for August 20, 1866, reprinted an article from *Kirkelig Maanedstidende,* edited by H. A. Preus and J. A. Ottesen, headed "A Warning to all Christians against *Marcus Thrane's Norske Amerikaner*"; the letter denounced it "as a newspaper that works to undermine the Christian religion and the existing civic order."

During its short existence Thrane's publication was exposed to many similar pronouncements. In a supplement in July, *Fædrelandet*'s editor Fleischer addressed "The Readers of *Fædrelandet* and *Marcus Thrane's Norske Amerikaner*" and identified what it found to be the "principles defended" already in the newspaper's first issue.

> A free and moral press is one of the greatest public goods, an adornment for the people and a promoter of morality, but a press that jests about Christianity's saving doctrine, our most sacred possession, and wishes to overthrow civic order is a nation's greatest evil. That Marcus Thrane's newspaper aims at doing this we believe we can find evidence of in his own words on page one of the first issue.

Fleischer also commented on Schrøder's "Inaugural Address" in Thrane's second issue, which appealed to the hesitant that they must not judge the new publication before they "have read the newspaper a half year's time, in the same way as one cannot judge food's quality before tasting it." "If any one should bring Mr. Schrøder a row of rotten oysters," Fleischer responded with considerable sarcasm, "we assume that he will ask to be excused from the obligation to taste it before he gives his opinion of whether it is good or bad." Thrane's outspoken criticism of the clergy, Protestant and Catholic, and even his support for the controversial idea of an eight-hour workday, as well as his reputation as a political radical, caused his fellow Norwegians to perceive him as a threat to their social and religious order. Thrane's newspaper never gained a sufficient circulation; Thrane himself reported two thousand subscribers when he sold it to *Skandinaven.* In a letter printed in *Skan-*

dinaven September 13, 1866, Thrane announced that "Inasmuch as the *Norske Amerikaner* for want of necessary financial resources has had to be discontinued its subscribers will hereafter receive *Skandinaven* in its stead." Thrane considered *Skandinaven* to be the most independent and best edited of the Norwegian newspapers in America; thus he perceived the new arrangement to be the best possible under the circumstances.[27]

On May 5, 1869, *Skandinaven* reported on the publication of the first issue of the monthly *Dagslyset* (The Light of Day), a philosophical and religious monthly *(Filosofiskreligiøst Maanedsblad)* edited and published by Marcus Thrane. It became the visible organ of the Scandinavian Society of Progress *(Den Skandinaviske Fremskridts-Forening),* organized June 25, 1869, in Chicago, though Thrane owned the monthly independently. The freethinking Dr. Paoli was the Society's first president and Thrane its secretary; its membership was largely Norwegian. The name was altered in 1875 to the Scandinavian Freethinker Society *(Den Skandinaviske Fritænkerforening).* The Society became the core of the Scandinavian Section 4, organized in November 1871, of the socialist International Workingmen's Association—the famed First International devoted to Marxist socialism. Thrane frequently lectured at Section 4's meetings at the "old" Aurora Hall on *Dagslyset*'s stated purpose to spread "free religious inquiry and radical political views."

Dagslyset faced financial uncertainty and a precarious existence; at its height in 1874 the monthly had only four hundred subscribers, which suggests the extent of the receptiveness of its socialistic and radical message. *Dagslyset* frequently skipped months of publication: the great fire caused a break of three months; it reappeared in January 1872 and continued monthly through December 1873; it did not appear in 1874; and it was revived in 1875 but with frequent delays and breaks. In January 1877 Thrane's close friend and financial benefactor, Christen Westergaard, a Dane from Thy in North Jutland, assumed publication and moved *Dagslyset* to Becker, Minnesota. Westergaard continued the monthly's aggressive radical political and religious message through the final issue, February 1878. Wist saw its survival under difficult circumstances as evidence of "great fighting zeal and willingness to sacrifice among that time's most extreme Norwegian American men in opposition, because their flock could not have been particularly large." Even so, a radical political agenda and the tenets of materialistic socialism were heard well beyond the circle of converts to *Dagslyset*'s cause.[28]

In 1878, the year *Dagslyset* ceased publication, Danish Socialists started *Den Nye Tid* (The New Age), with Louis Pio as editor. Pio, considered the founder of the Danish Social Democratic Party, was bribed to emigrate by Danish officials fearful of his socialistic agitation. Thrane occasionally wrote for *Den Nye Tid,* but he was not, as some historians have stated, involved in its founding or editing. A copy of his blistering satire on the Norwegian Lutheran clergy, "The Old Wisconsin Bible," was offered as a premium for subscribing one year to the newspaper. The pioneer Norwegian feminist Aasta Hansteen, who during the years 1880–89 resided in the United States, two years in Chicago, agitated for women's rights on its pages. A printer in the shop where *Den Nye Tid* was typeset related in later correspondence visits by Thrane and Hansteen.

> Among the writers were Marcus Thrane, then in his 60s . . . and Aasta Hansteen, a woman's rights fighter. She was already old but flamed up when anyone opposed her ideas. She and Thrane often came in and talked with the typesetters. They liked their glass of beer, too, and often shared it there.

Pio, "no longer the fiery agitator," according to the same correspondent, left the editorship after a few months. For most of its life *Den Nye Tid* was edited by the popular Norwegian Socialist and violinist Peter Peterson. In an editorial he claimed it to be the only Scandinavian newspaper in America to "fearlessly and clearly speak the cause of the worker and free thought." Arriving from Trondheim, Norway, in the 1880s, Olaf O. Ray, newspaperman and lawyer, was associated with *Den Nye Tid* during its final years; the newspaper folded in 1884, lacking resources so that, again quoting the contemporary observer, "the printers were paid some Saturdays; sometimes not."

Until 1881, *Den Nye Tid* served as a voice for the Workingmen's or Socialist Labor Party. A breach in the Socialist ranks occurred at a meeting of social revolutionary groups in Chicago in October 1881. August Spies, editor of the German-language *Arbeiter-Zeitung*

(Workers' Times), published in Chicago, urged for the Socialist platform to support the democratic political process. Peterson rejected using the ballot and instead advocated revolutionary methods. After the split, *Den Nye Tid,* edited by Peterson, became the Norwegian and Danish organ of the anarchistic Revolutionary Socialist Party. Its offices were on Erie Street close to Milwaukee Avenue and consequently this Scandinavian agent of revolution, much reviled by the dominant Scandinavian Republican electorate and Lutheran worshipers, was a visible member of the Norwegian community.[29]

The Press and Women's Rights in the Civil War Era

The asylum the Norwegian champion of women's rights Aasta Hansteen sought in the United States bespoke the greater freedom and opportunity for women in the nineteenth century in the New World. Nevertheless, the subordination of women continued on both sides of the Atlantic. Immigrant editors were aware of the similarity between Norway and America in this regard and gave space to the feminist movement in the old homeland as well as the new. Agitation for equality between the sexes was voiced not only in the columns of radical journals such as *Den Nye Tid,* but also in a few more traditional news organs. This leaning was by no means universal; parity for women at the polls met with opposing arguments in both secular and church publications. Advocates of female political involvement were in fact viewed with a suspicious eye by most of the major Norwegian American newspapers launched in the decades after the Civil War.

The women's suffragette cause was inspired to move forward with greater zeal following Lincoln's Emancipation Proclamation. Many of the activists had worked to abolish slavery; after its accomplishment they concentrated on their own political rights. The Norwegian-language press for the most part did not get involved until the founding of the National Woman Suffrage Association in 1869. Historian Arlow Andersen noted two exceptions. In November 1868 editor Just M. Kahn of *Fremad* in Milwaukee declared the following under the captions "Universal Suffrage!" and "Long Live the Republic!":

> Let it be understood that an Indian and a Chinese have as much right as a Negro, and let it be understood that our wives, mothers, and sisters, who must be annoyed by our political debates and must listen to the political preachers in the American churches with reverence every Sunday, should have the right to vote.

Fædrelandet og Emigranten, edited by Frederick Fleischer, in spring 1869, following a meeting of the American Equal Rights Society in New York, was provoked to state an opposing view:

> The American ladies no longer wish to be women and wear skirts. They wish to forsake family life for public life, skirts for trousers, and in those trousers to roam about the country carrying on political intrigues and delivering public addresses.

The public role of women—in Norway and the United States—as reported in the Norwegian immigrant newspapers will be more fully referenced in chapter five. Social limitations explain the great absence of Norwegian immigrant women in American public affairs at midcentury, the era of the Civil War, and later. One can, however, cite at least one early anomaly. Elise Tvede Wærenskjold stood out as a gifted and industrious feminist before her move from Norway to Texas in late summer 1847; in Norway she had edited the second and also last volume of the magazine *Norge og Amerika* (Norway and America). In her activities after her arrival in Texas as the "lady with the pen," she demonstrated the crosscurrent relationship between Norway and the United States. She spoke warmly for Texas, against slavery, deeming it "contrary to the law of God," and clearly "refused to be confined within the narrow bounds which at that time circumscribed the activities of her sex." Her views may be gleaned from her many letters addressed to individuals or published in newspapers in Norway or in such Norwegian American journals as *Billed-Magazin, Fædrelandet og Emigranten,* and *Norden* (The North) in Chicago.[30]

Concluding Commentary

Political engagement was emblematic of the early Norwegian American press; it educated its compatriots about the social issues of the day and assisted in their full participation in life in the new society. In her biography of her father Laur. Larsen, Karen Larsen explained how "To the Norwegian pioneers politics was an absorbing interest, second only to the affairs of the church," thanks to the Norwegian-language newspapers. However, the press did not speak with one voice. A Republican Party loyalty did not preclude divisive forces surfacing among editors of like political conviction; the strong influence of leading Lutheran clerics might stoke the fires of controversy. In writing about the lack of unity in the Swedish-language Republican press, Beijbom claimed that it caused "political impotence" and explained "the meager results of Swedish Republican activities in Chicago." A similar analysis may well apply to the political circumstances among Norwegians. Control over immigrant newspapers, however, supplied political credentials, as reflected in the important political appointments obtained by immigrant editors of both nationalities.

The Norwegian American newsmen at their rolltop desks, as determined in the Swedish American case, "represented the thin layer of immigrant intellectuals," even though some had risen to that level through self-education. Many were graduates of Norwegian educational institutions and well educated in the Western tradition. They gained their readers' respect and trust and became community leaders. A number of these men, and eventually also women, made journalism a lifelong vocation. Their religious instruction since childhood encouraged social and moral responsiveness, even among those who rebelled against a Lutheran heritage. It also had an impact on their understanding of American life and in their political involvement. In general, their loyalty to their Norwegian identity became a strength as they guided their compatriots' adjustment to American ways. The foreign-language press's role as a promoter of both ethnicity and cultural assimilation was clearly reflected in the activities of Norwegian American journalism.

In his empirical research on the non-English-language press, Robert Park distinguished between a provincial and a cosmopolitan press, arguing, "To the provincial, the most acceptable news is news about people whom he knows or places with which he is familiar." Historians Dirk Hoerder and Marion Marzolf rejected Park's categorization, which, they held, required thorough revision. Marzolf, in fact, found that "the rural weeklies retained a broader outlook and coverage of world and national news longer than the urban weeklies." When considering the Norwegian American press, even only in its early decades, one may with certainty conclude that it was not "provincial" in Park's terms, whether published in La Crosse, Wisconsin, or in the bustling metropolis of Chicago. In Hoerder's estimation, "the ethnic press, whether published in small towns or in cities, provided a link with the old country and access to the new society."[31]

Minneapolis Tidende

CHAPTER 3

A Flourishing Midwestern Press

For many years I have considered Minnesota the best state for newspaper literature.[1]

THE GEOGRAPHICAL SPREAD of the Norwegian American press and the time of founding of individual journals relate closely to immigration and the advance of settlement. Land and immigration were the major ingredients in the peopling of the Upper Midwest; newspaper publishing is one measure of where Norwegians settled most heavily. Nearly 80 percent of all weekly and daily Norwegian-language journals, counting all titles from first to last, had their home in the states of Illinois, Wisconsin, Iowa, Minnesota, and North and South Dakota; more than 26 percent of all secular newspaper titles were based in Minnesota, Wisconsin as second registered about 18 percent, North Dakota 16 percent, Illinois 12 percent, Iowa 4 percent, and South Dakota 3 percent. These percentages reflect the dominance of large urban centers like Chicago and Minneapolis in ethnic journalism, but they also strongly suggest the great expansion of newspaper publishing to local centers of Norwegian settlement throughout the region. Immigrant journals featured promotional advertising from railroad companies, private colonization organizers, state agencies, and speculators of many kinds offering land. These optimistic notices were directed both at immigrants already in the United States and at the many in Norway seeking to become landholders in America.

A major number of new journals appeared from the late 1870s for about thirty years, coinciding with, and extending beyond, the second and largest wave of mass emigration. A postwar economic boom in the United States ended with the panic of 1873, but economic life recovered rapidly. The new growth required the import of labor in all branches of the economy. The Oslo, Norway, newspaper *Morgenbladet*'s Chicago correspondent reported in December 1879 that while hard economic times continued in Europe, "America has gradually risen from the hard blow suffered during the crisis of 1873." Emigration from Europe was sensitive to such market fluctuations.

The year 1880 heralded a new beginning in Norwegian mass departures to the United States, lasting until 1893. On the average 18,900 Norwegians left annually, equaling ten of every one thousand inhabitants and giving Norway one of the highest rates of emigration in Europe. The second mass exodus culminated in 1882 with 28,804 departures, a number that exceeded the natural population increase. From the beginning of the first mass emigration wave in 1866 and until the end of 1900, some 441,000 Norwegians immigrated to America. In spite of the heavy drain, Norway's population continued to increase, so that it passed two million around 1890.[2]

It was to a great extent a rural-to-rural movement, fueled by a desire to continue an accustomed way of life and to preserve traditional values associated with a rural existence. Suggesting foresight and knowledge, *Morgenbladet* in September 1880 carried a long descriptive article titled "The New, Great Wheat Land in North America." Such enticing reports encouraged footloose, land-hungry Norwegian peasants to become farmers in America. Migration from the countryside dominated in absolute numbers, but from the mid-1870s the intensity of the urban overseas exodus surpassed the rural. The composition of the annual emigrant contingents changed; the earlier family emigration gradually became a youth movement; by 1900, 70 percent of all men and 62 percent of women who moved to America were between the ages of fifteen and thirty; whether urban or rural, the emigration became increasingly more male. These statistics represent the demographic circumstances that sustained the expansion of the immigrant press.

Norwegians were statistically the most rural of major nineteenth-century immigrant groups; a dedication to land and farming—and to farming as a way of life—was an idiosyncratic trait. A strong rural orientation has in fact characterized Norwegians in America from generation to generation. Of course not all became farmers. Many found a livelihood in the small towns and villages that sprang up in regions of Norwegian settlement; these marketplaces frequently took on an ethnic Norwegian quality and became centers for the Norwegian agricultural communities in their hinterlands. A strong rural attachment may even have reinforced nationalistic and ethnocentric emotions.

Even though Norwegian immigrants and their descendants resisted the pull of the city, they like other ethnic groups formed identifiable enclaves in the urban environment of a metropolis like Chicago. "Little Norway" came into being alongside competing ethnic colonies of other nationalities; in 1900 Chicago had, as recorded in the federal census, 22,011 Norwegian-born residents and almost twice as many of Norwegian heritage born in America. Minneapolis, with a dominance of Scandinavian and German populations, did not experience the same ethnic diversity as Chicago; it had 11,532 Norwegian immigrants and its twin city St. Paul 3,000 at the turn of the last century; combined the two cities sheltered 26,000 citizens of the second generation. Chicago surpassed all other American cities in numbers of Norwegians. However, Minneapolis with its smaller Norwegian concentration, located as it was in the heart of Norwegian settlement in the Upper Midwest, from the 1890s gradually replaced Chicago as the new Norwegian American capital.

The Norwegian stock in 1900—first and second generations—in the six midwestern states listed in Table 1, according to the federal census, numbered 272,074 of the total number of 336,985 Norwegian-born immigrants to the United States, or 81 percent, and 270,776 had at least one parent born in Norway, equaling 64 percent of the total 420,199.

Concentrations of Norwegians and resultant newspaper publishing were to be found in such towns on the rise as Eau Claire, La Crosse, Madison, Milwaukee, Stoughton, and Superior, Wisconsin; Albert Lea, Crookston, Duluth, Fergus Falls, Madison, Moorhead, and Rochester, Minnesota; Cedar Rapids, Decorah, Lake Mills, Sioux City, and Story City, Iowa; Devils Lake, Fargo,

Table 1: Norwegian Immigrants in the Midwest, 1900

STATE	FIRST GENERATION	SECOND GENERATION	TOTAL
Minnesota	104,895	103,995	208,890
Wisconsin	61,575	61,645	123,220
Illinois	29,979	29,870	59,849
Iowa	25,631	25,500	51,131
North Dakota	30,206	30,171	60,377
South Dakota	19,788	19,595	39,383
Total	272,074	270,776	542,850

Grafton, Grand Forks, Hillsboro, and Minot, North Dakota; and Brookings, Flandreau, and Sioux Falls, South Dakota. A large Norwegian-speaking population powered a flourishing of the Norwegian American press; nearly half, 49.9 percent, were of the second generation. The American-born generations increasingly assumed leadership roles in journalism and in public service.[3]

A Norwegian American Press in Minnesota

The year 1868, disregarding the brief showing of *Folkets Røst* in St. Paul ten years earlier, witnessed the beginnings of a Norwegian immigrant press in Minnesota. Counting the first and second generations, Norwegians numbered 49,569 in the state in 1870, demonstrating a need for a Norwegian-language publication. *Nordisk Folkeblad* (Nordic People's Newspaper) appeared with its first number March 12, 1868, in Rochester; it was in the words of Johannes Wist "the first Norwegian-Danish or Danish-Norwegian newspaper in Minnesota." In order to trace the nature and growth of Norwegian American journalism and its political actions, the lot of a number of short-lived and failed periodical ventures must be recorded. To avoid an excessively detailed, overly crowded narrative, this text will limit the number of fleeting journals it references. Appendix 1 lists a complete register of all secular news organs. Readers may discern the historical path of publications excised from the narrative in the addendum or in supplemental data in the endnotes.

Two other weeklies appeared in 1868. *Folkevennen* (Friend of the People), a Republican campaign sheet, was published in Winona during the 1868 fall election. *Amerika,* which began publication in La Crosse, Wisconsin, in August 1868, was a continuation of *Skandiaviske Demokrat* (Scandinavian Democrat). Debuting in La Crosse June 18, *Amerika* continued volume numbering from that date; its publisher and editor was Knud Knudson, a prosperous property owner. *Amerika* declared itself an independent Union organ; it thus differed politically from its predecessor, which during its brief existence spoke for Wisconsin's Democrats. *Amerika* editorially praised Lincoln, Knudson declaring that his own political belief was in the strictest sense the same as the late president's.

When Johan Schrøder assumed ownership and editorial responsibility October 29, *Amerika* placed itself firmly in the Republican camp, to the chagrin of the established journals. *Fædrelandet*—edited by Frederick Fleischer and soon to merge with *Emigranten* to form *Fædrelandet og Emigranten*—continued to have its publication home in La Crosse and perceived *Amerika* as a disturbing rival; praising the early founding of *Emigranten,* while disparaging *Amerika,* Fleischer encouraged, as advertised, "the public 'to go to the oldest and best' newspaper." Schrøder, a cofounder of *Fædrelandet* in 1864, claimed that the attack by "our colleague" simply had convinced some people to subscribe to *Amerika.*

Under the title "Minnesota My Future Home," printed in *Amerika* December 23, 1868, Schrøder explained why *Amerika* from that issue would be published in Rochester; he had "for many years . . . considered Minnesota the best state for newspaper literature." He had, he stated, encouraged "the establishment of *Nordisk Folkeblad,*" which by then had been moved to Minneapolis, leaving room for a new Norwegian-language news organ. "In my eyes," Schrøder continued, "southern Minnesota and northern Iowa are still the main regions for Norwegians." The newspaper faced financial problems in the new location as it had in the old; the last issue published in Rochester is dated January 21, 1869. The next issue, dated May 11, was published in Winona, Minnesota; Winona was listed as place of publication until the final issue, dated December 30, 1872. Schrøder moved on to new ventures in immigrant journalism, though little is known of his activities until the 1880s.[4]

Nordisk Folkeblad, the first Norwegian newspaper in Minnesota, was not a Norwegian undertaking, but in fact one by the publishers of the *Rochester Post,* Leonard & Booth, in Rochester, the seat of Olmsted County. They were motivated by a relatively large Norwegian migration into the state, especially into Olmsted and neighboring counties. It was not uncommon for individuals outside the Norwegian community to address the immigrants in their own language, if, as in this case, they anticipated financial gain and political influence. Edited by Danish-born F. Sneedorff Christensen, *Nordisk Folkeblad,* as the name suggested, appealed in the Dano-Norwegian language to all three Nordic populations. Through the weekly *Nordisk Folkeblad,* Sneedorff Christensen advocated for the greatest possible participation by Nordics in the political life of the state; he is thought to be the first person in Minnesota to have publicly engaged in such agitation. The election of the prominent Swedish immigrant Colonel Hans Mattson, of Civil War fame, as secretary of state in 1869 was to a great degree attributed to Sneedorff Christensen's strong public statements in support of his candidacy.

The American founders, disappointed in the newspaper as a business venture, sold *Nordisk Folkeblad* to Sneedorff Christensen in fall 1868, the year of its founding; he moved publication to Minneapolis and put out the first weekly issue there March 17, 1869. Danish-born Søren Listoe, a well-educated twenty-year-old immigrant in 1866, initially found employment on *Fremad* in Milwaukee and *Emigranten* in Madison; in 1869 he became assistant editor of *Nordisk Folkeblad* after its move to Minneapolis, a position he held until 1871.

Nordisk Folkeblad, beginning July 14, published articles penned by Listoe about Minnesota's benefits. These propaganda reports were later published in the form of a pamphlet: the English translation of the suggestive title reads, *The State of Minnesota in North America. Its Advantages for the Scandinavian Immigrant Especially with Respect to the Farmer.* Perhaps the most memorable contributions calling attention to Minnesota's suitability for Scandinavian settlement were made by the Norwegian immigrant Paul Hjelm-Hansen, who served as a special agent of the state of Minnesota in 1869 to promote Scandinavian settlement in the region. He was recognized through his articles in the Norwegian American press as the discoverer of the Red River Valley for Scandinavian settlers. Hjelm-Hansen was a mature and experienced man of fifty-seven when in 1867 he landed in America. In Norway he had belonged to a small group of liberal journalists who sympathized with the common man; he was a lawyer by training and had practiced law for several years. Hjelm-Hansen's concern for the loss of Norwegian citizens to emigration led him to go to America to find evidence of America's dangers, which would convince Norwegians to remain at home. After arriving in America, however, Hjelm-Hansen became convinced of the reality of America's opportunities, and he became the immigrants' defender. Their aspirations could, he insisted, best be fulfilled as landowning farmers; he believed that hard work on the land would preserve the strength of the Norwegian character and develop high moral qualities.

Hjelm-Hansen's philosophical reflections from the strenuous journey from his home in La Crosse to the "Red River Country" were printed in fourteen travel letters in *Nordisk Folkeblad* and *Fædrelandet og Emigranten;* their propaganda was thus most directly aimed at the Norwegians. His first letter from Alexandria appeared in *Nordisk Folkeblad* July 14 and his final September 22, 1869. His lengthy letter dated July 31, written after his return to Alexandria following a trip of three weeks through the Red River Valley, titled "From the Red River Country," was perhaps the most interesting, and also most significant from a promotional point of view. It reads in part:

> I have made a journey, a real American pioneer trip into the wilderness with oxen and farm wagon. I have spent the nights in the open wagon with a buffalo hide as a mattress, a hundred-pound flour sack as a pillow, and, like Frithjof's Vikings, I have had the blue sky for a tent. In storm, lightening, thunder, and rain I have lain thus under the open sky. I have been so tortured and tormented by mosquitoes that I have had to sit upright in the wagon throughout the night, hitting about me unceasingly with my handkerchief, in order to guard myself against these little creatures, so greedy for human blood.

The main message was nevertheless settlement promotion:

> On Minnesota's high plains I have become rid of my rheumatism, and in place of it, I have gained physical strength and a cheerful dis-

> position . . . as the air here is just as wondrously invigorating as the land is beautiful and fertile. . . . In ten years this tract of land will be built up and under cultivation, and that it then will become one of the richest and most beautiful regions in America. The soil is fertile to the highest degree and is exceptionally easy to cultivate, for there is not as much as a stone in the way of the plow.

Hjelm-Hansen's observations were surely compelling arguments for land-hungry Norwegian immigrants. *Nordisk Folkeblad* carried Hjelm-Hansen's complete report to the State Board of Immigration on February 2, 1870.

In 1870 Sneedorff Christensen was appointed land commissioner for the St. Paul & Duluth Railroad Company and sold the newspaper. *Nordisk Folkeblad* continued its regular weekly appearance, changing ownership and editors several times, until July 7, 1875, when its subscription list was sold to *Skandinaven* in Chicago. *Nordisk Folkeblad* had no monopoly on the state's Norwegian newspaper field but rather competed desperately with other Norwegian-language publications. This was especially the case with the newspaper *Minnesota,* founded in Minneapolis in 1872 by the earlier publisher and editor of *Emigranten,* Carl Fredrik Solberg; Solberg, as related in the previous chapter, sold *Emigranten* to *Fædrelandet*'s publisher and editor, Frederick Fleischer, and after a sojourn in La Crosse moved to St. Paul.

In 1873 Solberg sold the weekly journal to Hjalmar Eger, who became editor upon Solberg's appointment as assistant secretary of state. In 1870 Eger had actually purchased *Nordisk Folkeblad* together with W. T. Rambusch and published it for a year or more before again transferring ownership to a new set of publishers. Eger enjoyed a reputation as a good writer, humorist, and speaker; he moved *Minnesota* toward the Democratic Party and employed his extrovert skills in vitriolic attacks on the Republican *Nordisk Folkeblad. Minnesota,* its political capital exhausted, ceased publication in October 1873.

Michael F. Wesenberg joined Eger in his bellicose exchanges with *Nordisk Folkeblad.* Wesenberg, according to Wist, was "by far the Norwegian newspaperman in America most inclined to do battle." He eventually became publisher and editor of *Duluth Skandinav,* established in 1887, a position "suitable to his needs and relish for strife." The petty quarrels, factious polemics, and personal disagreements that appeared in Norwegian American newspapers at this time created an impression of great inner dissension in the ethnic group despite its outward appearance of solidarity. Norwegian American life was afflicted with dissent and divided into factions of many kinds—political, religious, social, and cultural. These immigrants were not above the universal human desire to succeed, gain acceptance, and be recognized, nor were they immune to pettiness or envy. The ambitious young men who under unfamiliar circumstances shaped the Norwegian American press did so in a competitive spirit with rival Norwegian newspaper ventures; consequently, confident in their own judgment, their rivalry from time to time descended into heated personal accusations against competitors, even when the rivals shared political and religious faith. Nineteenth-century political discourse—in general, not limited to the immigrant press—was nothing less than strident.

Wesenberg had "made his first bow to a Norwegian American public" as co-worker on the weekly *Nordlyset* (Northern Lights, unrelated to the earlier Wisconsin paper of the same name), established in Northfield, Minnesota, in 1870 and financed by Harald Thorson. Thorson was the wealthy benefactor of St. Olaf's School (later St. Olaf College), founded in 1874. As a public-spirited citizen, Thorson was likely moved by his wish to enlighten his fellow Norwegians and perhaps concurrently advance his own business interests. *Nordlyset* appeared irregularly; its initial move into immigrant journalism was in fact fleeting and it folded after a brief publication period. It was revived in 1878, albeit shakily, and was discontinued in 1879. A publisher could start a newspaper with relative ease; the challenge was to attract a sufficient number of paying subscribers and advertising to make publishing a news organ a profitable business. The Norwegian American newspaper enterprise suffered a high mortality rate; many ventures were short-lived, suggesting the difficulty in making a profit in the uncertain world of immigrant journalism.[5]

Budstikken—Minneapolis Tidende

The newspaper *Budstikken* (The Messenger) became the primary Norwegian press organ in Minnesota during the late 1800s. Its first number appeared in Minneapolis September 2, 1873; Gudmund F. Johnson, Johan B. Gjedde, and Paul Hjelm-Hansen are listed as publishers. Hjelm-Hansen became the weekly's first editor. "The undersigned," the publishers' bluntly stated preamble began, "who have determined that the time has finally arrived when our countrymen have become thoroughly averse to receiving political news, information, and advice from newspapers owned by American politicians, have resolved to publish a weekly under the name *Budstikken*." The reference was here just as much to Norwegian-language publications—*Nordisk Folkeblad,* for example—such as short-term political campaign sheets and regular news organs, which were subsidized by American political parties and candidates. Norwegian American newspaper publishers accused each other of selling out to Yankee politicians. These accusations were likely unfounded, though the extent of American financial involvement in the foreign-language press cannot be reliably ascertained. In selecting the name *Budstikken*—literally the message stick—the publishers evoked the ancient Norse custom of sending a specially designed stick from farm to farm to call the people together, in many instances for defense or raids. The name itself was thus a symbolically powerful declaration of Norwegian strength and independence and a refusal to accept "financial assistance from political persons and coteries."

Budstikken found great fault with both major political parties, as explained in an editorial, but supported the Republican ticket, because that party "preserved the Union and freed the slaves." But *Budstikken* also supported "the farmers' revolt . . . against oppression and plundering by political beasts of prey," which it considered to be "the most warranted movement that has ever existed in this country." The reference was to the Grange, an organized farmer movement represented in the state by the Minnesota State Grange, formed in 1869. In the 1870s local granges numbered 379. Promoted by newspapers like the *St. Paul Pioneer Press,* and clearly joined by *Budstikken,* the Grange worked for regulatory legislation of railroad freight and grain storage elevator charges against high-handed capitalist abuse of power and money.

Budstikken's social views and anticapitalist stance moved it to support the Democratic Party toward the end of the decade. At the time of its founding, however, competition came from Republican rivals. In the September 16, 1873, issue, Hjelm-Hansen explained why he had sold his share in *Budstikken* to Ferdinand A. Husher, at the time associate editor of *Fædrelandet og Emigranten* in La Crosse, Wisconsin. Hjelm-Hansen had learned a few days after the launching of *Budstikken* that Husher intended to start a new Norwegian newspaper in Red Wing, Minnesota; in Hjelm-Hansen's opinion Norwegians in the state could not support three Republican journals, *Budstikken, Nordisk Folkeblad,* and the proposed rival, and he feared that Husher's personal qualities, as he defined them—a man in his prime with great knowledge, intelligence, experience, and energy—would give Husher "the best chance to succeed" at the expense of a man like himself "already with one foot in the grave." Husher became part owner and from December 9 succeeded Hjelm-Hansen as editor of *Budstikken*. Husher was born in Viborg, Denmark, in 1825 but grew up in Norway from the age of three. He received theological training and served as a teacher, school superintendent, and parish pastor before moving to America in 1869. His entry into immigrant journalism and active participation in Republican politics secured him important political appointments. Husher, according to Wist, through his extensive travels to Norwegian settlements had "in his time a more intimate relationship with the newspaper's public than perhaps any other Norwegian American newspaperman." He left his editorship and returned to La Crosse in 1875 to edit *Fædrelandet og Emigranten;* in March 1879 he overtook ownership of the journal after Frederick Fleischer, who had continued as publisher until his death in November 1878.[6]

Hjelm-Hansen returned as editor of *Budstikken* for about a year following Husher's departure. The most influential editor, however, was undoubtedly Luth Jaeger, editor from 1877 until 1885. Jaeger immigrated to America in 1871 at the age of twenty from the Arendal region of Norway; he had studied at the University of Oslo before his departure and continued his studies at the Uni-

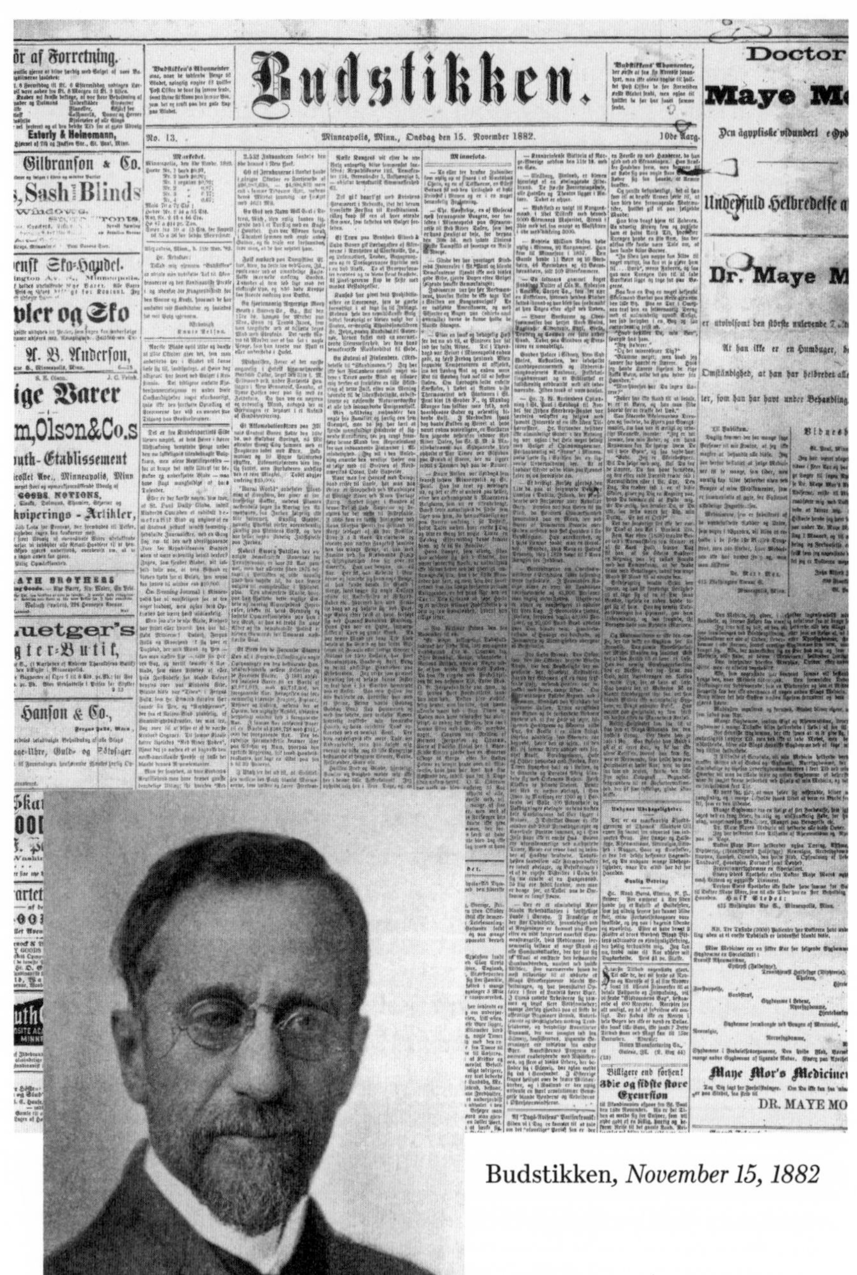

Budstikken.

No. 13. Minneapolis, Minn., Onsdag den 15. November 1882. 10de Aarg.

Gilbranson & Co.

Sash, Blinds

A. B. Anderson,

Luetger's

Hanson & Co.,

Doctor

Maye M

Dr. Maye M

Maye Mor's Medicine

DR. MAYE MO

Budstikken, *November 15, 1882*

Luth Jaeger, pioneer newspaper-man and prominent citizen of Minneapolis, became a spokesman for rapid Americanization.

versity of Wisconsin in Madison. Jaeger laid great stress on the study of English; in his journalistic career he was admired for his complete mastery of both Norwegian and English. Before assuming editorial responsibility for *Budstikken,* he cooperated with Sigvart Sørensen, later editor of *Minneapolis Tidende,* in founding the literary monthly *Norsk Maanedskrift* (Norwegian Monthly) in 1874 in La Crosse; it folded the following year. In 1876 Jaeger moved on to the weekly *Norden* (The North) in Chicago as associate editor.

Jaeger assumed his editorial responsibilities of *Budstikken* with the issue dated October 17, 1877. Due to disagreement with the two publishers, Gjedde and Johnson, in regard to editorial autonomy, Jaeger resigned from his position January 1, 1884, but continued to edit the weekly until early the following year.[7]

Luth Jaeger's liberal editorials, on religion, politics, and social affairs, troubled the publishers and the reading Norwegian American public alike. However, Jaeger kept the journal's columns open for free discussion; prominent individuals offered their views on many of the burning issues of the day. Jaeger's opposition to anything that seemed to retard Americanization and agitation to abandon the Norwegian language in favor of English more than anything else generated strong denouncement. He expressed his views on the situation for American-born youth in *Symra* 1913:

> The work for Norsedom has nearly become a national cause in churches, schools, societies, and organizations of different kinds. . . . The tendency of work for Norsedom is to create disunion and confusion, ambiguity, and uncertainty between the old and the new, a generation that nearly does not know whether it is Norwegian or American. In choosing between Norwegian and American, the young must choose the latter, they cannot split themselves.

Jaeger became a prominent and influential citizen of Minneapolis; his editorship greatly enhanced *Budstikken*'s quality as an original news medium; his tenure shines bright; after his departure *Budstikken* lost much of its popularity. In 1890 *Budstikken* reported a circulation of ten thousand; it was distributed throughout the state and beyond. One of the regular contributors during Jaeger's tenure was the Episcopal minister Erik L. Petersen in Faribault, Minnesota; in his regular column, "Studies at My Desk," he presented book reviews, historical articles, and commentary on social issues. His "biting sarcastic style and his ability to shroud inconsiderate commentary in humor" captivated readers, but also generated bitter rejoinders in *Budstikken* by those he had offended.[8]

Reporting on scandals, as Jaeger himself admitted, increased circulation. *Budstikken* covered fully the conflict that led to Oline Muus suing for divorce from her husband the Reverend Bernt Julius Muus, the founder of St. Olaf College and pastor of Holden Church in Goodhue County, Minnesota. The marital antagonism injected into the public sphere was naturally a great embarrassment for the Norwegian Synod, whose leadership in general supported Pastor Muus. The discord also energized the discussion in *Budstikken* and other immigrant newspapers of the rights of women. The main point of controversy, aggravated by domestic mistreatment on the part of Pastor Muus, was his attempt, in keeping with Norwegian law, to appropriate an inheritance Oline had received from Norway. The district court in Red Wing, Goodhue's county seat, ruled in Oline's favor in a case that commenced January 5, 1881. Oline was later granted legal separation. "Norwegian laws concerning the relationship between husband and wife we could easily do without in this country," a contributor wrote in *Skandinaven*. Many seconded this view.

Luth Jaeger and Judge Andreas Ueland were among the liberal spokesmen who served as hosts in Minneapolis for the renowned Norwegian man of letters Bjørnstjerne Bjørnson on his lecture tour in America during the winter of 1880–81. Bjørnson had earlier proclaimed the loss of his childhood Christian faith and held himself to be an unbeliever. Bjørnson considered the Norwegian Synod pastors to be hopeless bigots, so his sympathy was clearly with Oline Muus. *Budstikken* carried detailed reports on Bjørnson's lecture tour and his strident confrontations with the Synod clergy. The newspaper also printed lectures by the Unitarian minister Kristofer Janson, who had preceded Bjørnson on his own six-month American lecture tour beginning in September 1879. His free humanistic thoughts were apparent in *Budstikken*. Jaeger, a Unitarian, welcomed his contributions and in addition reprinted accounts of Janson's lectures gleaned from other Norwegian American newspapers. In his published lectures Janson, too, expressed support of Oline Muus while castigating Pastor Muus and the Norwegian Synod. Janson published his own monthly, *Saamanden* (The Sower), in Minneapolis 1887–94; its themes, in the spirit of Unitarianism, called attention to social injustices and promoted liberal humanism on the principles of the Social Gospel movement framed to create a social order that conformed to the teachings of Christ.[9]

The many splits among Norwegians were made conspicuous by unremitting confrontational dispatches from different quarters. Opposing political loyalties were strong forces of dissent. There were, however, instances where nationality trumped politics. As the Grange lost ground, *Budstikken* gave its support to the Farmers' Alliance, launched in Chicago in 1880. In Minnesota, the Alliance's stronghold was in the regions of agricultural disaffection in the western portion of the state, most especially among Norwegian farmers. *Budstikken* consequently found a receptive audience among these compatriots.

Budstikken continued its Democratic orientation. In the historic election in 1882, however, Knute Nelson challenged the American Charles F. Kindred for the Republican nomination for the House of Representatives in Minnesota's fifth congressional district. Luth Jaeger editorially in *Budstikken* not only encouraged Nelson to become a candidate, but also persisted in supporting him throughout the campaign, which Nelson won. The hard-fought election, which launched Nelson on his career of national leadership, led to the district's designation as the "Bloody Fifth."

Throughout the election, Kindred had also turned to the Norwegian voters in their mother tongue. A corporation interested in supporting Kindred purchased *Nordstjernen* (The North Star), which Michael Wesenberg established in Grand Forks in 1879; it moved to Fargo in 1881. Wesenberg had begun publishing *Red River Posten* in Fargo in 1878, the first Norwegian-language journal in North Dakota. Its support of Kindred in the 1882 political race greatly reduced its popularity among Norwegians. Wesenberg was instrumental in starting a number of Norwegian-language newspapers; his activities demonstrated the fluidity in immigrant journalism. He had published an earlier *Nordstjernen* briefly in Whitehall, Wisconsin, and after leaving the Fargo journal *Red River Posten* some months after its founding, he started *Minnesota Posten* in Red Wing, Minnesota, the same year. Like most of his newspaper ventures it was short-lived and had little political influence. The weekly *Tiden* (The Age), the organ of Nelson's adversaries, in Fergus Falls, published 1881–82, failed as well in its endorsement of Kindred. Johan Schrøder joined the fray by moving to Fergus Falls where he published the strongly pro-Nelson *Normanna Banner* (Norman Banner), also from 1881 to 1882. In addition, *Budstikken*'s enthusiastic endorsement of Knute Nelson's candidacy certainly influenced the favorable outcome; on November 15, 1882, Nelson expressed his gratitude for the Democratic newspaper's "warmth and might" in securing his election. The Democratic Party lost again in the fall 1886 election, but out of appreciation for editor Luth Jaeger's dedication made him their candidate for state auditor.[10]

Minneapolis, as the metropolis of the Upper Midwest, was obviously an attractive location for Norwegian American journalism. In July 1886 Ferdinand Husher, publisher and editor, sought a larger field of action by moving *Fædrelandet og Emigranten* from La Crosse to Minneapolis. Putting out a newspaper, Husher complained, was no easy matter: "The longer one publishes a newspaper and writes about people and events, the better one understands how extremely difficult it is to stroke every man where he likes it the most." Formidable competition from *Budstikken,* the successful Republican newspaper *Nordvesten* (The Northwest), established in St. Paul in 1881, and the appearance in January 1887 of *Minneapolis Daglig Tidende* (Minneapolis Daily Times) sealed the fate of the venerable news organ. The economic burden overwhelmed Husher and in July 1889 *Fædrelandet og Emigranten* went bankrupt; the newspaper, as announced, would continue regularly "on the estate's account" *(for Boets Regning).* Additional funds came from friends; in March 1890, however, Husher in a long letter bade farewell to the weekly's readers, explaining that he was leaving to accept the position of U.S. consul in Port Stanley and St. Thomas, Canada, appointed by President Benjamin Harrison. In September that year Thorvald Gulbrandsen, publisher of *Minneapolis Daglig Tidende* as well as of the weekly *Minneapolis Tidende,* begun in 1888, purchased *Fædrelandet og Emigranten* and contiued its publication until the end of 1892. In January 1893, it was consolidated with *Minneapolis Tidende.*[11]

Thorvald Gulbrandsen, born in Moss, Norway, in 1854, had learned the book printing business and spent a year in Hamburg, Germany, before he moved to America in 1874. He initially found employment within his trade, typography, at a Swedish newspaper in New York and as a typesetter in American printing shops in Chicago. Following the path of many other immigrant pressmen, he had ambitions of advancing into newspaper publishing. He moved to Grand Forks, North Dakota, in 1879; "the brisk growth taking place in the Red River Valley had a great attraction on him," stated his 1934 obituary. Grand Forks was at the time, however, a pioneer village. He worked for a while in the weekly *Nordstjernen* in Grand Forks and *Red River Posten* in Fargo before he became business manager at the *Grand Forks Tidende* (The Grand Forks Times). Like its peers in the frontier press, it worked to attract settlers to

Cedar Avenue in Minneapolis looking north across the intersection of Fifth Street South about 1890. Dania Hall, at right, served as an assembly hall for Scandinavian entertainment and organizational activities. Norwegians owned businesses of many kinds nearby and cultivated an ethnic life. The daily and Sunday Minneapolis Tidende *could be delivered for six cents a week within city limits.*

the territory. *Grand Forks Tidende* was founded in 1880 by Tellef Grundysen as a weekly newspaper. Grundysen emigrated from Bygland in Setesdalen, Norway, when he was just seven; he is credited with writing the first novel to deal with life in a Norwegian settlement in America. Gulbrandsen took over *Grand Forks Tidende* as owner and publisher in 1882.

As the publisher of *Grand Forks Tidende,* a promising local weekly, Gulbrandsen sought even "a greater calling" by harboring "the bold idea that Minneapolis ought to have its own daily Norwegian newspaper like Chicago." The weekly Chicago *Skandinaven* competed successfully in the Minneapolis market; its daily edition, however, was mainly limited to Chicago. Most of the hundreds of local journals, irrespective of language, published in villages and towns throughout Minnesota were weeklies; it was thus a risky enterprise, and "hardly anyone but himself thought it feasible." Gulbrandsen undertook several inspection tours and became convinced that Minneapolis, full of activity and excitement and with "more countrymen gathered than in any other city in America," would welcome a daily journal in the homeland's language. The initial issue of *Minneapolis Daglig Tidende* appeared January 24, 1887, as a small four-page journal. It heralded a successful venture in Norwegian American journalism.[12]

Minneapolis Daglig Tidende's first editor was the Populist Tom Overland, who in 1885 had succeeded Luth Jaeger as *Budstikken*'s editor until July 1886 and served *Grand Forks Tidende* in that capacity when Gulbrandsen launched *Daglig Tidende.* In bidding farewell to *Budstikken*'s readers he extolled the People's Party *(Folkepartiet)* and expressed his confidence that the newspaper would persist as "a spokesman for people's needs and wants." Overland's confidence was well placed; in succeeding years the newspaper embraced both the Farmers' Alliance and the Populist Party. In June 1888, however, *Budstikken* went into receivership with Luth Jaeger functioning as receiver. December 8 that year Thorvald Gulbrandsen assumed ownership. His declaration to *Budstikken*'s subscribers stated his guiding principles as a Norwegian American newspaper publisher:

> The change in ownership of *Budstikken* will not bring about any change in the newspaper's positions. It is our determination to keep the newspaper out of all church strife, to contend the rampant

> monopoly rule that threatens our free constitution, to oppose all fanaticism, and on the whole it will be our endeavor to make *Budstikken* as worthy an organ for the liberal, reformist element in our Scandinavian population as anyone rightfully might expect.

In January 1888 Gulbrandsen began publication of the weekly *Minneapolis Tidende;* it continued the volume numbering of *Grand Forks Tidende,* which Gulbrandsen had published until that time. Thus, Wist contended, the new weekly might be seen as a continuation of the Grand Forks journal. Gulbrandsen enjoyed a steady and solid growth in his publishing business, yet expressed disappointment about the Norwegian public's lack of interest—complaints that were valid in light of Gulbrandsen's considerable financial challenges. He actively recruited subscribers, appointed agents, and appealed to new groups of readers. His decision to begin *Minneapolis Søndag Tidende,* a Sunday offering, November 24, 1889, increased circulation; it replaced the regular Saturday edition. The Sunday edition had a circulation of six thousand in 1890 while the daily had about half as many subscribers. The daily and Sunday editions could either be mailed or within city limits be delivered *(ombragt)* to the door for six cents a week. In 1891, Gulbrandsen incorporated his publishing firm as T. Gulbrandsen Publishing Company with himself as president. The daily newspaper was offered alongside two weekly journals, *Budstikken* and *Minneapolis Tidende.* In the December 25, 1894, issue Gulbrandsen announced the decision to merge the two newspapers under the name of *Minneapolis Tidende,* describing it as "a completely independent news and family journal, which has made so much progress that it is now one of the most widely circulated Scandinavian newspapers in America."

The regular features from *Budstikken* and *Tidende* were continued in the merged weekly, welcome and familiar to readers. Among these were "Church Vistas" *(Kirkelig Rundskue),* "For the Woman" *(For Kvinden),* "The Home and the Farm" *(Hjemmet og Farmen),* "From Norway" "From Denmark," "From Sweden," "From Foreign Countries" *(Fra Udlandet)*—the Nordic countries were homelands—"Questions and Answers" *(Spørgsmaal og Svar),* letters from subscribers, and columns on local and national business activities, as well as news from regions of Norwegian settlement in neighboring and more distant states. These informative features created an impression of comprehensive coverage and also suggested a close relationship between the newspaper and its subscribers. The questions to the editor, the majority on legal issues, are especially illustrative in this regard as are the many submitted letters. In May 1898 someone asked where he might find a map of available homestead land in the Red Lake Reservation in Minnesota, another requested information about citizenship, and a third expressed concern about the possible consequences of having cast a false vote.

The weekly edition had indeed, like *Skandinaven* before it, become a national newspaper. By 1900 *Minneapolis Tidende* had an average circulation in excess of twenty-nine thousand. The absorption of *Emigranten og Fædrelandet* in January 1893 gave it boasting rights to lay claim to being the second-oldest Norwegian American journal, after *Nordlyset,* dating its history back to *Emigranten*'s founding in Inmansville, Wisconsin, January 23, 1852. The daily and the weekly editions of *Tidende* continued publication into the 1930s.[13]

An Expanding Small-Town Press

Albert Lea, county seat of Freeborn County, was a large Norwegian center; in 1875 the Norwegian stock, first and second generation, numbered 5,191, close to 40 percent of the total county population. Norwegian settlement expanded in Freeborn and neighboring counties on both sides of the Minnesota-Iowa border. Several transient Norwegian local newspaper ventures were made in Albert Lea; these exemplify small-town limitations in attracting a sufficient geographical readership and advertising base. As the newspaper list in Appendix 1 denotes, only *Albert Lea Posten* (The Albert Lea Post), the final of five undertakings, enjoyed a measure of success. It was published by the Albert Lea Publishing Company, a stockholding company formed by local businessmen; its first issue is dated July 5, 1882; from early 1883 Erik S. Gjellum, Albert Lea lawyer and later editor of the Iowa journal *Decorah-Posten,* assumed editorial responsibility. Born in Utica, Wisconsin, he was an early example of second-generation entry into Norwegian American journalism. In the March 17, 1885, issue, Gjellum explained that due to "difficult times" *(haarde Tider), Albert Lea Posten* had been sold to Chr. Brandt & Co., publishers of *Nordvesten* in St. Paul.

The preserved files of *Albert Lea Posten* provide a vivid portrait of life in a "Norwegian" small town during the early 1880s: Carlsen & Amberson offered "air-dried fish from Bergen" *(Tør-Fisk)* and other Norwegian delicacies; ethnic societies and Norwegian Lutheran churches were active; and lawyers and medical doctors advertised their services in Norwegian. A feeling of a Norwegian immigrant world prevailed. May 17, 1883, was celebrated with a parade through the streets of the city to the opera house, where the observance held forth with music, several speeches, and cheers to "The kingdom of Norway and Sweden" and to their new hometown; in the evening a local dramatic troupe presented C. P. Riis's "To the Mountains" *(Til Sæters),* with its medley of folk songs and nationalistic affirmation, then "the festivity concluded with dancing." Politically *Albert Lea Posten* was strictly Republican. Following Democrat Grover Cleveland's election as president in 1884, the editor deplored that "The result is not what we had expected and worked for." Local small-town journals like *Albert Lea Posten,* as well as larger metropolitan newspapers, provide a window into life in the Norwegian American community.

In the competition for subscribers, village and town newspapers often lost out to the widely circulated big-city journals. Small-town publishers' reasonable expectations were rarely fulfilled. Spring Grove in southern Houston County provides an illustrative example. It was an important distribution point for the Norwegian movement westward; the town itself and its surroundings were filled with Norwegian settlers. One might reason that a small Norwegian-language journal here would attract an interested readership. Sven H. Ellestad, born in Wilmington Township in Houston County of parents from Hallingdal, Norway, started the weekly *Spring Grove Posten* (The Spring Grove Post) in April 1880, viewing his prospects for journalistic success to be good. Instead, as Johannes Wist recorded, "after a miserable existence of about a year it was discontinued."

Many publishing endeavors ended in the same disappointing fate; it was a common experience for "small newspapers—the expenses were greater than the income." According to Carlton Qualey, western Houston and eastern Fillmore counties in southeastern Minnesota likely had the greatest concentration of Norwegian settlement in the state. Visiting the area in October 1874, Ferdinand Husher, *Budstikken*'s editor, reported how impressed he was by the density of the Norwegian population and the denizens' use of the Norwegian language. In spite of favoring prospects, the weekly *Det utflyttede Norge* (The Emigrated Norway) lasted only from 1888 to 1889 as a Norwegian news medium in Lanesboro in Fillmore County. Its initial publisher and editor was the Norwegian Synod pastor Erik Knudsen Thuland of Lanesboro; during its last few months, the newspaper was published and edited by American-born Samuel A. Langum, who moved the newspaper to the county seat of Preston. Langum in association with *Det utflyttede Norge* published and edited the *Preston Times,* begun in 1886, and served in the Minnesota state legislature for many years. The weighty credentials of the two newsmen were clearly not the determining factors in how the weekly fared.

Across the Mississippi River in Wisconsin, La Crosse early on established itself as a hub of Norwegian American journalism, yet the city's days as a publication center for Norwegian-language newspapers came to a close before the end of the 1800s. A second *Varden* (The Beacon), following the one published by T. J. Widvey, cast its light in La Crosse in the early 1890s. Lars A. Stenholt, the controversial writer of popular sensational novels and journalistic exposés, edited *Varden* for a while; he was succeeded by Ole A. Buslett, author of tales in the nationalistic style of Bjørnson. The two men represented very different standards of immigrant fiction; neither author can be viewed as a great interpreter of Norwegian American life. Creative writers frequently labored in the service of the press; as an example, Stenholt was a contributor to *Budstikken.* Buslett edited the La Crosse weekly *Folkevennen* (The People's Friend) for some time. In 1895, after nearly two years of publication, *Folkevennen* was absorbed by *Norden* in Chicago.

Jacob L. Hjort launched *La Crosse Tidende* (The La Crosse Times) in September 1895. Hjort was born in Allamakee County, Iowa, the son of pastor Ove Jakob Hjort. The weekly journal's expansion to twice weekly indicated, as Wist reported, that the journal "should amount to something." It was, however, not to be. In September 1897 *La Crosse Tidende* merged with the Milwaukee weekly *Fram* (Forward) and was published as *La Crosse Tidende og Milwaukee Fram* until its demise after a few weeks. Jacob Hjort found employment on other immigrant newspapers. The second generation had obviously come of age in the world of Norwegian American journalism.

Kristian Prestgard, who was to earn fame as *Decorah-Posten*'s longstanding editor, had in 1897 edited *La Crosse Tidende* during the last few months of its existence. *La Crosse-Posten* (The La Crosse Post), the last Norwegian-language newspaper published in La Crosse, expired in 1898 after being published for about a year as a special La Crosse edition of *Decorah-Posten. Decorah-Posten,* founded in 1874, had its roots in La Crosse, which explains the connection. The history of the venerable Iowa journal can be traced back to the literary magazine *Ved Arnen* (By the Fireplace) begun in La Crosse 1866. The detailed historical recounting of immigrant journalism makes evident the persistent energy and optimism, as well as political and financial motives, that powered the floundering Norwegian American press in small towns and villages throughout the Midwest.[14]

The Press in St. Paul, Minnesota

The Republican Party organ *Nordvesten* (The Northwest), founded in St. Paul the summer of 1881, initially gained considerable political influence; its political clout diminished with the Populist advances toward the end of the decade. Frequently unsuccessful Democratic challenges to the Republican Party began at an earlier date. The Democratic weekly *Tiden* (The Age) started in 1878 by the politician Erik N. Falk was discontinued the following year. *Nordvesten* had a more promising future, given the Republican strength in the state, as well as the support of the railroad executive James J. Hill, the politically powerful creator of the famed Great Northern Railway. Democratic *Budstikken* in 1886 went a step further and claimed that the publisher had tried to conceal that *Nordvesten* in fact was owned by Hill; even liberal Republican *Skandinaven* sarcastically described *Nordvesten* as "a Norwegian newspaper published by an American railroad magnate and edited by a German professor." The latter was in reference to Christian Brandt, who edited *Nordvesten* from fall 1881; his rejoinder to early accusations by the church-related Minneapolis weekly *Folkebladet* and other Norwegian-language journals of having sold out to American capitalism expressed a wish "to clarify a question that seems to 'trouble' several of our colleagues" by insisting that "no railroad company owns as much as a cent in *Nordvesten.*" Even so, the positions of the men associated with *Nordvesten* suggest at the very least a shared political advocacy with Hill's railroad empire.

A stockholding company, organized by familiar actors in the early Norwegian American press, stood as *Nordvesten*'s publishers. F. Sneedorff Christensen was its secretary; Søren Listoe and other politically engaged newsmen served on the board of directors. The president of the group was Lars K. Aaker, a successful entrepreneur and politician from Goodhue County. In 1869 he was appointed to the important position of registrar at the federal land office in Alexandria, Douglas County, Minnesota; he served until 1875 and worked tirelessly to attract Norwegian settlers to the region. Land grant railroads encouraged and financially supported colonization efforts along their lines; pamphlets and newspaper promotion were important propaganda organs in the recruitment of settlers. In the fall of 1881 Aaker was elected state senator.[15]

Nordvesten experienced a series of owners and editors during its publication life. Christian Brandt purchased the St. Paul weekly in 1883, the firm registered as Chr. Brandt & Co., and published it until he sold it in 1887. During Brandt's ownership, Wist wrote, "the newspaper had a really exceptional growth and became one of the most circulated political news organs in the Norwegian language in this country." Brandt was born in Vestre Slidre in Valdres, Norway in 1853. Before immigrating to the United States in 1876, he had attended the military school, became a lieutenant in the Norwegian army, and for a year had studied civil engineering in Aachen, Germany. In America he entered journalism, first as city editor of the *Daglige Skandinaven* (The Daily Scandinavian), then as assistant editor of *Fædrelandet og Emigranten* before he assumed the editorship of *Nordvesten.*

Brandt left *Nordvesten* to serve as inspector general of the Minnesota National Guard—an appointment secured through political networking—with the rank of brigadier general. In December 1891, Brandt returned to newspaper publishing by launching the weekly *Heimdal,* "published every Sunday morning"; several Danish and Norwegian journals bore the name of the Norse god Heimdal, the guard of the gods, born of nine maidens, with the uncanny ability to hear grass grow, indeed an excellent metaphor for a journalistic endeavor. The god himself drawing his sword and with his famed Gjallarhorn—the blowing of which would proclaim the end of the world—at his side adorned the masthead. Reminders of ancient Viking roots fueled a positive Norwegian American identity.

Like *Nordvesten, Heimdal* advocated the policies and candidates of the Republican Party. Brandt sold the weekly in August 1893. *Heimdal* initially claimed to be "The only Norwegian illustrated Sunday newspaper in the United States," and by 1896 it somewhat questionably advertised itself as "the only newspaper in the Norwegian language in St. Paul." It continued publication as a "Norsk" newspaper until February 1902; *Heimdal* was then bought by Danish-born Christian Rasmussen, whose publishing company issued a number of Scandinavian journal titles, and continued as the Danish weekly *St. Paul Tidende.*

Heimdal's and other Norwegian American editors often referred to each other as "brothers"; family feuds were, however, bitter at times, as exemplified by *Heimdal*'s reference to its rival the Republican *Nationaltidende* (The National Times) as being full of nonsense *(sludder). Nationaltidende* began publication in St. Paul in 1893; it moved to Duluth in 1895. In its December 3, 1896, issue Søren Listoe, then editor of *Nordvesten,* announced that the newspaper had added two thousand "new names to our subscription list" by purchasing *Nationaltidende*'s list. The weekly *Scandia* in Duluth, with a pronounced political opposition agenda, immediately accused "Colonel Soren the Penman" Listoe of gross exaggeration, insisting that *Nationaltidende* never had more than two hundred subscribers and hardly gained twenty new readers in Duluth. It was brought to Duluth, *Scandia* claimed, "to freeze out the *Scandia*" but could not raise money to continue. The final accusation by *Scandia* is illustrative of the prevailing antagonism, although its accuracy cannot be verified:

> When James J. Hill appointed Soren the Penman editor and proprietor of the *Nordvesten,* this paper had 10,000 subscribers which the "colonel" has now managed down to 3,000; while as a writer and editor only those who can't read his paper consider him more than a rank failure. And his valuable newspaper has cost Mr. J. J. Hill over $50,000.[16]

Nordvesten's circulation was declining, but due more to the shifting political winds of the 1890s than to incompetent management. The historic reform of the Democratic Party and its alliance with the Populist Party fortified a tradition of great involvement among Scandinavian voters and politicians. The fusion between the Democrats and Populists represented a major political realignment; the fusion party mobilized small farmers and urban laborers and advocated economic radicalism. The election of Swedish-born John Lind, the fusion party's gubernatorial candidate, as governor in 1898 highlighted the shift in political loyalties. It was the first time after the Civil War that a Republican had not won the governorship of the state. Democratic *Minneapolis Tidende* and other Norwegian-language reform media in the state gave Lind their support.

Christian Brandt had returned to edit *Nordvesten* the previous year and made it less of a party organ. Lowering partisan rhetoric did not, however, protect the weekly from its sinking popularity. Inheriting insolvent rivals' subscription lists might of course improve a journal's prospects. In December 1899, *Red River Tidende* in Crookston, owned by Iowa-born E. G. Mellem, was consolidated with *Nordvesten,* providing a potential three thousand new subscribers. However, it does not seem to have been a done deal, even though *Red River Tidende* appeared on *Nordvesten*'s masthead. In September 1900 the Norwegian Synod–friendly newspaper *Amerika,* then published in Madison, Wisconsin, carried the startling news that Mellem had transferred ownership of his journal's subscription list to *Amerika,* which in subsequent issues listed *Red River Tidende* on its opinion page. An explanation for the abrupt change of business partner might be found in *Red River Tidende*'s history. It was established in 1895 by Hans Johnson, a former pastor in the Norwegian Synod, and owned by Mellem only since early 1899; the Synod organ *Kirketidende* expressed its pleasure that "our newspapers are placed in the hands of men who stand up for Christianity and the Church."

A second consolidation came about. In 1905 *Minneapolis Tidende* sold its literary supplement *Aftenlæsning* (Evening Reading) to *Nordvesten;* the publishers a second time reassuring its readers that "the consolidation gives a considerably increased circulation." The final years of *Nordvesten* suggest the precarious and shifting environment in which the ethnic press operated. In its June 27, 1907, issue, *Nordvesten* announced that it "from next week will be merged with *Minneapolis Tidende* . . . since the newspaper as a business enterprise no longer turns a profit."[17]

Journalistic Reform Vistas

A bevy of Norwegian-language newspapers gave significant support to the agrarian reform message advocated by the Farmers' Alliance and the succeeding program of the Populist Party. In his compelling analysis of political dissent among Norwegian Americans, historian Lowell Soike discussed how from the 1880s "Main Street versus the countryside loomed." Norwegian immigrant farmers were pulled into the Alliance movement and agrarian militancy in disproportionate numbers. Yet A. J. Underwood, owner and publisher of the Republican organ the *Fergus Falls Weekly Journal,* founded Republican mouthpiece *Fergus Falls Ugeblad* (Fergus Falls Weekly), continuing the volume numbering of *Normanna Banner,* in January 1883 in Fergus Falls, Minnesota. This outsider's venture was clearly a Republican attempt to reach Norwegians in Otter Tail and neighboring counties and to perhaps mediate small town and country conflict.

Factionalism within the Farmers' Alliance movement, the activism of proponents of Populism, as well as individual political ambitions complicate the role played by the Norwegian American press in political dissidence. *Fergus Falls Ugeblad* soon shifted its political course. In 1884, Anfin Solem acquired ownership and for the most part edited the Otter Tail weekly, moving it into the Farmers' Alliance camp. It became a considerable political force in its area of distribution; in 1890 it celebrated the formation of the Minnesota Farmers' Alliance Party. By the 1890s Norwegians in Otter

Tail County abandoned the Republican Party in droves and, to cite Soike, "provided the core of support for Alliance and subsequent Populist party candidates." Solem published *Fergus Falls Ugeblad* until 1908. He was born in Strinda, now a part of Trondheim, in 1850, graduated from Klæbu normal school—as Svein Nilsson had done before him—then studied at the technical school in Trondheim before coming to America in 1879.[18]

Upheavals within the Alliance party had repercussions on Norwegian American journalism. Leaders antagonistic to Ignatius Donnelly and his influence controlled Alliance politics at the state level. Donnelly, a lawyer from Philadelphia, is perhaps best known for being a spokesman for rural discontent and his role in forming the Populist Party at a meeting of Farmers' Alliances in Cincinnati in 1891. He also organized the Minnesota People's Party, and as a distinguished agrarian orator he gave the keynote address at the Populist Party's convention in Omaha, Nebraska, in July 1892, where the strongly reformatory Omaha platform was adopted. In Otter Tail County Donnelly was joined by Norwegian-born Haldor E. Boen, a strong spokesman for the Norwegian farmers in the county. Boen

The printing shop of Fergus Falls Ugeblad *in 1915. In its area of distribution, the weekly journal became a political force in support of the Minnesota Farmers' Alliance party.*

edited the Populist *Fergus Falls Globe,* established in 1887; in 1892 he was elected to Congress as a Populist.

On November 28, 1893, Boen gained a Norwegian voice with the launching of *Rodhuggeren* (The Radical) in Fergus Falls by Norwegian immigrants Ole E. Hagen, born in Gudbrandsdalen, and Torkel Oftelie, from Telemark; Oftelie had for several years been on *Fergus Falls Ugeblad*'s staff. In the first issue, addressed to "Friends and Opponents," the two editors stated:

> When we today send *Rodhuggeren* out to thousands of homes, perhaps even delivered to your door, we wish foremost to announce that *Rodhuggeren* is a People's Party newspaper and that we to our best ability will work for the principles that party is founded on.

Torkel Oftelie edited the Populist Rodhuggeren, *which competed politically with* Fergus Fall Ugeblad. *Oftelie was active in the* bygdelag *movement, a cofounder of Telelaget of America, and the editor of its journal* Telesoga *(The Telemark History).*

When the Alliance split apart, Anfin Solem of *Fergus Falls Ugeblad* joined forces with the anti-Donnelly faction. On November 8, 1893, in anticipation of the start of *Rodhuggeren, Fergus Falls Ugeblad,* still professing to support Populism, commented critically on its coming rival.

> The new journal, *Rodhuggeren,* is generally thought to be Congressman Boen's organ. . . . It will be a People's Party organ, but in part it will likely also be a Unitarian and freethinker organ. Mr. Oftelie is as everyone knows a Unitarian, and Hagen is as seen in newspaper articles and pamphlets a pronounced freethinker.

The criticism reveals much about *Fergus Falls Ugeblad.* The weekly had a circulation of about fifteen hundred and augmented its political stance by providing considerable space to matters relating to religion, temperance, and literature. In the 1892 election campaign, Solem editorially endorsed Republican Knute Nelson for the state's governorship against Donnelly. Boen was made congressman from Minnesota's seventh district, in spite of Solem's endorsement of his German Republican opponent, gaining an average of 62 percent of the votes in the strongly Norwegian precincts in Otter Tail County.

The two Fergus Falls journals continued to endorse separate candidates for political office. By 1895 *Rodhuggeren* had surpassed *Fergus Falls Ugeblad* to become the principal Norwegian-language weekly in Otter Tail County, with a reported subscription list of four thousand and a substantial circulation in northwestern Minnesota and eastern North Dakota. In the heated 1896 election, *Fergus Falls Ugeblad* appeared to have even suggested that freethinkers should not be elected to public office in the state, a recommendation described as un-American and dumb by the more radical *Rodhuggeren.* The conflict obviously moved beyond political concerns. Editor Hagen's radicalism at times appeared as wanton and fearless attacks on churchly affairs. The fused Democratic-Populist Party went down to defeat nationally, and it steadily declined in Otter Tail County. The change in fortunes affected both journals. *Fergus Falls Ugeblad,* after the People's Party's amalgamation with the Democratic Party in 1902, declared itself "an independent reform paper" and served as a local news organ until it was discontinued in 1946. In May 1898 *Rodhuggeren* informed its readers that it would move to Fargo, North Dakota, and merge with the Populist *Fjerde Juli og Dakota* (Fourth of July and Dakota); the merged journals would continue as the weekly *Fram* (Forward).[19]

The Red River Valley of North Dakota experienced strong reformist journalism, which will be dealt with more fully in the following chapter. Hans A. Foss—perhaps best known for his popular immigrant novel *Husmands-Gutten* (The Cotter Boy)—as editor of *Normanden* (The Norseman) in Grand Forks, North Dakota, became a strong political voice among Norwegians in the state. He was born at Modum, Norway, and emigrated in 1877 at the age of twenty-six. In the mid-1880s he became a forceful spokesman for the temperance movement. *Normanden* was established by L. K. Hassell in April 1887 to promote the cause of temperance; he saw an opportunity for a second newspaper when *Grand Forks Tidende,* which he earlier had edited, moved to Minneapolis in January 1888, where it continued as the weekly *Minneapolis Tidende.* In

1888 a corporation purchased *Normanden* and hired Foss as editor; Foss together with the printer Edvard Lund purchased *Normanden* about two years later and published it until 1893. Foss as editor of *Normanden* gave strong support to the Farmers' Alliance, and with the formation of the Populist Party, the weekly became the party's official organ. The victory for the Populist Party in the state election in 1892 was also a victory for Foss.

Financial reality set in—the depression of 1893 and Populism's decline—and *Normanden* shifted owners as a consequence. The new publishers were closely associated with the Republican Party; accusations of selling out to the enemy were hurled at Foss. Foss himself claimed in a letter printed in *Rodhuggeren* December 1893 to have been overrun by *Normanden*'s shareholders. The aging Republican Ferdinand A. Husher, "who neither in theory nor in practice is a temperance man and prohibitionist," Foss complained, was hired to edit the newspaper.

Foss responded to the personal offense he felt at being accused of aiding an American Republican elite by launching the weekly *Nye Normanden* (The New Norseman) in January 1894, again in partnership with Lund, as a radical Populist advocate. It was begun in Moorhead but moved to Minneapolis in spring of the following year.

Nye Normanden, advocating the principles of the Populist Omaha platform, questioned the claimed People's Party credentials of its weekly rival *Red River Dalen* (The Red River Valley) in Crookston, Minnesota. It began publication fall 1889; Adolf Bydal served as editor and from January 1893 also publisher until its demise some three years later. Bydal's Populist convictions were genuine, though *Red River Dalen* might more accurately be described as a politically independent organ with Populist tendencies. Bydal studied law and classical Germanic philology at university before moving to America in the late 1870s; he entered Norwegian American journalism shortly after his arrival. In 1897 he moved on to express the concerns of the Norwegian farming population by publishing and editing *Madison Tidende* (The Madison Times), founded in Madison, the county seat of the heavily Norwegian Lac qui Parle County, Minnesota, in 1894. In August 1897 he purchased the subscription list of *Minnesota Folkeblad* (People's Newspaper), a local newspaper published in Canby, Minnesota, 1892–96, and changed the name to *Minnesota Tidende.* Bydal advocated for agrarian reform measures through aggressive editorials and strong political involvement; despite his popularity among Norwegian farmers, Bydal's tone and tactics exposed him to the determined actions of his stalwart political opponents, which likely caused the journal to fold in 1899.[20]

Radical advocacy characterized *Nye Normanden* as well. Editor Foss gained great disfavor with *Rodhuggeren* by joining *Fergus Falls Ugeblad* in castigating Haldor Boen, finding among other faults Boen's insinuated hypocrisy in his stance on temperance reform. *Rodhuggeren* showed its dissatisfaction by refusing to establish an exchange relationship with *Nye Normanden,* a common courtesy among newspaper publishers. In the heavily competitive newspaper market in Minneapolis, Johannes Wist wrote, the journal "was moreover excessively radical for the average Norwegian public" and lost out in the competition with other Norwegian-language newspapers. A high point for *Nye Normanden* was Democratic-Populist presidential candidate William Jennings Bryan's visit in October 1896. *Nye Normanden* printed the Norwegian translation of his speech and predicted victory for the Populist/Democratic ticket. Bryan's disappointing loss to the Republican William McKinley in November 1896 and again in 1900 was seen as an endorsement by the American people of imperialism, trust monopoly, militarism, tariff, anti-prohibition, and false patriotism. The newspaper's growing debt and resulting financial straits led to foreclosure and sale to a shareholding company in the summer of 1904.

Nye Normanden continued as the weekly *Politiken* (The Politics), the initial issue dated June 26, 1904. The last preserved number bears the date January 8, 1907; in November that year the journal began a two-year run as the freethinking monthly *Ny Tid* (New Age). Editorially *Politiken* explained in its first issue that the new name "was intended to imply that we hereafter will concentrate more on political news and on issues that are of general interest and practical importance." Though *Politiken* began as a Democratic news organ, it insisted that "Socialism is one of the strong currents in our time and cannot be dropped from consideration." The newspaper assured advocates of Socialism that they would be heard.

When Laurits Larsen Stavnheim in September 1905 became *Politiken*'s publisher and editor, the Minneapolis journal did indeed adorn a pure Socialist dress. Editorially Stavnheim included farmers in the labor class and welcomed them to the Socialist camp, though he seemed to give the urban worker greater attention than the tiller of the soil. Stavnheim was born at Sandnes, Norway, in 1863 and gained considerable experience in editorial positions before he emigrated in 1889, influenced by the political liberalism of the set around the Norwegian author Arne Garborg; in his new location he continued to engage in journalism and political reform movements. Notwithstanding *Politiken*'s financial problems, Stavnheim in launching the weekly was confident that many "freethinking men and women would rally around and support . . . a Norwegian newspaper that dared state its opinion where other newspapers thought it wisest to keep quiet." In March 1906 *Politiken* published the platform of the Minnesota Socialist Party and endorsed "the brave *[kjekk]* Norwegian" Ole E. Loftus, the Socialist or Public Ownership Party candidate, for governor. Socialism was for Stavnheim "equal opportunity for everyone" and "economic freedom and independence."[21]

From Duluth-Superior to Chicago

Like the Twin Cities of Minneapolis and St. Paul, Duluth on the Minnesota side and Superior in Wisconsin were, as Theodore Blegen described them, "immediate neighbors." They formed a comprehensive urban area at the western end of Lake Superior at the mouth of the St. Louis River. The twin port cities became a major transportation center on the Great Lakes–St. Lawrence Seaway. From the final two decades of the nineteenth century Norwegians moved to the region, but not in any great numbers. In 1900 Duluth had 2,655 Norwegian-born residents and 4,638 of the second generation and Superior 2,026 and 3,430 respectively; the two central places grew as hubs for Norwegian church life, business entrepreneurship, social and cultural activity, and newspaper publishing. Duluth remained the larger of the two cities.

Duluth Skandinav (Duluth Scandinavian) made its appearance as early as December 7, 1887, one of the many newspaper ventures made by Michael Wesenberg; in contrast to his earlier efforts, this one enjoyed great success. Wesenberg was born in Bergen in 1841 into one of Norway's oldest and most noted families; he came to the United States at the age of eighteen. His obituary in 1919 describes his life as a struggle, much of it devoted to "the newspaper he established," which "he carried forward and upheld as long as he could wield his pen in defense of everything he believed in." His pen, as suggested by Johannes Wist as well as in his published eulogy and evidenced in the columns of *Duluth Skandinav,* was on occasion cutting.

The weekly *Duluth Skandinav* informed the Norwegian community in Duluth and environs until 1965—a period of nearly eighty years. In early 1888, *Superior Posten* (The Superior Post) became a rival journal across the bay, launched by Charles Lagro, a noted property owner in Superior, as a Democratic medium. The paper switched hands in 1891. In 1893 Lagro resumed ownership, but due to declining health he sold it that same year; the new publishers changed the name to *Superior Tidende.* Under that name it persisted until 1962. These two journals enjoyed a remarkable length of publication; they clearly filled a need in the Norwegian community. Documenting their early history is difficult, however, since no issues of *Duluth Skandinav* have been preserved before 1916. *Superior Tidende* has files from 1896 to 1902, but then there is a long lacuna until December 1925.[22]

Aspects of the histories of the two newspapers can be traced in celebratory newspaper supplements; the first commemorative publication that exists is a 1937 fiftieth anniversary tribute to both journals. They by then shared publisher and editorial leadership. In November 1917 Jørgen Jansen Fuhr purchased *Duluth Skandinav* from Wesenberg's son John C. Wesenberg and the typographer Severin Simonsen, who each in 1912 got half ownership of the journal. Fuhr had served as editor for a year or more when he acquired *Duluth Skandinav;* in 1918 Fuhr organized the Fuhr Publishing and Printing Company; the first issue of *Duluth Skandinav* published by the new company is dated February 1. In 1919 Fuhr gained ownership of *Superior Tidende* as well.[23]

In 1896, the shareholding company that then published *Superior Tidende* hired Henry P. Petersen as editor. Petersen later acquired principal ownership of *Superior Tidende.* The Republican ticket was listed as "Our Slate" *(Vor Valgliste)* in the 1896 presidential election; it celebrated the election of William McKinley: "the four years of Democratic rule . . . now belong to history." In state politics the *Superior Tidende* under Petersen's leadership opposed the Old Guard—the Republican League—and sided with the Reform element in the Republican Party. It involved itself in the rise to power of Robert M. LaFollette and his progressive program of reform and anti-machine politics that assured him Wisconsin's governorship in 1900—later with heavy Norwegian support reelected in 1902 and 1904.

Petersen left *Superior Tidende* in October 1901 to become factory inspector in Wisconsin's northern district. In his farewell letter he committed himself "to work for [*Superior Tidende*'s] circulation and influence across its wide field among Scandinavians in northern Wisconsin." At that time it had fewer than three thousand subscribers. Petersen's political appointment likely had more to do with his role as president of the Grand Lodge *(Storlogen)* of the fraternal mutual aid association the Independent Scandinavian Workers Association (ISWA) *(Den uavhængige skandinaviske Arbeiderforening)* than as newspaper publisher. Its declared political neutrality notwithstanding, ISWA did not entirely refrain from political involvement; leaders within ISWA frequently used their positions to achieve political goals. Petersen's weekly publication served as ISWA's official organ from 1898 until 1901. The insurance fraternity published its own monthly journal at its headquarters in Eau Claire 1907–14.[24]

Several newspaper ventures were started in the Twin Ports. Anton B. Lange was a notable Norwegian newsman in Duluth and later Chicago, earning a reputation as a controversial figure in the service of the Norwegian American press. He was born in Bergen, Norway, in 1857 of German parents; his father made a living as a merchant on Bergen's German Wharf *(Bryggen).* Lange entered business and attended the city's best schools before immigrating in 1880 to the United States. With his tendency to openly ridicule individuals and causes he disfavored, he found that journalism suited his temperament better than commercial enterprise in America. The Socialist Emil Lauritz Mengshoel described Lange, evidently sharing his view of the Norwegian American press, in his weekly *Gaa Paa* (Press Forward):

> He soon found his way to journalism, and with Lange there came a new, refreshing element into the Norwegian American newspaper world, which earlier had produced little more than church piety and bourgeois matter-of-factness. Sheer dullness and tedium. He worked for different newspapers in Minnesota, among these one that for a time existed in St. Paul and was called *Nordvesten*. But, to be sure, he did not stay long with any of them—likely precisely because of his superior talent and penchant to write the truth; for these qualities were little appreciated by the people who publish the Norwegian American organs for the petty bourgeois propriety. And Lange was least of all the man who let himself be browbeaten.

Mengshoel's opinion viewed through the prism of Socialism simply provides more evidence of the diversity of loyalties and affiliations that sustained Norwegian American journalism. Lange started the weekly *Scandia* in Duluth in April 1888; it spent its infancy there until it moved to Chicago in 1899. In spite of his liberal leanings, during the Populist era Lange declared his journal to be Republican and strongly anti-Populist, finding many Populist causes objectionable, among these prohibition of alcohol.

Colleagues described Lange as "one of Norsedom's most gifted and least 'diplomatic' journalists." He was the son of Michael Wesenberg's sister, which did not prevent him from filling *Scandia* with bitter attacks against his uncle. Wesenberg on his part described his nephew as that "Stiff *[Kadaver]* who puts out the yellow journal *[Smudsbladet] Scandia.*" Lange's strident Norwegian patriotism as well as prideful loyalty to his Norwegian place of birth fueled his critical nature; the newspaper colleagues he castigated jested that "he was not only a Norwegian Norseman all the time, but in addition from Bergen"; Lange thought his rival Norwegian newsmen were far too American, making them blind to the eminence of conditions elsewhere.

Scandia continued its journey among Norwegians in the bustling metropolis until its cessation in May 1940. Lange edited and published *Scandia* after its move to Chicago until his death in October 1910. Commenting on *Scandia*'s entry into the competitive world of newspaper publishing in the metropolis, Lange in November 1900 complained, "last year *Skandinaven*'s rabbits got busy sneaking around to warn against us." Possible subscribers were cautioned not to pay in advance, Lange wrote, "since we would not live four weeks—three months—longer than to the end of the year." And indeed, Lange's regular conflicts with leaders in Norwegian Chicago, his personal and often unfair attacks, and his tendency to make sarcastic observations in regular news reporting negatively affected his publication venture. The number of subscribers, never great, shrank. His views, regularly combative—a practice begun in Duluth—were expressed in every issue under the title "Reflections and Aspersions" *(Indfald og Udfald).* "Lange was *Scandia* personified," H. Sundby-Hansen surmised. "He was the newspaper's founder, editor, typographer, and personal distributor to the outlets for single copies sales . . . and he himself took care of the mailing to his regular subscribers." It was indeed to a great extent a one-man show.

In late 1910, following Lange's death, Sundby-Hansen and Ludvig H. Lund assumed ownership of *Scandia,* with Sundby-Hansen as editor. Sundby-Hansen, born in Moss, Norway, arrived in Chicago from Norway in 1887 at the age of eleven together with his younger brother and mother to join his father who had emigrated earlier; he graduated from Chicago University and created an impressive career in journalism, mainly on the staff of American newspapers, but also in the Norwegian immigrant press. In 1913 Lund, the proprietor of Lund's bookstore in Chicago, took over as both publisher and editor. He was born in Oslo in April 1870, and from childhood exhibited a great interest in works of literature; before coming to America in 1890, he had learned the book trade by employment in Oslo bookstores and one year of study in Germany. Lund retained ownership and editorial responsibility until his death in November 1935, five years before *Scandia*'s demise.

These two men transformed *Scandia* into a much-respected local newspaper for the Norwegian colony in Chicago. They adopted an inclusive editorial policy: unfair personal assaults belonged to the past. *Scandia* declared itself politically neutral "but gave its support to all genuinely liberal trends and the labor movement"; in churchly matters it likewise maintained its neutrality but "favored above all the views of contemporary rationalism." *Scandia* considered itself to be the colony's liberal voice and gave freehanded space to Norwegian clubs, societies, organizations, "and to all genuine work for Norsedom." A new popular column "Minor and Major" *(Moll og Dur)* was a free forum for contributors to express their opinions on "the issues of the day and any other matter of general interest that they had at heart." An enlarged *Scandia* provided room for Lund's literary selections. The subscription list and the number of single copy sales grew quickly, as did advertising.[25]

Metropolitan Chicago and Church Controversy

Scandia identified five distinct classes within the Norwegian colony in Chicago: an aristocracy, a middle class, a working class, a very poor class, and a class of the permanently unemployed and shiftless. Undeniably, class differences among Norwegians in Chicago were quite likely greater than in other regions of Norwegian settlement, due in part to the economic opportunities in a rapidly expanding urban economy as well as the colony's early founding. The divisions among the social groupings were hardly as sharp as *Scandia* suggested. Individuals of different classes interacted considerably and could breach the social distance. Social, political, and religious entities clearly competed for influence and standing in the community. Its location in a central port city—and even more the force of its institutions, cultural and financial resources, prominent leaders, and national publications—made Chicago's Norwegian colony a decisive factor in shaping the entire Norwegian American subculture.[26]

Religious controversy seemed to engender an intensity rarely experienced in other circumstances. Secular journals continued throughout the nineteenth century to be pulled into the fray, not to mention the church publications. Dissensions, generally revolving around doctrine and church polity, among Norwegian Lutheran communions were not dampened by a common Lutheran confession of faith; the common confessionalism of Norwegian American Lutheranism, on the other hand, served to distance it from non-Lutheran denominations and also distinguished it from American Lutheranism. "Norwegian" and "Lutheran" might indeed have been the same for most Norwegians in America in spite of a rampant denominationalism. By the 1880s Norwegian Lutherans were mainly divided among the liturgical high-church Norwegian Synod, the more moderately pietistic Conference of the Norwegian-Danish Evangelical Lutheran Church in America, and the highly pietistic Hauge's Synod, which was organized in Chicago in 1876 as a successor to Eielsen's Synod. The Conference, organized in 1870, with roots back to the Scandinavian Augustana Synod, represented a broad, intermediate position in the pietist-liturgical divide in Norwegian American Lutheranism. The formal organization of the Conference, the name generally used, took place in C. L. Clausen's church in St. Ansgar, Iowa; Clausen, separating himself from the Norwegian Synod in 1868, played a decisive role in forming the new church body and became its first president.[27]

The Norwegian Synod's theological controversy with other Norwegian Lutherans waned considerably toward the end of the 1870s as learned and lay in the Synod became engrossed in a bitter and destructive internal controversy in regard to the doctrine of election or predestination *(Naadevalget)*—"God's election of men to salvation." The conflict—even more acrid than the slavery discord—represented a growing antagonism against the dominance of the Missouri Synod, especially among younger American-trained ministers as well as among new pastors arriving from Norway; they revolted against the blind obedience by the church leaders to Missourian theology. The Synod could clearly not accommodate the two opposing theological views that became apparent on the teachings of predestination; the friction split the Synod clergy into an anti-Missourian and a Missourian camp. The clerical disputants moved the debate into public space, pulling the laity into turbulent warfare over abstract theological interpretations.[28]

The Norwegian Publishing Company, organized in July 1884 by ministers and prominent leaders in the Norwegian Synod, launched the first regular issue of *Amerika* in Chicago December 9, 1884, following sample copies October 1 and 15 (not to be confused with two earlier journals with identical titles). Volume numbering began with *Amerika*'s January 7, 1885, number. By 1890 it enjoyed a circulation of about six thousand. Editor Thrond Bothne announced *Amerika* as "a political news organ published in a Christian spirit . . . and as long as the Republican Party is faithful to its principles will place itself by its side." The editor stated as well that "we as little as possible will involve ourselves in the work that falls to the church organs, in the same way as we will not as a rule participate in the theological or dogmatic controversies that are carried on between the different synods or that arise in their midst." *Amerika* would compete with the secular press on its terms. In its review of its first year, the weekly journal editorially described itself as "a Synod newspaper," but *Amerika* refuted other newspapers' accusations that "it was founded to provide a fortress for the Missourians in the Election conflict." Bothne did, however, admit, "we have censured *(dadlet)* Pastor Muus and his supporters because they seek to split the Norwegian Synod." *Amerika*'s Missouri proclivities were made crystal clear when the schism became a reality in 1887 after the anti-Missourian party the previous year—well led by among others Bernt Julius Muus and the learned German dialectician F. A. Schmidt—established its own seminary at St. Olaf's School in Northfield, Minnesota.

Institutional affiliations gave evidence of synodical loyalties; Laur. Larsen, president of Luther College, Decorah, Iowa, and the venerable Synod leader Pastor U. V. Koren, who had selected the site for the college, were leaders of the Missourian forces. *Amerika*'s first editor, Thrond Bothne, born in Vikør, Hardanger, Norway, in 1835, is yet another example of a career based on teacher training. He taught school and held appointments as newspaper editor before moving to America in 1875 to accept a teaching position at Luther College. He was a stimulating personality and enticed students with his favorite subjects: Norwegian and history. In 1882 he turned to editorial work and made a successful entry into Norwegian American journalism. O. M. Kalheim succeeded Bothne as *Amerika*'s editor in 1887, leaving his position as a Latin instructor at St. Olaf College to accept the post, which he held until his death in October 1895. Kalheim arrived in America at the age of three in 1867 and had studied at Luther College under Bothne's tutelage.[29]

Begun in Chicago October 13, 1874, the weekly newspaper *Norden* (The North) was ten years older than *Amerika* but considered it to be a serious rival. *Norden,* like its younger competitor, was closely associated with the Norwegian Synod and engaged in heated church polemics and regular critical attacks on the more powerful *Skandinaven. Norden* accused *Skandinaven* of being unchristian and the promoter of freethinking, based on *Skandinaven*'s printing of Marcus Thrane's *Dagslyset;* its defense of the Norwegian politician Søren Jaabæk, found guilty of "blasphemy" *(Gudsbespottelse)* by the Norwegian courts; and its correspondence from Norway that placed itself on the side of the freethinking Dane Georg Brandes, "who has made it his life's work to combat Christianity." *Norden Dagbladet* (The Daily Newspaper), published by *Norden* 1889–91 as a competitor to the daily *Skandinaven,* failed. Yet, in 1890 *Norden* reported for its weekly edition an impressive circulation of 14,390. Even when compared to *Skandinaven*'s larger weekly circulation of thirty-two thousand, *Norden* at the time wielded considerable influence among Chicago's Norwegians. During the Election controversy *Norden,* siding with the anti-Missourians, made the Missourian *Amerika* its most arrant foe.[30]

I. T. Relling established *Norden* together with the Swedish Norwegian vice-consul Peter Svanoe. Relling later became sole owner. His Norwegian bookstore housed *Norden* and sold steamship tickets and bank notes; it was on Milwaukee Avenue, centrally located in the Norwegian neighborhoods on Chicago's northwest side. Born in the Nordal parish, Sunnmøre, Norway, in 1840, Relling found employment as a clerk in Ålesund and Oslo; his educational pursuit thwarted by lack of funds, he moved in 1867 to Chicago, where he worked on *Skandinaven*'s editorial staff, but soon returned to Norway, where he sojourned until he in 1870 made Chicago his permanent home. Relling typified the upwardly mobile Norwegian immigrant; newspaper publishing gave visible evidence of his success.

Hallvard Hande, a former minister in the Norwegian Synod, edited *Norden* from its beginning in 1874 until 1887, save for two years, July 1882 until September 1884, when Thrond Bothne, *Amerika*'s later editor, held that position. Hande, born in Valdres in 1846, completed his theological training in Norway before immigrating to America in 1872. He was called as pastor for Estherville and annexed congregations in Iowa until he accepted the editorship of *Norden.* "He was an unusually gifted man with great journalistic competence," recorded Johannes Wist, "especially . . . as a quick-witted disputant, a faculty, which the state-of-affairs of the Norwegian American press gave ample opportunity to foster." Hande's perspectives were greatly colored by his religious beliefs, and perhaps also by his poor health, which caused his death in 1887 at the age of forty-one: in reviewing the year 1881 he posited how short a year is "compared to eternity." He wished the best for "the many thousands of our countrymen who the last year have come over to us to seek a better temporal livelihood." "In our churchly affairs," Hande deplored, "there is still much unrest and ferment." "Personal strife and doctrinal controversy," he continued, "the most serious we so far have experienced, threaten to split our church community."

In this building on Milwaukee Avenue in Chicago, I. T. Relling published the newspaper Norden, *operated a Scandinavian bookstore and a steamship agency, and sold bank notes on Scandinavian banks.*

Among the many letters debating the election controversy, the ones from East Norway Lake congregation in west-central Minnesota may be cited to exemplify the intensity of the conflict. In March 1882 the majority of the congregational council in negotiations concerning predestination had adopted the anti-Missourian position; only after intense pressure did the congregational pastor Lars J. Markhus disclose his standpoint, which turned out to be the Missourian view. In arriving at their disavowal of the Missourian interpretation, the council members relied on their religious instruction from childhood *(Børnelærdom)* contained in Luther's Catechism as explained in 1737 by Erik Pontoppidan in "Truth unto Godliness" *(Sandhed til Gudfrygtighed),* which had been a major textbook in Norwegian primary schools for nearly 150 years. Norwegian ethnic emotions were clearly stirred; the Missourian position could easily be seen as an affront to their childhood faith. The issue festered in the East Norway Lake congregation until July 24, 1885, when Pastor Markhus had the humiliating experience of being carried out of his church by the anti-Missourian party.[31]

Hande wrote in November 1885 that *Norden* had, with the exception of two years (a clear reference to Bothne's tenure), been led in the same spirit and direction since its founding eleven years before. The theological conflict between Hande and Bothne intensified during the remainder of Hande's editorship. Both men engaged in name-calling and personal accusations as well as defensive rebuttals; a particularly heated exchange was recorded in *Norden* in October 1886, where ill-tempered adjectives such as "quarrelsome, incompetent, blasphemous, hateful, dishonest" were exchanged.

January 31, 1888, Peer O. Strømme took over as editor of *Norden;* he claimed to know more Norwegian Americans than anyone else through his extensive engagements as a traveling correspondent worldwide, lecture tours, political prominence, and newspaper activity. Knowledge about the editors in the service of the Norwegian American press, their educational and occupational background and their recruitment, is essential to an understanding of the nature and functioning of immigrant journalism. Strømme, like a number of his journalist colleagues, studied for the Lutheran ministry; he was, however, of the second generation, born in 1856 in the Winchester settlement, Winnebago County, Wisconsin, to immigrant parents from Vrådal, Telemark, Norway. He graduated from Luther College and not yet twenty years old entered theological studies at Concordia Seminary, St. Louis, Missouri. After ordination in 1879, officiated by Pastor Muus in Northfield, he served as pastor for several congregations, but, as he writes in his memoirs, it was a wrong choice. He returned to Northfield in 1887 to teach at St. Olaf College, then the center of anti-Missourian organizational activity. The congregations departing from the Norwegian Synod had by then united in a temporary association called the Anti-Missourian Brotherhood *(Det antimissouriske Broderskab).*

Meanwhile in Northfield, the editorship of *Norden* was offered to Strømme, as suggested by Hallvard Hande himself shortly before his death. *Norden* declared itself a Republican organ from its founding, but because of its occasional support of Democratic causes and candidates was regularly accused by Republican rivals of not being true to the party. With Strømme as editor *Norden* moved entirely into the Democratic political camp. However, Strømme related, "*Norden* had under Hande's leadership been more or less a church-political newspaper, and during the Election controversy was considered to be the Anti-Missourian Brotherhood's semi-official organ." It would persist in that direction, although the Election controversy subsided with the formation in Minneapolis in June 1890 of the United Norwegian Lutheran Church *(Den forenede Kirke),* organically merging the Conference, the Anti-Missourian Brotherhood, and the Norwegian Augustana, the latter dating from 1870, into one church body. Strømme was a close friend of O. M. Kalheim, then *Amerika*'s editor, which did not appear to dampen the polemics. In fact, Strømme insisted, they became sharper, "but Kalheim and I were just as good friends in spite of it." Strømme's account illustrates a latent comradeship, even among rival editors; the limited immigrant world of journalism encouraged a sense of being a member of a league. These opponents might even have realized that controversy sold newspapers. Strømme related the following:

> In Chicago I had to begin with [before my family arrived], a room in the home of Mrs. Hande and was well taken care of. Otherwise I spent most of my free time together with Kalheim, who at that time was still a bachelor. And we frequently sat together and composed

our editorials; he attacked me and *Norden* and I attacked him and *Amerika.* We did not spare each other. But we read aloud for each other what we had written.[32]

Strømme edited *Norden* only until June 1892. In March of that year a special local *Chicago Norden*—published every Saturday—was launched in addition to the regular *Norden;* rather than a sign of growth, the local edition was an effort to attract additional advertising from Chicago businesses. *Norden* had entered a period of decline, perhaps, as has been suggested, a consequence of its change of political loyalty during a period of upheaval as well as the economic hard times. R. S. N. Sartz succeeded Strømme as *Norden*'s editor July 1, 1892. Sartz, born in Nordfjord, Norway, in 1852, was a lawyer by training when he emigrated in 1879; he had a varied journalistic career, eventually moving to Washington, D.C., as a newspaper correspondent. Editor Kalheim expressed his misgivings about the editorial shift since "the new editor has no churchly interest whereas the one who left enjoyed the church party's confidence." Sartz responded by promising to "cover churchly issues and church news, but for the future merely reporting the news without making judgmental partisan comments."

Sartz served as editor until 1895, when he retired, more due to poor health than to lack of journalistic aptitude or disregard for a failing newspaper venture. In July 1894 *Norden* acquired the subscription list of the weekly *Varden,* published in La Crosse, Wisconsin; the publisher emphasized that *Norden* had without ever wavering expressed "the opinions and principles for which *Varden* consistently has fought for." As stated earlier, in December 1895 *Norden* reported that it had assumed ownership of a second La Crosse newspaper, the short-lived *Folkevennen.* The infusion of new subscribers did not save *Norden;* the many strong appeals to subscribers to pay "both for earlier and new subscriptions" indicate existing financial straits. The last publisher was Andrew Jensen in Edgerton, Wisconsin; he purchased *Norden* simply to keep a Democratic organ alive. In October 1897, however, he merged *Norden* with *Amerika* to become *Amerika og Norden.*

Amerika moved from Chicago to Madison, Wisconsin, in April 1896. The fall of 1895 Peer Strømme, moved by Kalheim's illness and death, had returned to Chicago to edit and acquire part ownership in *Amerika* together with four other men, including Andrew Jensen, three Democrats and two Republicans, all residing in Madison or its vicinity. It was thus natural to move publication closer to their residences. To eliminate competition the new owners first purchased the briefly published Madison weekly *Wisconsin Nordmanden* (Norseman), owned and edited by the poet Ole A. Buslett. Strømme as editor made *Amerika* a Democratic organ; his strong advocacy for William Jennings Bryan in the 1896 presidential election met with great protest from the two Republican owners, especially since the newspaper lost subscribers. In *Amerika og Norden*'s October 12, 1898, number Strømme bid the readers farewell, explaining in an editorial that his position had become "unfortunate" since he was unable to write "with force and conviction without offending some of the owners, whose political belief is the opposite of mine." *Amerika* again shifted publishers, this time to Rasmus B. Anderson, a dominating, if controversial, figure in the Norwegian American community, and thus commenced the final—and clearly the most colorful—period of its history. It expired in 1922; this last era will be treated in chapter six.[33]

Skandinaven—regularly assailed by church journals for its alleged lack of Christian tenets—opposed the liturgical high church tradition. As a proclaimed advocate for the common man, it was generally sympathetic with laymen and tended toward low-church practice. In its rejoinders to *Amerika, Norden,* as well as other church-related publications, *Skandinaven* indeed invested intellectual power into religious controversy. It had a running battle with the Conference organ *Folkebladet* (The People's Newspaper) in Minneapolis; two professors at Augsburg Seminary, Sven Oftedal and Georg Sverdrup, owned and edited the weekly in the early 1880s. *Skandinaven* dismissed *Folkebladet* as "that professor organ in Minneapolis" and rejected as "spiteful diatribe" contentions that "in regard to Christianity and improvements in churchly and religious life, or if one with heavy hand touches upon public and private morals, *Skandinaven* wants no part in." *Skandinaven*'s greater tolerance and anti-elitist stance met with success; the flood of Norwegian newcomers from the early 1880s burgeoned the newspaper's subscription rolls. In 1886 *Skandinaven* proudly declared its weekly edition to have the largest circulation of any Norwegian

Danish newspaper in the world. It published a special "Northwestern Edition" for Minnesota and the Dakotas, enclosing a page with expanded local news coverage; separate offices were opened in St. Paul and Minneapolis. The weekly *Skandinaven* enjoyed national distribution beyond the Upper Midwest; the daily, according to promotional statements, was also moving beyond Chicago's Norwegian community. In 1878, as a broad outreach, John Anderson, then *Skandinaven*'s sole publisher, had launched the weekly *Verdens Gang* (The Way of the World) as a low-price edition mainly for the Chicago market, with an annual subscription price of fifty cents, compared to the two-dollar annual fee for the weekly *Skandinaven;* when *Verdens Gang* was discontinued in 1919, a year's subscription had increased only by a quarter. Imaginative business acumen in a competitive marketplace assured success for the John Anderson Publishing Company where other newspaper ventures failed.

Anderson continued to expand *Skandinaven*'s circulation by purchasing the subscription lists of defunct rivals. In July 1888, "the several thousand readers" of the short-lived *Skandinaviske Tribune* in Madison, Wisconsin, were editorially welcomed "into the large brotherhood of *Skandinaven*'s circle of readers." The *Tribune* had been founded in 1887 as a newspaper for Norwegians in Wisconsin, liberated from "personal attacks and quarrels and speculative political rings." It was thus, *Skandinaven* noted, a "people's newspaper" *(Folkets Avis),* published in the same spirit as *Skandinaven* itself. David Monrad Schøyen, lawyer by training, entered journalism after arriving in America in the late 1860s; he gained experience on *Skandinaven*'s editorial staff. Later on he was hired to edit *Verdens Gang,* until he became editor of the newly established *Skandinaviske Tribune* in 1887.

Editors of marked talent served *Skandinaven.* In 1886 Peter Hendrickson became the newspaper's third editor, succeeding Knud Langeland and Svein Nilsson; in 1892, editorial responsibility was passed on to Nicolay A. Grevstad. Hendrickson grew up in Racine, Wisconsin, from the age of three, immigrating to America with his parents from Telemark, Norway, in 1845. His experience was thus that of the second generation. His education in the United States, Norway, and Germany prepared him for an academic career; after leaving the editorship, he bought Albion Academy, in Albion,

Wisconsin, a school started by Seventh Day Baptists, where many leading Norwegian Americans were educated. Hendrickson engaged in farming and authored a much-read book titled *Farming med Hoved og Hænder* (Farming with Head and Hands). *Skandinaven,* even though presenting itself as an independent Republican newspaper, on occasion voiced support for the Farmers' Alliance; it reflected the journal's enthusiasm for the common man and optimistic faith in democracy and the possibilities America offered for self-improvement.

Skandinaven reached its peak as a political force during Grevstad's editorship, which lasted until 1911; he returned as editor in chief a second time in 1930 and held that position until his death ten years later. In the meantime he had pursued a successful career in journalism, in the U.S. diplomatic service, and in political appointments. Grevstad rose from humble origins in Norway; he was born in 1851 into a cottar's family of poor means on the farm Grevstad in Sykkylven, Sunnmøre. As a highly gifted young man, he earned a law degree, worked as a lawyer, was employed by the Norwegian Justice Department, and found employment as editor of the liberal newspaper *Dagbladet* (The Daily Newspaper) before he moved to the United States in 1883.

In 1905, *Skandinaven,* then published in daily and semiweekly editions, had a circulation of 48,335 for its twice-weekly edition. Grevstad, while not altering the key principles of *Skandinaven,* was cognizant of the transformation that had taken place among Norwegian Americans since the newspaper's founding in 1866, and he gave it a more contemporary stamp. Johannes Wist explained as follows: "The first settlers, who in Langeland's day struggled with poverty, had become prosperous, many of them had gained honor and distinction in politics, in business, and in other fields. . . . The Norwegians had moved from being a small undistinguished group of pioneers to being a great power that had to be considered in politics and otherwise." Wist's rosy evaluation notwithstanding, *Skandinaven*'s editorial leadership was equal to the task at hand. Norwegian American politicians eagerly sought the newspaper's editorial endorsement. In her analysis of *Skandinaven*'s editorial policy from 1900 to 1903, Agnes Larson concluded that "On most matters *Skandinaven* was fairly conservative, though it was critically so—it was more open-minded and independent than most of the English newspapers in the United States."[34]

Final Observations

Historian Marcus Lee Hansen was certainly correct in his assertion that "A favorite occupation of the immigrant intellectual was journalism." A mobile journalistic class emerged, easily moving from one newspaper venture to another, as editors and publishers, making a living in the shifting and uncertain world of Norwegian American newspaper publishing. For some a sojourn in journalism led to careers in public office or in business enterprise. Most belonged to the immigrant generation, but American-born editors also made an entrance into ethnic journalistic enterprise. Educational background and occupational experience varied greatly. Norwegian-trained lawyers, individuals with familiarity in newspaper production, normal school graduates, theologians, and others with typographical skills, together with immigrants with few journalistic qualifications, moved to America to take part in the challenging mission of educating their compatriots about life in America while assuring contact with and affection for the homeland and pride in being Norwegian American. The newspapers they produced, mainly weeklies, did not in appearance differ from contemporary American weeklies.

In the nineteenth century, Johannes Wist claimed, "the church was for so many years the eye of the tempest in nearly all intellectual movements among Norwegians in America." The competing factions within the Norwegian Lutheran church in America had a strong voice in the immigrant press; theologically trained editors gained prominence in its service. Historian Laurence Larson contended that the energy and learning of the Norwegian American church was poured into religious controversy; the controversial issues hindered original intellectual contributions or great advances in human knowledge. Larson presented these circumstances to explain why the Norwegian element had achieved only a modest place in American scholarship. Making a living and love of land preoccupied nineteenth-century rural Norwegian immigrants who "followed the advance of rural settlements over the beckoning prairies of the free land." The intellectual interests Norwegian pioneers possessed were greatly centered on the church; the Lutheran ministry was the single honorable profession they recognized.

"Immigrant journalism," Theodore Blegen wrote, "meanwhile offered a challenge that attracted some of the most gifted minds among Norwegian Americans." Blegen continued, "It was close to actual life and opinion, responsive to changes, and wide in its interests." As the Norwegian American community matured, adjusted to life in America, and responded to the new impulses carried across the Atlantic by waves of immigrants, the Norwegian American press kept pace. It adapted to the ever-changing nature of its patrons on their historical journey—together with many other distinct ethnic populations—as active participants in a unique process of nation building.[35]

Washington Posten

Largest Circulation Of Any Foreign Language Paper In The Pacific Northwest

SEATTLE, WASH., FREDAG 13, MAI, 1938

CHAPTER 4

The Rise of a National Norwegian American Press

In the years before 1914 probably the class of ordinary American citizens best read in international affairs were not the residents of Boston or New York, but the older generation of immigrant farmers in the Middle West.[1]

ACCORDING TO Marcus Lee Hansen, "The distant continent of Europe was never wholly forgotten" by the immigrant press, even though as time passed the focus shifted to American news, "and, in particular . . . the activities and interests of the immigrant group in the United States." Hansen's generalization surely also applied to the Norwegian American press. Newspapers began to place greater emphasis on the ethnic community's life in America without excluding news from across the ocean. The Norwegian homeland and its Nordic neighbors still earned a special degree of attention.

An intense competitive spirit did not preclude early endeavors—not consistently successful—at cooperation among rival publishers; in theory, working together should strengthen the position of the Norwegian American press as a whole and benefit its individual members. Press associations were organized, even on a pan-Scandinavian basis, to "cultivate a closer contact among the Scandinavian newspapermen." The earliest press associations, however, were created to publish, as previously explained, politically partisan journals. The Scandinavian Press Association of the Northwest, established in Minneapolis in 1883, was the first attempt to organize the Norwegian newspapers in one association. Its initial meeting on December 13, where *Budstikken*'s editor Luth Jaeger was elected president, displayed a shared Scandinavian, or more correctly Norwegian and Swedish, complexion. Magnus Lunnow, *Svenska Folkets Tidning*'s (The Swedish People's Times) editor was elected vice-president. The group comprised five Norwegian and three Swedish immigrant newspapers. However, as Alfred Söderström, the Association's corresponding secretary, concluded in his book *Minneapolis-Minnen* (Minneapolis Recollections), the Association achieved little in its short existence, "because in this as in so many earlier cases it was impossible for the respective newspapers due to their dissimilar interests to bring about a more harmonious *(helgjuten)* outcome." Publishing rivalry, amplified by national differences, clearly trumped collaborative initiatives.[2]

The Norwegian-Danish Press Association of the United States *(Den norsk-danske Presseforening av De forenede Stater),* founded at an organizing meeting in St. Paul, Minnesota, July 18 and 19, 1895, was a more successful venture in terms of durability and social interaction among its members, but its attempts at joint action in business affairs had no more success than the efforts of the Scandinavian Press Association of the Northwest. The Swedish-Norwegian Union crisis, reaching a grave point in 1895, made a broader Scandinavian fellowship inconceivable. The Norwegian-Danish Press Association's constitution defined its objectives as follows:

> The Association's purpose is to apply itself to the interests of the Norwegian-Danish press in the United States, promote cooperation and collective action in business affairs and endeavor to create a friendly collegial relationship among the members.

The Norwegian-Danish Press Association made notable progress in realizing its friendly collegial objectives; Danes and Norwegians had of course cooperated in immigrant journalism from the start; the cherished common Dano-Norwegian literary language served as a bond. Since there were more successful large Norwegian newspapers than Danish, thousands of Danes became regular subscribers to the Norwegian American journals; Danish immigrant publications attracted Norwegian readers as well.

A joint invitation to convene for the organizing meeting was issued by Brynild Anundsen of *Decorah-Posten,* Thorvald Gulbrandsen of *Minneapolis Tidende,* Søren Listoe of *Nordvesten,* Anfin Solem of *Fergus Falls Ugeblad,* and G. Bie Ravndahl of *Syd Dakota Ekko* (South Dakota Echo). More than twenty Norwegian and Danish publishers and journalists embraced the idea of a common Norwegian-Danish organization and attended the July meeting in St. Paul. Anundsen was elected president by acclamation; Listoe accepted the position of first vice president, H. O. Oppedal second vice president, Bie Ravndahl secretary, and Laurits Stavnheim treasurer. All elections were made with unanimous consent. Oppedal was from 1894 associated with *Norden* in Chicago and listed as sole editor following R. S. N. Sartz's retirement in early 1895. Shortly after 1897, and *Norden*'s merger with *Amerika,* Oppedal returned to Norway. He that year represented the Association at the International Journalist Congress in Stockholm.

The Association mainly limited its activities to the Midwest and functioned until, as Carl G. O. Hansen writes, it "expired by default" in the mid-1930s. It honored its own. In 1924 a plaque with the following inscription was unveiled in the Minnesota Historical Society building in St. Paul:

> To the memory of the Norwegian-American editor, Paul Hjelm-Hansen. Born in Bergen, Norway, 1810. Died in Goodhue County, Minn., 1881. Who blazed the way for Scandinavian settlers to the Red River Valley. Presented by the Norwegian-Danish Press Association.

The Norwegian American press continued its westward movement to the Pacific Coast; it advanced and gained support wherever Norwegians made their homes; it thrived among Norwegians on the eastern seaboard where the midwestern connection was less firmly established. The present chapter, while following the course of the midwestern immigrant press, will expand beyond this main region of Norwegian American newspaper activity to include the appearance of a Norwegian-language press in the far West, with stops along the way in Montana and Utah. It will include publication ventures in the East, in Brooklyn, New York, and elsewhere. A national Norwegian American press became a visible reality. Major midwestern journals, such as *Skandinaven, Minneapolis Ti-*

dende, and *Decorah-Posten,* as national news organs, early on had substantial circulations throughout the United States and reached Norwegians in places like Texas and Alaska, where a separate immigrant press did not emerge. The Norwegian American press served and drew its support from Norwegians scattered throughout the country and carried news from a wide expanse. People of similar cultural backgrounds were welded together, Theodore Blegen wrote, "in common interests, to give reality to the geographically nebulous concept of a 'Norwegian America.'"

Annual meetings, planned excursions, specific projects, and representation at public events furthered the program of the Norwegian-Danish Press Association. Minneapolis became the most common meeting place, but the Association also convened in Chicago, Madison, Wisconsin, St. Paul, Sioux Falls, and Decorah. The fifth annual "press meeting" *(Pressemøde)* in 1899 was held in Decorah "so that the members would have an opportunity to attend the celebration on September 19 of B. Anundsen's twenty-fifth anniversary as publisher of *Decorah-Posten.*"[3]

Brynild Anundsen and Decorah-Posten

Wist, longtime editor of *Decorah-Posten,* portrayed Brynild Anundsen as having "a richly gifted disposition with a strong strain of true generosity." His experience in early childhood and youth "had taught him the value of money." He was born in Skien, Norway, in 1844 and as a child of seven "began the struggle for existence that would last far into the years of his manhood." He worked in a cigar factory, a stone quarry, a flour mill, and then at age twelve or thirteen as an apprentice in a book printing shop, a foreshadowing of his life's work as a newspaper publisher—a common path for many other men in the service of the immigrant press. After completing his training as a typographer, Anundsen sailed in the Norwegian merchant fleet for a couple of years; then in 1864 he immigrated to America. The young Anundsen settled in La Crosse, Wisconsin, where he found employment as compositor on the newspaper *Fædrelandet.*

Decorah-Posten's first regular issue was dated September 5, 1874; production difficulties delayed distribution until the eighteenth. For nearly a hundred years, *Decorah-Posten* served the Norwegian American community; its name and history were intimately associated with immigrant life. Unlike the other two leading midwestern journals, which both derived benefits from the easier access to advertising and subscribers in large metropolitan settings, *Decorah-Posten* established itself and attained its national position in a small-town environment. Its humble beginnings, as indicated earlier, were rooted in La Crosse and the literary monthly magazine *Ved Arnen: Et Tidsskrift for Skjønliteratur* (By the Fireside: A Periodical for Belle-Lettres) founded September 1, 1866, with only sixty subscribers.

The magazine did not provide a living for Anundsen and his wife, the former Mathilda Hoffstrøm, whom he had married in 1865. Anundsen's fortunes changed when he accepted an invitation by the Norwegian Synod to move to Decorah and assume responsibility for printing its official organ *Kirkelig Maanedstidende* (Church Monthly), which the Synod leaders had moved from Madison, Wisconsin, to Decorah so that its publication could be supervised by the Luther College faculty. In December 1867 Anundsen "marched into the Synod's vested stronghold of Decorah," as Wist has it, with his printing press and all his worldly possessions transported in two small horse-drawn wagons. *Ved Arnen* did no better in the new location; his attempt in 1869 to publish the weekly *Fra Fjernt og Nær* (From Far and Near), first as a supplement to *Ved Arnen* and later independently, fared no better. Both were discontinued the following year.

Ved Arnen would later be revived as a literary supplement to *Decorah-Posten,* which owed its existence to the two earlier publication ventures. About three months after its launching it had gained about one thousand subscribers; it was initially intended as a local "news and advertisement paper for Decorah and vicinity." Decorah was the seat of Winneshiek County, which in 1870 had 8,302 Norwegian residents out of a total population of 23,570; there was consequently some justification for hoping for success. By 1875 in fact, *Decorah-Posten* had outdistanced its two English-language competitors to become the county's official newspaper. In its first number, September 5, 1874, Anundsen announced *Decorah-Posten*'s purpose:

> I hope in a very short time to have a subscription list larger than any other newspaper in the county. The paper will contain NO POLITICS, but local and other news from the new and the old world besides novels and other interesting reading matter.

The avoidance of controversial issues, pledged in the first number, was a prudent business policy. Political and religious controversy had, as Anundsen well knew, destroyed many an earlier journal. Anundsen, as publisher and editor in chief, therefore took a position of merely reporting objectively on public issues. He continued this policy even after *Decorah-Posten* became a major national enterprise. In time, however, especially from the mid-1890s, in editorials the newspaper showed sympathy for the progressive Republican sentiments of the vast majority of its midwestern subscribers. It was not entirely able to exercise strict neutrality in religious matters either; Anundsen's close ties with Luther College, the church magazine's publisher until 1877, made it inevitable for the Norwegian Synod to be shown some preference. Nevertheless, *Decorah-Posten*'s endeavor to inform rather than direct its readers was an important factor in attracting new subscribers.[4]

In 1877 the Synod established its own press, thereby depriving Anundsen of print jobs and causing financial duress for him and his newspaper enterprise. It encouraged him to make the bold decision to move beyond the local market and launch *Decorah-Posten* as a national Norwegian-language news organ. Anundsen increased the size of the newspaper and in fall 1882 revived *Ved Arnen* as a monthly supplement; from 1887 it was a weekly edition. He had some success. In October that year he explained to the newspaper's readers,

> Already at first sight will everyone discover that *Decorah-Posten* now comes out in "an improved edition" inasmuch as types and other makeup is entirely new. When to that is added that a serial hereafter accompanies as a separate thirty-two-page pamphlet once a month, our subscribers will surely realize that we according to our best ability strive to give recompense for the considerable support the newspaper has found in the reading public.

A smaller advertising income was compensated for by the lower publication costs in a small-town commercial environment. Suc-

Decorah-Posten og Ved Arnen

cess was largely due to Anundsen's sound judgment and business sense; he showed great executive leadership and kept abreast of the times in printing and distribution. His promotional initiatives in awarding prizes to new subscribers contributed to the newspaper's growing circulation. Norwegian Americans moving to other locations took the newspaper with them; subscription agents introduced it to new subscribers. "Wherever Norwegians go, *Decorah-Posten* follows," became a popular slogan. By 1885 its circulation passed twenty thousand; for the remainder of its long life, the newspaper gave its publisher a good profit. From 1894 until 1942 *Decorah-Posten* was published semiweekly. Around 1900 it found its way into thirty-seven thousand Norwegian American homes, the majority in the Upper Midwest but also from coast to coast. Of the three major midwestern newspapers only *Skandinaven* surpassed it in the number of subscribers. Like these, *Decorah-Posten*'s growth resulted from the crests of mass Norwegian immigration in the 1880s and the decade and a half before World War I. At his death in March 1913, Brynild Anundsen left behind considerable wealth.

Brynild Anundsen founded and published Decorah-Posten og Ved Arnen.

Decorah-Posten's editors were in many instances recruited from the teaching profession: several were graduates from a Norwegian folk high school *(folkehøyskole)* or teachers' seminary; few were specifically trained for careers as journalists. Lyder Siewers had taught in secondary schools in Oslo, Norway, before he began as a teacher at Luther College in 1863. In 1877 he joined *Decorah-Posten* and spent thirty years at the paper, for a time as co-editor and editor. *Decorah-Posten*'s first co-editor—Anundsen never fully abandoned the editorship—Bernt Askevold, in 1874 a recent immigrant from Sunnfjord, moved on to become a Synod minister. In 1885, when *Decorah-Posten*'s expanded size and distribution required additional help, Erik S. Gjellum was hired as co-editor. Gjellum later assumed full editorial responsibility. Born in Utica, Wisconsin, in 1852, he became the only American-born person to occupy the position of editor. A Luther College graduate and a lawyer by training, he came to *Decorah-Posten* with experience as editor of *Albert Lea Posten.*

Johannes B. Wist and Kristian Prestgard became the two most influential men to serve *Decorah-Posten.* Prestgard came to assist Gjellum in 1898 after having edited newspapers in La Crosse. In 1901 Wist became editor in chief and Prestgard continued as co-editor with editorial responsibility for *Ved Arnen.* Wist, born in 1864 at Inderøy, North-Trøndelag, had in Norway been engaged as a private tutor *(Huslærer)* and as newspaper correspondent during the stormy political rallies of the 1880s. The national and liberal issues raised at the time influenced Wist's career and his progressive political and social philosophy, as well as his patriotic cultural view and an idealistic regard for his own profession. He arrived in America in 1884 and served in various journalistic capacities, among these the founding of two Norwegian-language newspapers.

In 1885, only a year after his arrival, he began publishing the weekly *Fakkelen* (The Torch) in Glenwood in west-central Minnesota with little success. Wist again tried his hand as a newspaper publisher when in August 1899 he launched the weekly *Norge* (Norway) in Granite Falls, Minnesota. In the first number, Wist explained that he had started the newspaper because "several Norwegians in Yellow Medicine, Chippewa, and Renville counties have urged us to begin this undertaking, inasmuch as they believe there is room for a Norwegian local newspaper in these parts." As a local apolitical news organ, *Norge* enjoyed some success. In its advertising in 1900, the weekly claimed to "have from two to three times as large a circulation as any other newspaper published within the territory where we have our circle of readers *(Læsekreds)"*; consequently it was "the best newspaper for advertising in this part of the State of Minnesota." In September of that year, however, Wist sold *Norge* to accept the editorial position at *Decorah-Posten;* on September 24, 1901, *Norge* bid its readers farewell and announced that the newspaper would merge with *Amerika,* then published in Madison, Wisconsin.

Prestgard was born in Heidal, Gudbrandsdalen, in 1866; he attended folk high schools in both Norway and Denmark, among the latter the great Askov Folk High School in Askov, Jutland, established in 1865 and Denmark's largest educational institution of its kind. The folk high schools reflected the outline established by the Danish theologian and writer N. F. S. Grundtvig; the mother tongue and national histories were central subjects, as well as a Christian faith that emphasized the human experience—the "happy Christianity"—which caused strife with Lutheran pietists. Grundtvig's philosophy influenced the formulation of a modern Danish national consciousness; his followers in Norway nurtured similar nationalistic sentiments. Norwegian immigrant editors such as Prestgard, because of their exposure at home to Grundtvigian political liberalism and even a decidedly romantic cultural view, commonly harbored anti-official convictions and a nationalistic perspective. Like their fellow folk high school graduates who remained at home, and there engaged in liberal political ventures, they were democratic and showed a deep and idealistic interest in the immigrant experience.

Following his return from Denmark in 1888, Prestgard taught at a folk high school for one year; illness then forced him to give up all work for two years; he thereafter found employment on the liberal Grundtvigian-inspired daily newspaper *Oplandenes Avis* (Oplandene's Newspaper) in Hamar. In 1893 Prestgard came to America as a newspaper correspondent to the World's Columbian Exposition in Chicago. Instead of returning to Norway, he found employment as editor of several newspapers in Minneapolis published by the Dane Christian Rasmussen, whose company brought out an impressive number of journals and magazines. His sojourn in La Crosse followed, then Decorah, where he served as co-editor of *Decorah-Posten* until upon the death of Johannes Wist in 1923 he moved into the top editorial position. Although they were different in temperament and outlook, during their years as co-workers the two men formed an efficient and productive team.[5]

The Iowa Setting for Norwegian-Language Journalism

The state of Iowa's scattered Norwegian areas of settlement housed a total of eleven weekly or semiweekly newspapers and twelve semimonthly or monthly magazines. Of these, *Decorah-Posten,* published in the northeastern corner of the state, heavy with Norwegian settlement, achieved the greatest success and recognition beyond the state's boundaries. Cedar Rapids, located on both banks of the Cedar River in east-central Iowa, was the home of *Kvinden og Hjemmet* (The Woman and the Home), a major monthly magazine; its history and influence will be a topic in the following chapter. The final decade of the nineteenth century witnessed the greatest period of growth in Norwegian-language journalism in the state. Sioux City in Woodbury County at the Missouri River's navigational head in the northwestern part of the state early on had Norwegian residents but only some 150 in 1870, nearly all immigrants. Considerable and rapid growth followed; by 1900 the Norwegian-born numbered 1,054 and those of the second generation 2,818 among a total population of about thirty-three thousand.

Sioux City Tilskuer (Sioux City Observer) appeared on the scene in 1887, published by A. M. Olmen & Company; the following year it altered its name to *Vesterheimen* (The Western Home) and the name of the firm to Vesterheimen Publishing Company with Olmen as director. Such expeditious shifts suggest failed cooperative efforts and the lack of resources immigrant publishers regularly experienced; *Vesterheimen* as a consequence soon went out of business. *Sioux City Tidende* (Sioux City Times) succeeded it in early 1890. Publishers Bergman & Levang advertised *Sioux City Tidende* as "a weekly Newspaper in the Norwegian-Danish language." Few newspaper ventures, small and large, relied exclusively on subscription and advertising revenue but, like *Sioux City Tidende,* offered job printing—"all kinds of printing," as it announced—and sold tickets and transferred money to Norway. During its first year of publication it promised any subscriber the newspaper free for one year contingent on "recruiting three new paying subscribers before New Year."

Sioux City Tidende served a local community but, like other immigrant news organs, had a focus beyond the hometown. It was a typical small four-page journal; the front page carried news from Norway and the United States alongside advertising by local businesses. Major world events and "From Abroad" *(Udlandet)* were regular features; happenings in the local as well as larger Norwegian American community were not neglected but were given adequate space. During its first year, *Sioux City Tidende,* pursuant to another common practice, serialized Alexander Kielland's social-critical novel *Fortuna* (English translation *Professor Lovdahl*).

Politically *Sioux City Tidende* declared itself Democratic and celebrated the great Democratic victory in November 1890. In December O. M. Levang became the sole publisher and editor. Levang emigrated from Nordland, Norway, in 1886; he worked as a compositor in Chicago and Cedar Rapids before moving to Sioux City. The November 5, 1892, number announced that John Story (Støre) had purchased *Sioux City Tidende* and would serve as its publisher and editor. Story announced a change in political faith: "The newspaper will now be Republican on the whole, but in local elections political identity is less important." The change in political affiliation resulted from the supremacy of the Republican Party in the state. Beginning in 1892 in Iowa, in contrast to most neighboring states, Republicans dominated over a period of forty years.

Story was born in Levanger, Norway, and he had considerable journalistic experience on Norwegian American newspapers before assuming ownership of *Sioux City Tidende.* In April 1897, Story changed the name of the newspaper to *Republikaneren* (The Republican) and announced it would move to Lake Mills, "where it will have a much larger territory . . . in such richly Norwegian settled counties as Winnebago, Worth, Kossuth, Humboldt, Webster, and Hamilton, which together form a little Norway." It continued the volume numbering of *Sioux City Tidende.*[6]

The May 7, 1897, *Republikaneren* listed Lake Mills, Iowa, as its location; it carried an article titled "Our New Home" *(Vort nye hjem),* where editor Story admits he was too new in the city to have an opinion, but the many Lake Mills advertisements held great promises. For a period *Republikaneren*'s circulation surpassed its county competitors and thus earned the privilege of becoming the "Official Paper of Winnebago County." The weekly often expressed its Republican loyalties in terms of educating its Danish and Norwegian readers to greater political participation, as it did in September 1897:

> The Norwegians in Iowa have been and continue to be in a political immaturity that is to little honor for our nationality. The Norwegians have never been represented in any federal or state office in Iowa. . . . And yet Norwegians hold majorities in five Congressional districts in Iowa! This is a disgrace for our Norwegian people.

John Story thought the lack of public service could be explained by the fact that "the Norwegian people are not cognizant of their duty as American citizens." His solution called for more "general education" *(Folkeoplysning)*. Story admired greatly "the Norwegian people's honesty," which would make them good public servants, he insisted, but they must first be "Americanized" so that they understood American institutions and political culture. Only "by having a passable comprehension of the true state of affairs" could Norwegians in America become "an independent people." Story's editorial is an insightful opinion of how immigrant adjustment to the new society could be achieved while celebrating an ethnic identity; no apparent conflict of loyalties existed in this process.

In March 1901, Story announced that he had been invited by the Republican governor of Iowa, Leslie M. Shaw, to visit the Scandinavian homelands on behalf of the state of Iowa, likely as a reward for his work for the Republican Party among Scandinavian residents in the state; as a consequence he leased his offices for a year to the Republican press room, which would be responsible for publishing *Republikaneren*. Subsequent issues printed Story's travel accounts. In his second letter, published May 24, 1901, he related his impressions of the first sight of the coast of Norway on April 16; Story emotionally introduced the newspaper's readers to a clear Norwegian starlit and moonlit sky, "and the sight of Mother Norway brought us all into high spirits." It was a high to which *Republikaneren*'s readers could easily relate. On his return from Norway in March the following year, Story again edited *Republikaneren,* but by June 6 he announced that he had sold the newspaper to Lake Mills Publishing Company. The following year, however, the new owners discontinued publication. Small-town politically partisan journals were greatly challenged by the strong position of successful newspapers like *Decorah-Posten* and regularly succumbed to the competition.[7]

The Varied Journey of Visergutten

The weekly *Visergutten* (The Errand Boy) was started in Story City in 1894 as a local newspaper for Story County, Iowa. It succeeded the short-lived *Vor Republik* (Our Republic), 1890–91, edited by A. C. Hurst, born in Hammerfest, Norway, in 1855; he came to America in 1873 after having attended the Latin school in Tromsø. Before moving to Story City, he was associated with other Norwegian American journals. Hurst was also a certified lawyer, a profession he pursued after *Vor Republik* ceased publication.

The Norwegian settlement in central Iowa centering on Story City, launched in 1855 by a party of immigrants from Sunnhordland, became one of the largest and most famous Norwegian settlements in Iowa. The immigrants had first come to Lisbon in the Fox River area of Illinois, but since all or most land had been taken there, they moved on in response to news of government land farther west. In all 196 persons—twenty-one families, five young men, and one widow—moved west in wagons drawn by oxen and six teams of horses. The party constituted itself a Lutheran congregation before starting out. A party of Haugeans in the farm communities by the Fox River sent agents, as the earlier group had done, to central Iowa and formed a colony farther north. Both settlements consisted of people from the same general regions in Norway, the southwestern coastal districts of Sunnhordland and Rogaland, but religious conviction, while giving internal strength and cohesion, separated the two communities.

The regional origin of the settlers in Norway carried weight with *Visergutten*'s publishers during its years in Story City; in 1917 publication was moved to Canton, South Dakota; *Visergutten* made a third change of address in 1944 when it moved to Fargo, North

Viserguiten
Udkommer hver Torsdag
Story City, Iowa.
Viserguiten Publishing Co.

Viserguiten.

Visergutten
Published every Thursday
at Story City, Iowa.
Over 40.000 Readers.

Nr. 4. Story City, Iowa, Torsdag, den 26de Januar, 1911. 17de Aargang

Kari Melleuil død

Elias J. Stoalnre

Mrs. Biel Myrah

Fra Newhall, Iowa

OLE O. ROE
ATTORNEY AT LAW
Des Moines, Iowa.
Will practice in all Courts in the State.—Corporation and Insurance Law a Specialty.

Til Finnsbuerne i Amerika

Fra Bergen, Norge

Fra Valevaag, Norge

Col. Henry Knutson

O. Bielland
fra Minneapolis

Huron, S. Dak.

Religiöse Möder

Første Kvinde i Norges Storting

Fra Iowas Legislatur

Efterspørgsel

Indremissionsmøde

En smuk residens for salg i Story City

Aarsmøde

Norske Billeder

Dusker en Automobile!

Visergutten, *Story City, Iowa, January 25, 1911. This newspaper played a unique role as a medium of correspondence for its readers.*

Dakota, where it was brought out until it expired in 1955. As a local news organ, edited by H. Halleland, it had a modest beginning, published in four six-column pages, with an annual subscription rate of only fifty cents; it advertised itself as "the only Scandinavian advertising medium for Story, Boone, Hardin, and Hamilton Counties." Local news and advertising generally filled *Visergutten*'s columns; the latter documented Norwegian business enterprise in Story City, from a Norwegian Drug Store *(Norsk Drugstore)* selling "Scandinavian medicines," to M. Mathiason's Meat Market, to Ole T. Hovde, Contractor, to Dr. A. J. Schwartz, highlighting his Norwegian medical degree from Christiania University. The editor even felt obliged to apologize for "the increased advertising and too little space for reading material" and promised to do better in the future.

Politically *Visergutten* declared itself Republican. The editor perhaps felt discriminated against as a non-English journal; in 1899 *Visergutten* took legal action against the county board for its refusal to approve it as the official county organ and thereby secure county printing, even though, editor Halleland claimed, the newspaper—with a readership of four thousand—had nearly as many subscribers as all the other county newspapers combined. Contrary to the law, as *Visergutten* and *Republikaneren* in Lake Mills both argued, the presiding Yankee judge J. E. Whitaker ruled "that newspapers in other languages than English can not be considered official organs." Story County was a Scandinavian stronghold and overwhelmingly Republican; it might thus have been as much a question of lacking the political patronage enjoyed by rivals as it was a case of discrimination against a Norwegian-language newspaper, though the ruling was of course discriminatory and did not conform to practice elsewhere in Iowa, as evidenced by *Republikaneren*'s position as official organ in Winnebago County.[8]

In fall 1901, *Visergutten* was sold to Gustav Amlund, born in Gjøvik, Norway, in 1850; he immigrated to Story City at age twenty-one with his wife Mathea Hansen Amlund. From 1891 to 1896 he published the semimonthly *Skolen og Hjemmet* (The School and the Home); contrary to what the title might suggest, the content consisted of short stories and other entertaining literature. As publisher and editor of *Visergutten,* Amlund turned the weekly into "a medium of correspondence for the circle of readers." All Norwegian

American newspapers carried correspondence from their readers in every issue; it was a practice that indicated the intimate relationship between newspapers and their public. Amlund took the idea to a logical conclusion by substantially filling its columns with such letters, alongside local news items, announcements, and advertising; *Visergutten* thus became a connecting link among thousands of people, not only immigrants but reaching across the Atlantic to the old homeland as well. The newspaper was expanded to eight pages with the low annual subscription price of sixty-five cents paid in advance in the United States and ninety cents for subscriptions to Norway. Editor Amlund explained *Visergutten*'s policy:

> We have set the price for the newspaper low [to Norway] so that everyone can have an opportunity to send it to their friends and family there. Make your dear ones happy in the homeland by sending them *Visergutten;* it is of great interest to them because they then can get news about their friends every week. Then they in return will send letters to the newspaper, which are of great interest in this country.

The concept was genial, unique, and well received. In January 1905 Amlund explained that the amount of letters received in advent of the holidays far surpassed *Visergutten*'s capacity; it listed in excess of sixty letters, mainly from the Upper Midwest, that had yet to be printed. The number of subscribers rose to ninety-six hundred by 1910, making *Visergutten* a profitable enterprise.

A content analysis of the correspondence published in *Visergutten* would surely illuminate individual and personal dimensions associated with the immigration saga; even a cursory examination of the many volumes of the newspaper leaves a deep impression of the human need to share the joys and warmth as well as the trials and tribulations that define the human condition. In the newspaper's columns the subscribers exchanged opinions about whatever they had at heart, wrote about all kinds of news from where they lived, and inserted letters to friends and kin who lived far away throughout the United States and Norway; a single family newsletter to *Visergutten* reached interested kin wherever they might reside. Occasional references to *Visergutten* simply as *Gutten* (The Boy), and the use of "Kjære Gutt" (Dear Boy) as a salutation suggest readers' intimate relationship to the newspaper.[9]

Onward to South Dakota

In South Dakota, Norwegians settled in large numbers in the valleys of the Big Sioux River and its tributaries in the eastern part of the state and in the northern counties. Many Norwegians found a new home in Minnehaha and Brookings counties; notable in the latter county is the Trønder settlement by Lake Hendricks founded in 1873. The two towns of Sioux Falls in Minnehaha County and Canton in Lincoln County farther south became important centers of Norwegian American life; substantial Norwegian populations resided as well in the seats Brookings of Brookings County and Sisseton of Roberts County. These small urban centers all hosted Norwegian-language newspapers.

Folketidende (The People's Times) in Sioux Falls, the state's major city, was the first exemplar of the immigrant press in its westward march in South Dakota, or more correctly Dakota Territory until statehood was granted in 1889, creating the two states of North and South Dakota. *Folketidende* was launched in 1879, but, as Wist described, the weekly "evidently lived only a short and barren life." *Vesterheimen* (The Western Home) had a longer and more productive life; it was founded in 1884 in Flandreau in Moody County, which by 1900 had some eighteen hundred Norwegian residents. Sivert O. Nordvold purchased *Vesterheimen* the following year and moved publication to Sioux Falls (Sioux City, Iowa, also given as place of publication). Nordvold, born in Lesja, Gudbrandsdalen, Norway, in 1847, was, like many who later entered into the service of the immigrant press, a *seminarist,* a normal school graduate; after emigrating to America in 1867, he was enrolled at Luther College for a time and later found employment for several years as a teacher in Norwegian congregational schools. In fall 1880 he and his family settled on a claim by Lake Benton in western Minnesota and remained there until Nordvold in 1885 took over ownership of *Vesterheimen.*

Editor and publisher Nordvold described *Vesterheimen* as "A Newspaper in the Norwegian Language," departing from the usual "Norwegian-Danish language." He consequently appealed directly to the Norwegian people in the newspaper's circulation area. Of the surviving issues, May 17 orations appeared on the front page in 1887 and 1888. Politically, *Vesterheimen* strictly espoused the Republican cause. *Vesterheimen* merged with *Syd Dakota Ekko* (South Dakota Echo) in Brookings in 1889. Sivert Nordvold moved to South Dakota's capital, Pierre, where he published twelve numbers of a Republican political weekly titled *Almuevennen* (The Friend of the People), beginning August 5, 1890 and ending October 21. Nordvold, as he explained in the initial issue, published his newspaper in Pierre to campaign for the city's selection as state capital, opposing *Syd Dakota Ekko* and others who advocated the city of Huron as a better site. The South Dakota electorate on November 1 decided in favor of Pierre.[10]

Syd Dakota Ekko, launched in Brookings August 1889 by a shareholder company formed by men active in South Dakota politics, like its rival *Almuevennen,* declared itself a Republican political weekly. During the editorship of G. Bie Ravndahl, 1890–98, *Syd Dakota Ekko* exerted itself forcefully in the political arena, even though Ravndahl and his political cohorts in 1890 lost their bid for Huron as state capital. Ravndahl typifies the intellectual and politically engaged Norwegian American newsman; he arrived in America in 1885, at the age of twenty, following university studies. Ravndahl edited Norwegian-language newspapers in North Dakota before moving to South Dakota; in South Dakota he served two years in the state legislature. In 1898 Ravndahl entered a diplomatic career; his first appointment was as American consul in Beirut, Syria. *Syd Dakota Ekko* continued to serve a Norwegian readership in South Dakota guided by serial editorial tenures until it was discontinued in 1906.[11]

During the 1890s the Populist weekly *Fremad* (Forward), published in Sioux Falls, stood forth as a strident political opponent to Republican *Syd Dakota Ekko.* The two journals appealed to different segments in a divided Norwegian American electorate; the basic conservative and Republican nature of South Dakota politics, however, soon made the Populist Party lose its identity and filter into the progressive wing of the Republican Party. Populism's effect, historians have pointed out, was felt in the progressive administration of Norwegian American Republican Peter Norbeck, elected South Dakota governor in 1916. His policy of reform gave greater voice to the people; legislation favoring wheat growers gained him the vote of Norwegian farmers.

Fremad.

3die Aargang Nummer 19. Sioux Falls, South Dakota, Thorsdag 24de September 1896. Løbenummer 123.

Syd Dakotas næste Guvernør, Nordmanden

Hon. Andrew E. Lee, af Vermillion.

"FREMAD"
"FORWARD"
The only Scandinavian People's Party Journal in the State.
Published every Thursday in Sioux Falls, S. D.
J. F. STRASS, Publisher.
Office: Mulhall Block, Main Ave.

10 Cents

Nogle Ord til Overveielse for Landsmænd.

Fra Brookings, S. D.

Fra Toronto, S. D.

Standinaver!

The Populist, later independent, Fremad *of Sioux Falls became the most important Norwegian-language newspaper in the state. This issue is dated September 24, 1896.*

As Populism evaporated by slow degrees, *Fremad* moved toward an independent political position without losing a reformist bent, siding with Republican progressives like Governor Norbeck, as the majority of South Dakota Norwegians did. It became the most successful representative of the Norwegian-language press in the state, informing the Norwegian American community until 1935. In the annals of immigrant journalism, *Fremad* thus stands out as a major news organ. The loss of competitors—including *Syd Dakota Ekko* in 1906—strengthened its position. Before World War I, two other newspaper ventures competed with *Fremad*. Eivind Trockstad, an immigrant from Norway at age eighteen in 1888, started *Sisseton Posten* (The Sisseton Post) in Sisseton in 1902 as a local news organ for Roberts County, South Dakota, later moving publication to nearby Effington. *Sisseton Posten* continued publication until 1912, its final issue in June blaming "lack of support from advertisers" as the cause of its demise. In November 1907, Helge Opland, an immigrant from Voss, Norway, and correspondent for the Chicago journal *Skandinaven*, launched the Progressive Republican four-page weekly *Sioux Falls-Posten* (The Sioux Falls Post) for Norwegians in South Dakota and western Minnesota; in 1910 Opland reported a circulation of thirteen hundred. Until its demise in 1916, *Sioux Falls-Posten* was a lively participant in state politics.[12]

The history of the first decade or so of *Fremad* is illustrative of the active role Norwegians played in shaping the infant state's political culture, even if *Fremad*'s Socialist message might find its greatest response mainly among voters historian John Milton described as "a bloc of East River farmers of Scandinavian background." Typographer Johan F. Strass established the eight-page weekly *Fremad* in 1894, the initial issue dated May 17; he served as both publisher and editor. Strass emigrated from Trondheim, Norway, in 1878, only sixteen years old, and in America followed a familiar path of employment on Norwegian American journals, among these the Populist *Fergus Falls Ugeblad*, where he was employed as printing shop foreman, before moving to Sioux Falls. He declared *Fremad* to be "the only Scandinavian People's Party journal in the State."

The agrarian revolt in the West, due to drought and falling farm prices, reached its climax between 1894 and 1896; the cause of

Populism became a holy crusade. The People's or Populist Party looked forward to the election of 1896 with high hopes. *Fremad* endorsed the Populist candidate for governor, Norwegian-born Andrew E. Lee. Lee lived in Vermillion, South Dakota, where he operated a large business firm. He had emigrated in 1851 at the age of four with his parents and thus by experience was of the second generation. To its readers, *Fremad* defined the coming election as the most serious in the history of the republic. The newspaper devoted prominent space to the Norwegian translation of the state Populist Party platform adopted in Huron; like the national platform it advocated the free coinage of silver and the liberal reforms contained in the Omaha Platform of 1892. Following the election, *Fremad* declared victory for the People's Party in South Dakota, where the Democratic and Populist presidential candidate William Jennings Bryan, while losing by a wide margin nationally to Republican William McKinley, carried the state by only a 185-vote majority. The election of Norwegian American Lee as Populist governor of South Dakota was an especially precious victory.

Fremad mocked its rival *Syd Dakota Ekko* for being on the losing side, even though its "decision to go from silver to gold [currency] made it fleet in milk and honey." *Fremad* on the other hand won while rejecting "blood money," because it "sought to throw off the gold party's slavery yoke it had placed around the workingman's neck." The encouraging reelection of Governor Lee in the 1898 election, as well as the election of the Democratic-Populist fusion candidate John Lind to the governorship of Minnesota notwithstanding, *Fremad* editorially, while reprinting *Nye Normanden*'s article praising Lind, deplored that "some voters had betrayed their own party by splitting their vote," which caused two of Populism's leaders in South Dakota to lose the election: the candidate for state treasurer John O. Langness and candidate for reelection state senator Lasse Bothun, both born in Norway and emigrating as young men. The 1900 election gave *Fremad* more reason for concern. The Populist and Democratic candidate for South Dakota governor, Norwegian American Burre (Børre) H. Lien from Minnehaha County, born near Spirit Lake, Iowa, in December 1859 to Norwegian-born parents, failed to win the governorship. Nationally, the reelection of William McKinley and the election of Theodore Roosevelt, president and vice-president respectively, confirmed for editor Strass in no uncertain terms that

> The intrigues and panegyrics of the money power and corporations proved to be so much more powerful than the opposing party's appeal to people's common sense that the so-called Republican Party also this time won with a crushing majority.[13]

The Story of North Dakota

In North Dakota, radical politics made a stronger showing than in its neighbor to the south. Progressive Republican movements such as Republican Nonpartisan League's Socialist public ownership platform influenced the political life in the state for a long time. "Norwegian immigrants brought radicalism . . . to North Dakota," wrote North Dakota historian Elwyn B. Robinson. During the Populist interlude of the 1890s Norwegian farmers in western Minnesota and eastern North Dakota, powered by agrarian dissatisfaction, sought through political action to gain control over crop marketing, to diminish railroad companies' power, and to establish a better credit system.

The Norwegian-language Populist press advocated the farmers' cause cooperatively. The extensive exchange of newspapers *(Bytteblad)* among the publishers was not limited to journals of the same political view; mutual commentary, not infrequently critical, was commonplace in all instances; rival journalistic enterprises regularly gleaned news items from each other. Reform newspapers frequently reprinted entire articles from Populist colleagues. *Normanden,* the largest newspaper in North Dakota, served as the official organ of the Populist Party from the party's founding in 1890 until 1893, when it converted to Republicanism. Other Norwegian-language newspapers in the state joined the Populists. Laurits Stavnheim, later publisher of the Socialist *Politiken* in Minneapolis, received publishing and editing experience in North Dakota journalism. In 1890 he was hired as editor of *Dakota*—a newspaper started in Fargo in 1889—when G. Bie Ravndahl, the initial editor, moved to Sioux Falls to edit *Syd Dakota Ekko;* during the election campaign of 1892 *Dakota* switched from the Republican to the Populist Party. Stavnheim became part owner in March 1895, from December of that

Normanden.

The Normanden has a higher circulation than is accorded to any paper in Grand Forks or in the State of North Dakota.
From Printers' Ink, Aug. 12, 1903.

Grand Forks, Nord Dakota, Onsdag den 13de Juli 1904. | 13de Aarg.

Minnesota.

600 druknede.

Figarens Resolutioner.

Normanden *out of Grand Forks was the most important Norwegian-language newspaper in the state. This issue is dated July 13, 1904. H. A. Foss edited and published the newspaper early on. He is likely best known for his romantic novel* Husmands-Gutten *(The Cotter Boy).*

year together with Amandus E. Norman, a graduate of the Unitarian Theological Seminary at Meadville, Pennsylvania; he was a close associate of the Norwegian Unitarian minister Kristofer Janson. In March 1896 he established on the ruins of the Populist weekly *Red River Dalen,* published by Adolf Bydal in Crookston, Minnesota, the newspaper *Den Fjerde Juli* (The Fourth of July), continuing Bydal's political course, and moved publication to Grand Forks. The two publishers, sharing political affiliation and ownership of *Dakota,* decided to merge their journalistic enterprises in March 1897, giving it the rather awkward name *Fjerde Juli og Dakota,* with a Fargo publication address.

Fremad, as the South Dakota voice of the Populists, from its start in 1894 cultivated a close relationship with such Populist news organs as *Nye Normanden, Fergus Falls Ugeblad,* and *Rodhuggeren,* all in Minnesota, as well as Populist colleagues in North Dakota. *Fremad* manifestly sided with both *Den Fjerde Juli* and *Fjerde Juli og Dakota* in their refusal to acknowledge the decline of Populism; the two weeklies assured *Normanden,* the Republican organ in Grand Forks, that the Populists had no intention of lying down peacefully to die. However, progressive newspapers consolidated in an attempt to strengthen their political agenda. In May 1898, as indicated earlier, *Fjerde Juli og Dakota* merged with *Rodhuggeren,* Ole E. Hagen's and Torkel Oftelie's radical weekly in Fergus Falls, Minnesota. The consolidated journals then became the Fargo newspaper *Fram* (Forward); Stavnheim and Hagen served jointly as editors for two years or more, Hagen continuing on alone until April 1903; they moved *Fram* from the Populist to the Socialist political camp and displayed marked anti-Christian and antichurch tendencies. The change of owners and political alignments thereafter altered *Fram*'s content radically and secured a measure of success.

Norwegian American newspaper readers could choose from a wide selection of publications and might subscribe to more than one newspaper; this practice offered a broad geographical distribution of the major journals. *Skandinaven*'s special edition for Minnesota and the Dakotas, headquartered in St. Paul, added additional local information to its regular Chicago edition, securing it a wide circulation in the region. A former resident of Hatton, North Dakota, exemplifies a Norwegian American readership in his letter to *Normanden*'s editor in April 1908 from Grygla in northwestern Minnesota, where he had moved in 1900:

> Mr. Editor! We read many letters in *Normanden,* and I also want to send a little letter. I do not subscribe to the paper, but as three of my neighbors get it, I have the honor of reading it every week. I subscribe to many newspapers, but not *Normanden;* it is very reasonable, more reasonable than *Decorah-Posten,* and I also get *Minneapolis Tidende* and *Praktisk Farming* [Practical Farming]; but these are all the same not like *Normanden;* because I there can read so much more about North Dakota.[14]

Norwegian settlement in North Dakota had a modest beginning in 1869 when Norwegian pioneers began to take land on the west side of the Red River Valley; massive movement into the territory took place with the "great Dakota land boom" from 1879 to 1886. North Dakota was destined to become the most Norwegian of all states. The highest Norwegian settlement density took place on the slightly sloping plain created by the Red River—a valley if you like—and its tributaries; Norwegians settled heavily in the two eastern tiers of counties and established marketplaces along the valley. Fargo and Grand Forks became important commercial centers alongside such smaller towns as Hatton, Mayville, and Hillsboro. In the northern part of the state Norwegians moved westward along the main line of the Great Northern Railroad. In the early 1880s they reached the Devils Lake region as they continued their westward trek; Norwegians took land along the Mouse (now Souris) River and farther west to the Montana border. Minot became the main urban center for Norwegian settlers. By 1900 North Dakota's Norwegian stock numbered nearly seventy-five thousand, equal to 23 percent of the state's population; their number increased to some 125,000 during the following decade. Like their compatriots in the other states of the Upper Midwest they engaged heavily in farming; the opportunity to become land-holding farmers on the American frontier motivated their movement west. The Norwegian American press—reminiscent of Paul Hjelm-Hansen's previous advocacy of the "Red River Country" published in *Nordisk Folkeblad* and *Fædrelandet og Emigranten*—persisted in the practice of printing letters that promoted land ownership. *Budstikken*'s editor Ferdinand A. Husher personally visited Fargo in 1874 and reported on the Norwegian farmers in the Sheyenne River settlement; by the mid-1880s letters to the Norwegian-language press about the Mouse River region were nearly as numerous as earlier had been published about the Red River country; the Chicago newspaper *Amerika,* St. Paul's *Nordvesten,* and Iowa's *Decorah-Posten,* among others, were significant outlets for homestead and settlement propaganda aimed at Norwegian land-seekers. In 1914 Norwegian farmers owned about one-fifth of North Dakota's fertile farmland.[15]

A Wealth of Newspaper Publishing

Only Minnesota and Wisconsin surpassed North Dakota in the number of Norwegian-language publications. *Fram* and *Normanden* were the most significant news organs in the state, but other journals also competed for the attention of Norwegian American readers. The initial issue of *Normanden* was dated April 15, 1887. In its May 1, 1917, issue celebrating its thirtieth anniversary, *Normanden* presented its early history written by L. K. Hassell, the weekly's founder. In his account, Hassell gave much credit to the newsman Jørgen Jensen, without whose assistance, Hassell wrote, the idea of starting a local newspaper for Grand Forks and surrounding communities "would have been stillborn." He described Jensen as "the most quick-witted of Norwegian American journalists." "His unforgettable style," Hassell continued, "brilliant logics and biting satire will be remembered with mixed feelings by his contemporaries." Jensen was born in Stjørdalen, North Trøndelag, in 1851; as a gifted youngster, he passed university entrance exams and studied at the university in Oslo until he immigrated to America in 1873. Among his early positions were employment in congregational schools, as a tutor in the home of Pastor Bernt Julius Muus, and finally as a teacher at Augsburg Seminary in Minneapolis. From 1878 he entered the world of Norwegian American journalism full time, working on such newspapers as *Budstikken* and *Minneapolis Daglig Tidende.* Hassell's own birthplace in Norway in 1862 was Biri; he graduated from middle school before he emigrated and moved to Grand Forks with his family in 1881. Both men typify persons with intellectual talent and interest who for shorter or longer periods served the immigrant press.

Hassell was editor of *Grand Forks Tidende* before founding *Normanden.* In 1888 he sold *Normanden* to a corporation that hired H. A. Foss as editor; Foss, as related in chapter three, together with the printer Edvard Lund about two years later purchased *Normanden* and published it until 1893. It then became the property of a Republican share company. Functioning as a Republican organ, it moved away from the conservative stalwart political ring of the state Republican Party, represented by Alexander McKenzie, the political agent in North Dakota of the Northern Pacific and of the powerful interests of Minneapolis and St. Paul, which held the region as a colony. McKenzie became known as "Alexander the Great, Boss of North Dakota." *Normanden* joined forces with those who opposed "boss McKenzie" and the dominance of Twin Cities capitalist interests in the state's political and economic affairs. *Normanden*'s political influence was highlighted in 1890, when it supported the Farmers' Alliance nomination for Congress: the Norwegian American Alliance leader Martin N. Johnson. McKenzie's henchman established *Statstidende* (The State Times) in Devils Lake to promote Johnson's competitor, Henry C. Hansbrough, in a language that would appeal to Norwegian voters. Hansbrough's loss ended the rationale for the Norwegian-language organ, so *Statstidende* ceased publication shortly after the November election. *Normanden* became an independent and progressive Republican voice among Norwegians in North Dakota. It made several declarations about its political stance to its readers:

> *Normanden* supports a government of, by, and for the people, and we demand that this should not only be used for show by political parties, but that it should be fulfilled in our public life. We support "*a square deal for all,*" and we by no means applaud high-handed cliquishness—regardless whether it calls itself Republican or bears another name.

The Normanden Publishing Company, the name taken by the new owners, published *Normanden* from 1893 until 1925. P. O. Thorson was hired as manager and soon became the major stockowner in the corporation. Acting as manager until 1922, he made the business one of the nation's most profitable Norwegian American newspaper ventures. Born in Scandinavia, Wisconsin, in 1867 to immigrant parents from Gudbrandsdalen, he moved to Grand Forks in 1888. His travels throughout the state acquainted him with people and places and the political thinking of his fellow Norwegian Americans; he and the journal he managed enjoyed great respect. Its progressive Republican political stance, though challenged both from the left and the right, was akin to that of large segments of the Norwegian American electorate. A parade of editors, well known as well as inexperienced—some serving periodically—represented a notable difference from many of the major journals, such as *Decorah-Posten* and *Minneapolis Tidende,* where single long-term editorial tenures left an indelible personal stamp.[16]

Normanden published sworn circulation figures to attract advertisers; in 1902 average circulation stood at 4,869. Not to be outdone, Laurits Stavnheim and Ole Hagen, as publishers of *Fram,* which, if truth be told, was under their management not a very profitable business, announced "that We Guarantee the largest circulation of any paper in N. Dak. and northwestern Minnesota," and thus *Fram* was the "best advertising medium." Even in 1904, *Fram* had a smaller circulation of 4,640. On its masthead *Fram* declared itself "the oldest and most widely distributed paper in the Red River Valley." It dated its beginning to the founding of *Red River Posten* (The Red River Post) in Fargo in 1878 and used its volume numbering, making the first issue of *Fram,* May 18, 1898, number 20 in volume 20. *Red River Posten* had a checkered history. Its founder, the restless Michael Wesenberg, sold the weekly to Major Alanson Edwards, publisher of the English-language Fargo newspaper *Argus,* who held ownership twice. Edwards was a strong supporter of Alexander McKenzie, a longtime opponent of the Farmers' Alliance, and in the "Bloody Fifth" campaign in Minnesota he gave *Posten*'s backing to Charles Kindred's candidacy against Knute Nelson's.

After Kindred's loss to Nelson in the historic congressional election, Edwards no longer had use for a Norwegian-language political proxy and transferred possession of *Red River Posten* to P. T. Julseth in 1883. He became a connecting link that could possibly give credence to *Fram*'s claim of being the oldest Norwegian-language journal in North Dakota. Julseth, a graduate of Augsburg Seminary in Minneapolis, exemplified the fluid state of the immigrant press: the many failed newspaper ventures and the great mobility of the newsmen in its employ. Julseth had earlier in 1883 established *Den Norske Amerikaner* in Fargo but like *Red River Posten* enjoyed little success. In 1884 Christian Brandt, then publisher and editor of the weekly *Nordvesten* in St. Paul, purchased *Red River Posten* and merged it with his journal. Brandt had previously held possession of *Red River Posten* between Edwards's proprietorships.

Julseth's second attempt at establishing a Norwegian American weekly failed; in fall 1884 he started the short-lived *Amerikaneren* (The American). Sufficient support for the journal was not forthcoming. His third attempt, *Fargo-Posten,* launched January 24, 1885; advertised as a successor to *Den Norske Amerikaner* and *Amerikaneren, Fargo-Posten* fared better. Julseth had learned his lesson; subscribers who were unwilling to settle their accounts with the new weekly's two predecessors had their names listed in *Fargo-Posten* under the heading "deadbeats," using the American term rather than a Norwegian equivalent. In 1887, indicating recognition of the four-page weekly's accomplishments, A. A. Trovaten purchased a half interest in *Fargo-Posten.* Trovaten was to play a major role in Norwegian American journalism in North Dakota and in particular in *Fram*'s history. Trovaten, born in Telemark, Norway, came to America with his parents at the age of seven in 1867. A dynamic personality, inexhaustible in his many ventures, Trovaten quickly gained the respect of his fellow Norwegians.

Politically *Fargo-Posten* declared itself independent, backing or opposing whom and what it desired; it did, however, align itself with the Farmers' Alliance ticket in 1886 against the political ring in control of Cass County, of which Fargo was the county seat. *Fargo-Posten* saw Edwards, publisher of rival *Argus*, as a true example of a corrupt ringleader. The *Argus* enjoyed the support of the railroad king James J. Hill of Great Northern Railway fame, who in the view of *Fargo-Posten* represented the interests that exploited the farmers, kept the territory under the control of outside interests, and prolonged the power of the corrupt leaders. In the extensive debate over granting Dakota Territory statehood, *Fargo-Posten* advocated the entrance of the territory into the Union as one state. The division into two states planned by a small Yankee oligarchy, *Fargo-Posten* argued, had developed from the greed of politicians who had only personal interests at heart. The journal considered the territory a natural entity with a largely homogeneous population.

Trovaten left *Fargo-Posten* in May 1888, and the following month started a rival weekly in Fargo titled *Vesten* (The West). Jørgen Jensen and G. Bie Ravndahl were both associated with *Vesten* as editors. *Vesten* promoted itself as the first Norwegian-language newspaper intended for the entire Red River Valley, all competitors dismissed as local sheets. *Vesten* initially favored the Democratic Party's program and agreed with the objectives of the Farmers' Alliance movement. Showing an intense competitive spirit, *Fargo-Posten* and *Vesten* hurled accusations at each other of being in league with the old political ring in Cass County. When *Vesten* in September 1888 was ceded to a Republican corporation, *Fargo-Posten*'s accusations seemed justified. Now controlled by straight Republican policies, *Vesten* insisted on dividing the territory into two states, agitating for Republican victory—the platform in 1888 called for admission of two states—and for the removal of the national Democratic administration whose policy it was, *Vesten* editorialized, to keep Dakota in its territorial status. However, both Republicans and Democrats voted for the omnibus bill of February 22, 1889, authorizing North Dakota, South Dakota, Montana, and Washington to frame constitutions.

In May 1889, Trovaten resumed his ownership of *Vesten* and purchased *Fargo-Posten* as well, merging the two weeklies as *Fargo-Posten og Vesten* (The Fargo Post and the West). He pledged support for the Republican administration of the infant state but simultaneously asserted an independent and liberal stance within the party. Trovaten soon altered the name of the consolidated journal to the much simpler and direct *Dakota*. The history and changing political affiliations of *Dakota, Den Fjerde Juli,* and *Fjerde Juli og Dakota* up to the founding of *Fram* in May 1898 was told earlier in this book. In July 1903, A. A. Trovaten entered the picture as *Fram*'s sole publisher, after having been part owner and manager since April. By 1910, *Fram* could report an estimated 7,500 subscribers, compared to *Normanden*'s 9,367. The two journals had achieved a secure position as North Dakota's major Norwegian American publications. Other journals made contributions as well. From first to last, when all are counted, some forty-five secular weekly or semiweekly newspapers hit the stands.[17]

The Mineral Kingdom

Norwegian settlers followed the general westward movement of the American population; from the mid-1830s to 1900 Norwegian land-seekers moved from the southern tip of Lake Michigan across Wisconsin, Iowa, Minnesota, South Dakota, North Dakota, and the Great Plains in eastern Montana. Along the route some chose to live in the small urban centers that sprang up and dotted the agricultural landscape. The Norwegian agricultural communities in the eastern counties of Montana represented a natural extension westward from the dawn of the twentieth century after settlement had advanced across North Dakota.

The mining counties in western Montana were settled with the far West; permanent and extensive Norwegian settlements developed in western and northwestern Montana, in Idaho, and in eastern Colorado. The Norwegian American press early on gave much attention to Montana's opportunities. Numerous letters from Norwegian settlers as well as articles about the territory were published in Norwegian-language journals circulating in the core regions of Norwegian settlement to the east. In 1889 the St. Paul weekly *Nordvesten,* as an example, published a series of eight articles titled "Montana Territory: What It Has to Offer to Scandinavian Immigrants." Even though eastern Montana's agricultural regions were far more attractive to Norwegian settlers than the mining and lumbering opportunities farther west, there were by 1900 identifiable clusters of Norwegians in that part of Montana. The settlers concentrated in the small urban centers and in various mining communities.[18]

A local Norwegian American press had a presence in the cities of Great Falls, Helena, and Butte and served Montana's Norwegian community. The first issue of *Montana Posten* (The Montana Post), published and edited by John Wessel, came out in Helena on October 11, 1890. It advertised itself as "A Political Weekly Journal"; it broadened its potential readership by employing both "the Dano-Norwegian and Swedish languages" and claimed to be "the only Scandinavian Democratic newspaper in the State of Montana." Nationality might, however, on occasion trump party loyalty. Swedish and Danish immigrants settled alongside Norwegians and found common ground as a minority population. Darrell J. Christofferson made the following observations to the author in a 1995 letter from Kalispell about the movement of his Scandinavian forebears from Norway, Sweden, and Denmark into the Flathead Valley in northwestern Montana:

> It is my understanding that Norwegian and Swedish were spoken here more than English at one time, and in my mind and in my long-ago memories, the Scandinavian influence was quite strong. I can still see how the attitude of "strong wholesome values" influences our community.

A long editorial in August 1891 reminded the weekly's readers that "Anyone who is acquainted with Scandinavians knows that they are among the most intelligent citizens of this country and that they examine and have an independent opinion about the issues of the day." The *Montana Posten* compared the greater success of the local Scandinavian Democratic Club to the lukewarm support enjoyed by the Scandinavian Republican Club. Even so, in the March 1893 city election, the editor urged Scandinavian voters to cast their vote for "a countryman . . . [and] let us not consider politics and be divided, but let us unite around him and let him win." In August 1893, after only about three years, *Montana Posten* ended publication.[19]

Helena sheltered a second Norwegian-language journal, *Montana Folkeblad* (Montana People's Newspaper), started in 1890 and the following year continued as *Montana Statstidende* (The Montana State Times) until it was discontinued in 1892. The single extant issue of *Montana Folkeblad,* dated October 28, 1891, carried several letters from mining operations, which indicate subscribers' wide geographical distribution. In a letter from Wickes, Jefferson County, Colorado, the weekly's readers learn that *Montana Folkeblad* "has not so few subscribers among the mountains . . . that the new smelting works in Boulder will give impetus to the mining operation in Jefferson County . . . that there are many Scandinavians, but they are not so easy to find, since most of them have their day labor under the earth's surface." Local news from "Helena and Environs" and from the three Scandinavian homelands enjoyed separate columns.

The Scandinavian Publishing Company started the four-page weekly *Montana Skandinav* (Montana Scandinavian) in Butte, Montana, January 26, 1893; the same year it merged with *Montana Tidende* (The Montana Times), also launched in Butte in 1893, to form the weekly *Montana Tidende og Skandinav* (Montana Times and Scandinavian). The bilingual—Swedish and Dano-Norwegian—newspaper survived only until 1895 in spite of its pan-Scandinavian appeal. No evidence exists to suggest that the impasse in the Swedish-Norwegian Union crisis, which in 1895 threatened to descend into a military conflict between the two homelands, directly caused the demise of *Montana Tidende og Skandinav;* tensions, however, between the "brother people" were tangible on both sides of the Atlantic. The initial editorial of *Montana Skandinav* expressed trepidation at the prospects for success; the editor stated, "a sufficient number of examples . . . [show] how difficult it was to make a Scandinavian newspaper endure in the state of Montana." However, *Montana Skandinav* intended to be an exception. Unlike the failed journalistic ventures that had relied on political affiliation for success, *Montana Skandinav,* the editorial insisted, would never become a party organ, but would be free to express its opinion unencumbered by partisanship. The depressed economic times of the 1890s, and the limited number of potential subscribers—in 1900 there were fewer than five thousand Norwegians in the state—combined with the high bar set for non-English small-town journals, as evidenced by the many short-lived Norwegian American newspapers throughout the heartland, doomed the Montana ventures to failure.

A decade after *Montana Tidende og Skandinav* ceased publication, an ultimate exertion to secure a Norwegian-language journal in Montana took its course. In the summer of 1915 H. Schmidt, as publisher and editor, presented the eight-page *Indlandsposten* (The Inland Post), with publication address in Great Falls, as the only Scandinavian newspaper in Montana. From November 1916 it came out in Fairfield, Montana. *Indlandsposten* ceased publication in 1917, at the time of the U.S. entry into the European conflict; it was not a propitious environment in which to launch a newspaper in a language unfamiliar to most Americans. World War I and the Norwegian American press will be dealt with in a later chapter; suffice it to say that official and public xenophobia against immigrant populations was a deathblow to many a foreign-language publication.[20]

The Norwegian Mormon Experience

In his foreword to *Homeword to Zion* by William Mulder, Oscar Handlin, distinguished historian of immigration, reminded the reader, "the migration of Mormons to Utah was but a part of a larger American westward movement." Many Americans were hostile toward the Church of Jesus Christ of Latter-day Saints, regarding the movement as foreign and even threatening. The Norwegian American press in its columns reiterated the misconceptions about the Mormon faith and Scandinavian Latter-day Saints gleaned from both American and Norwegian published sources. Scandinavia yielded 46,497 converts between 1850—when the Scandinavian mission was launched—and 1905, half of which were Danish, less than 36 percent Swedish, and nearly 14 percent Norwegian. "Of the 22,653 of these 'members of record' who emigrated," Mulder wrote, "56 percent were Danish, a little over 32 percent were Swedish, 11 percent Norwegian." The headquarters of the Scandinavian mission was located in Copenhagen, Denmark, whose liberal 1849 constitution guaranteed free religious worship. Danish authorities as a consequence did not—as might be the case in Norway and Sweden—take action to hinder missionary activity. Mormon missionaries encouraged emigration. Norwegians, the smallest contingent, numbered fewer than twenty-five hundred converts to Mormonism who during the half century moved overseas to the Mormon religious colony in Utah. A few converts from older frontiers joined them; some had even participated in the great Mormon trek westward in 1846. After that time Mormons made only modest advances among Norwegians in the Midwest. The strength of the Norwegian Lutheran church and its forceful anti-Mormon campaign greatly limited the number of new converts. Even so, Norwegians and other Scandinavians established a visible presence in Utah.[21]

The Norwegian Mormon agricultural communities in Utah can be included in the large Norwegian settlement area of the "mineral kingdom" in western Montana, Idaho, and eastern Colorado. The principal region of Scandinavian settlement in Utah was in the Sanpete Valley, south of Great Salt Lake. As reported by *Decorah-Posten* in 1883, the valley contained a total population of about twenty thousand, mostly Scandinavians, primarily Danes and Swedes. The 1930 census showed the relative strength of the Scandinavian nationalities in Utah: the Norwegian element numbered only 6,198, as against 24,895 Danes and 15,839 Swedes. Salt Lake County had by far become the main Mormon settlement in the number of Norwegians. Farming became the principal livelihood for Norwegians, as well as for all the rest; a growing portion of settlers worked as laborers and artisans in a variety of trades, and even as proprietors. Craftsmen tended to settle in Salt Lake City, the capital.

Mulder described Scandinavian Mormon settlers "as yeomen developing Zion," where "the idea of the Kingdom encouraged survival when lesser hopes failed" and fostered the daily cooperation endemic to Mormon society. This made them different from their compatriots in America. The Saints became Mormon villagers and lived a closely knit community life. As pioneers, Scandinavian Mormons resembled their countrymen building homes in Dakota or Nebraska or Minnesota. Their distinction, Mulder explained, embodied the following unique properties:

> their religious motivation as dissenters from the old Establishment and as converts to a new American authority, the Kingdom of Zion; their union as Scandinavians overriding Danish, Swedish, and Norwegian divisions, a union which had characterized them as proselytes, as emigrants, and as settlers; their self-help under an American doctrine and program and an American leadership, effecting their transformation from despised ugly ducklings to respected Saints and citizens, members of a flourishing church and a prosperous community they themselves helped to build.[22]

In their process of adjustment and community building, they communicated, following an established practice, in the

Dano-Norwegian and Swedish languages through a separate immigrant press. The Danish-Norwegian *Bikuben* (The Beehive), launched in 1876 in Salt Lake City (or *Saltsö Stad,* as listed on the masthead), enjoyed a continuous life of fifty-nine years, until it was suspended in 1935. It was the most significant journalistic achievement, though the weekly *Bikuben* was not the earliest venture into journalism. The Danish-Norwegian *Utah-Posten* (The Utah Post) made its appearance in Salt Lake City December 20, 1873, edited by Peter Olaf Thomassen, an immigrant from Drammen, Norway, in 1863. He brought to the Scandinavian Saints, as he wrote, "the address of the Presidency and the doctrine of the Church in a language which reaches the heart." He feared the Liberal Party, in opposition to the church, and its design to win immigrants over to its side, and reproduced the People's Party ticket—the Mormon Church party—in the municipal election. *Utah-Posten* was destined for failure in spite of its warm reception since, as Thomassen explained, "it had been launched "without help or assistance from anyone." Only thirty-six issues saw print, the final one dated September 5, 1874; thus the first foreign-language publication in Utah became a victim of hard economic times and lack of adequate financial support.

The Liberal Party gained Scandinavian members among those who had left the Mormon Church, although the liberal *Salt Lake Tribune* seems to have exaggerated in its 1889 assertion that half the Scandinavians in Salt Lake had left and were then members of the Liberal Party. In refuting the claim, the Utah journal *Svenska Härolden* (The Swedish Herald) editorially insisted that there were fifty Scandinavians in the People's Party to every five in the Liberal. Despite dissenting voices, the Mormon faithful were united from more than 25 nations; they sang and praised God, as *Bikuben* had it, with one heart and one mind and were one people in a political and a religious sense. Dissatisfaction was common, however, among Scandinavians as well as among other nationalities, resulting in high rates of desertion from the mother church; migration figures and the story of mission activity revealed that about one-third left Mormonism.

The anti-Mormon liberal weekly *Utah Skandinav* (Utah Scandinavian), printed in Dano-Norwegian, Swedish, and English, succeeded *Utah-Posten* in Salt Lake City on October 22, 1874. Its editor, Colonel B. A. M. Froiseth, expressed enlightened goals for the weekly and gave the journalistic venture vigorous and serious leadership; since there are no extant copies of *Utah Skandinav,* however, information about it relies on contemporary descriptions in other journals; *Bikuben* commented that *Utah Skandinav* had received strong financial and moral support from "local apostates and heathens." Froiseth's apparent libelous methods against the Mormon Church and its members offended many. *Bikuben* for August 2, 1877, related how a certain Colonel M. M. Kaighn felt "his inner being in uproar" from Froiseth's false accusations, and when they happened to meet on a street in Salt Lake City, to quote *Bikuben,* "The editor of *Utah Skandinav* got caned *(Stokkeprygl).*" In the judgment of the Mormon Church, the newspaper was "apostate" and a "plague." Before *Bikuben,* Scandinavian Saints had no organ to defend themselves against the weekly attacks.[23]

Bikuben was launched by Anders W. Winberg in August 1876 to counteract what he claimed was *Utah Skandinav*'s venom. In the initial issue Winberg explained that his "little Beehive" was intended to meet a long-felt need for a newspaper "that would speak the truth and work for people's interest and welfare" in the Scandinavian, or more precisely Dano-Norwegian, language for the many "who cannot read the English language or even understand it." Winberg, a Swedish blacksmith by training, had an adventurous life journey, becoming Patriarch Winberg before his death in 1909. He was born in Lund, Sweden, in 1830; his apprentice journey took him to Denmark, where in 1851, following a dream where God had revealed that Mormonism was the only pure and true faith, he converted and engaged in a fertile proselytizing activity. He became a traveling missionary in the Nordic lands as well as in America; in 1853 he immigrated to Utah. He was publisher and editor of *Bikuben* from 1876 to 1891, whereupon he became superintendent of the Norden Mercantile Company, selling Norwegian-imported delicacies.

On January 1, 1885, after nearly a decade of publication, *Bikuben* was faced with a rival when Winberg's fellow churchman, the Dane Andrew Jenson, launched the weekly *Utah-Posten,* reviving the old title with Peter Thomassen's permission. Jenson's reason for starting a competing Mormon journal was his dissatisfaction with *Bikuben*'s lack of an engaging literary style; Winberg never laid any claim to learning and was more in tune with the practical rather than the cultural side of newspaper work. Jenson outlined an ambitious journalistic program in the weekly's first number. Like *Bikuben, Utah-Posten* presented in Dano-Norwegian translation material—Mormon speeches and reports of church conferences—gleaned from the Salt Lake City Mormon journal *Deseret News*.

Jenson announced in the first number that he published *Utah-Posten* with "the consent and recommendation of the Church authorities." Several weeks later, Jenson explained that the Church had authorized him to start the new journal because "people wanted a better newspaper than the one they until then had had." Winberg refused to yield the field to *Utah-Posten;* Jenson heeded church advice to give *Bikuben* its priority, printing *Utah-Posten*'s final number April 8. The two rivals joined forces; the April 16, 1885, issue of *Bikuben* listed both Winberg and Jenson as publishers and editors. When Thomassen—who in 1891 purchased *Bikuben* from Winberg—unexpectedly died that same year, a shareholding company, Bikuben Publishing Company, took over ownership. In 1895 *Bikuben* became church property. Jenson was then called to manage and co-edit *Bikuben,* an appointment he held for nearly fifteen years. As assistant church historian, Jenson was a prolific author and collector of records. His 1879 biography of Joseph Smith, the Mormon prophet, in Danish was Utah's first book in a foreign language.[24]

Bikuben throughout its history never lost the common touch, even though it changed its emphasis and added new features. In its later years it serialized mainly religious books; throughout it contained reports and correspondence from settlements and news from the homelands and elsewhere where Mormon converts resided. The early issues contained on the front page translations into Dano-Norwegian of sermons by the founder and president of the Mormon colony, Brigham Young, as well as by other church leaders in defense of the faith. Young's death August 29, 1877, and funeral a few days later produced a series of front-page articles about his life given in speeches in his honor.

In the nineteenth century, no aspect of Mormon teaching required greater defense from anti-Mormon forces than the practice of polygamy. Brigham Young making the doctrine of plural marriage public in August 1852 produced massive opposition and a series of federal measures to outlaw polygamy and cohabitation. Norwegian American newspapers joined in the attacks on this social institution. The Synod-influenced *Emigranten,* citing stories written by Scandinavians in Utah, described polygamy as worse than slavery. In an article in May 1856, the newspaper actually carried a story about a market in which women, due to money shortage, were bartered off in exchange for produce.

The Saints naturally objected to these fanciful and false charges. The Danish-Norwegian newspapers *Utah-Posten* and *Bikuben* vigorously protested the falsehoods spread by their Norwegian journalistic colleagues to the east. Occasionally defenders made light of less than Christian provocations, as when the Danish-Norwegian Methodist organ *Den kristelige Talsmand* (The Christian Spokesman) in 1884 reported that a pastor "prays that Mormonism will be eradicated from the earth." *Bikuben*'s laconic rejoinder was to state that "for us it will be interesting to observe the outcome so that we can learn the effect of prayer . . . but we are not fearful even though the Methodist pastor is a little more than usually deranged in regard to the Latter-day Saints." The Edmunds Act of 1882, reinforced by the Edmunds-Tucker Act of 1887, represented stringent measures to end the practice of plural marriage. In the mid-1880s, scores of federal marshals were sent to Utah Territory in what would be described as "the Raid"; they arrested and prosecuted men who practiced polygamy and unlawful cohabitation. Some Scandinavians were polygamous, but like the rest of Mormon society the great majority lived in monogamous relationships. Nevertheless, in 1888, 28 percent of the 219 violators in the Utah Penitentiary were Scandinavian. On December 1, 1886, Winberg, a polygamist, editorialized how he had been arrested on November 21 and charged with five counts of cohabitation; he served the customary six months in the penitentiary and paid a fine.

Bikuben gave great prominence to the discussion concerning polygamy given in the Tabernacle in Salt Lake City in 1890. September 24 President Wilford Woodruff proclaimed that he went to the Lord; the result was the issuance of the "Manifesto," a document announcing that the church no longer sanctioned plural marriage. On October 6 in General Conference, the Latter-day Saints voted unanimously to accept the Manifesto. Polygamy was severely restricted but not discontinued. In fact, polygamy was not completely abolished until the second "Manifesto," issued in 1904 by Latter-day Saints President Joseph F. Smith; the punishment for further practice would be excommunication.

On January 4, 1896, Utah was admitted to the Union as a state. In 1891 the People's Party, the Mormon political party, was disbanded. The Saints were directed to join Republican and Democratic parties. In 1896 the state of Utah sent its first two senators and one representative to Congress, all members of the Republican Party. In 1900 the church reported a total membership of 268,331. *Bikuben*'s circulation grew from 1,250 in 1910 to 2,050 in 1929; it demonstrated Scandinavian cooperation by having had editors from all three Nordic countries at various times in its history. The Mormon Church discontinued *Bikuben* in 1935, together with three other foreign-language newspapers, a German, a Swedish, and a Dutch.[25]

A San Francisco Story and the Norwegian American Press

The Norwegian story in San Francisco dates back to the 1849 gold rush and thus predates all other Norwegian settlements on the Pacific Coast. Their number was small but reinforced by the arrival of Danes and Swedes. The Argonauts set out from their homes in Norway and the Midwest in an adventurous quest of gold; sailors abandoned ships when they docked in San Francisco. The small urban colony had a decidedly pan-Scandinavian appearance; when their numbers were small, Danes, Swedes, and Norwegians in the New World united in the multiethnic world of America's cities; they cooperated in religious, political, and social activities. The Scandinavian Society of San Francisco, organized in 1857, typifies a common Nordic spirit; it gave aid to sick members, burial service, and a place to gather. There were newspapers from the three mother countries and a library for the free use of the members.

In the years and decades after the gold rush the immigrant press informed midwestern Norwegian settlers about the many opportunities that awaited in the far West. *Skandinaven* followed the progress of the Northern Pacific Railroad in 1871 from its terminus on its way westward and called attention to its importance for Norwegian settlement, announcing in a leading article in 1873 that it had reached the Missouri River and would soon continue laying tracks toward the Pacific; in 1883 it finished its line to Portland, Oregon, and to the Puget Sound. The first transcontinental railroad was, however, completed in 1869 by the Union Pacific and Central Pacific railroads between Council Bluffs, Iowa, and Alameda, California. The driving of the last spike at Promontory Summit, Utah, where the two companies' tracks met, on May 10, 1869, established a transportation network that revolutionized the population and economy of the American West.

In *West of the Great Divide* Kenneth Bjork showed that several Norwegians who settled there, even before the gold rush subsided, were businessmen and men in finance, in trade, and in shipping who had been attracted to the city during a time of speculation and easily amassed fortunes. The early colony had a clearly elitist character. Bjork described its history from the 1850s into the 1870s as "a chronicle of outstanding individuals." The majority in 1870, as reported by the Reverend Christian Hvistendahl, a contributor to secular Norwegian American newspapers in the Midwest, were seamen and sailors. Norwegians arrived in greater numbers after 1874, adding to the labor supply called for by building projects or finding work as store porters, as longshoremen, or in other occupations. Norwegian girls were eagerly sought as housemaids. By the turn of the century the Norwegian-born in San Francisco numbered 2,172 in addition to 2,818 of the second generation; Norwegians settled in Oakland and other towns on the east side of San Francisco Bay as well.[26]

A letter by Andrew H. Lange from San Francisco appeared in the Chicago journal *Skandinaven* in January 1884; it was written in response to an earlier correspondence in the same newspaper deploring that Scandinavians on the West Coast were losing their cultural heritage. Lange conceded that for some Scandinavians that might be the case but noted that at least in part it was due to the lack of adequate Norwegian or Danish newspapers in the community. Two newspapers printed in Dano-Norwegian offered their services at that time, the semimonthly *Bien* (The Bee) and the weekly *Valkyrien* (The Valkyrie).

The reality was, however, that the Norwegian American press

did not enjoy great success in California. Norwegians were at a disadvantage in newspaper publishing since they were greatly outnumbered by Danes as well as Swedes. In most instances the Norwegian community stuck to journals run by Danes; *Bien* at its founding in 1882 and *Pacific Posten* from 1904 were exceptions to Danish journalistic dominance; Danish-Norwegian interplay was, however, apparent on the columns of these two journals as well. *California-Posten* (The California Post), the first Danish-Norwegian newspaper on the Pacific Coast, saw the light of day as early as Christmas Day 1874.

Midwestern newspapers regularly carried stories from California; newspapers like *Norden* in Chicago, *Fædrelandet og Emigranten* in La Crosse, and *Budstikken* in Minneapolis reprinted stories from *California-Posten*'s founding and later from other San Francisco journals. *Budstikken*'s column was titled "News Bits from the Pacific Coast." By consulting *California-Posten,* the midwestern news organs could give their readers detailed information about wages in specific occupations and employment opportunities in California. In February 1875 *Budstikken* reprinted two articles titled "About California's and San Francisco's Development" and "About California's Prospects"; the previous month *Norden* carried *California-Posten*'s praise of California as the state where "one lives best and most cheaply." Bjork observed that positive stories "breathed a strong spirit of optimism and hope." They acquaint us as well with early San Francisco and California and with *California-Posten*'s brief history. Two young Danish typographers, Peter Freese and Ferdinand Iversen, started the journal. Freese soon left and Iversen struggled to publish the newspaper alone; for how long is not completely clear, but it likely ceased publication sometime in 1876.[27]

The weekly *Valkyrien,* started in 1878 under W. Hartvigsen's editorship, represented a continuation of *California-Posten;* in Norse mythology the Valkyries were Odin's armored goddesses of fate who elected to Valhalla those chosen to die in battle; the Age of the Vikings bestowed ethnic identity and pride. The journal had strong literary tendencies but functioned as a regular news organ. *Valkyrien* was basically a Danish publication; nevertheless it appealed to a Norwegian readership as well. Until it was discontinued in 1886, stories in its columns were regularly reprinted in Norwegian newspapers in the Midwest. For example, in January 1884, *Skandinaven* reprinted articles from *Valkyrien* praising the large stretches of good land in the foothills of the Sierra Nevada Mountains.

Founded and edited by the Norwegian Synod minister I. L. P. Dietrichson—then pastor in San Francisco—on April 22, 1882, the illustrated literary weekly *Bien* (The Bee) was a unique journalistic contribution to the local Norwegian community and beyond. Claiming to publish "for the intelligent Scandinavians on the West Coast," it initially had sixteen pages, four to six of which were devoted to pictures, plus features, short stories, and about two pages to advertising. Its size decreased greatly over the years. In 1890 it came under Danish management, and the following year it was revived as a regular weekly news organ. The Danish American typographer and historian Sophus Hartwick began as a co-owner but after a few years assumed full ownership; he secured *Bien*'s prosperity and gave the Danes of California their own voice. *Bien* in 2009 continued as a semimonthly publication.[28]

The summer of 1886, after the weekly *Valkyrien* ceased publication, *Pacific Skandinav* launched as its intended Danish-Norwegian continuation. Copenhagener J. C. Hansen held the editorship and after a few years purchased the weekly from the original publisher. It advertised itself as "the oldest, best, and most widely circulated Danish-Norwegian weekly on the Pacific Coast." *Pacific Skandinav* pledged to print only "interesting and exciting stories by the best authors, [and] in every number bring original articles about the burning issues of the day." Politically the newspaper affiliated with the Republican Party and in the 1896 election voiced intense opposition to William Jennings Bryan and free silver; the preelection editorial predicted that should these political forces gain the majority, "then the door would be open for all kinds of calamities . . . destitution, bankruptcies, and unemployment . . . and even the breakout of a large social revolution." Scandinavian voters hardly needed *Pacific Skandinav*'s dire warnings to be convinced to vote the Republican tickets.

In a December 18, 1896, editorial, *Pacific Skandinav* announced "to Danes and Norwegians on the Pacific Coast" that from January 1 ownership would shift to Michael Salomon and Wm. Mörck, with Salomon in the editor's chair. The new publishers expanded the weekly's distribution to "the northern Pacific states." *Pacific Skandinav*'s masthead for a time listed Portland, Oregon, and Seattle, Washington, along with San Francisco and Oakland as publication addresses. Salomon and Mörck identified the challenging circumstances that had convinced Hansen to sell the newspaper. "Our press out here has for quite a few years struggled with financial scarcity, insufficient support, lack of interest in the public." But the prospects were good "for a newspaper in our own mother tongue—mind you, only for a good one." That was precisely what the new publishers promised, and they were convinced of success because "a strong national sentiment is stirring among our countrymen out here on the Pacific Coast." Unmistakable enormous progress held great promises for the future. Salomon had considerable experience in journalism in Denmark before coming to the United States. *Pacific Skandinav* benefited greatly from his editorial skills.

The publishers' Danish orientation is evident in the major focus given circumstances in Denmark and among Danes in the New World; it paid special attention to South Jutland and reported regularly on the Society for the Preservation of the Danish Language in North Slesvig *(Foreningen til det danske Sprogs Bevarelse i Nordslesvig)*. Perhaps the concern for the protection of the Danish language against German encroachment at home encouraged *Pacific Skandinav* to take the lead in petitioning for the creation of a Scandinavian Department at the University of California, Berkeley. In March 1897 *Pacific Skandinav* heralded the notion that "the Nordic Spirit Awakens" in support of "the establishment of a Scandinavian faculty"; the petition submitted on May 11, 1897, with five thousand signatures, called for "a Chair for the teaching of the Old Norse Language and Literature and Lectures on Modern Scandinavian Literature." To the petitioners' disappointment, the response from the board of regents was negative, due to "the present financial stringency."

In April 1899, declaring itself "the best edited Danish newspaper in California," *Pacific Skandinav* announced that it had entered into an agreement with *Tacoma Tidende* (The Tacoma Times) in Tacoma, Washington, so that subscribers could receive both for the low annual price of $1.35. *Pacific Skandinav*'s primary competitor was the San Francisco journal *Pacific Posten.*[29]

Politically *Pacific Posten* took a different path than its rival. Under the heading "What We Want," its introductory editorial, dated September 15, 1904, explained that in regard to religion and politics it would be tolerant and gather the Norwegian people around a common heritage. The president of the Pacific Posten Publishing Company, the weekly's publisher, was the noted Olaf Anders Tveitmoe, who after his arrival in San Francisco in 1898 rose to power and high position in the labor movement. When the San Francisco Buildings Trade Council—a separate federation for the building trades—on February 3, 1900, started its own newspaper, *Organized Labor,* Tveitmoe became its first editor. *Pacific Posten* served as the Norwegian voice of workers' rights. Tveitmoe, born in Valdres, Norway, in 1865, came to the Holden community in Minnesota in 1882 and spent two academic years at nearby St. Olaf's School (later St. Olaf College) in Northfield. He then turned his attention to the Farmers' Alliance movement and found employment for a while on the still-Populist *Normanden* in Grand Forks, North Dakota, before moving on to California. In San Francisco he encountered a city becoming the most unionized in the nation; Tveitmoe easily transferred the ideology of the Farmers' Alliance movement to the cause of labor.

Pacific Posten earned the distinction of having the first female Norwegian American editor in chief, Hanna Astrup Larsen. Larsen, the daughter of Laur. Larsen, president of Luther College, was born in Decorah, Iowa, in 1873; she exhibited exceptional journalistic and literary powers. In addition to her work on *Pacific Posten,* her career included editing *Den Norske Amerikaner* (The Norwegian American) in Brooklyn, New York, editing the English-language *American-Scandinavian Review*, and other writing and translation work.

As editor of *Pacific Posten* Hanna Astrup Larsen engaged in editorial exchanges with the Hauge Synod's *Pacific-Emissæren* (The Pacific Lay Preacher) in Tacoma, Washington, with Tveitmoe's separate commentary; *Pacific-Emissæren* questioned the editor's lack of originality and ability to explain the meaning of tolerance in religious affairs. "Does that mean to be tolerant toward heathenism and freethinkers?" *Emissæren* wondered. Tveitmoe dismissed the criticism as "religious quackery." The weekly was not antichurch; in fact, a Norwegian Synod pastor sat on its administrative board. Even though Norwegians in the city united around the newspaper, the community on the whole could not concur; churchly elements in time distanced themselves from *Pacific Posten*. As a consequence Hanna Astrup Larsen in February 1906 resigned from the editorship.

Pacific Posten's reporting gave glimpses into a developing urban Norwegian American community and news from Norway and Norwegian settlements in America; it reprinted items from immigrant journals and newspapers in the homeland; and it announced church services and organizational meetings, concerts by the local Norwegian male choir, as well as other significant events in San Francisco.

Pacific Posten's advocacy for the laboring classes, especially through the actions of Tveitmoe, is clearly featured in its columns. The newspaper covered the American Federation of Labor (AFL) meeting in San Francisco in November 1904 and the reelection of Samuel Gompers as AFL president; it heralded the AFL as "A Great Power."

A sense of class-consciousness among Scandinavian workers in California appeared in the 1870s and 1880s. In September 1877 Dennis Kearney organized the Workingmen's Party of California. By the spring of 1878 midwestern newspapers reprinted articles about the Scandinavian branch of the Workingmen's Party in San Francisco. It worked against vested interests but also against Chinese immigration. Outspoken opposition to the Chinese cropped up repeatedly in the story of Norwegian migration to the West Coast. A general anti-Chinese sentiment led in 1882 to the Chinese Exclusion Act. The Workingmen's Party's agitation for Chinese exclusion led directly to the organization of the Japanese and Korean Exclusion League on May 14, 1905 (renamed the Asiatic Exclusion League in 1908). O. A. Tveitmoe served for a number of years as its president. The Japanese had replaced the Chinese as "cheap labor"; *Pacific Posten* in a piece titled "The Yellow Menace" reported how Japanese and Korean workers entered a surprising number of branches of industry, "and where they come in they work for lower wages than white workers are able to, and these are thus squeezed out." The league had free voices in labor newspapers like *Pacific*

Posten; on May 11, 1905, it headlined Tveitmoe's role under the heading "A Norwegian Leading the Anti-Japanese Movement." The editor might not have seen the irony in placing on the same page an editorial that asked, "Why do we Norwegians celebrate May 17?" The response in part: "We Norwegians have our faults, but there clearly are powerful elements in the Norwegian national character *(Folkekarakter)* that are greatly needed in the development of the American nation."

In November 1905, *Pacific Posten* merged with its former rival, *Pacific Skandinav*. Michael Salomon, then *Pacific Skandinav*'s sole publisher, thus gained part ownership and editorial input in *Pacific Posten*. Salomon explained, "a distinctly Danish edited [and] a distinctly Norwegian edited" newspaper would be combined "to reach a joint public and expand the field of action." The final number of *Pacific Posten* is dated April 12, 1906. Only six days later, on April 18 at 5:12 AM, a major earthquake struck San Francisco and the coast of northern California; residents from Oregon to Los Angeles and inland as far as central Nevada felt the shaking. The earthquake and its aftershocks caused tremendous damage, but the fires that burned out of control afterward were much more destructive. *Pacific Posten* suffered great loss along with everyone else in San Francisco and could not get back on its feet again. A renewed attempt at publishing *Pacific Posten* after the earthquake and fire was short lived.[30]

The Pacific Northwest—A Major Norwegian American Center

Norwegian settlement in Oregon and Washington was closely related to the completion of transcontinental railroads; as noted, Northern Pacific was first with a line to the region in 1883. Ten years after Northern Pacific's initial arrival, Great Northern in 1893 connected to Seattle; a third line, built by Chicago, Milwaukee, and St. Paul, reached Tacoma in 1909. From the late 1880s a considerable number of midwesterners left for the Pacific Coast. Norwegians who had earlier farmed in the Midwest took land in the northern part of the Willamette Valley in Oregon, where they grew wheat, corn, hops, and fruit. Many Norwegians were attracted to Alaska and the northern Pacific Coast; the landscape was reminiscent of the coastal districts of Norway, with familiar modes of livelihood in lumbering, fishing, and shipping. In the cities many men entered the building trades—a special ethnic niche in all urban environments where Norwegians concentrated. The largest grouping of Norwegians was in the Puget Sound; separate communities formed in the protected sea-lanes and bays in the sound.

Some Norwegian American newspapers, mainly transitory ventures lasting a year or two, appeared before the turn of the twentieth century; the Norwegian numbers were apparently not sufficient to sustain a separate press. Of the twenty-seven secular weeklies established in Oregon and Washington, more than half came into being after 1900 (their stories are dealt with in a later chapter). Norwegian American newspapers appeared in Portland, Oregon, and Seattle, Tacoma, Everett, and Spokane, Washington. The first three Norwegian-language journals in the Pacific Northwest began in 1889: *Stillehavs-Posten* (Pacific Ocean Post) in Portland, *Washington Posten* (The Washington Post) in Seattle, and the short-lived *Tacoma Budstikke* (Tacoma Messenger) in Tacoma, edited by P. O. Bergan. Ten or so additional journalistic ventures all failed in the 1890s after a brief existence, with the exception of *Tacoma-Tidende* (The Tacoma Times). *Tacoma Tidende*'s first issue was dated July 4, 1890; it continued publication under that masthead until 1925. Only sporadic information has been uncovered about the majority of these publications; they are all listed in Appendix 1. Newspapers could be started with relative ease; overly optimistic anticipations of success and income were, however, frequently shattered when the publisher confronted the reality of inadequate subscriptions and advertising to finance the enterprise.

Stillehavs-Posten represented the effort of J. P. Holm to offer a Danish-Norwegian news organ to residents of those nationalities. Holm had operated a bookstore in Fergus Falls, Minnesota, before moving to Oregon. He managed to publish *Stillehavs-Posten* for about two years. Holm represented the mobile serial immigrant newspaper publisher, common to journalistic careers. He later lived in Perth Emboy, New Jersey, as Danish vice consul and publisher of the Danish *Perth Amboy Folkeblad* (Perth Amboy People's Newspaper); served as publisher in New York of *Dansk-Amerikaneren* (The Danish American); and filled a longer-term post at *Den Nor-*

ske Amerikaner (The Norwegian American), where Hanna Astrup Larsen moved after she left the editorship of *Pacific Posten.*[31]

Despite its shaky start, *Washington Posten* was destined to become a major Norwegian American newspaper on the Pacific Coast. Its inception is illustrative of the spread of Norwegian-language journalistic enterprise. The fact that no local immigrant newspaper existed did not deprive the Norwegian American community on the Pacific Coast of news organs in their native tongue. People moving to the coast from the Midwest continued to subscribe to familiar journals. In 1938 Frank Oleson, an immigrant from Trondheim, Norway, described on the fiftieth anniversary of *Washington Posten* in 1938 how he had happened to establish the newspaper:

> Early in 1888 I was employed as a distribution clerk at the post office in Seattle. . . . The entire staff consisted of four persons in addition to five letter carriers. As a clerk at the post office, I discovered that many bundles of *Decorah-Posten, Skandinaven, Budstikken,* and other Norwegian American newspapers were being sent to subscribers here. They were not only for people in Seattle, but many were addressed to post offices in the surrounding area for which Seattle served as a distribution point. This circumstance gave me and my brother Richard, who also worked in the post office, the idea of publishing a Norwegian newspaper in Seattle. I was at that time twenty-six years old and my brother two years younger. We had no experience whatsoever in the publishing business and even less experience in editorial work.

Oleson then launched *Washington Posten* on May 17 the following year; it was Seattle's first celebration of the homeland's constitution day. "It had not really occurred to me," Oleson later recalled, "how many Norwegians there were here until we began to celebrate May 17." In the same article he gave insight into the "cut-and-paste" newsgathering procedure of the immigrant press. "We had no time to get newspapers from Norway, so items from the homeland were taken from newspapers farther east which in turn had taken them from the Norwegian newspapers," Oleson explained. It was truly an extension of the Norwegian American press westward. In February 1890, Oleson bought *Washington Tidende* (The Washington Times), which had just been launched in Tacoma by Erik Thuland, and combined it with his own journal. *Washington*

Posten addressed itself more directly to the local community than the large national Norwegian-language newspapers could; it was more a city-oriented journal than most of the midwestern newspapers and wrote mainly for urban Norwegian Americans with many secular and nonchurchly interests. *Washington Posten* may in fact be described as a window on a developing Norwegian urban colony.

Washington Posten joined American and Swedish American newspapers in recruiting immigrants from the Nordic homelands as well as midwestern Scandinavians to the Puget Sound region; travel accounts, letters, and news articles from the Puget Sound appeared early in the midwestern Scandinavian press. In 1890, Seattle, located in King County, with a population of nearly forty-three thousand had only 1,353 Norwegian-born citizens, a figure that by 1900 had increased to 1,642 plus 2,577 of the second generation. Seattle developed on Elliott Bay, an arm of Puget Sound, which provided an excellent harbor. As the presence of Nordics grew, the city acquired a Scandinavian flavor; in the northwest part of the city, Ballard—a separate municipality from 1889 to 1907—contained the largest concentration of Norwegians.

Oleson left *Washington Posten* in September 1891; the newspaper was faced with grave financial difficulties and mismanagement, and from the early part of that year had been owned by the newly formed Scandinavian Publishing Company, which published Swedish and Norwegian journals in both Seattle and Tacoma. The company experienced further deterioration of revenue and was dissolved in 1892; that year *Washington Posten*'s circulation fell to only 1,345 weekly copies. The depression in 1893 further aggravated its situation as it went from owner to owner. On September 24, 1896, A. J. Thuland, an immigrant in 1884 at the age of thirteen from Vestfossen in Buskerud, announced that he had taken over the publication of the newspaper; he struggled to keep *Washington Posten* alive, but it was not a paying proposition, even though the number of subscribers increased steadily. Circulation stood at about twenty-four hundred in 1899. In 1902, Thuland sold *Washington Posten* and it again commenced on a succession of changes in ownership and editorial leadership. Only after Gunnar Lund took over as publisher and editor in November 1905 did *Washington Posten* gradually attain its position as the Norwegian voice of the Pacific Northwest—a role it may still claim though now mainly in English and under a different title.

Norwegians on the West Coast harbored the same partisan cleavages and interests in religion and politics as their compatriots in the Upper Midwest. Historian Kenneth Bjork, however, convincingly argued that they became less involved and, especially in Washington, leaned more to the liberal side than their more prosperous friends and kin farther east. West Coast leaders were less committed to conservatism than men in commerce and professions in the midwestern states. The influence of the Lutheran faith was reduced; the percentage of Lutheran Church members lagged far behind the Midwest. These circumstances were reflected in *Washington Posten*'s columns. Norwegian-language newspapers in the Midwest, with their large readerships of churchgoing rural people, gave considerably more attention to religion than did *Washington Posten.*

During its initial five or six years it held to liberal Democratic or Populist views; the immigrant commercial elite briefly and unsuccessfully attempted to move *Washington Posten* into the con-

The business district in Ballard about 1910. Annexed by Seattle in 1907, Ballard housed the largest concentration of Norwegians in the city.

servative camp. In 1896 Populists and Democrats gained political control of the state. *Washington Posten* had a forceful colleague in the Populist weekly *Vestens Skandinav* (The West's Scandinavian), published 1892–93 by the Danish immigrant J. C. Auen in Spokane, Washington. Auen accused both *Normanden* in Grand Forks, North Dakota, and *Fergus Falls Ugeblad* in Fergus Falls, Minnesota, of being remiss in their support of the Farmers' Alliance and overly friendly with the railroad king Jim Hill and the corporations. Auen had earlier published *Spokane Falls Ekko* (Spokane Falls Echo), 1890–91, but as reported in St. Paul's *Nordvesten* had to leave the weekly "because of chicanery." *Spokane Falls Ekko* continued for a time as *Vor Tid* (Our Age) in Portland. Auen raised money to launch *Vestens Skandinav.* During the depression of the 1890s, which stimulated liberal and radical thought, many Norwegian workers and small farmers supported liberal causes; Populism gained strength in both western and eastern Washington.

In the 1896 election Thuland, *Washington Posten*'s new owner, was well connected in the Republican Party; he and the conservative Norwegian business community deplored the loss of the immigrant vote. But as Thuland stated editorially, the Republicans had put up a good fight. The newspaper's declared political affiliation was independent Republican; later commentary revealed Thuland's regard for political convictions to the left. When the short-lived Seattle Populist weekly *Fram* (Forward), published by Julius Sunde, a regular correspondent to Norwegian-language newspapers in the Midwest, in 1897 was acquired by *Washington Posten,* Thuland assured readers that the Populists would get "all the latitude they wished" if they only steered clear of "religious controversies."[32]

Tacoma in Pierce County sheltered about the same number of first- and second-generation Norwegians as Seattle to the north; it was second only to Seattle in Norwegian American newspaper publishing on the coast. The first number of *Tacoma-Tidende,* the most important Norwegian-language weekly in the city, was dated July 4, 1890, published by Tacoma Tidende Publishing Company, which was organized by Dirk Blaauw with local businessmen as shareholders. Blaauw, a conservative Republican, unlike the more inclusive Thuland, dueled constantly with *Washington Posten*'s liberal political positions as expounded by its editor Peter Røthe, an immigrant from Hardanger, Norway, who likely expressed the social and political sentiments of most Puget Sound Norwegians; the sharp mutual attacks were fueled by personal as well as ideological differences. The two cities, Seattle and Tacoma, were also rivals.

Tacoma-Tidende sought a wide circulation. It operated an office in Portland to court the Norwegian population in the city and surrounding areas. Replicating *Washington Posten* and other immigrant journals, *Tacoma-Tidende* proclaimed itself "The Most Widely Circulating Organ of the Scandinavians in the States of Washington and Oregon, in Alaska and in British Columbia" to solicit precious advertising and subscriptions. To give some veracity to such promotional hype, newspapers like *Tacoma-Tidende* were obligated to carry local news from all points in their claimed field of circulation. *Tacoma-Tidende*'s regular contacts with and reports from the planned Norwegian colony of Bella Coola, founded in 1894 as the northernmost coastal settlement in British Columbia, provide insight into Canada's organized settlement policy as well as the travails in the life of a colony. Most of the settlers were from the Crookston area in Minnesota. The trek to the goldfields in the Klondike and Alaska 1897–98 was highlighted in both *Tacoma-Tidende* and *Washington Posten,* the latter observing that people arrived in the embarkation port of Seattle believing that "the gold grows as pears on the trees." Both newspapers covered individual experiences of miners.[33]

Tacoma-Tidende shifted ownership and editorial management in late 1897: John Blaauw, its representative in Portland, purchased the newspaper and changed places with Dirk Blaauw in the editor's chair; financial straits had convinced him to move on to other livelihoods. John Blaauw expanded *Tacoma-Tidende* from four to eight pages, advertising it as the largest weekly in the area, and regularly printed sworn circulation figures that varied from 2,150 to 2,500. He expanded its reach by cooperating with other journals; in July 1900 subscribers were offered *Tacoma-Tidende* together with *Det Frie Ord* (The Free Word), published in Grafton, North Dakota, by "the uniquely creative" K. P. Wig for $1.10 for a year's subscription. Beginning in September 1901, John Blaauw published a monthly edition of the weekly and also made a successful effort to enter the Seattle market in competition with *Washington Posten. Tacoma-Tidende*'s monthly in 1900 claimed to have four hundred subscribers in Seattle, ninety in Ballard, and more than one hundred in Poulsbo. While continuing its Republican loyalty and engaging actively in political issues, *Tacoma-Tidende* declared itself to be a temperance journal. Editor Blaauw wrote, "We feel that our countrymen now will fully understand that this newspaper is untainted so that they need not smell the stench of whiskey and charlatan advertising." As a temperance voice, it dissociated itself from May 17 celebrations, specifically the one in Seattle in 1901, where alcohol and "fallen women" entered into the festivities. Blaauw held such practices to reflect poorly on Norwegians:

> *Tacoma-Tidende* . . . is of the opinion that if Norwegian Americans wish to celebrate that day [May 17] in America it must be from high and pure motivations, and it should be celebrated so that our fellow citizens will understand that we belong to a great nationality, a race, which in culture and intelligence stands on the highest level.

John Blaauw published and edited *Tacoma-Tidende,* save for one year, until 1911. Extant copies give a clear impression of growing focus on Norway and Norwegian nationality. The front page carried news from Norway under the title "From Home" *(Hjemmefra)* while setting apart news items from other Nordic countries as well as world news. *Tacoma-Tidende* responded to need in the homeland by fundraising and selected serial literature by classical Norwegian authors like Jonas Lie and Alexander Kielland. These developments are not unique to *Tacoma-Tidende;* they apply to the Norwegian immigrant press in general; it increasingly gave its major attention to the Norwegian community in America and to the old fatherland.[34]

The Newspaper Story in the East

Norwegian settlement westward to the Pacific Coast represented an extension of the agricultural and urban Norwegian communities in the Upper Midwest. The bonds were close and strengthened by kinship and shared historical experience. Norwegians on the eastern seaboard on the other hand, while surely interacting with religious and cultural institutions in the Midwest, experienced a greater nearness to the homeland. Writing in the literary monthly magazine *Symra* (The Anemone) in 1907, the Reverend Sigurd Folkestad, who had extensive editorial experience from Norway and in New York, described the Norwegian colony in greater New York as "From Norway—to Norway." The core of the early settlement was made up of sailors who abandoned ship. Historian David Mauk aptly designated Brooklyn, which in time became the largest urban colony of Norwegian-born people outside Norway, as "The Colony that Rose from the Sea." Thousands of Norwegian sailors deserted ship when they landed in New York, attracted by higher American wages and increased employment opportunities. The first Norwegians settled in Lower Manhattan; shipyard and dock work appealed to sailors who had deserted as well as later arrivals.

Bridges and ferries linking Manhattan with Brooklyn encouraged movement across the East River. The Bay Ridge district became the center of the colony and was practically considered a suburb of Bergen or Oslo. A. N. Rygg referred to the migration as "the invasion of Brooklyn." From the 1880s the permanent Norwegian population increased substantially; shipyards on Staten Island recruited workers from Brooklyn's Norwegian districts, thus creating a permanent Norwegian colony on the island. Norwegians formed urban colonies only in New York, but Norwegians settled in Boston as early as the mid-nineteenth century; Norwegians later made their homes in other parts of New England as well as in the mid-Atlantic states. Largely due to the many mariners who settled there, the Brooklyn colony was dominated by immigrants from Agder on the southern coast of Norway and Rogaland, the southernmost county on the west coast. The regional origin of the majority residents bestowed a local Norwegian flavor on the colony.

In his history of *Nordisk Tidende* (The Nordic Times), Karsten Roedder commented on the 1890 federal census, which reported 8,602 Norwegian-born residents in New York State and another 1,317 in New Jersey. This represented a greatly improved market for a Norwegian-language newspaper compared to a decade earlier, when only two thousand Norwegian immigrants lived in the state. The Norwegians in Brooklyn "concentrated in the southern part of the city and across Bay Ridge," Roedder wrote, constituting "a group that could easily assert itself."[35]

Discounting the joint Swedish-Danish-Norwegian journalistic efforts beginning with *Skandinavia* in 1847, *Nordiske Blade* (Nordic Newspapers), started in New York in 1878 by the printer Martin Nielsen, an immigrant from Drammen, Norway, was the earliest Norwegian American newspaper of any significance in the city. Peter S. Christensen, earlier associated with *Nordisk Tidende,* in 1914 described Nielsen as a man with many friends who assisted him through "dilemmas in connection with getting the newspaper out . . . because even though it was only a small slip of four pages, it nevertheless was a precious bond between the old and the new country." *Nordiske Blade* began as a semimonthly journal, but as its circulation expanded, it became an eight-page weekly. Published in Brooklyn's Red Hook, it nonetheless faithfully represented Manhattan colony views throughout its existence; according to Mauk, the Manhattan colony for some time "held the most important elements in the bay area elite—the consulate and major old-country shipping agencies, as well as the loyalty of *Nordiske Blade.*"

Nordiske Blade prospered sufficiently to employ editorial staff to assist Nielsen; R. N. S. Sartz edited the newspaper for several years before he moved to Minneapolis in 1887, where from 1889 he edited *Budstikken* and *Minneapolis Daglig Tidende,* and then on to Chicago to accept an editorial appointment to *Norden.* Nielsen himself was recognized for his front-page "Week in Review"; a person in the literature referred to only as "Barber" Andersen, a Dane who had resided in Trondheim several years, served as Nielsen's right hand by dividing his time "between his barber shop and the editorial office." Andersen translated popular German novels for serialization in *Nordiske Blade*; these added to the newspaper's popularity. Consolidations with other publications promoted growth as well. Sartz and Louis Lorange in 1885 consolidated the humor magazine *Krydseren* (The Voyager) with *Nordiske Blade* after having published it for six or more months; the newspaper in 1901 absorbed the short-lived Danish-oriented weekly *Connecticut Folkeblad* (Connecticut People's Newspaper) published in Hartford. Many years earlier Nielsen had abandoned his newspaper venture, which by 1901 had changed owners several times and was experiencing serious decline.

Nordiske Blade's good fortune turned in 1890. Its difficulties related to the weekly's scathing editorials of how the secular Norwegian-American Seamen's Association of Brooklyn conducted its affairs. Organized as a benevolent society and free of the seamen's pastor's paternalistic attempts at reforming seamen's behavior, the Association offered a comprehensive assistance program in aid of mariners. One of its early traditions was establishing parties in sailor-town bars following each weekly meeting and arranging monthly welcoming meetings for crewmen on newly arrived vessels; these activities before long gave the Association a reputation of rowdiness and hearty alcohol consumption. The issue's exposure was limited to disparaging gossip among colony residents until *Nordiske Blade* publicly criticized the situation in 1890. The Association responded with both reform and counterattacks.

The launching of the weekly *Nordisk Tidende* January 3, 1891, was perhaps a part of the Association's counteroffensive. Printer Emil Bernhard Nielsen established the paper with start-up capital provided by the Association, of which he was an early member. Mauk explained that Nielsen used the newspaper "to cudgel not only *Nordiske Blade* but the whole array of reactionary upper-class groups he felt it represented," which included Our Savior's Lutheran Church in Manhattan as well as the economic groups with vested interests in Norwegian shipping that exploited seamen. The aging Martin Nielsen sold *Nordiske Blade* to a shareholding company; medical doctor Hans Volckmar became the editor. Volckmar returned to the homeland after a few years to edit the Oslo daily *Dagbladet*. In the pages of *Nordiske Blade,* Volckmar engaged in a hostile conflict with Emil Nielsen, whom he dubbed "the fanciful printer" for his ingenious and rich store of combative and condescending words.

Nordiske Blade shifted publishers several times, including Finnish-born Axel Hornborg, who experienced difficulty in hiring qualified editors. The most interesting person in the newspaper's later history was undoubtedly Sigurd Folkestad, who while an assistant at the Norwegian Seamen's Church in Brooklyn began writing for *Nordiske Blade*. He was able to organize a new shareholding publishing company in 1903 and assumed the editorship; in 1906 he changed the newspaper's title to appeal exclusively to the Norwegian colony—*Den Norske Amerikaner*—and give the weekly a new start. Folkestad declared war on Emil Nielsen and attacked him for his reckless speech; but, as Roedder wrote, "it ran like water from a duck's back."

The internal war between the two rivals was apparently rather ugly, and even though one might assume that controversy had its own appeal, Roedder posited that readers began to harbor a certain distaste for both publications. New capital that might have saved *Den Norske Amerikaner* was not forthcoming, while *Nordisk Tidende* found backing from the Seamen's Association. Folkestad left for the Midwest to study theology; after ordination in the Norwegian Synod he served as pastor in Strum, Wisconsin. He later returned to Norway to assume editorial responsibility for *Nordmanns-Forbundet,* the eponymous magazine of the Norsemen's Federation in Oslo. It was more evidence of transatlantic relations. The newspaper venture he had departed in New York could not be rejuvenated, even with changes of owners and editorship. *Den Norske Amerikaner*'s last publisher was J. P. Holm, then Danish vice consul, who faced dire financial prospects; with Hanna Astrup Larsen in the editorial chair, he managed to keep the newspaper going until it folded in 1910.

The limited market impeded success, as illustrated by the brief appearances of *Norges-Posten* (The Norway Post), published by A. G. Gulliksen 1903–4, and several humor magazines, among these *Kolonies Argus* (The Colony's Argus), 1895–96. *Nordisk Tidende* also struggled to establish itself as a profitable enterprise; early attempts to make it a daily or even semiweekly were soon given up. Its eccentric and outspoken founder Emil Nielsen was born in Horten, Norway, in 1859; he became a printer at age eighteen and sojourned in Germany and Finland before returning to the Norwegian capital in 1888. There he became one of the leaders in the ongoing typographer strike. After they lost the strike, many of the most capable printers found employment abroad; Nielsen immigrated to America and arrived in New York in July 1889. From the start, Nielsen filled the pages of *Nordisk Tidende* with sensational rumors, scandals, and murder stories. An exchange newspaper, *Everett Ekko* (Everett Echo) in Everett, Washington, in 1907 had the following censorious comments: "So far *Nordisk Tidende* has been an organ that even the worst rowdy among Scandinavians would have to blush at having to recognize as a Norwegian American product." Nielsen introduced all contributed pieces and objections "with his own commentary and brushed aside all arguments before there was an opportunity to read them," wrote Karsten Roedder, who labeled *Nordisk Tidende*'s history from its founding in 1891 until 1911 as the "subjective period."

A series of editors came and left; Nielsen himself functioned as editor, though he described himself as "owner and responsible publisher." Aside from Nielsen, there was Ingvald Kopperud, earlier assistant editor of *Oplandenes Avis,* the liberal Hamar newspaper where Kristian Prestgard found employment. It was Kopperud who for many years as editor secured *Nordisk Tidende*'s success. Christensen summarized, "His intimate knowledge of everything Norwegian,[and] his bold, and straightforward style were to the readers' taste and the number of subscribers increased." "It was in these years," Christensen concluded, that "*Tidende* beat *Blade.*" He acknowledged the real war between the two journals, but in the small Norwegian colony encountering each other was inevitable, and when the "two Nielsens met, they readily shared a beaker and 'warmed up' about the olden days."

Emil Nielsen died unexpectedly of pneumonia in his forty-ninth year, the winter of 1907. *Nordisk Tidende*'s March 14 obituary described him as "a unique person . . . [who] liked a good fight and always did battle with what he believed to be wrong." Peter Christensen, who for many years had been in the employ of the newspaper, managed and edited *Nordisk Tidende* for Nielsen's widow, Sofie Wikberg Nielsen, whom Nielsen had married when living in Finland. The Norwegian News Company, formed by E. T. Christensen and David Tulloch, shortly purchased the newspaper. The colony in 1910 consisted of 22,280 Norwegian-born residents and 10,899 of the second generation; the crews of the thousand or so Norwegian ships that annually called at the port of New York placed their stamp on the colony. Affluent men sponsored *Nordisk Tidende,* and, Roedder affirmed, "also it—satisfactorily or less satisfactorily edited—could in 1909 register that it lived on own resources with an edition of about seven to eight thousand—half of which went to paying subscribers and the remainder for single sales." It was then, as Christensen asserted, the only Norwegian newspaper in the East; even so, he predicted, "a distribution like the large Scandinavian newspapers in the West have, is and will be out of the question." The national journals published in the Upper Midwest would indeed for decades to come dominate Norwegian American newspaper distribution.[36]

A National Communications Network

"It was a foregone conclusion," stated Kenneth Bjork, "that wherever Norwegians—alone or in combination with Danes—were at all numerous, someone with a bit of capital would organize a publishing company and put out a newspaper in the Danish-Norwegian language." Many journals as a consequence saw the light of day in small and large towns and in large metropolitan areas; most perished very shortly. The least successful ventures were often partisan journals published to promote a specific cause or political candidacy. Expectations of success were frequently unrealistic given rival publications and limited numbers of potential subscribers. Means to begin a newspaper might come from supporting groups and individuals or, as the present chapter suggests, were accumulated by immigrant printers, who might in addition to publishing a Norwegian-language journal print other jobs on the side. Success escaped the majority. The initial challenge was to entice subscribers, then to convince them to honor the annual subscription fee. The publishers put forth compelling bonuses for new subscribers, lowered the subscription price, and regularly printed strong editorial urgings for delinquent subscribers to pay up.

Hardships and failures notwithstanding, by 1900 a national interactive Norwegian American press was a functioning reality; small and large journals cited each other, engaged in heated exchanges of opinions, cooperated, and created a Norwegian-language journalistic network from coast to coast. The press promoted a sense of a Norwegian America that stretched from the eastern seaboard, across the midwestern states and Rocky Mountains, all the way to the Pacific Coast. The many newspapers informed their readers about Norwegians living in other parts of the United States; they carried local news from a wide area. The individual newspapers filled their columns as well with news from the Nordic homelands and other parts of the world, news frequently gleaned from newspapers published in Norway, or from the Yankee press, as it was referred to, and then translated into Dano-Norwegian. The close cooperation between Danish and Norwegian journals, and the many Danes who found employment in ostensibly Norwegian publications, prevent a clear national distinction. The immigrant newspapers were the main source of information for individuals lacking a reading knowledge of English; in addition to local, national, and world news, they gave advice on a great number of issues, responded to questions from their readers, and offered special columns on farming, market prices, and appeals for the assistance of immigrants in need. The newspapers took part in every aspect of the immigrants' lives and came to be considered personal friends. They were distinctly democratic and projected a popular image.

In addition to the so-called Big Three, *Skandinaven, Decorah-Posten,* and *Minneapolis Tidende,* regional newspapers rose above failed competitors to become a representative voice. *Normanden* in North Dakota, *Fremad* in South Dakota, and *Bikuben* in Utah are examples of developments in the Norwegian American world of journalism. In the Pacific Northwest *Washington Posten* secured a prominent position; Minnesota's *Duluth Skandinav* and across the bay *Superior Tidende* in Wisconsin both exercised considerable journalistic influence. On the East Coast *Nordisk Tidende* surfaced as the major news organ. Other regional newspapers can be included in the list of journals with continuing service for some length. The point, however, is the reality that the Norwegian community in the United States had access to publications in a familiar language wherever they settled.[37]

Visergutten.

Story City, Iowa, Torsdag, den 26de Januar, 1911.

CHAPTER 5

Community and Public Affairs

The press—with its servants and subscribers—constitutes in a sense the concept often designated “Norwegian America.” It is the framework around everything else, even when the picture has gained such bright colors and impressive forms that the frame itself seems to disappear.[1]

HISTORIAN ARLOW ANDERSEN posited that “Norwegian American newspapers provided the window through which readers viewed the nation and the world from their secluded habitats in rural settlements and urban enclaves.” The weekly visitors were naturally, as has been demonstrated, a significant medium for news and opinion; politics and other public affairs received editorial attention. The newspapers entertained their readers with short stories and serialized novels, advertised services and products—both patent medicine and imported ethnic food items—and printed letters from readers filled with trifling local reports as well as polemics; journals announced cultural events, social meetings, and religious services. In a parallel fashion the ethnic press—of which the Norwegian American was a constituent part—socialized its readers to life in America as it educated them and gave them a sense of citizenship in the new society.

The Norwegian American press unified the ethnic group and transmitted shared national values, religious views, and cultural heritage from the homeland, while giving voice to an evolving reinvented sense of ethnic identity in the new environment. As a tool of adjustment, the press promoted pride in Norwegian ancestry as well as economic and political power. The Norwegian-language journals reported extensively on political, social, and cultural stirrings in the homeland. They interacted with newspapers published in Norway; indeed, their columns depended on news clipped from their colleagues "back home." "Judging from newly arrived Norwegian newspapers" was a common introductory sentence for news from Norway, or, more disappointing, "All mail from Norway was this time so delayed that we in this number could not include the regular stock of Norway news." The many correspondents who year after year reported from various parts of the homeland gave local and national news a personal bent. Telegraphic connection allowed for more immediate news releases; the mainstream English-language dailies enjoying news service became main sources. News releases from the Nordic consulates in Washington, D.C., were another significant avenue for information about public events. In 1916 *Minneapolis Tidende* became a United Press subscriber and in 1928 gleefully announced that through United Press it had established "its own telegraphic service, which is printed every Wednesday, without having to wait to see what the American newspapers bring." It therefore could avoid reliance upon what the American press deemed newsworthy. Relations between the Norwegian and Norwegian American press represented a two-way street. From the Norwegian American newspapers' genesis at mid-nineteenth century, their publishers sought to inform about, and at times defend, the experience of Norwegians in America by exchange arrangements with the homeland's press and by acquiring subscribers in Norway.

The current chapter will consider the historic developments leading to the dissolution of the Swedish-Norwegian Union as reported by Norwegian American journalists; the role played by the Norwegian American press in Norway itself; and the interpretation of the Norwegian community given by the Norwegian-language newspapers. Literary magazines of many kinds gained interest, as did serialized literature in the individual newspapers. Publishers devoted special columns and entire magazines to women's issues. In the reform agitation carried by the Norwegian American newspapers, women's rights were regularly featured, though by no means consistently in support of gender equality; even more pervasive was the agitation for the temperance cause where women played a significant role. The editorials and reports by columnists provide an educational journey into the Norwegian American press and its cognate audiences in the United States and in Norway.[2]

The Norwegian American Press and the Union Crisis

Decorah-Posten's longtime editor Kristian Prestgard described the Norwegian American newspapers "as a large, clear window that faces toward the home community and the immigrants' youth with all its precious memories." Immigrants and later generations harbored great concern for the welfare of the ancestral homeland; those born in Norway might in their memories recall sorrow as well as joy, and they were much aware of the poverty and limited opportunities that propelled their own departures. Relief for Norway was forthcoming, usually initiated and administered by Norwegian newspaper publishers; such disasters as the huge landslide in Verdal, east of Trondheim, in 1893 with 112 casualties or a raging storm in the Lofoten fishing grounds the same year, also with great loss of life, had immediate repercussions in the Norwegian population in America; appeals for aid and lists of donors appeared promptly in the columns of Norwegian American newspapers.

The Norwegian American press kept its readers well informed about happenings in the homeland; the constant stream of immigrants, reaching a high mark in the 1880s, also conveyed impulses from political movements and social reforms. Newspapers covered political movement toward greater democracy in opposition to royal power and the ensuing constitutional conflict; from 1883, when the conflict moved toward impeachment of the sitting Norwegian government, *Budstikken* regularly carried articles explaining the nature of the controversy. Nicolay Grevstad, earlier editor of the liberal *Dagbladet* in Norway and active in the Norwegian American press, predicted that the conflict would not end "without bloodshed" and was convinced that a coup would occur. Norwegian Americans, intensely interested in Norway's political battles between liberals and conservatives about constitutional principles, formed the Norwegian American Liberal Society *(Den Norsk-Amerikanske Venstreforening)* in January 1884 in Minneapolis. Its appeal, printed in Norwegian American newspapers, read:

> Our old fatherland's independence and freedom are at stake. Threats against its constitution reach over to us, and we would be poor sons of a freedom-loving people and even poorer citizens of America if this would be a matter of indifference to us.

In April the Liberal Society, whose treasurer was Luth Jæger, editor of *Budstikken,* sent four thousand *kroner* to Johan Sverdrup, the leader of the Liberal Party *(Venstre). Budtsikken* editorialized, "contributions were made by a considerable number of Swedes," and attacked the royalist editor of *Svenska Folkets Tidning* (Swedish People's Times) in Minneapolis for his "hatred of Norwegians." The liberal and secular Swedish-language Chicago weekly *Svenska Tribunen* (The Swedish Tribune) opined "that the opinion of Swedish Americans on this serious issue is by and large completely pro-liberal." These sentiments would change radically as the union crisis deepened in the 1890s and put an end to an urban Scandinavianism carried forward by a Nordic elite. May 17, as an example, changed from a pan-Scandinavian festival day to an exclusively Norwegian observance.

In Norway impeachment proceedings against the government were set and in the course of the first few months of 1884 the sitting prime minister and his ministers were removed from office. In June, circumstances convinced the union king Oscar II to appoint Sverdrup, the leader of the largest political party in the *Storting,* prime minister, thereby introducing a parliamentary system. The Liberal Society, soon to be dissolved, sent a telegram with good wishes "for the democratic victory which has been won in Norway by the newly accomplished constitutional reforms." This radical change strengthened democratic forces and weakened royal power; it also weakened the union, because the monarchy had been the single unifying power. *Skandinaven* printed a thank-you letter from Sverdrup for Chicago's Norwegian community's assistance: "I accept, gentlemen, with more gratitude than I am able to express the testimonial you give me about confidence and approval." Regardless of political color in the United States, the entire Norwegian American press seemingly gave its support to the most nationalistic political initiatives in Norway.

The cause that led to the dissolution of the Swedish-Norwegian Union was Norway's desire to establish its own foreign consular service. From the Norwegian viewpoint, the joint diplomatic corps favored Swedish interests, especially since the nationality of the joint foreign minister by unilateral Swedish action would be Swedish. The conflict over foreign representation began with the introduction of parliamentary control of the government and intensified in the 1890s. The need for a separate consular service related to not only national pride but also the reality of basic economic and commercial differences between Sweden and Norway. Provocations from the Norwegian government, in serial actions insisting on Norway's right to conduct its own affairs and allocations of funds for a separate Norwegian foreign representation, led to perilous confrontations. These were given front-page attention and strident editorial commentary in America. *Skandinaven* printed a regular column titled "The Crisis in Norway" that encouraged an emotional response from its readers from coast to coast.

Throughout the nation, Norwegian American newspapers reported with great sadness on the *Storting*'s June 7, 1895, resolution and the humiliating retreat it represented from the bold course the Liberal Party had pursued in "its demands for Norway's complete independence in all national issues." The Norwegian representatives had backed down under the possible use of Swedish military might; Norway's subordinate position in the Union was made visible. In the resolution Norway had agreed to negotiate with Sweden about the state of the Union and to abandon the policy of confrontation. The Norwegian American press persisted in its close reporting on "the period of negotiation," beginning in 1895, and Norway's rapid military armament the political defeat gave rise to. The final phase of the controversy between the two Union partners may be dated to 1898, when the *Storting* adopted universal male suffrage as a further democratization of society and in December unilaterally declared the "pure" flag *(rene Flag)* the law of the land. "The time has now come for every patriotic Norwegian to display our country's flag," announced an advertiser for "the Pure Flag" in

Skandinaven.

SEMI-WEEKLY—PART I

Nummer 23—B. Chicago, St. Paul og Minneapolis, Fredag 9de Juni 1905. 40de Aargang.

Kong Oscar har ophørt at regjere i Norge—Regjeringen styrer.

Storthinget erklærer Kongen afsat og Unionen opløst.

En provisorisk Regjering organiseret med Michelsen som Statschef—Kongen anmodes om at samvirke ved Valg af ny Konge—Proklamation til Folket—Norges Folk tolker sin Tilslutning til Storthinget med værdig Ro—Afgjørende Vendepunkt i Norges Historie.

Mæglingen.

Diktatoren.

Following the June 7, 1905, resolution by the Storting, Skandinaven *(June 9, 1905) proudly announced "King Oscar has ceased to govern Norway—the Norwegian government rules." The paper's publisher, John Anderson, at his rolltop desk in his office on Peoria Avenue, headed the efforts of the Norwegian National League in Chicago to gain international recognition of the new Norwegian government.*

Skandinaven in February 1898 in advance of the December parliamentary declaration. The Norwegian national emblem without the Union insignia in the corner had been flown earlier both in Norway and among Norwegians in America.

Negotiations between Norway and Sweden ultimately failed; Norwegian national self-consciousness had been a strong deciding factor. On June 7, 1905, the *Storting* declared the Norwegian throne vacant and the union with Sweden dissolved. Few events have had a more powerful impact on Norwegian American society. "King Oscar has ceased to govern Norway—the Norwegian government rules," *Skandinaven* declared in its June 9 issue. John Anderson, *Skandinaven*'s publisher, headed the efforts of the Norwegian National League in Chicago to come to the aid of the homeland and gain international recognition of the new Norwegian government, as the situation between Norway and Sweden deteriorated and the possibility of war between "the brother people" loomed. Petitions, lobbying activity, and mass meetings promoted the cause of diplomatic recognition of Norway's independence. War was averted; following a national referendum on dissolution and a September accord signed at Karlstad, Sweden, the United States joined Russia and Belgium on October 30 to be the first nations to officially recognize a fully independent Norway. "Finally," *Washington Posten* reported in Seattle, "it has come to the point that Norwegian men and women can have a say in their own destiny."

The ultimate confirmation of the homeland's complete sovereignty was the ascension of King Haakon VII to Norway's throne. *Skandinaven* provided a detailed account of the royal coronation in the Nidaros Cathedral in Trondheim in late June 1906 and the reception of a Norwegian American delegation by King Haakon and Queen Maud at the royal mansion. As reported by the newspaper, the delegation was warmly greeted by His Majesty and assured that he was "fully cognizant of and grateful for the powerful moral support that the Norwegian American stand during the crisis the previous year had rendered Norway." One may easily conclude that the new monarchy and the homeland's greater national visibility strengthened a positive Norwegian American self-image.[3]

Norwegian Readers and Correspondents

Official Norway was slow in trying to establish a closer systematic contact with the Norwegian American community; in the years after 1900 a greater appreciation of the life of Norwegians and their descendants in America gained public notice. At the individual level, of course, emigrated kin kept up close relations through letters and visits to the home turf. The connection was for a long time cultivated rather one-sidedly by Norwegian Americans. The Norwegian American newspapers played a significant role in acquainting people back home with the growth and functioning of a Norwegian American subculture. In 1948, Didrik Arup Seip, professor of Nordic linguistics and for a period president of the University of Oslo, related how Norwegians in America kept considerable contact with the most isolated communities—like Åseral where he grew up—and the outside world:

> When I was a boy, I learned to know the name America before I heard about any other foreign country. And I heard about New York and Chicago before I heard about London and Berlin. Names like Dakota and Minnesota I heard more often than Spain and France. The reason was that I grew up in a Norwegian mountain community that had sent many of its young men and also women to America; there came continuously letters and there came Norwegian American newspapers. We read about life on the prairie and in the forests. Every Christmas there came Norwegian Americans who told us about the world there on the other side of the ocean. . . . High up in our mountain community we had a lively cultural contact with America; news from there gave us a broader outlook, and nourished the imagination.

Professor Arup Seip, as a young man in his mountain community, would also find news items about Norway in the Norwegian American journals; all major journals had correspondents and contacts in many parts of the country. In 1924, for instance, *Decorah-Posten* reported that it had twenty-five correspondents in Norway; these contributed local news, "of great and small things from town and country, births and deaths, weather and wind, old ways of livelihood and new enterprises, in other words, everything that occurred in the old home districts." No newspaper in Norway could do the same. Norwegians joked that people in Norway subscribed to *Decorah-Posten* or other Norwegian American newspapers to keep informed about what was going on in their own country.

Most subscriptions in Norway were gifts from emigrated kin and friends in America; in addition several journals formed exchange relationships with Norwegian newspapers. News about the Norwegian American community as well as letters from individual Norwegian Americans, generally from people of prominence, appeared on the pages of Norway's urban newspapers. The press indeed functioned as an international bridge. Even in current times, a number of people in Norway have reported excitedly the discovery of old copies of Norwegian American newspapers in attics and in nearly forgotten chests of drawers. The circulation and influence in Norway of the products of immigrant journalism constitute an important, but alas greatly neglected, chapter in the history of Norwegian immigration to America. These newspapers have left surprisingly little archival or library evidence. Contacts with Norway's National Archives, Postal Museum, Central Bureau of Statistics, local historical societies, the Norwegian Institute of Local History, the Norwegian Association of Media History, and articles in appropriate journals have garnered much good will but precious few resources. One is tempted to conclude that keepers of historical records in an earlier generation did not consider Norwegian American publications and related materials worthy of preservation despite clear evidence of their contemporary importance.

In 1897, Olav Kringen, who had served as contributing editor of *Nye Normanden* from its founding in 1894 and then returned to his native Norway, wrote: "Here came *Rodhuggeren, Fremad, Vesterheimen* and *Nye Normanden* with fresh news from America." Kringen became a leading personality in the Norwegian labor movement; his journalistic career and Socialist associations in the United States, as well as his selection of Norwegian American dissenting weeklies, suggest a continuous influence of Norwegian American political journals on his political reform efforts in Norway. Kringen edited the Labor Party's official organ, *Social-Demokraten* (The Social Democrat); he belonged to the moderate reform wing of the party, which advocated social-democratic processes. His contributions to the radical Socialist newspaper *Gaa Paa* (Press Forward) in Minneapolis and correspondence with its publisher Emil Lauritz Mengshoel are further evidence of an exchange of impulses between political idealists in Norway and the United States.[4]

The main, often only, source of knowledge about the presence of the Norwegian American press in the homeland remains the information provided in newspapers' columns. From pioneer days on, Norwegian American newspaper publishers have sought a readership in Norway. In September 1853, *Emigranten* assured its readers that the newspaper could be sent weekly "to the most distant regions, within and also outside the United States, even all the way to Norway." It was, however, as *Emigranten* explained in a later issue, a circuitous and costly route. All the same, *Fædrelandet* announced in 1864 that it had "not an insignificant number of subscribers in Norway."

The improved transportation and postal service following the American Civil War made the procedure simpler and less expensive. An Oslo letter dated October 1866 and published in *Skandinaven* began: "I keep up with the American newspapers as much as possible: then I read *Emigranten,* then *Fædrelandet,* and then *Skandinaven.*" The correspondent indicated the value the newspapers had in broadly disseminating news about the Norwegian American community. "Your Synod affair is a strange commodity," he stated, "I do not believe there are many here who agree with 'the Slavery Synod,' which it usually is called here." From the Civil War issues, he moves on to let *Skandinaven*'s readers know that "There is much ado in the newspapers here about the emigration, especially in regard to the direct steamship connection between America and Scandinavia."

In the weeks before the Christmas holidays, throughout the history of the Norwegian-language press in America, publishers regularly recommended their newspaper as an excellent Christmas gift. *Nye Normanden* in its holiday greetings consistently addressed its readers on both sides of the Atlantic, clearly having secured a readership also in Norway. *Budstikken* asked in 1883: "Ought not *Budstikken* sent home every week from now until next Christmas be one of the most valuable presents one could send? This for consideration by the many who have family and friends in Norway or Denmark"; similarly *Minneapolis Tidende* in 1934 suggested: "Give a year's subscription on *Minneapolis Tidende* to father, mother, sister or brother. In case you have family in Norway, you have no doubt seen from experience how happy they are when they hear from America. . . . The newspaper will be a weekly greeting from you for an entire year."

Skandinaven took the next logical step in January 1874 by offering potential readers in Norway and Denmark a special semimonthly European edition of the newspaper. It would be different from the American version:

> Since the number of the newspapers weekly sent to Europe, especially to Norway and Denmark, has grown, and convinced that if the [subscription] price, which until now, because of the postage, has been very high, could become more reasonable, many more would subscribe and send the newspaper to family and acquaintances at home, we have resolved to publish a European edition of *Skandinaven*. It will come out every two weeks, but as the serial stories, and also foreign news and advertising, which have no interest for European readers, will not be included, this edition for our people at home will be just as valuable as the weekly. Contributed pieces of news, correspondence etc. from the daily and weekly editions, with the exception of the above-mentioned, will have space in the European edition, which is of the same size as the weekly, namely 10 columns, so that the European reader will get 40 columns of reading material.

The annual subscription price was $2.50 in advance—later reduced to $2.00. No extant copy of the European edition has been located, but it clearly enjoyed success. In November 1875 *Skandinaven* reported that during the last few weeks, more than one hundred new subscribers had signed up, making the editor note that "this fully shows that it can look forward to a steadily increasing favor and a growing interest among our countrymen on both sides of the Atlantic Ocean." It thus found a readership in Norway from its first issue in January 1874 until it was discontinued in September 1893; the weekly edition of *Skandinaven* was thereafter offered to European subscribers. In May 1891, Fredrik Bagge submitted a long letter of gratitude from Oslo to *Skandinaven*: "Through my brother Einar Bagge, who works at a large watch and jewelry store in Chicago, I have become acquainted with *Skandinaven,* which by

A promotional advertisement for Skandinaven *from around 1900 described the periodical as "The oldest and largest Norwegian newspaper in America." The sales pitch, translated in part, continued: "Published in a daily, semi-weekly, and Sunday edition"; "A spokesman and guide for the Norwegian people in America"; "A connecting link between the homes on both sides of the ocean"; "A number of prominent men and women living over here or in Norway are regular contributors to* Skandinaven*"; "Subscribe to* Skandinaven*"; "Send the newspaper to family and friends in the old country as a greeting from kinsmen on this side of the ocean."*

him is sent us every fourteenth day, and we are very happy every time the newspaper comes. There is so much news and different from what we are accustomed to." Surely, as Bagge suggested in his correspondence, the newspaper was a connecting link across the Atlantic and familiarized the Norwegian public with conditions among their compatriots in America.[5]

The Artist Printer in 1891 gave this assessment of how *Skandinaven*'s European edition was received:

> The European edition, made up entirely of American home news, having its circulation almost exclusively in Norway, Denmark, and Sweden, and there regarded as authority on all matters pertaining to America, and which, with the exception of the New York *Herald,* is the only newspaper in the United States, prepared especially for European circulation.

The circulation of Norwegian American newspapers in Norway is difficult to estimate; no official registry exists. The newspapers themselves from time to time emphasized the extent of their presence in the homeland. Augsburg Seminary professor Sven Oftedal's weekly *Folkebladet* in Minneapolis announced December 2, 1880, that "of this number, of which 500 go to Norway, will be sent some sample copies." The weekly, which from 1881 was co-owned by the two prominent Lutheran church leaders Oftedal and Georg Sverdrup, likely had easy access to low-church Lutheran circles in the homeland. All evidence, however, shows that *Decorah-Posten* had the honor of being the most widely circulated Norwegian American newspaper; the publisher in 1885 reminded gift recipients in Norway that they could extend the subscription by sending "us six *kroner* in Norwegian currency." By 1901, *Decorah-Posten,* then published twice weekly, reported 980 foreign subscribers, mainly in Norway; by 1924 the number of subscribers abroad, not including Canada, had grown to 1,183. The newspaper had a much larger readership than subscription figures indicate; it circulated in the neighborhood and encouraged lively commentary about a world most readers only encountered in its columns.

Decorah-Posten's distribution spanned the disparate regions of Norway's lengthy and sparsely populated territory. In a long series of installments in 1900 and 1901 under the title "Greetings from

Decorah-Posten's subscribers to family and friends in the old countries," the newspaper listed the names and addresses of those who received the newspaper in Denmark and Norway; there were only a few Danish recipients, but even a cursory examination of Norwegian benefactors shows that *Decorah-Posten* arrived at addresses throughout the length of the country, from north to south. Heavy emigration districts, as expected, were the most deluged by the Norwegian American press; most donors were residents of the Upper Midwest, where the journal had its densest circulation, though the newspaper had gift subscribers in other parts of the United States as well. Helga Balstad's letter from Kristiansund, Norway, dated November 25, 1918, to her brother, Daniel C. Jordahl in Minnesota might be illustrative of *Decorah-Posten*'s everyday familiarity for many people in the old country. "I read *Decorah-Posten,*" she related, "(I don't know who gives it to me. Is it you?) and full of terror I begin with the list of casualties [from World War I]—thank and praise God that I until now have been spared finding the names of those who are closest to us." Letters with wide references to *Decorah-Posten*'s content were surely commonplace during the era of Norwegian emigration. The newspaper also became a source for family histories. In 1950, following extensive collection efforts, Ola Kvisle published genealogy charts for residents and emigrants from the rural Numedal and Sigdal communities in Buskerud County; *Decorah-Posten*'s published obituaries furnished the information from America.

Unlike *Decorah-Posten*'s national outreach, *Visergutten* had a pronounced local focus. Reflecting the origin in Norway of the newspaper's American subscribers and their contact with kin and acquaintances in Norway, 435 of the beneficiaries lived in Rogaland and 239 in Hordaland; these two counties on Norway's southwest coast thus represented about 96 percent of all Norwegian subscriptions; these were spread throughout the region, touching isolated farm communities in west Norway's fjord districts and on coastal islands, as well as commercial centers like Haugesund, Sandnes, and Stavanger.

Visergutten also reached Mosterhamn in Rogaland County, the home of one of the newspaper's most productive correspondents: Håkon Pedersen, known as "the shoemaker scribe in Mosterhamn," who beginning in 1909 and until toward the end of his life in 1925, at the age of seventy-eight, wrote some seventy letters to *Visergutten* under the signature dePers. Pedersen was likely more productive than most contributors to the Norwegian American press; his literary missives from Norway to a reading public in America are emblematic of a much larger practice. Throughout the land individuals from all walks of life took pen in hand to communicate with emigrated compatriots through the columns of Norwegian-language journals across the Atlantic; Pedersen was likely more passionate and talented in his press dispatches than most, albeit his was not an exceptional pursuit. Martin Nag collected and edited the letters made available in two publications titled *America Letters from Moster.*

The letters revealed the creative intellect of a man well versed in literature and Norse mythology. In their descriptions of life in an island community, they moved beyond the mundane—which certainly also was present in descriptions of the fisheries, harvesting, economic woes, greetings from and to named persons, weddings, and funerals—to engage in philosophical debates over the nature of Christianity in particular and religion in general. Pedersen was at odds with many of the beliefs of Lutheran pastors in America and did not hesitate to find fault with emigrants from the community, especially "how they fly at one another in scribblings in *Visergutten*'s columns." *Visergutten*'s subscribers in Norway as well as America read his observations. His obituary, as cited by Nag, stated that his religious concepts and view of life made him a controversial figure in his home community. As a bridge-building project his correspondence may as a consequence assume added primacy and interest.[6]

The Norwegian Language in America

Norwegian immigrants in the nineteenth century and even later arrived in America with two linguistic traditions. A multitude of local urban and rural vernaculars conveyed the warmth of family togetherness and a sense of kinship with others who shared the local Norwegian dialect; in settlements of fellow Norwegians they proceeded to use it in daily associations and pass a local linguistic heritage on to later generations. The Dano-Norwegian literary language assumed a near sacred standing, consecrated by its oral usage in religious services and the written word of the Bible. Formal Dano-Norwegian speech, impacted by Norwegian pronunciation, began in the church, spread to colleges and seminaries, and was taken up by the literati and political office-seekers. It was a cherished and familiar idiom, which Norwegian Americans understood to be Norwegian. All literature the Norwegian American community encountered in educational, religious, and secular spheres was written in the standard Norwegian of the nineteenth century; it was, as stated previously, a norm taken from Danish.

The fact that the literary forms did not conform well to Norwegian speech habits, social and cultural forces, and awakening Norwegian nationalist sentiments launched two seemingly irreconcilable movements to create a separate Norwegian written language and eliminate Danish. Educator and linguist Knud Knudsen headed a determined effort to Norwegianize the written language—in style, word selection, spelling, and sentence structure—in accord with urban speech; the self-taught linguist Ivar Aasen on the other hand worked for a totally Norwegian written language based on rural speech. In his extensive studies, Aasen showed a clear continuity between Old Norse and the many rural dialects and set out to create a new Norwegian literary form based on these rural vernaculars. Aasen called the new written language *Landsmaal* (nation-wide language); it gained legal equality with Danish in 1885. Knudsen's linguistic reform, *Rigsmaal* (later spelled *Riksmål*)—national language—was officially adopted in Norway in 1907, replacing the Danish standard, followed by further linguistic reforms in 1917 and 1938. Around 1900, strong objections to Aasen's version of Norwegian politicized an already emotional debate between the two language camps. In a letter to *Visergutten* in May 1912, Håkon Pedersen shared his distaste for Aasen's *Landsmaal* with the newspaper's readers: "I have written against these advocates of *Landsmaal,* but I have been reprimanded to a degree that is horrible to read." Pedersen found solace, as he wrote, in the thought that his critics "stood on a low rung in their breeding."[7]

Aasen's *Landsmaal,* from 1929 termed *Nynorsk* (New Norwegian), gained few adherents among Norwegians in America. Newspaper publishers occasionally printed letters and poems written in that standard but generally expressed hostility toward the new linguistic creation. However, in 1897 reform-minded Hans A. Foss serialized the *Landsmaal* author Hans Seland in *Nye Normanden.* Those expressing their support for the *Landsmaal* standard offered it and the culture it emanated from as a more genuinely Norwegian alternative to the Dano-Norwegian literary forms. In 1900 Peer Storeygard launched the monthly *Norrøna. Det fyrste Blad paa Norskt Maal i Vesterheimen* (The Norse. The First Magazine in the Norwegian Language in the Western Home) in Walnut Grove, Minnesota, as a voice of the cause of *Landsmaal* among Norwegians in America. It was discontinued in 1901, and after being inactive for many years, it was revived in Fargo, North Dakota, and published there from 1914 to 1915. Storeygard's second attempt to make a success of *Norrøna* was prompted by the unveiling of a bust of Ivar Aasen in 1913 on the campus of Concordia College in Moorhead, Minnesota; the magazine held language to be the most significant part of the national culture and expressed an idealistic, national, and romantic language policy. The monthly was, however, inferior to competing Norwegian American magazines and hardly reached a thousand subscribers. In 1902–3, the author Jon Norstog, then a recent immigrant from Telemark, put out six issues of another *Landsmaal* magazine titled *Dølen. Tidsskrift paa Norsk Maal* (The Dalesman. Magazine in the Norwegian Language) in Joice, Iowa; he was later a regular contributor to *Norrøna.* Most Norwegian immigrants dismissed *Landsmaal* and the later *Nynorsk* as old-fashioned and irrelevant.

In reality, a Norwegianization of the Dano-Norwegian written forms did not gain much favor in the Norwegian American community either; *Rigsmaal,* from 1929 *Bokmål* (Book Language), with its series of orthographic reforms, was possibly even viewed as a betrayal of a common cultural heritage. A letter writer to *Sioux Falls Posten* in Sioux Falls, South Dakota, in 1910 expressed a common Norwegian American sentiment in regard to both *Rigsmaal* and *Landsmaal:*

> Indeed, if the good gentlemen in Norway wish in the future to have contact with us Norwegian Americans on this side of the ocean, then do not in any way adopt any new language, which we will have

> trouble understanding, because then we will soon turn our back to you, and only employ this country's valid language.

All major Norwegian American newspapers initially refused to adopt the new and changing standard: for their aging readers, having learned Dano-Norwegian before emigrating, the Danish standard represented a treasured literary legacy; besides, a move away from Dano-Norwegian put at risk the hard-won subscriptions from Danish American readers. A major concern was the preservation of any Norwegian language in a multicultural environment; confusion from linguistic reform challenged efforts to maintain the mother tongue. In 1926, Kristian Prestgard summed up the situation in *Decorah-Posten:*

> We newly examined the first volume of *Decorah-Posten* and found that the newspaper's linguistic form in 1874 was to a high degree exactly the same as the one now in 1926. And this is how it is with all Norwegian newspapers here in the Northwest. But this has brought us into the quite curious situation that our newspapers maintain a language dress that no longer exists in Norway or Denmark. We have become something for ourselves between the two.

In his memoirs, Prestgard explained that *Decorah-Posten* had five thousand Danish readers, whereas a newspaper like *Minneapolis Tidende* had only few Danish subscribers, a fact that encouraged *Decorah-Posten*'s conservative linguistic form. Only in 1939 did *Decorah-Posten* bring its orthography into line with the minor changes adopted in 1907, ignoring the more substantial reform in the written language in 1917 and the much greater changes in 1938. News releases from Norway and articles taken from Norwegian journals were edited to conform to *Decorah-Posten*'s use of the 1907 *Rigsmaal* standard. It continued to capitalize nouns until 1961, to use Danish-voiced consonants after vowels almost to the end, and to print the newspaper in Gothic type until 1952. Immigrants were clearly conservative in their cultural preferences, especially in the Norwegian heartland; even so *Decorah-Posten* was clearly more loyal to tradition than many of its colleagues. Erling Innvik, one of *Decorah-Posten*'s later editors, explained that the paper survived most of its Norwegian-language competitors, so it became "a newspaper written for old people by old people."

Newspaper publishers on the Atlantic and Pacific coasts, however, replaced Gothic with Latin types early on, as did a few newspapers in the Midwest; in August 1912, however, when the Fargo newspaper *Fram*—adhering to common practice in Norway—instigated Latin types, readers' negative response prompted a return to Gothic after only three issues. During the interwar years most Norwegian American newspapers made some accommodation to the Norwegian 1917 language reform; *Washington Posten* even modernized its orthography through the substantial 1938 revision of standard *Bokmål.* The adoption of English words and terminology into the journalistic language mix in order to explain American political and social circumstances distanced Norwegian American language usage even further from the homeland's written standard. For example, newspapers consistently used the word "bill" for a legislative motion, even adding the Norwegian inflection *-en (Billen)* for "the bill," rather than a Norwegian equivalent; they used words like "office" for a government position instead of *Embede,* "trustees," no Norwegian equivalent being immediate, and *Legislaturen* for the legislature, or the use of the word "store" for a commercial site since the Norwegian *Butikk* perhaps gave a different mental image; these and many other Anglicisms appeared in the Norwegian American press. This part of the acculturation process deserves its own systematic study beyond what the Norwegian American linguist Einar Haugen found.[8]

The Rural Culture Makes Its Mark

The Norwegian American community's organizational life was accorded prominence in the group's publications. Societies of many kinds and their publications had a direct influence on the press and consequently deserve a place in its history. The many organizations known as *bygdelag* (old home societies) represented a rural heritage; they sought to legitimize their rural cultural heritage as an accepted and respected expression of Norwegian identity. Each society gathered immigrants—and to a certain extent the children of immigrants—with common roots in a particular community or group of communities or a general district, fjord region, or valley. In these nationwide societies, the majority of members were thus rural, midwestern, Lutheran, and Norwegian-born. At annual reunions, termed *stevne,* members in a sense festively re-created and celebrated the Norwegian ancestral *bygd,* or rural community. As this author wrote in a previous work, "Their identity was tied to the home and geographical place they had left behind, making the *bygdelag* a strategy to enable them to return to a pre-modern rural world and the sense of permanence and place it accorded."

The first *bygdelag,* Valdres Samband (Valdres Union), convened in 1899; by 1913 the thirty-one major societies had all been organized. Their names proclaimed members' Norwegian home district with designations like Hallinglaget and Telelaget (both formed in 1907), Sognalaget and Trønderlaget (1908), Vosselaget, Gudbrandsdalslaget, Setesdalslaget, Nordfjordlaget, and Nordlandslaget (1909), Hardangerlaget and the large Stavanger Amt Laget (1911). Special columns in Norwegian American newspapers throughout the land announced their annual reunions and gave extensive reports on the two- to three-day festivities. *Normanden* in Grand Forks printed separate pages under the heading "Normandens Bygdelag Tidende" (*Normanden*'s Bygdelag Times), and *Skandinaven* and *Decorah-Posten* both had a section simply titled "Bygdelagene" (The Bygdelag). Leaders and loyal members contributed a bevy of letters to the Norwegian American press. These give insight into the motivating forces that gathered people at large colorful events to celebrate a particular local rural heritage in speech, culinary dishes, dress, and social conventions. Surely the small towns and central marketplaces that hosted the reunions welcomed the revenue they contributed to the local economy; the Norwegian-language press noted these commercial benefits as well.[9]

Some journals, depending on subscribers' and publishers' origin in Norway, showed a certain bias in their news coverage for specific societies, though no *bygdelag* was excluded from any newspaper's columns. *Nordvesten* in St. Paul, edited by Christian Brandt from Valdres, spoke for Valdres Samband; *Visergutten* in Canton, occasionally referred to as *Rogalandbladet*—the Rogaland newspaper—declared itself the special organ of the twin societies of Sunnhordlandslaget and Stavanger Amt Laget; the Fargo newspaper *Fram,* as edited by A. A. Trovaten from Telemark, carried a special Tele column and with the Halling immigrant Ingvald H. Ulsaker in charge frequently added special news about Hallinglaget. *Duluth Skandinav* and *Superior Tidende,* which shared a publisher, devoted an entire page to *Trønder Tidende* (The Trønder Times), where they filled their columns with news about Trøndelag and its natives—Trønders—in America and their precious Trønderlaget; Nordlandslaget and correspondence from north Norway were also popular features.

The Norwegian American press made it possible to communicate with the individual *bygdelag*'s membership. Such societies as Telelaget, Sognalaget, and Setesdalslaget did so in their local dialect. The annual reunions gave opportunity to speak the local vernacular with enthusiasm and pride; immigrants treasured the occasion to use these rustic expressions of home, which created self-confidence and interest in regional lore and traditions. In few other venues would peasant speech gain comparable acceptance. In their own publications—annual, quarterly, or monthly magazines—the *bygdelag* mainly used standard Dano-Norwegian, although a few tried to write in the local dialect. Its absence need not be seen as a lack of pride, but simply the inability of people trained in the literary Dano-Norwegian to use or even understand renderings of untutored peasant speech. Andrew A. Veblen, a founder of Valdres Samband, in *Valdris Helsing* (Valdres Greetings), published from 1903 to 1910, regularly employed dialect writing in articles, poems, and anecdotes. Torkel Oftelie as editor of *Telesoga* (The Telemark Saga) from 1909 to 1924 most consistently used dialect. He was here influenced by the orthography of *Landsmaal;* the difficult task of creating a written norm from dialect speech would discourage most people from even trying. The most successful efforts to use dialect material in printed form were made by immigrants from the mountain valleys and fjord districts of Norway.[10]

Hands across the Sea

The many *bygdelag* cultivated their kinship with the Norwegian home community; they collected aid money and arranged visits to the home sod. Local Norwegian youth societies *(ungdomslag)* in turn collected money to buy banners *(faner)* with motifs from the home district to send to America. The banners were there dedicated with great ceremony, treasured as a memento from home, and displayed in colorful processions. The *bygdelag* folk assembled around their individual emblems; the bonds with Norway were strengthened.

In the early 1900s a greater appreciation for what was commonly designated "Norwegian America" was made evident. Inspired by the fervent nationalism and dramatic events that in 1905 created a national Norwegian monarchy, a new organization taking the title Nordmanns-Forbundet—currently rendered in English as the Norse Federation—was founded in the Norwegian capital on June 21, 1907. The prospering Norwegian American community was heavily involved in its founding. It declared itself to be an international league of Norwegians in order "to gather the bloodline *[ætt]*, the Norwegian people, wherever they live in the world." In the columns of its journal, *Nordmanns-Forbundet,* it promulgated the romantic concept of "a greater Norway" *(et større Norge)* "together with the notion of 'the emigrated Norway' and the idea of *vor egen Stamme*—our own race or nation—to which Norwegians outside Norway also belonged." Unlike the *bygdelag,* the Federation had strong elitist qualities and cultivated prestigious and influential persons. The Federation didn't exclude commoners; in fact it eventually formed a close affiliation with the American *bygd* societies. The extreme parochialism the *bygdelag* fostered, however, conflicted with the Federation's advocacy of a common Norwegian national identity.

Nordmanns-Forbundet's inception and history call attention to a much-neglected aspect of emigration history: namely, national attitudes toward emigrated citizens. The proposition of "a greater Norway," if indeed accepted by Norwegians at home and abroad, would suggest a reinterpretation of Norwegian nationality fueled by the country's historic emigration experience. No doubt, a collective sense of Norwegian nationality, unifying all Norwegians—wherever they made their home—in a common cause to expand Norwegian culture and influence, would give Norway a greater voice in world affairs and enhance its international reputation. The United States became the Federation's most productive field of operation; in time members constituted local chapters throughout the country. The Norwegian American press and *Nordmanns-Forbundet,* the organization's membership journal, detailed the activities of the chapters and the home office in Norway. The latter publication featured the experience of Norwegians in the United States and around the world.

The Norwegian passenger company the Norwegian America Line adopted the slogan "Hands across the Sea," symbolizing the strength of ethnic bonds. In 1913 the line established direct service between Norway and the United States. Nordmanns-Forbundet had championed the initiative from the start. The idea of a Norwegian steamship that would ply between Norway and New York, carrying passengers and cargo, was appropriate in the context of the strong patriotic emotions regularly espoused during the post-Union years. The projected venture was received very favorably by the Norwegian American press; in its columns E. H. Hobe, Norwegian consul in St. Paul, promoted the sale of the company's stock in America. Prominently placed stock-subscription invitations appeared in newspapers from coast to coast; large stock purchases subsequently gave evidence of the appeal of a passenger line under the Norwegian flag. The first ship built, the SS *Kristianiafjord,* honored the Norwegian capital Kristiania (Oslo). *Pacific Skandinaven* in Portland, Oregon, in 1911, joining other members of the press, reassured its readers that in Norway "the country's best men support it . . . and not alone because it is a matter of national honor but also because it is a profitable enterprise." Constituted in August 1910, the steamship company in fact raised half of its capital among Norwegian Americans, which serves as an example of Norwegian American financial resources. Shortly before World War I, then, Norwegian immigrants and Norwegian Americans visiting Norway could travel on a Norwegian ship.

The author states the following in an earlier publication:

> In order to unite in a greater Norway the two homes of Norwegians—one in the west, the Western Home *(Vesterheimen),* and one in the east, Norway itself—a common historical narrative had to be realized. . . . The success of Norwegian Americans clearly bolstered the idea of a greater Norway, in which Norwegian America represented the other half of the Norwegian nation.

There were surely shared historical memories and national symbols, but the depiction of a common and uniting past was really only achieved with the two historical monographs by Ingrid Semmingsen, published in 1941 and 1950 and titled *Veien mot vest* (The Way West). The undertaking was initiated and supported by Nordmanns-Forbundet. Professor Semmingsen made Norwegian Americans an integral part of Norway's history. Norwegian Americans thus at last had been validated as true Norwegians by the homeland.

Norway and the Norwegian American community, even so, surely exhibited many disconnects. The Norwegian American press not only engaged in explaining and defending the Norwegian immigrant community when criticism and even condescension on occasion reached it from Norway, but also went so far as to lecture the homeland when it felt called to do so. Norwegian officialdom, cultural institutions, and even ordinary citizens were from time to time insensitive to their emigrated citizens and the changing circumstances of their life in America. *Vestkysten* (The West Coast) in Tacoma, Washington, as an example, editorially opened a campaign against a 1929 article in the Oslo magazine *Vor Verden* (Our World) by Tharald M. Hansen, who asked the question: "Do we in Norway overrate the significance of the contributions of Norwegians in America?" His strong affirmative response to his own query raised editor John Soley's dander. Hansen concluded that Norwegians are "a quite ordinary race" with few achievements. Soley rebuked his negative view, expressed without evidence, and assured him and Norway that they need not be ashamed of "the Norwegian immigrant [because] he has made a great mark on American society . . . even though the Norwegians make up an insignificant part of the American population." "We are much closer to the truth," editor Soley concluded, "by saying that instead of being overrated, Norwegian Americans have been regarded with a certain mock superiority in Norway."

Even Nordmanns-Forbundet, as late as the 1930s, received reminders of the differences that existed between Norway and the United States. In a July 1938 editorial in *Duluth Skandinav,* Anna Dahl Fuhr urged the Federation to consider well who it sent to speak to "Norwegian America" in its planned exchange program, so that it did not invite speakers with an academic degree or professor title unless they possessed "an open eye and an understanding heart," contending that "Nothing raises a Norwegian Ameri-

Kvinden og Hjemmet

og „Vort Bibliothek."

Et Maanedskrift for den skandinaviske Kvinde i Amerika.

CEDAR RAPIDS, IOWA. Vol. XVI. | ——: APRIL 1903. :—— | MINNEAPOLIS, MINN. No. 4.

En venlig Anmodning.

En „Haand" paatrykt ved denne Meddelelse betyder, at Modtageren endnu ikke har indbetalt sin Fornyelse.

Vi tiltrænger vore Penge, og vil derfor anmode Vedkommende om at indsende det lille Beløb nu.

Naar nogen skyldte dem en lille Sum og de anmodede Vedkommende i Venlighed om at indbetale Beløbet, og hun ikke gjorde det, hvad vilde de saa tro? Tør vi derfor haabe, at enhver, der skylder os, nu vil indsende sit Kontingent strax. Med venlig Hilsen,

Ida Hansen.

For „Kvinden og Hjemmet."

Hvem skal regjere i Hjemmet—Manden eller Hustruen?

(Af Josephine Brincell.)

Naar der bliver Spørgsmaal om Familielivet, saa er Ordet „regjere" et stygt Ord, og selve Sagen endnu styggere. Om nogetsteds Fællesstyrelse og Medregentskab burde forekomme, saa er det netop i Hjemmet. Ogsaa har vi da allerede i Begyndelsen af vor lille Opsats sagt ifra, hvad vor Hensigt er. Med et Ord, vi har indirekte givet Svar paa Spørgsmaalet.

Ingen Kvinde kan nogensinde blive saa lykkelig, som Gud har tilegnet hende at blive, ved ægteskabelig Forbindelse med den Mand, der har begjæret hende til sin Livsledsagerinde og givet hende Løfte om Værn og Beskyttelse, om denne Mand stadigt lader hende føle, at hun bør være den underordnede og han den styrende. Hvor eftergiven en Kvinde end maa bøie sig under Mandens Villie, saa findes der dog hos enhver ædel Kvinde noget vist noget, som aldrig lader sig bøie under et andet Menneskes Villie. Jo mere begavet hun er med et sundt Omdømme og klar Forstand, jo umuligere bliver det for hende at i sit inderste Hjerte opgive alle egne Ideer, Tanker, Omdømme og omfatte sin Mands eller lade ham alene tænke for hende og dømme over Sager og Forholde, som angaar dem begge eller hende alene. I Almindelighed vilde næsten enhver foragte den Kvinde, der gjorde saa, forsaavidt denne Kvinde ikke var hans Hustru. Men en Kvinde kan lære sig at tie og at aldrig diskutere eller argumentere, selv om hendes Overbevisning er aldeles snorret mod Mandens. Jo, det kan til og med hænde, at en trofast og hengiven Hustru ikke anser det for nogen Byrde at give efter og lade Manden helt og holdent bestemme over hele hendes Tilværelse uden at tage noget Hensyn til hendes Ønsker, Anlæg, Tilbøieligheder og forrige Vaner. Men ingen forstandig og tænkende Kvinde kan saa tabe sin egen Individualitet, at hun i sin Mands Hænder bliver kun som Leret i Pottemagerens. Der bliver altid saadanne Stunder, da hun i sit Hjertes Inderste spørger: Jeg undres, om min Mand nogensinde kommer ihu, at ogsaa jeg er ansvarlig ligeoverfor Gud for det Pund, jeg har faaet at forvalte, og at jeg selv — ikke min Mand — vil have at svare for, hvorledes jeg har forvaltet det? Naar han søger at forme mine Ønsker, mine Handlinger og mit Tankesæt efter sin Villie alene, saa undres jeg, om han paa den Dag, da alt skal dømmes, ogsaa vil svare for mig, ifald det, hvad han formaaet at udrette med og gjennem mig, ikke bliver taget gyldigt af Gud, eller om han da vil lade mig staa alene for min Dommer?

Om en Mands Kjærlighed og Fortrolighed til sin Hustru formaar at fremkaste og udvikle de ædleste Træk i hendes Karakter, saa har hans tyraniske Enevælde netop den modsatte Virkning. Hun vil under hans Jernhaand krympe sammen til et villieløst og frygtsomt Væsen, der vandrer omkring i sit Hjem som en Skygge. Hun vil, som en Hustru en Gang udtrykte sig, kjende sig „som en Ting, men ikke som et følende, tænkende og med Villie udrustet Væsen." Ved det Hjem, hvori der hersker et saadant Forhold. Det kan neppe kaldes et Hjem, denne Plads, hvor to Mennesker er sammenbundne, den ene for at regjere og den anden for at regjeres. Det er en Ulykke for dem begge; thi Manden paa sin Side kan heller ikke komme til den Karakterens Ædelhed, som han ellers vilde opnaa, om han paa sin Side forsagede sig selv for den Kvinde, som han har lovet at elske i Sorg og Glæde. Selvopofrelse er Karakterens Prøvesten, og aldrig høiner et Menneske sig mere til sit Ideal, end netop ved de Tilfælder, hvor det kan og maa forsage for en anden.

Det er denne selvtagne Ret til at regjere med en alt andet end moderat Myndighed, der har skabt saa mange ulykkelige Hustruer og derfor ulykkelige Hjem. Om enhver Mand fra Begyndelsen af sit Ægteskab kunde indse, hvilke Forskjel der ligger i den opofrende Tjeneste og de aldrig trættende Omsorger, som en Kvinde frit og utvungen skjænker den Kjærlighed, som næst Gud skattes høiest, saa vilde han aldrig forsøge paa at indføre Despotismens afskyelige Vælde i sit Hjem. En Hustru ofrer med Glæde hele sit Liv for den Mand, hvis Ord og Handlinger viser, at hun er hans dyrebareste Skat, at hun er uvurderet, ikke derfor at hun helt simpelt behøves i Huset, men derfor,

Kvinden og Hjemmet, *April 1903, has the subtitle "A monthly for the Scandinavian woman in America." This particular issue carries a discussion of "Who shall govern in the home—the husband or the wife," indicating the influential magazine's feminist agenda.*

can's hackles more than to stab him with class distinctions or beat the drum about university exams." The editor here posited a common Norwegian American self-image and explained further that in America, Norwegians learned tolerance and the ability to adjust, "something many of Norway's cultural bearers have not learned." The allusion to condescension toward emigrated citizens is clear. In a later issue, editor Dahl Fuhr suggested that more knowledge in Norway about those who crossed the ocean to begin a new life in America would go a long way to create respect for the Norwegian American community. Alas, she continued, "the Norwegian history books, even the most recent, do not, with only one exception, have a single word about the large Norwegian emigration or settlement in America." Anna Dahl Fuhr expressed her confidence in Nordmanns-Forbundet and Ingrid Semmingsen, née Gaustad; on her research forays in America in preparation for writing the history of the Norwegian emigration, the young and single Ingrid Gaustad had also visited Duluth.[11]

Women's Rights and Norwegian-Language Publications

The struggle for equal suffrage and public service for women did not gain much speed in the male-dominated Norwegian American press. The opinions expressed in the various journals cannot be easily classified, but some newsmen recognized women's inequality. Before the American Civil War, women engaged in temperance and abolition movements; they sought equal rights to pursue higher education and to enter the professions. Norwegian immigrant women were indeed poorly prepared to participate in American affairs; the gender inequality in the social and public spheres they had experienced before emigrating—the rule of men in the church and in the classroom—all contributed to lowered expectations for advancement to full equality with men in the New World; Norwegian American columnists were more likely to emphasize the traditional role of women than to agitate for greater opportunities in public life for their female compatriots.

As suggested earlier, despite obstacles, women in nineteenth century America had greater opportunity than their peers in the Norwegian homeland. Some Norwegian immigrant women benefited from the improved circumstances, as evidenced in such institutions as the Women's Medical School in Chicago, founded in 1870. Dr. Helga Ruud, from Kongsberg, Norway, was the first of many Norwegian-born women to graduate, in 1889; her sister Marie Ruud took up teaching, a common occupation for educated women. Their writings in *Skandinaven* show their active role in female organizations and their social engagement. In spring 1890 the University of Zurich, Switzerland, conferred a doctor of philosophy degree upon Agnes Wergeland. Wergeland became the first Norwegian woman to hold a doctorate; studies and commensurate positions were denied women in Norway and she had therefore explored possibilities overseas. Earlier she had consulted the Norwegian feminist Aasta Hansteen, who responded to Wergeland from Boston on New Year's Day, 1886: "America is the best place on earth for women." Wergeland moved to America in fall 1890; she is best known for her professorship in history at the University of Wyoming, in Laramie, from 1902 until her death in 1914. She raised the banner of women's rights, impressed by the practice of woman suffrage in the state. The Norwegian American press, notably *Skandinaven* and *Decorah-Posten,* did not give much attention to her work and carried no tributes after her death. Noteworthy exceptions were Waldemar Ager in his *Kvartalskrift* (Quarterly), Peter Myrvold in *Fram,* and Carl G. O. Hansen in *Minneapolis Tidende,* who praised her academic accomplishments.

Budstikken, under the editorships of Jørgen Jensen and R. S. N. Sartz, 1887–91, espoused opinions against the women's movement. These did not remain unchallenged. Drude Krog Janson, then living in Minneapolis with her husband Kristofer Janson, the Unitarian champion of women's rights, took *Budstikken* to task for its criticism of feminist leaders. Her defense of women's rights was a positive influence in the Norwegian American community. Supporting male voices were also heard. In the short life of *Almuevennen* in Pierre, South Dakota, its editor S. O. Nordvold in 1890 defended the feminist Susan B. Anthony and her agitation for "woman's equality before the law and the courts—as the woman is a human being created in God's image, endowed with the same intellectual and physical qualifications for development and progress as the man and therefore also has just as much right to express her opinion and have it recognized by the law as the man." During the 1890s, with the formation of the American Suffrage Association and a younger and more aggressive leadership, Norwegian American male editors and publishers remained largely silent on the efforts to improve the status of women; newspapers like *Folkebladet, Decorah-Posten,* and *Nordvesten* seemed to harbor a certain resentment toward the greater involvement of women in political life.

After 1900, journalists increasingly acknowledged women's demands, evidenced in the introduction of special features for a female readership in a number of Norwegian American journals and the success of literary magazines directed toward women. However, *Decorah-Posten* and *Nordisk Tidende,* even when publishing special woman's departments, opposed the ballot for women and encouraged a traditional gender role. Contrasting opinions were drowned out by Norwegian American editorial commentary, yet Ager in his newspaper *Reform,* for example, voiced his ardent support for a federal woman suffrage amendment.

The final impetus to the woman suffrage movement was spurred on by World War I. Norwegian American newspapers, together with the American press in general, then joined the patriotic and popular chorus for equal rights; in fact by 1914 women had full suffrage in a number of states. Women in Norway had won full equality with men at the polls in 1913. The slogan "Women can vote in Norway" became for Norwegian women's groups an additional argument for a federal amendment. The progress for women's rights in Norway was taken to heart by the immigrant press as well, and both Andreas Rygg of *Nordisk Tidende* and Johannes B. Wist of *Decorah-Posten* abandoned their skepticism of feminist arguments; Wist admitted in 1917, "no one sneers at the woman's movement today." The Nineteenth Amendment to the Constitution giving women the right to vote was ratified August 18, 1920. *Normanden*'s editorial in October likely summed up a prevailing query: "How will women vote?"[12]

The Literary Tradition in Magazines and Newspapers

Monthly magazines intended for women became a regular part of Norwegian American print journalism. The most successful was the monthly *Kvinden og Hjemmet* (The Woman and the Home), published in Cedar Rapids, Iowa, from May 1888 until August 1947. It engaged itself strongly in the feminist movement and, as announced, was written "by, for, and about Scandinavian women in America"; a clear correlation seems evident between an expressed wish for equality within the marriage and the suffrage movement, which became a singular early issue for the magazine. Its reporting on progress of the movement in Scandinavia directly influenced the attitude of women immigrants in America. The question of suffrage became entwined with temperance and prohibition; the right to vote would enable women to work against the evil of the saloons. A supplement titled *Vort Bibliothek* (Our Library) provided novels and short stories for "a thousand homes in America."

Kvinden og Hjemmet's founder and editor was Ida Hansen, who emigrated from Ringsaker, Norway, in 1870 at age seventeen with her parents and siblings, including her sister Mina Jensen, four years her junior, who was the magazine's printer. *Kvinden og Hjemmet* may be seen as a continuation of the magazine *Fra alle Lande* (From all Nations), published in Cedar Rapids from 1885 to 1888 by Ida Hansen's husband, Danish American Niels Frederick Hansen, who continued as publisher and business manager in the new venture. Ida Hansen had edited "Husmoderen" (The Housewife) in *Fra alle Lande* and Mina learned the printing trade there.

Kvinden og Hjemmet grew in popularity. Most of the readers and subscribers were women; it circulated widely in the United States, Canada, and Scandinavia. In 1901 it boasted a circulation of forty-five thousand, which by 1924 had been reduced to thirty-four thousand; it remained a family business throughout the sixty years of publication. Beginning modestly with eight pages, the magazine became a forty-page journal with many illustrations and numerous advertisements. The editors were women and homemakers, which colored the content of the magazine; they created an awareness of women's significance. Other female-oriented magazines and columns were generally directed by male publishers and editors; *Skandinaven*'s women's section on the other hand was edited by Dr. Ingeborg Rasmussen, also a graduate of the Women's Medical School.

Hans A. Foss, after leaving *Nye Normanden* in 1905, offered women readers *Kvindens Magasin* (The Woman's Magazine); published in Minneapolis until 1917, it was only the second Norwegian American woman's magazine. Later editors were also male. In March 1915, N. N. Rønning, the longtime editor of the Synod monthly *Ungdommens Ven* (The Friend of Youth), assumed editorial responsibility; *Decorah-Posten* praised him as the right man to produce "a first class woman's magazine." *Kvindens Magasin*'s strong focus on a Norwegian heritage and well-selected literary copy assured the magazine a wide circulation.

Kvinden og Hjemmet as well expressed a dynamic ethnic culture—though with less sentimentality than its competitor—while guiding women's adjustment to life in America. Perhaps, as students of the magazine have concluded, its women readers may be seen "more as promoters of Americanization than as defenders of ethnic retention." One might of course argue that these two roles did not conflict but were played out simultaneously and complemented each other in the demanding process of adjustment to a new society. The changing social and political world as it related to women and their response to it is in any event charted from a gendered perspective throughout *Kvinden og Hjemmet*'s six decades. The female immigrant experience it portrays thus provides a greater nuance in the historical exegesis.

The many reading clubs and literary societies formed in Norwegian American rural and urban settings satisfied a great cultural need. These associations collected money to purchase books and created local libraries; they often subscribed to magazines and newspapers as well. Such reading societies appeared in Norwegian settlements from the 1870s; Martin Ulvestad, a contemporary chronicler, thought that in 1902 they numbered close to three hundred and could be found in all regions of Norwegian settlement from coast to coast. Norwegian Americans were clearly a literate people with a varied literary taste. Easy access to reading material, especially for isolated rural communities, however, came only in the twentieth century with public libraries and free rural postal service. The many reading societies persisted alongside the public institutions.[13]

Most literary magazines as well as those with a set purpose such as music or athletics were short-lived—with the possible exception of a few membership periodicals. Some publications with a literary bent can be noted here; additional titles will be introduced in a different context in the following chapter. The value of *Billed-Magazin,* 1868–70, edited by Svein Nilsson, as a historical source deserves to be reiterated (from chapter one); Svein Nilsson furthermore served as editor of the monthly *Skandinavisk Billed-Magazin* (Scandinavian Picture Magazine), published in Madison, Wisconsin, the same years as *Billed-Magazin* by the printer B. W. Suckow. With its mixture of entertaining, public-spirited, and instructive content it was much the same as *Skilling-Magazin* (Penny Magazine) during the same period; it was published in Norway's capital, as the subtitle stated, "to spread knowledge beneficial to all." The influence across the ocean was evident.

The semimonthly magazine *For Hjemmet* came out in Decorah, Iowa, 1870–88, and was advertised as "an entertaining and educational periodical in a Christian spirit." Wist reported it had a "creditable distribution and was much read." As mentioned earlier, the strongly literary influenced *Norsk Maanedskrift* (Norwegian Monthly) appeared only briefly—1874–75—in La Crosse, Wisconsin; not even the capable leadership of Luth Jaeger and Sigvard Sørensen, the later successful editor of *Minneapolis Tidende,* could save it. Other publishing ventures suffered the same fate. The well-edited *I ledige Timer* (In Idle Hours) published in Chicago by the Icelander Jon Olafsson from 1895 to 1896 lacked an adequate subscription base, as did *Skirnir,* published 1895–97 in Tacoma, Washington, notwithstanding such highly recognized and capable contributors as Drude Krog Janson and Kristian Prestgard. *Vor Tid. Maanedsskrift for Litteratur og Samfundsspørgsmaal* (Our Times. Monthly for Literature and Social Issues), published in Minneapolis from 1904 to 1908, was a highly anticipated and for some time a widely circulated literary and civic-oriented magazine; Peer Strømme and Laurits Stavnheim at different times gave editorial direction. *Vor Tid*'s impressive distribution, though fleeting, indicated, Wist claimed, that the editors "struck the keynote in the Norwegian American mindset."

The literary magazines failed largely because they were no match for the less costly and more accessible newspapers' literary supplements, serials, and stories. Wist observed in 1914 that competition also came from "the many excellent and inexpensive magazines in the English language . . . the older [readers] are content with their Norwegian newspapers, while the younger, if they do not belong to the later years' arrivals, divide their interest between dailies and magazines published in the English language."

The book trade among Norwegian American newspaper publishers beginning in the late 1850s gained increasing importance in the following decade; bookstores advertised Norwegian books and in time offered a diversified stock of religious and educational books as well as titles in fiction and history; books were also marketed directly by individual newspapers through mail order arrangements, even by traveling salesmen, and offered as bonuses to new subscribers. Norwegian Americans consequently had access to diverse reading materials. Most of these books were imported from Norway and Denmark; the percentage of those produced in America, however, grew. Large-scale U.S. book publishing in the Norwegian language began only with the founding of *Skandinaven* in Chicago in 1866. John Anderson opened *Skandinaven*'s Boghandel (*Skandinaven*'s Bookstore) in December 1876; it competed with the large bookstore opened in Chicago by I. T. Relling in 1870. In research for her master's thesis, Jean Skogerboe Hansen identified more than four hundred titles published or printed by the John Anderson Publishing Company. Most of the books published were fiction. Among these titles were works by prominent Norwegian authors such as Henrik Ibsen and Bjørnstjerne Bjørnson, but also translations of Charles Dickens and Mark Twain.

The merged *Skandinaven og Amerika* in September 1873 announced the publication of *Husbibliothek* (House Library), a literary monthly. From 1882 it became a literary supplement to *Skandinaven;* all serial fiction was then moved to the supplement to devote more space to news in the regular newspaper. The publisher later changed the name to *Illustreret Husbibliothek* to denote its focus on the arts as well as literature. A major stated purpose was "to be instrumental in preserving the mother tongue among the Scandinavian young people by giving them entertaining and at the same time sound and instructive reading." Likely encouraged by the exclusive lecture and debate group named the Arne Garborg Club formed in 1891 by technically trained Norwegian immigrants in honor of the *Landsmaal* author, the literary supplement the following year serialized his novel *Trætte Mænd* (Weary Men), given a Dano-Norwegian attire by the author.

In the fall of 1882 Brynild Anundsen revived *Ved Arnen* as a literary supplement to *Decorah-Posten;* its publication was somewhat irregular until 1887, when it became a weekly addition. A literary heritage was preserved in the selected stories and novels. Bjørnstjerne Bjørnson's idealized peasant tales were popular regular features; legends, poems, and tales by the Telemark writer John Lie were featured, as were regional writers from the romantic revival of the 1890s—men like Bernt Lie, Jacob Breda Bull, and Hans Aanrud. The mighty novels of Johan Falkberget depicting the life of the mountain people and miners in Røros found an interested readership. The novelist Jonas Lie was the most widely serialized in the immigrant newspapers; many of his novels, such as *The Family at Gilje,* depicting the home life of a country army officer in Valdres, were serialized soon after their publication in Norway. The nostalgic and the sentimental homeland tales appealed to the immigrant mind. Scholar Haldor L. Hove discussed how the Norwegian American press shaped and defined a literary culture inherited from the mother country in the decades before 1890; it was, he argued, a literary culture conceived of in the spirit of romanticism. The new literary realism came later—protested by some newsmen—and will be dealt with in chapter six.

Ved Arnen and other outlets typically printed imaginative prose such as translated novels and short stories from both well-known and marginal authors in Europe and the United States; numerous overly sentimental novels and short narratives with great variations in quality won favor with Norwegian Americans. *Ved Arnen*'s library of fiction included the products of immigrant writers. These also gained popularity. One often-cited example is *Husmands-Gutten. En Fortælling fra Sigdal* (The Cotter Boy: A Tale from Sigdal) by Hans A. Foss, which when it was serialized in *Decorah-Posten* the winter of 1884–85 was said to have produced six thousand new subscribers. People were so eager to read the novel, Foss later recalled, that it seemed to the publisher "as if people were competing to mail in new subscriptions."

Serialized novels played a significant role in broadening the popularity and thus distribution of most journals published by Norwegians in America. Their selected stories and novels were much like those in *Husbibliothek* and *Ved Arnen* and did not vary much from one journal to the next. The genre most readily serialized in weekly installments was the lengthy historical novel; *Ved Arnen* was unique, however, in taking pains to present and encourage creative writing by "our own people": Norwegian Americans. New serialized fiction was announced in all journals with great fanfare. Typesetters frequently set up the installments to appear at the bottom of the page for readers to clip out and reassemble in the form of a book. Many preserved journals consequently are missing the fictional accounts. These literary successes indicate that they filled a real need among the immigrants for entertaining reading material.[14]

The Press and the War on Demon Rum

In 1901 Minnesota Total Temperance Society, the joint state organization of local Norwegian total temperance societies, extended its sincere gratitude to temperance journals in the Upper Midwest, among these *Nye Normanden, Lutheraneren, Reform, Folkebladet,* and *Fergus Falls Ugeblad.* The issues of temperance, total abstinence, and prohibition became a broadly debated cause célèbre in the Norwegian American press; no publisher could remain entirely neutral or indifferent. A balance between personal liberty and the public welfare became an elusive goal for most journals; Luth Jaeger in the 1870s in *Budstikken,* while deploring drunkenness, voiced objections to prohibiting the sale of alcoholic beverages as it would deprive everyone of the freedom of choice. The Norwegian Synod leadership as well displayed displeasure with organized temperance work. In 1879 it warned parishioners from joining temperance societies. Their argument was that for Christians the congregation was the only temperance society required since they "at baptism and confirmation had pledged to God to refrain from all sin." The Synod here clearly expressed a fear of organizations it did not control. The liturgical Synod held a moderate approach to temperance: stimulating beverages were one of God's gifts to mankind; neither abuse nor prohibition but moderation would thus be the accepted principle. The pietistic Hauge's Synod and the United Church did not agree. Temperance advocates instead promoted "moderation in enjoying that which is good and total abstinence from that which is evil." Toward the end of the century the historian of the temperance cause J. L. Nydahl found a change in the Synod's position in that "a large part of our Norwegian-Lutheran pastors in this country are now temperance men and almost no one takes a strong stance against" temperance. They joined forces with American and immigrant pietists to promote the temperance cause.

Many Norwegian columnists voiced concerns about intemperance and its ills. Before the turn of the century temperance became equal to total abstinence; journals were moreover founded as official organs for the abstinence-prohibition movement and had declarative names such as *Afholds-Basunen* (The Temperance Trumpet), founded in Hillsboro, North Dakota, in 1887. A pietistic condemnation of intoxicants represented moral tenets carried across the Atlantic; immigrants were abundantly familiar with overindulgence from home. For Norwegians and other Scandinavians drinking was a culturally conditioned practice. The pioneer Norwegian sociologist Eilert Sundt in the 1850s opined that "the bad custom and vice" of alcohol abuse "more than anything has been the misfortune and destruction of our people," indulged in at baptisms, weddings, and funerals.

In the United States, the per capita increase in beer and whiskey consumption in the decades after the Civil War, along with other social evils, were blamed on the saloons and the brewing industry. Enmity against the saloons at times resulted in direct actions to rid society of their presence. In his programmatic *Trediveaarskrigen mod Drikkeondet* (The Thirty Year War against the Evil of Drinking), Foss related how in February 1890, a group of about fourteen women, "armed with small axes," entered the saloons in Hatton, North Dakota, and destroyed everything they could lay their hands on. The incident became known as "the great battle in Hatton" and proved that the state had its own Carrie Nation in the fight against liquor and the saloons.[15]

Women were much involved in the fight against the saloon element. Norwegian-born Ulrikka Feldtman Bruun traveled for the Woman's Christian Temperance Union (WCTU); from its headquarters in Evanston, Illinois, she visited midwestern states to organize "unions" of Scandinavian women. She was also responsible for the temperance monthly *Det hvide Baand* (The White Ribbon). At both the local and the state level Norwegian women took part in organizing temperance societies. Women's temperance work moved them into the political arena; voting rights surfaced as an important cause. The Republican Party moved decisively toward "dry" legislation from the 1870s; anti-Democratic bias among Norwegian Americans was reinforced by an increase in temperance sentiment and a rising anti-Catholic agitation. The fight against drinking became a leading issue and pulled many Norwegians into the progressive fervor within the Republican Party and third party movements advocating reform; the temperance cause gave Norwegian politicians an edge as they promised to keep the sale of alcohol out of the community. The local option—adopted in Dakota Territory in 1887 and in Minnesota in 1915—and state and national prohibition became vehicles for Norwegian and Swedish politicians to rally their compatriots behind their candidacies.

Much of the temperance work among Norwegians in Chicago—unlike states in the Upper Midwest where the cause of temperance was dominated by the Lutheran clergy and the Republican Party—was connected with the Prohibition Party, organized in 1869. Members were evangelicals and public-minded—at times unchurched—Norwegian American businessmen and civic leaders. In 1878, Norwegian Methodists and liberals formed the Harmony Total Abstinence Society. Ole Br. Olson, who entered the temperance cause through conversion to Methodism, was the leading figure; John Anderson of *Skandinaven* was among the liberal members. In 1880 Olson launched the monthly *Afholdsbladet* (Temperance Paper). Although the third-party affiliation was not likely to result in election to public office, members were mobilized by social issues, such as woman suffrage and a clear platform of prohibition of the manufacture and sale of alcohol. *Skandinaven* and *Verdens Gang* in their columns advocated "public morals" and the defeat of the political corruption surrounding the liquor trade.[16]

The 1889 division of Dakota Territory into North Dakota and South Dakota led to a great victory for the prohibitionists; following the example of Kansas in 1881, both states' constitutions prohibited the sale and consumption of alcohol at the time of their creation. As a consequence the saloons closed the following year. In South Dakota resubmission brought repeal in 1895, but

North Dakota did not repeal prohibition until the 1930s. Ole Br. Olson and *Afholdsbladet* were well known in Dakota Territory in the 1880s; he spoke with great force to large crowds in the Red River Valley advocating abstinence and prohibition. In Madison in South Dakota *For Fattig og Rig* (For Poor and Rich) in the 1880s spread an identical message; in 1886 Foss purchased the weekly and restarted it in Portland, in Traill County, North Dakota, with the masthead altered to *Dakota-Bladet* (The Dakota Newspaper). It was a radical temperance organ that engaged in local politics. In spring 1887 financial straits convinced the publishers to sell the subscription list to *Folkebladet* in Minneapolis—a low-church organ of the Norwegian-Danish Conference eagerly engaged in the temperance cause.

Afholds-Basunen then began publication in Hillsboro, North Dakota, the summer of 1887; it had actually been started the previous year as *Folkets Røst* (The Voice of the People). The leader of this undertaking was Pastor Jens Lønne of the Conference, an immigrant from Vik in Sogn in 1876; *Afholds-Basunen* was discontinued in 1896. *Normanden* in Grand Forks became a competing temperance voice; in 1888 with Foss as editor, *Normanden* engaged in a bitter debate with the Hillsboro journal, causing a split in the Norwegian prohibition forces in the state. While both newspapers agreed on a prohibition article in the state constitution, *Afholds-Basunen* inclined toward the Republican Party and *Normanden* agitated for accomplishing this through the Populist movement. The rift among prohibitionists harmed their cause. However, both journals together with temperance pamphlets flooded the state with the message: "local option is good, state prohibition is better, national prohibition—the real goal—is best." The electorate approved the constitution with its prohibition clause—though with a small margin.[17]

Normanden advocated temperance, but with varying degrees of conviction, throughout its existence. In 1911 the Fargo weekly *Fram* became the official organ of the North Dakota Temperance Association and as its voice a strong proponent of national prohibition; *Fram* then enjoyed a circulation of about seventy-five hundred. Salt Lake City's *Bikuben*, in keeping with the Mormon teachings, condemned any use of alcoholic beverages. National prohibition was of course the ultimate ambition for most people in the total abstinence camp. However, aside from *Fram* after 1911 and *Reform,* which will be discussed shortly, Norwegian American newspapers in their agitation for temperance did not make a clear demand for complete prohibition at the national level until the years following World War I. Many continued to advertise alcoholic beverages; Carl G. O. Hansen of *Minneapolis Tidende,* as an example, during the prewar years defended his advertising Duffy's Pure Malt Whiskey, since, as he claimed, the old-timers had suffered no ill effects from many years of consumption; in fact the advertisement claimed that "it was the only Whiskey approved by physicians everywhere as a family medicine." In actuality, during this era, physicians widely prescribed alcohol for therapeutic purposes. Hansen favored local option, the ability of each community to determine the legality of the sale and consumption of alcohol.

Hostility to saloons and their influence became widespread in the Progressive Era from the turn of the twentieth century; the exigencies of the worldwide conflagration after 1914 united public opinion behind the "dries" and their demand for prohibition as the best remedy to eradicate a destructive social malady. *Skandinaven* in 1915, as *Decorah-Posten* had done earlier, discontinued advertising alcoholic beverages. Both the Socialist *Folkets Røst* (The Voice of the People) and its predecessor *Gaa Paa,* however, expressed strong opposition to national prohibition; the newspapers saw it as a capitalist affront on the rights of the laboring man. Big industrialists, editor Mengshoel suggested, wished to see widespread unemployment in order to lower salaries; following its enactment, the editor's excoriation of the law reached new heights. By 1915, however, Johannes Wist noted in *Decorah-Posten,* "Considered in its entirety we believe that it can be said that the Norwegian American press takes a very well-disposed position in regard to prohibition." Prohibition against the sale of intoxicants had been enacted by a number of states prior to national prohibition, and other states were moving in that direction; under the local option ordinance, for example, sixty-three of Minnesota's eighty-seven counties were "dry" by 1919.

The ratification of the Eighteenth Amendment of the U.S. Constitution, along with the Volstead Act, which defined "intoxicating liquors," on January 29, 1919, established Prohibition in the United States—effective January 1920. The measure's sponsorship by Norwegian American Congressman Andrew J. Volstead of Minnesota made opponents label him as an extremist. Violations of the Volstead Act and a considerable growth in organized crime in response to public demand for illegal alcohol made it a very unpopular law; in fact it became fashionable to drink, especially in the big cities. The prohibition amendment was subsequently repealed by the Twenty-first Amendment on December 5, 1933.

In *Afholdsfolkets Festskrift 1914* (The Temperance People's Jubilee Publication 1914), Waldemar Ager claimed that "Norwegians in America viewed as a people have accomplished more for sobriety relative to their numbers than any other nationality in this country—the Yankees not excepted." Temperance and prohibition in the states of the Upper Midwest were largely the result of a persistent crusade that drew much of its leadership and strength from Norwegians and Swedes. Evidence of their engagement is apparent in the columns of the majority of newspapers published by these two nationalities.[18]

Waldemar Ager and His Newspaper Reform

The newspaper *Reform* in Eau Claire, Wisconsin, became the quintessential advocate of total abstinence and prohibition; its near absolute concentration on these issues placed *Reform* in a unique position among secular Norwegian American journals. Other Norwegian weeklies also wrote in favor of temperance and women's rights but were hardly ever as one-sided about sobriety as *Reform*. *Everett Ekko* was not alone in finding fault with a newspaper carrying the name "reform," considering, as *Everett Ekko* wrote in February 1908, that its message of reform was a limited and restrictive one; the caustic critique rebutted *Reform*'s editorial assaults on *Everett Ekko* for carrying advertisements for beer and other alcoholic beverages. The Everett weekly was not the only Norwegian American journal to feel *Reform*'s wrath for similar transgressions of its temperance policy.

Reform's history began with activities by Olson and Ager in Chicago. In 1888 Olson moved his monthly *Afholdsbladet* to Eau

Claire, Wisconsin, and merged it with the weekly *Arbeideren* (The Laborer), started in 1886. The merged journals were published under the masthead *Reform*. In its initial issue, dated February 9, 1886, *Arbeideren* explained its purpose; its founder and first editor was the Reverend Gjermund Hoyme, who with establishment of the United Church in 1890 became its first president. Editor Hoyme identified four objectives:

> The newspaper's main purpose will be to work for the laboring class's financial and spiritual interests by in a wholesome and calm manner standing up for its legitimate claims as well as its duties to its employer and capital. . . .
>
> In the political arena the newspaper will as far as possible adopt a neutral stance, inasmuch as it will impartially report the existing political situation. . . .
>
> Without being an organ for prohibition or the total abstinence movement, the newspaper will zealously oppose and fight against all saloon traffic. . . .
>
> The newspaper will work for the Lutheran church's growth, work for unity and merger of the present Lutheran church bodies on the foundation of truth.

Save for the portion about the Lutheran church—Olson having converted to Methodism—*Reform* could embrace, indeed strengthen, the position of *Arbeideren*, especially in regard to the temperance cause. Ole Br. Olson was the major figure in *Reform*, from 1890 published by Fremad Publishing Company; he sat at the rolltop desk as editor of the weekly until his death in 1903. In 1892, he needed a printer and hired Waldemar Ager, whom he knew from Chicago; Ager moved to Eau Claire and worked as printer until 1896 when he was promoted to manager and co-editor; he succeeded Olson in the editor's chair in 1903. Ager was born in Fredrikstad, Norway, in 1869; the city had a Methodist congregation, which his mother joined. In 1885, his mother together with Waldemar and his two siblings immigrated to Chicago, where his father had settled earlier. He found work as an apprentice and learned typesetting in the weekly *Norden*. He took a solemn pledge at the Harmony Total Abstinence Society not to touch alcoholic liquors; he became a contributor to Olson's *Afholdsbladet* and an avid and talented public speaker for its cause.

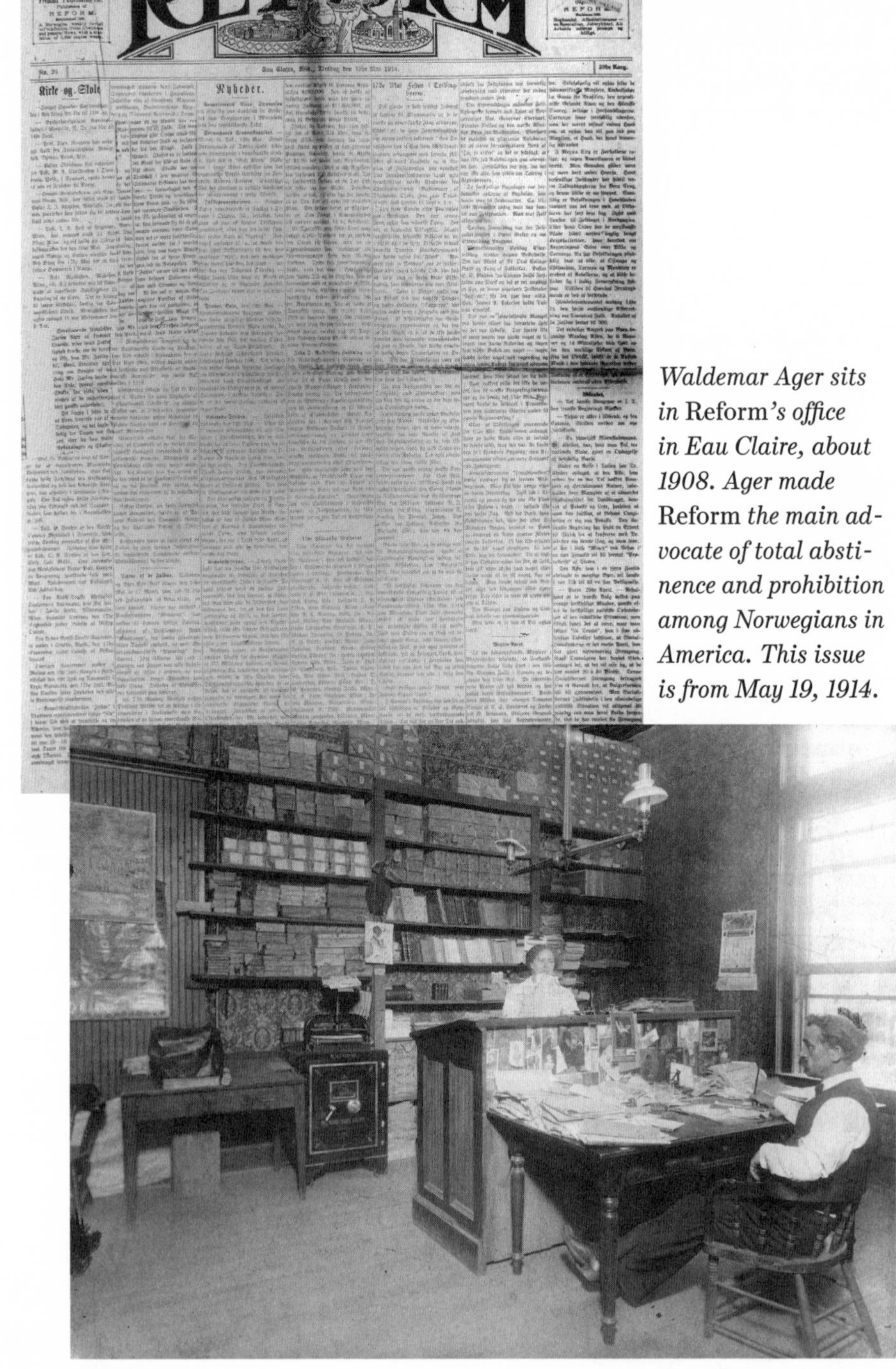

REFORM

Waldemar Ager sits in Reform*'s office in Eau Claire, about 1908. Ager made* Reform *the main advocate of total abstinence and prohibition among Norwegians in America. This issue is from May 19, 1914.*

Ager's obituary August 1, 1941, noted, "*Reform* was Ager and Ager was *Reform.*" The final issue of the newspaper is dated September 18, 1941. At a stockholder meeting of Fremad Publishing Company in Eau Claire April 12, 1929, all of "the property, assets and valuables of all kinds and description" were transferred to Waldemar Ager as the sole owner, the transfer motivated by financial adversity and decline of *Reform*'s profitability as a news organ. Ager's elation over his sole ownership and complete command did not alter this stark fact. Ager continued to reinforce his position against alcohol; his single-minded temperance advocacy likely repelled some advertisers and readers. In a 1927 editorial, he lamented the fact that many newspapers that once favored prohibition were changing their position; the acrimonious debate between "wets" and "dries" continued until the repeal of Prohibition in December 1933. It was to be sure a failure of a major ideal, though Ager gave no clear expression of his reaction to the repeal on the pages of *Reform.* More will be noted later about *Reform*'s and Ager's cultural engagement and ideals; in spite of its one-sidedness, *Reform* culturally deserves high marks as an outstanding Norwegian American journal.[19]

A Community and Press in Transition

Nordvesten in St. Paul announced June 3, 1897, the formation of a society called the Norwegian Pioneer Association of Deerfield [Wisconsin] and Surrounding Towns. Among its members were some of the earliest Norwegian settlers in the country. The Association's concern was to preserve the pioneer saga as a reminder of the passage of time as lifestyles and future prospects were changing.

The value it placed in preserving past achievements reveals a maturing and self-conscious Norwegian American community. Also signifying this vital subculture were the many social and cultural organizations and their variety of activities. Enthusiasm around the 1905 achievement of full independence for the fatherland encouraged a celebration of Norwegian heritage. Norwegian American journals—among these *Nordvesten,* which asked, "Will Norway be proclaimed a republic like France and Switzerland?"—abandoned their speculations about the Republic of Norway once a Norwegian monarchy became the preferred choice, stressed the unity of Norwegians at home and abroad, and hailed Norway as an independent kingdom.

The progress for women's rights was another sign of changing times, even though some Norwegian American columnists during the early stages of the feminist movement fell short of committing themselves to female equality and women's new opportunities in the twentieth century. After the Nineteenth Amendment gave women full suffrage, however, no editorial voice expressed a wish to rescind the measure. The experiment in national prohibition, with extensive involvement by women, though it failed, indicated conscious social engagement; it was an important force in state and local politics through the 1930s.

Visits back to the home sod strengthened bonds across the ocean. Norwegian Americans could sail proudly under the homeland's flag on the vessels of the Norwegian America Line; new arrivals from Norway, either for a brief sojourn or permanent settlement, could do the same. In magazines and newspapers a library of Norwegian and Norwegian American literature as well as translated short stories and novels entertained and educated a large readership. The Norwegian American press was indeed the framework and agent that made these changing circumstances a conscious reality among Norwegians in America. It extended its reach to Norway by encouraging subscriptions to individual newspapers and by correspondents in Norway who regularly informed expatriates about local and national circumstances. Though the concept of "a greater Norway" likely was overly romantic and unrealistic, increased Norwegian American organizational activity and the initiatives of immigrant penmen encouraged a sense of ethnic solidarity across the Atlantic.[20]

Decorah-Posten og Ved Arnen

CHAPTER 6

The Golden Age of Norwegian America

The Norwegian American press will exist and tend to its mission according to its ability as long as it is needed. Judging by all portents under the sun there will be a need for it a long, long time to come.

THE EXCERPT ABOVE WAS *Decorah-Posten*'s optimistic answer to its own question in its September 5, 1924, issue: "Are the days of the Norwegian American press soon counted?" "When its mission is done," editor Kristian Prestgard further wrote, "it will cease by itself just as quietly as it came into being." In Prestgard's opinion, this would not happen any time soon. This issue had been raised fifty years earlier, Prestgard suggested, and he stated with confidence that it would likely be asked fifty years later.[1]

The 1920s witnessed a last hurrah for many Norwegian American activities. Prestgard could not have foreseen the dire consequences of the deep depression that commenced at the end of that decade. Though severely challenged by the intolerant nativism of World War I, a Norwegian American community flourished from the mid-1890s until the end of the 1920s—in many respects the Golden Age of Norwegian America.

Norwegians were secure in their ethnic identity; it was a maturing ethnic subculture—confident of its place in America. By 1900 the second generation outnumbered the Norwegian-born population. These children of immigrants did not consistently embrace their parents' ethnic traditions; indeed, as their parents might lament, many rejected the foreign ways of the immigrant population. This disappointment notwithstanding, the Norwegian American community saw many promising developments: the emergence of a celebratory identity where the American-born generations were invited to take part, the success of secular and religious institutions, a flourishing of voluntary organizational life, and a new large influx of immigrants as the American economy revived after the economic slump of the 1890s. These circumstances brightened the future for the established Norwegian American newspapers at the start of the twentieth century: some journals modernized production; circulations were in general on the rise; and the major journals even turned a good profit. A large and growing Norwegian American national community welcomed news organs in the language of home. The jaundiced and xenophobic attitudes generated by World War I for the first time placed limitations on the foreign-language press; even so, many Norwegian Americans, several of them recent arrivals, found it easier to read about the hostilities and their impact on the old homeland in their native tongue. The decade of the 1920s, with loss of subscribers and advertising and increasing costs, produced a crisis for the Norwegian-language press, perhaps acknowledged by Prestgard in posing the question about its future. By then, for a large percentage of subscribers, the Norwegian-language newspapers supplemented a subscription to an American English-language daily.

The Norwegian American Community

In 1910, according to the federal census, nearly every third Norwegian, counting only the immigrants and their children, almost one million people in all, resided in the United States. Norway's population in 1910, toward the end of mass emigration, reached 2,391,782. That year the immigrant generation peaked at 403,858 persons as registered by census takers; the second generation, surpassing the first, numbered 577,377. The vast majority of the Norwegian American population still lived in the Upper Midwest, but, as the following table demonstrates, they resided in large numbers in many regions of the United States:

Table 2: Norwegian Immigrants by State, 1910

STATE	FIRST GENERATION	SECOND GENERATION	TOTAL
Minnesota	105,303	174,304	279,607
Wisconsin	57,000	100,701	157,701
Illinois	32,913	35,525	68,438
Iowa	21,924	44,978	66,902
North Dakota	45,937	77,347	123,284
South Dakota	20,918	39,828	60,746
Montana	7,169	6,773	13,942
Utah	2,304	3,205	5,509
Texas	1,784	2,661	4,445
Washington	28,363	24,361	52,724
Oregon	6,843	6,592	13,435
California	9,952	7,194	17,146
Michigan	7,638	9,136	16,774
New York	25,013	12,392	37,405
Total	373,061	544,997	918,058
All other states	30,797	32,380	63,177

Thirteenth Census of the United States, 1910: Population, I, 781, 804, 875, 893–95, 918–24.

The figures above reflect the third and final mass immigration wave from Norway, 1900–1914, and the greater U.S. geographical spread; the movement from the core Norwegian settlements in the Upper Midwest continued unabated to the Pacific Coast area. New opportunities in the fishing and lumber industries made the Pacific Northwest a particularly attractive terminus for immigrants from coastal Norway. Immigrants headed for the cities to a greater extent than earlier arrivals; even so, especially in the Upper Midwest, the children of the immigrants, following their parents' lead, resisted the pull of the city. In Minnesota in 1900, for example, second-generation Norwegians were only 18 percent urbanized, a percentage that increased to only 34 percent by 1920. The statistics for the immigrants for these same years were 28 and 39 percent respectively; the higher percentages for the immigrant generation evidence the impact of the post-1900 arrivals. Norwegians inhabited small towns or the surrounding farming communities in exceptional numbers, to a higher degree than other nationalities.

During the first decade and a half of the twentieth century 214,985 Norwegians left the homeland; the migration was a part of an international Atlantic labor market dating back to the late 1800s. From the late 1870s the exodus gradually shifted from family emigration toward individual departures. Toward the end of mass emigration, the overseas movement had largely become a youth migration, encompassing a mobile and less permanent population; the men's share had consistently increased. Many of the new arrivals sought employment as guest workers, intending to return to Norway when they had saved money. Clearly, a large percentage exhibited second thoughts and decided to become permanent residents of the United States. The changing composition of the Norwegian American community forms the backdrop to its gloried decades.[2]

The second generation, including those who found greater rewards in mastering the language and customs of the host society, became a force in shaping the Norwegian American community in urban as well as rural settings, even though, as Johannes Wist lamented, they might not in general be regular subscribers to Norwegian-language publications, preferring instead the more colorful American periodicals. By the early 1900s, the public life of the Norwegian urban colonies fell more and more under the influence of a rising class of professionals and businessmen. To quote an earlier analysis by the author, "Many of these leaders were American-born children of Norwegian immigrants. . . . The second-generation dynamics and a generational transformation during the last two decades of the century applied in how a Norwegian American identity was fashioned." To quote further:

> The American-born generations would have a greater concern for ethnicity than those born in Norway since it for them to a higher degree became a means of interacting with American society and of establishing acceptable credentials. They might promote mainstream American ideals and values as being specific to Norwegians and create myths of origin and descent. In other words, they demonstrated that their ethnoculture was compatible with American national norms and ideals.

Norwegian Americans, in the manner of other ethnic groups, celebrated invented and reinvented ethnic identities to set the group apart in a multicultural industrial society. This nationalism required an idealized past and symbolic order. Unifying ethnic festivities—in town and country—celebrated such national icons as patriotic May 17 observances, Leif Erickson's discovery of America, and the heroic age of the Vikings, all of which comprised a collective historical memory that embodied life in America as well as in Norway. These forces produced a final golden age as the Norwegian American community established its place as an integral part of the American nation. The Norwegian American press reflected and greatly influenced these developments.[3]

A Celebratory Ethnicity

Norwegian American journalists gave increased attention to the initiatives and actions of their compatriots in America; they announced in banner headlines and fastidiously covered the festive moments in the group's social and cultural affairs. Activities rooted in a nineteenth century context gained fresh vigor in the new; the expansion of urban settlement and the appearance of an influential leadership beyond the pulpit fueled a greater focus on a secular heritage, although the Norwegian American clergy by no means relinquished their hold on their congregants. The secular press in any case—while printing regular columns on church life and synodical processes—had long freed itself from the theological pronouncements and religious controversy of an earlier date; the disparate branches of Norwegian American Lutheranism were moving toward doctrinal unity, laying the foundation for merger. Increased secularization encouraged by the growth of urban enclaves and the arrival of newcomers who felt distant from the earlier religious controversy all strengthened an appeal to unite on ethnic grounds. The end result was the merger that in June 1917 created the Norwegian Lutheran Church of America *(Den Norsk Lutherske Kirke i Amerika);* the conciliated Norwegian Synod, Hauge's Synod, and United Church formed a national Lutheran communion.

A rich shared store of Lutheran hymnody appeared as a familiar and treasured possession; Norwegian musical activity received its strength and inspiration as well from a long tradition of folk songs and the music of Norwegian as well as Norwegian American composers. This musical heritage was cultivated by male choruses early on. Few events were headlined in the press to the same degree as the large song festivals. The male chorus movement followed organizational traditions established in mid-nineteenth-century Norway; as in Norway, male choruses became a cultural institution in Norwegian American communities throughout the land. Song festivals, assembling many choruses, began in the mid-1880s, advanced in the 1890s, and flourished during the first decades of the following century. A number of singing societies *(Sangforeninger)* and associations published their own song and music magazines; the most important one was launched in Minneapolis in 1910 with the title *Sanger Hilsen* (Singers' Greeting), published by the Norwegian Singers' Association of America (NSAA) *(Det Norske Sangerforbund),* organized in 1910. Under different names and composition NSAA actually dated back to 1897. It was the largest of the associations with as many as fifty member choruses by 1914. Its magazine continues to carry news about its activities, attesting to the longevity of a festival tradition in song and music.

Norwegian American newspapers were a significant part of its success. *Budstikken* reported enthusiastically on the "Great Minneapolis Sangerfest of 1891" in July of that year, judging it "a monumental success," with close to two thousand singers. It was arranged under the auspices of the United Scandinavian Singers of America; the following year united Scandinavian choruses became a victim of the Swedish-Norwegian conflict; the Swedish choruses withdrew and formed their own organization; the Danish and Norwegian United Scandinavian Singers, as Carl G. O. Hansen wrote, had a festival in Chicago during the Columbian Exposition in 1893, which became its swan song, as it soon after was dissolved. Hansen, who joined the editorial staff of *Minneapolis Tidende* in 1897, gained recognition for the newspaper as an organ in tune with the cultural life of the Norwegian American community, specifically in music and literature.

The Norwegian Student Singing Society's America Chorus *(Den Norske Studentersangforenings Amerikakor)* tour throughout the country in the crucial days in late May 1905, as the Union crisis came to a head, had a profound impact on Norwegians in America. The student society's concerts were announced in the Norwegian-language press long in advance of the arrival of the singers; it secured well-attended concerts. *Pacific-Posten* in San Francisco, prior to the anticipated concerts, cited the Oslo newspaper *Aftenposten* as claiming "anything better [than the chorus] has hardly ever left Norway." *Skandinaven* reported how "More than one thousand Norwegian men and women" welcomed the chorus at its arrival at the Illinois Central Railroad Station in Chicago. "An enthusiastic and jubilant five-thousand-large audience attended the concert—a spectacular and unforgettable festival—at the Chicago Auditorium." Hansen claimed that the student chorus from Norway stimulated a revival of male chorus singing and convinced many that "if a Norwegian chorus were to survive it would have to consist of Norwegians." Male song festivals had, however, continued unabated. *Pacific-Posten* in announcing the Norwegian student chorus reminded its readers of the third annual concert of the Pacific Coast Norwegian Singers Association (PCNSA) in Portland, Oregon, in August 1905; the year before *Normanden* had narrated with great pride and detail the program of the Sangerfest in Grand Forks offered by male choruses from all states of the Upper Midwest.[4]

At a time of heightened attachment to Norwegian roots, the Norwegian American press throughout the United States became an agent for and commentator of many public events that appealed to patriotic sentiments: the many ski meets and ski jumping competitions, where Norwegians excelled; the celebrations of Leif Erickson's discovery of America; the annual conventions of the *bygdelag*, welcomed by local chambers of commerce; and the most constant observances of all, the festivities associated with May 17, which for a while competed with June 7 as a national holiday, the date most Norwegians recognized as ending the Swedish-Norwegian Union. Tensions between Swedes and Norwegians in America faded rapidly after 1905, especially in the urban setting, where Swedes, Norwegians, and Danes frequently resided together in close-knit neighborhoods and met at public events, at Saturday night dances, and at many other venues, including religious services. *Everett Ekko* in Washington urged Scandinavian unity in political affairs and praised Scandinavians in Minnesota and Wisconsin for pulling together *(løfte i flokk)* politically. Additional moves toward unity included, for example, a gathering of Swedes and Norwegians in Webster, South Dakota, for "a Big June 7th Festival" to celebrate a peaceful separation, as mentioned in a 1911 *Sioux Falls-Posten.*[5]

The Eidsvoll Constitution's centennial on May 17, 1914, stirred Norwegian nationalistic emotions during the gloried post-Union years; Norway's Constitution Day was saluted with mounting passion as the primary symbol of Norwegian ethnicity. Norwegian patriotic pride was evident in the press and in new publications. Waldemar Ager helped to create the Norwegian Society of America *(Det Norske Selskab i Amerika)* in January 1903 to "unite all Norwegian Americans around the worthwhile cause of Norwegian language, literature, and immigrant history." To further the Society's program, Ager launched the magazine *Kvartalskrift* (Quarterly) in January 1905; as the Society's organ it promoted the literary scene among Norwegian Americans until it was discontinued in 1922. *Kvartalskrift* faced competition when Johannes B. Wist and Kristian Prestgard, both of *Decorah-Posten,* in 1905 started a literary periodical in Decorah, Iowa, with the ambitious title *Symra, en Aarbog for Norske paa begge Sider af Havet* (The Anemone, a Yearbook for Norwegians on Both Sides of the Ocean); like the national achievements of 1905, the anemone marked the advent of a spring full of promise and a following abundant summer. Considered the best literary magazine ever published by Norwegians in America, *Symra* featured original literary prose and poetry by authors in Norway and the United States; from 1909 until it ceased publication in 1914, *Symra* expanded from a yearbook to a quarterly magazine.[6]

Two literary magazines published in North Dakota both carried the name *Eidsvold* (now spelled Eidsvoll), which was the site of the constitution's signing, May 17, 1814. In May 1909 the monthly literary journal *Eidsvold* appeared in Grand Forks, North Dakota, with Kjetil Knutsson, editor of *Normanden* and former editor of the short-lived temperance organ *Afholds-Basunen* in Hillsboro, in the editor's chair, assisted by Peer Strømme. Knutsson soon became sole owner; he left *Normanden* to devote his full time to his new enterprise. It was a literary organ of high quality. The many contributions by Norwegian American authors indicated a need for a literary magazine open to their productions. Mindful of his temperance mission, Knutsson made nightly expeditions to the saloon city of East Grand Forks in Minnesota and exposed in *Eidsvold*—with photographs—the prohibition-struck North Dakotans crossing to the wet neighboring state to acquire their "booze." The magazine, discontinuing publication in September 1911, consequently had a moral message in addition to its literary content.

In Fargo in June 1912, Hans Astrup Jervell founded a second *Eidsvold* literary magazine. Jervell emigrated from Fræna, Norway, in 1905, then in his mid-thirties. Before emigrating, he had earned a law degree and engaged in journalism. Jervell opened the magazine to notable Norwegian American writers like Waldemar Ager and Simon Johnson. It did not succeed, however, shortly moving from a monthly to a quarterly magazine; in 1914 it ceased publication altogether.

American-born Peer Strømme, examining an issue of the newspaper Normanden, *was a force in Norwegian American journalism and active in many pursuits as a minister, a teacher, a journalist, a translator, a speaker, a novelist, a politician, and a worldwide traveler.*

Kjetil Knutsson had hoped through his magazine *Eidsvold* to convince the Norwegian population in America that an appropriate memorial gift *(Mindegave)* to present to Norway in 1914, when the old fatherland observed the centennial of its emancipation from Denmark, would be a people's college *(Folkeuniversitet)* built at Eidsvoll; Knutsson's idea met with enthusiasm in North Dakota but received only measured support elsewhere, and when he died in 1911, his suggestion for a memorial gift died with him.[7]

Few issues at the time consumed more ink and space in the Norwegian American press than the discussion of what would be the most timely memorial gift from "the emigrated Norway" on the occasion of the constitutional centenary jubilee; fundraising began and suggestions abounded. In June 1909, a national memorial committee assumed the charge; state senator Lars O. Thorpe of Willmar, Minnesota, headed the group, constituted in Minneapolis. The committee decided to establish an endowment fund from which accrued interest would be distributed to charitable and humane causes at the discretion of the Norwegian parliament, the *Storting.* On July 4, 1914, in a grand ceremony outside the parliament building in Oslo, an official representing Norway accepted a memorial gift of about a quarter million *kroner,* in 2009 equal to about twelve million *kroner,* approximately $1.7 million. The result of the prolonged collection drive was far below expectations. Many blamed the *bygdelag*—the old-home societies—since they declined to take part but instead collected money for their respective Norwegian home districts to the detriment of the larger undertaking. They presented gifts at large and small *bygd*—community—festivals for returning Norwegian Americans.

Nordmanns-Forbundet in a broad view of Norwegian nationalism took the initiative to have a separate pavilion for "emigrated countrymen, especially Norwegian Americans" at the centennial exposition at Frogner Park in Oslo. The later prominent statesman C. J. Hambro, in his capacity as the Federation's secretary general and editor of its well-received magazine, traveled in Canada and the United States to engage Norwegian Americans in the constitutional event and secure a worthy representation of "the emigrated Norway." The May 17, 1914, commemoration in Norway of the rebirth of its kingdom, due largely to Nordmanns-Forbundet's sustained commitment and actions, became "the Great Homecoming" in particular for Norwegians in America, with an estimated twenty thousand of them visiting the homeland. As a gift from his state in connection with the jubilee, Governor Louis Hanna of North Dakota on July 4, 1914, unveiled a bust of Abraham Lincoln in Frogner Park; the celebration featured a series of speeches extolling the virtues of the Great Emancipator and the ideals of the Norwegian American population.

The main celebration of the Eidsvoll Jubilee in the United States was held in the Twin Cities of Minneapolis and St. Paul May 16–18,

1914. Tensions between urban and rural cultural orientations were on full display in the years leading up to the centennial. The conflict represented a persistent divide among Norwegian Americans. The *bygdelag,* mainly organized among Norwegians residing in country towns and farming communities, challenged the Norwegian Society of America's sophisticated national cultural expressions and demanded respect for the old folk traditions. The *bygdelag*'s version was, however, a selective celebration of a transplanted folk culture, limited by the leadership of a pietistic clergy. Many feared that the *bygdelag* and their rural attachment, guided by a dominant Lutheran clergy, would have too much influence in shaping a Norwegian American cultural world. In an act of unity, the *bygdelag* initiated a common observance of the constitutional jubilee. The program, made public by a joint committee of the *bygdelag* in 1912, caused consternation and intensified attacks on these societies; a special provision of the program was that the *bygdelag* alone would plan and carry out the schedule of activities, which called for a full day of separate *bygdelag* meetings and one day reserved for church services. The newspaper *Scandia* in Chicago likely expressed the sentiment of many. "The peasants are coming! The peasants are coming!" it warned and accused the *bygdelag* committee of planning a celebration for "the glorification of *bygder* (rural communities) and Lutheranism," adding caustically: "How could anyone ever believe that one could make a *Norwegian* out of a Vossing or Sogning?"

A threat to arrange a competing celebration convinced the *bygdelag* committee to rescind its earlier resolutions and accept input from civic groups and Norwegian organizations in the Twin Cities. The three-day commemoration became ethnicity on parade—the creation of public memory—as interpreted by the expanded committee on arrangements. Some fifty thousand persons participated in the festivities. The eclectic images created, proclaimed in bold headings in Norwegian American journals, encouraged pride in a Norwegian heritage and acceptability by American society. It was a colorful festival, with two processions introducing the event on May 16, one from St. Paul and one from Minneapolis. They convened at the fairgrounds between the two cities. The unique peasant costumes, banners, flags, and floats, including bearded Vikings in a Viking ship and a float with a representation of the Eidsvoll constitutional assembly, were reminiscent of the land they had left. Survivors of the Fifteenth Wisconsin of Civil War fame on the other hand gave evidence of Norwegian Americans' place in American society and history. *Minneapolis Tidende* in its exuberant account saw the Minneapolis parade as "a magnificent demonstration of Norse organizational activity in Minneapolis"; *Decorah-Posten* described the program during the following two days as symbolizing "a triumphal march of Norsedom in America."[8]

The Norwegian American Press and World War I

War broke out at the end of July 1914, causing "the Great Homecoming"—for those centennial celebrants who had not already sailed home—to end in a somewhat panic-stricken return journey, not only to the United States, but to other nations with resident Norwegian populations as well. "By the autumn of 1914," noted historian Carl Chrislock, "the opposing armies of World War I were slaughtering each other on a scale unprecedented in world history." The opinions of the Norwegian American, indeed of the entire non-English press, were most cogent prior to the United States' entry into the Great War April 6, 1917; editorial views revealed existing divisions in regard to the belligerents. The roots of the rise of "the most strenuous nationalism," to cite John Higham, "and most pervasive nativism that the United States has known" had prewar origins in the crusade for Americanization; it became a xenophobic demand for 100 percent Americanism and an intolerant anti-hyphen campaign. Total loyalty to American war policies became the parole of the day. Higham observed, "Theodore Roosevelt stood out as the standard-bearer and personification of 'unhyphenated Americanism.'" Woodrow Wilson surrendered to the call for national solidarity and cultural uniformity and joined the campaign against hyphenate subcultures. President Roosevelt's call for English only and a militant nationalism found many adherents and affected the freedom and very existence of the foreign-language press. In 1914 he declared,

> We have room for but one language in this country, and that is the English language, for we intend to see that the crucible turns our people out as Americans, of American nationality, and not as dwellers in a polyglot boarding house.

An initial concern for Norwegian American newspapers with the outbreak of war in 1914 revolved around how the homeland would fare; all journals adopted regular columns on "The War" *(Krigen)* and "The War and Norway" *(Krigen og Norge)*. Many journals expressed strong antiwar sentiments before United States entry into the conflict; in March 1917, *Pacific Skandinav* asked: "Is it war we now want?" Once the war was a reality the press gave its support to America's engagement, if not consistently with enthusiasm. Until then, the Norwegian American press expressed both identifiable pro-Ally and pro-German positions.

The large *Minneapolis Tidende,* from August 14 through March 1917, had a discernable pro-Ally stance; its editorial line reflected distrust of Germany; Peter Myrvold in *Fram* and Waldemar Ager in *Reform*—like the Swedish American and German American newspapers—expressed sympathy for Germany. Many leading Norwegian Americans admired German civilization; the cultures had Lutheranism in common. The frequently controversial Rasmus B. Anderson of *Amerika* took the Norwegian Lutheran pastors to task for their pro-German tendencies; the politically left Torkel Oftelie in turn criticized Anderson for placing all blame for the war on Germany. Peer Strømme, writing in *Normanden,* found reason to defend the actions of the German Empire, finding fault for the outbreak of war with the Allies, in particular England. Nels T. Moen, editor of *Fergus Falls Ugeblad,* on the other hand, sided with the stance of most Norwegian Americans in the Upper Midwest—rejecting an involvement in Europe's old feuds—and advocated for American neutrality and peace. In general, with the exception of *Amerika,* the smaller Norwegian-language weeklies in the Midwest vigorously opposed the drift toward war. *Minneapolis Tidende,* however, leaned toward intervention, as did *Nordisk Tidende,* influenced by a strongly interventionist environment in the East; *Skandinaven,* though less directly, also advocated firmness toward Germany.[9]

The examples above illustrate conflicting positions shaped by the different regions' climate of opinion in the years leading up to America joining forces with the Allies against Germany. Public opinion had previously held German Americans to be one of the most assimilable and reputable of immigrant groups. Yet according to John Higham, after the war began they experienced the most spectacular reversal of judgment in the history of American nativism. No immigrant group was, however, entirely spared the hysterical outbursts of anti-foreign prejudice. The Nordic homelands of Scandinavian immigrants maintained neutrality throughout the conflict; it might have spared them the most severe questioning of their loyalty to America.

But even neutrality became an issue. The Norwegian journalist Einar Hilsen, publicist for the 1914 centennial and editor of its anniversary publication, in 1914 went on a speaking tour "to build bridges between Norwegians on both sides of the Atlantic." Following the tour, instead of returning to Norway, Hilsen settled in the United States and became a widely traveled speaker and a prolific columnist, especially in the two South Dakota journals *Fremad* and *Sioux Falls Posten* but also in *Scandia* in Chicago; he argued the pro-Ally case with intensity, with vitriolic attacks on the German position, and with appeals to Norway not to trade with Germany. In a piece titled "Letter to Norway from Einar Hilsen," published in *Fremad* July 12, 1917—several months after the April declaration of war—he strongly reproved Norway for its neutral stance, accusing the old homeland of letting others fight for its freedom. For Norway to keep its integrity and others' respect, Hilsen urged Norway "to enter the war and do your part to defeat the German Midgard Serpent." It was surely a radical exhortation.

The above statement by Hilsen may be interpreted as a declaration of loyalty to American war policies. Loyalty oaths abounded from many quarters. The May 12, 1917, letter to President Woodrow Wilson from seven hundred publishers of non-English newspapers was reprinted in *Fremad* in English and in Norwegian translation. It read in part:

> We the undersigned publishers of American foreign language newspapers circulating among eighteen millions of people who have left their native lands to enjoy the blessings of citizenship in the United

> States, knowing full well what is in the hearts of these people, assure you, Mr. President, that they cordially welcome the opportunity now offered them, in common with their fellow Americans, to assist the enlightened citizenship of other nations in establishing more firmly throughout the world the great principles of democracy.[10]

The declaration goes on to remind the president of the immigrants' contributions to "the agricultural, industrial, and commercial greatness of the United States," their gratitude to the land of their adoption, their loyalty to its government, and their willingness to make the sacrifices that might be expected of true patriots. A submissive compliance was not a matter of choice, however, but a matter of wartime legal code and rising patriotic hysteria. The U.S. government greatly infringed upon the freedom of speech. On October 6, 1917, Congress outlawed commerce with enemy nations and in a special provision of the act established censorship over the foreign-language press. Editors of non-English newspapers were required to file full and complete translations of all articles dealing with government policy or the war with the local postmaster or to secure presidential permits exempting them from the requirement. A number of newspapers protested, among these *Skandinaven,* which editorially declared that the provision signified that the U.S. administration would not tolerate any criticism of its policy in print.

In Minnesota, Nicolay Grevstad, past editor of *Skandinaven,* in advance of the October 6 provision was appointed assistant publicity director of the foreign press by the Minnesota Commission of Public Safety; his charge was to oversee the Scandinavian American press in the Upper Midwest and assure their proper patriotic spirit. Grevstad contributed articles with the appropriate loyalty focus. Scandinavian American newspapers, some on the recommendation of Grevstad, were soon displaying permit numbers on their mastheads, exempting them from the burden of translating all political articles. Socialist and other left-leaning journals, such as *Gaa Paa* and *Reform,* as well as Gilbert T. Hagen's liberal reform newspaper *Vesterheimen* (The Western Home) in Crookston, were obliged to submit translations of all their political articles and commentaries.

Agitation for monolingual education and the English-only movement further impeded support for non-English journalistic endeavors. The most flagrant example was the famous language proclamation issued by Governor William L. Harding of Iowa May 23, 1918, which would obtain during the war. English would be the only medium of instruction in all schools, private as well as public; conversations in public and over the telephone, as well as public addresses, had to be conducted in the English language. Because the prohibition applied only to the spoken word, it did not directly touch the foreign-language print media, and newspaper publishing continued under existing restrictions. *Washington Posten* feared the movement would spread to other states, as it indeed did before the armistice on November 11 discouraged legislative adoption of wartime ordinances; governors of at least fifteen states had proposed legislation prohibiting the teaching of all foreign languages in schools and limiting their religious use to private worship in the homes. Kristine Haugen, active in Norwegian American cultural affairs, sounded a strong note of protest against the Harding proclamation from Sioux City, Iowa; in letters written in Norwegian to several Norwegian-language newspapers, she accused Harding of wanting "to combat Prussianism in Europe and practice it in the American homeland . . . the very hotbed *(arnested)* of individual freedom." Even if the prohibition in practice would only apply to the German language, as some Iowa and South Dakota English-language journals opined, the Seattle weekly *Washington Posten* expressed a broader vision: "*Washington Posten* is of the opinion that we are on the wrong track in this country, even when we ban the enemy's language."[11]

The Voice of Socialism

Washington Posten's concern appeared well founded. In 1919 American xenophobia reached new heights under the weight of the First Red Scare, 1917–20, which was especially intense during the final two years. The seeming threat from the Russian Revolution of March 1917 and the ensuing Russian Civil War called forth a hysterical antiradical nativism and a widespread fear of anarchism, of a Communist uprising, and of the radicalization of political groups on the Far Left; anarchist bombings and radical political agitation fueled the anxiety. The official response to anti-government campaigns produced repressive measures. It was in this political climate that in 1919, as reported in the press, both the Minnesota Senate and the House of Representatives made motions requiring—here citing an interview around 1950 by John Bjørhus, earlier business manager and the final publisher of *Minneapolis Tidende*—"all foreign-language newspapers to print everything translated into English in a column alongside the foreign language material." Bjørhus described it "as a crackpot bill" that, if passed, would have killed the foreign-language newspapers in the state.

Representative Nels T. Moen of Fergus Falls led the opposition in the house on April 9, 1919; the Socialist *Folkets Røst* (The Voice of the People) rejoiced a few days later that the proposed legislation "did not find enough idiots and chauvinists to become law . . . it went down the drain." English-only advocates in Oregon's legislature had greater success. January 20, 1920, the governor signed into law an act "making it unlawful to print, publish, circulate, sell or offer for sale any newspaper and periodical in any language other than the English." Violations of the act would constitute a misdemeanor punishable by imprisonment and fine. It had a chilling effect on publishers of non-English material nationwide. *Normanden* in Grand Forks, edited by "the prairie writer" Simon Johnson, labeled Oregon *Molboerstaten* (The Molboer State), here referring to the tall Danish tales about the *molboer*—inhabitants of Mols in Jutland—invariably depicted as stupid and gullible.[12]

Socialist thought, as indicated earlier, was made public by penmen in a number of Norwegian American news organs, not only in declared Socialist journals, but in a newspaper like *Scandia* as well; others such as *Skandinaven* showed great sympathy for the working man and encouraged working-class consciousness without embracing socialism's message. Two Socialist newspapers—*Gaa Paa* and *Social-Demokraten* (The Social Democrat)—may be of special interest because of their roles in the Socialist Party of America (SP), a union of the various factions of American socialism formed the summer of 1901; Eugene V. Debs became the most prominent figure in the new party, as he had been in the Social Democratic Party, one of the SP's constituent groups formed three years earlier.

Gaa Paa represented the SP's Dano-Norwegian voice. In 1903 J. A. Wayland, the publisher of the widely circulated Socialist organ

Appeal to Reason in Girard, Kansas, decided to start a Scandinavian Socialist newspaper there. He invited Emil Lauritz Mengshoel and his wife Helle Crøger Mengshoel to Girard; they published the first issue of *Gaa Paa* on November 29. Wayland thereafter decided not to be publisher but instead give financial support to the venture. Mengshoel had editorial experience on the radical Populist *Nye Normanden* in Minneapolis and was a contributor to *Appeal to Reason*. Born out of wedlock in 1866 in the small town of Gjøvik, Norway, he moved away from his unfortunate situation at age eighteen, enrolled in the school for noncommissioned officers in Oslo, and after his 1888 graduation went to sea. He there suffered the maltreatment commonly the lot of ordinary sailors. This traumatic experience, and his earlier witnessing of the brutality of military units sent to break up strikes by workers in Oslo, engendered in him a strong sense of social justice. He jumped ship in Pensacola, Florida, in 1891 and began life in America.

In fall of 1904, Mengshoel moved *Gaa Paa* from Girard to Minneapolis, where a large Norwegian working-class reading public

Mastheads of Gaa Paa, *November 27, 1908, and* Folkets Røst, *January 4, 1919. The Socialist newspaper* Gaa Paa, *published in Minneapolis by Emil Lauritz Mengshoel, in October 1918 lost its second-class mailing privileges as a consequence of its Socialist agitation. It reappeared in December as* Folkets Røst.

would assure profitability; the newspaper commanded some influence in the Twin Cities working-class wards; by 1912 he had built a circulation of five thousand, which remained relatively stable into the 1920s. It found a readership far beyond Minnesota; debt-ridden small farmers in western Minnesota and North Dakota responded positively to its message, as did workers in Chicago, in Seattle, and in Astoria, Oregon, another Scandinavian radical powder keg. Mengshoel believed that the political process would transform America into a socialist society, and while appealing to class consciousness in Marxist terms, he rejected the idea of direct action and sabotage and embraced the nonviolence plank of the Socialist Party. The Socialist Party of America never became a major political party but was nonetheless a counterpart to social-democratic contemporaries in Europe. The Socialist movement's progress may be gauged by the election of Andrew O. Devold, Helle Crøger Mengshoel's son from a previous marriage, to the Minnesota House in 1914 and the Senate in 1918 on the Public Ownership Party, as the Minnesota Socialist Party was named.

Socialism drew strength from the waves of immigrants who arrived after 1900 with Socialist ideas and experience of labor conflicts. Because of their larger numbers, Swedes dominated the Scandinavian socialist movement in America; Scandinavian cooperation was obvious in socialist circles. In 1910 Scandinavian socialist clubs from all over the nation met in Chicago and organized the Scandinavian Socialist Federation under the Socialist Party of America. The Federation was headquartered in Chicago, which was the organizational center of Scandinavian American socialism; by its height in 1918, it had 3,735 members divided into sixty-eight clubs. In 1911, Danish and Norwegian clubs in the Federation launched the newspaper *Social-Demokraten* (The Social Democrat), with Danish immigrant Frank Hurop serving as its first editor; a lasting hostility developed between it and *Gaa Paa* as they competed in a restricted market.

The outbreak of war, and most evident after America's entry into the conflict, placed both *Gaa Paa* and *Social-Demokraten* at great risk because of advocating "peace in a country under arms." *Gaa Paa* expressed faith in the socialist peace movement, promoted international worker solidarity as a means of preventing capitalist interests from waging war, and took strong exception to the creation of the Minnesota Commission of Public Safety, which it feared would further suppress civil liberties and the rights of labor. As a consequence of its opinions, the newspaper lost its second-class mailing privileges in October 1918. It reappeared in December, a month or more after the armistice, rechristened *Folkets Røst* (The Voice of the People) by Mengshoel, and shortly employed *Gaa Paa*'s volume numbering. On the masthead, *Folkets Røst* declared "Vox Populi Vox Dei" (The People's Voice is God's Voice); the new name suggested a less blatant socialist tenor and reflected, as the Socialist Party virtually disappeared in the 1920s, the political reality at that time, locally as well as nationally, until its demise October 31, 1925.

Folkets Røst, while appealing to the people and labeling itself a Norwegian Socialist newspaper, opposed the radicalization that was taking place in the Socialist Party of America. Mengshoel was obviously out of step with the Scandinavian Socialist Federation, which, meeting in Chicago in 1920, voted itself out of the Socialist Party in favor of joining the Third Communist International. Konrad Knudsen, an immigrant from Drammen, Norway, was *Social-Demokraten*'s editor at that time; in 1920 he joined forces with the prevailing Communist faction in the Federation. Knudsen thereafter returned to Norway where he became active in labor journalism and had various positions within the Norwegian Labor Party. The victory of the radical wing in the Norwegian Labor Party led it to adopt the Moscow Theses for some years in the early 1920s; it was the only social-democratic party in western Europe to do so. Knudsen represented the Labor Party in the *Storting* from 1937 until 1957.[13]

The Midwestern Press in the New Century

Historians of the Norwegian American impact on upper midwestern politics have regularly speculated about how far left-of-center the Norwegian American electorate moved. Judging from the opinions of a vocal Norwegian American press, upper midwestern Norwegians to a considerable degree embraced progressivism after 1900, just as many had taken to heart the Democratic-Populist message in the previous decade. Progressivism was preeminently a Protestant middle-class movement; Progressives were leery of both the business elite and midwestern and western farmer and labor radical reformism; they favored government regulation of business practices that would ensure competition and free enterprise. Norwegian support for the Progressive movement suggested that many upper midwestern Norwegians had attained a middle-class status. Voting records provide a more nuanced political picture than the Norwegian-language press seemingly communicates. The Populist insurgency found little support, for example, in southeast Minnesota but had considerable Norwegian support in the west-central and northwest-central regions of the state. In addition, a number of Norwegians participated actively in the Socialist Party; many of the members joined after the demise of Populism. A larger number of Norwegian Populists resumed a loose affiliation with the insurgent wing of the Republican Party from which they easily could move into other reform movements when these emerged. The North Dakota insurgency of hard-pressed farmers, whether earlier Populists or not—discussed below—is a case in point. The newspapers analyzed in the present study communicate an apparent left-of-center slant in Norwegian political orientation. The political history of the Norwegian population, based on both election returns and the election of candidates on the political right, even so, suggests the presence of a traditional conservative orientation that counterbalanced a visible political reformist bent. Norwegian Americans played a role in shaping several aspects of the political culture of the Upper Midwest.

Folkets Røst on March 15, 1919, carried a laudatory obituary of Gilbert T. Hagen, the publisher and editor of *Vesterheimen*, out of Crookston, Minnesota. *Folkets Røst*'s editor, Mengshoel, eulogized Hagen as a man who, in spite of adversity, held firmly to his progressive, even quite radical convictions: "He was an active friend of temperance, just as much as he was a man of peace. On the whole he was liberal in all political issues, and in some directions he moved strongly toward the Socialists." The interests of the hard-pressed farmers in western Minnesota had highest priority in *Vesterheimen*'s columns. The newspaper began as the weekly *Banneret* (The Banner) in 1892 in Hatton, North Dakota; two years later Hagen purchased the newspaper, changed the name to *Vester-*

heimen, and moved publication first to Mayville, North Dakota, and then from 1900 until it was discontinued in 1919 to Crookston. Hagen emigrated from Sigdal, Norway, as a young man; before purchasing *Vesterheimen* he gained experience as copublisher of the Populist weekly *Samhold* (Solidarity) in Elbow Lake, Minnesota, which in 1894, when Hagen became owner of *Vesterheimen,* merged with the politically radical *Rodhuggeren.*

Across the state line in Fargo, North Dakota, the newspaper *Fram,* the official organ of the North Dakota Temperance Association—consistently in sympathy with the insurgent forces in the Republican Party—from 1916 expanded its political engagement to become the Norwegian voice of the Republican Nonpartisan League (NPL) in North Dakota, under the editorship of Peter Myrvold. The League, founded by Arthur C. Townley during the North Dakota legislative session in 1915, was a farmers' organization inspired by the message of the Socialist Party of America led by Eugene V. Debs; while keeping the League within the Republican Party and appealing to party loyalty, Townley adopted a platform of state ownership of such essential agricultural enterprises as elevators and mills, state inspection of grain and dockage, state hail insurance, and state rural banks. The movement spread rapidly through rural areas of North Dakota, Minnesota, and a dozen other states. Its own organ, *Nonpartisan Leader,* was, like *Fram,* published in Fargo; by the winter of 1915–16 it enjoyed a circulation of nearly thirty thousand and was by far the largest newspaper in the state. In a March 1916 editorial, *Fram* declared its endorsement and support of the League and in subsequent issues reported on its political convention and other League initiatives. The Ulsaker Brothers were then the publishers of *Fram.* Ingvald H. Ulsaker served as manager and likely did editorial work as well; he clearly did so following Myrvold's resignation in April 1916.

Fram, referring to the North Dakota legislature as "our *Storting*" *(Vort Storting),* could report with great elation that the Nonpartisan League was gaining control of state governance. It won control of the state legislature in the 1916 elections and placed Lynn Frazier, a farmer, in the governor's seat. After the 1918 elections, winning control of both houses, the League enacted a significant portion of its platform.

Normanden in Grand Forks took great exception to the Nonpartisan League and to *Fram*'s pro-League advocacy. The Grand Forks weekly was at the time edited by Lars Siljan, who in 1914 succeeded Peer Strømme in that position. Siljan was an immigrant from Skien, Norway, had worked on *Skandinaven*'s editorial staff, and had experience in failed attempts at newspaper publishing in Canada before coming to *Normanden*. Siljan wrote excellent editorials and increased the political influence of the newspaper and its place in the progressive Republican camp. Over several pages in March 1916 Siljan directed his extreme wrath against the Nonpartisan League, calling it "the most dangerous political machine in North Dakota." He directly addressed the many subscribers who belonged to the League and asked them to consider the damaging information about "The League's secret program" to gain full control of the state government and re-introduce the saloon. In fact, *Normanden* lost many subscribers because of its regular attacks on Townley and the League; by 1919 *Normanden*'s circulation dropped to 6,790 from 9,216 in 1911.

Heated polemics between the exuberantly pro-Ally *Normanden* and the pro-League *Fram* were regular fare. *Fram*'s and the League's antiwar position and Socialist politics produced accusations of disloyalty; once U.S. participation in the war was a reality, America's war efforts gained full, if not heartfelt, backing. In December 1917, *Normanden*'s publisher, P. O. Thorson, purchased *Fram* from Ulsaker, promising to continue its publication; motives are here unclear, but Thorson shortly merged the two journals under *Normanden*'s masthead, thereby eliminating a rival and increasing circulation.[14]

Norwegian Nonpartisan League forces were not ready to accept defeat and the loss of a Norwegian-language organ. On June 26, 1919, the Grand Forks American Company, a stock company owned by one thousand North Dakota and Minnesota farmers, issued a sample copy of *Nord Dakota Tidende* (The North Dakota Times); regular weekly publications commenced in August. J. L. Rindal, who briefly edited *Fram* and was a lawyer by training in Norway, played a major part in starting the League weekly and served as its editor. *Normanden* found comfort as it observed the decline of "Townleyism" in the 1920s. *Normanden* nonetheless engaged in serious diatribe against its "Socialist colleague" *Nord Dakota Tidende,* which never doubted its call for state control of issuing money, advocacy of industrial democracy, and opposition to capitalist interests and compulsory military training. Even as *Tidende*'s popularity receded, it believed it spoke for the people. A laudatory poem to Townley, composed by poet, farmer, and *bygdelag* luminary Bjørgulv Bjørnaraa, related how everything looked dark and despairing before the noble Townley caused freedom and hope to return to the despondent farmers. The newspaper enjoyed a circulation of four thousand before it was discontinued in July 1923.[15]

Political reform advocacy in the Norwegian language persisted in South Dakota as well, even if not lodged in the Republican Nonpartisan League. On June 2, 1924, at age sixty-two, editor and publisher of the reformist *Fremad* in Sioux Falls, Johan F. Strass, passed away or, as announced in the newspaper, "relinquished his mission after a thirty-year calling." It was a remarkable achievement, which commenced with the first issue of *Fremad,* dated May 17, 1894. As advertised on its masthead, it had for some time been "the only Scandinavian newspaper in South Dakota." The strong connection Strass had to Trøndelag, his place of birth, encouraged special news coverage and correspondence from that region of Norway. Wartime conditions, while not precluding a postal connection, delayed delivery greatly. Albertine Walstad regularly corresponded from Trondheim; her letter mailed at the end of January 1918, with news about hardships due to war, could not be printed in *Fremad* until early April. One Karl Otto Kleven, an eager subscriber to *Fremad,* wrote from Hegra in Trøndelag and lamented the negative impact on regular delivery caused by "the difficult postal transportation" but added that once received, "the newspaper is immediately read with the greatest appetite." Direct contact with Norway, even if impeded by war, was retained, evidenced in the columns of all Norwegian American journals.

In the manner of most foreign-language newspapers, *Fremad* proclaimed its loyalty on its editorial page, pledging that "this paper has enlisted in the cause of America for the period of the war"; it commended the *German-Herald* in Milwaukee, "one of the leading German newspapers in this country," for departing from its earlier German stance (having little choice but to do so) and siding with the American war policy. *Fremad* printed in Norwegian translation the stirring patriotic speech given by Norwegian-born senator Knute Nelson, a man described as "not having as much as a hyphen in his blood," at the massive Loyalty Rally in St. Paul in December 1917. *Fremad*'s pages, echoing what was occurring in the press nationwide, regardless of language, encouraged everyone to buy savings stamps and subscribe to Liberty loans. "Victory is won," *Fremad* declared in November 1918.

Strass continued to support progressives in the Republican Party; he responded to the Nineteenth Amendment enfranchising women, "it is about time." In the October 26, 1922, editorial page, he related his own life story. *Fremad,* unlike most Norwegian American journals of long endurance, was thus like Hagen's *Vesterheimen,* Mengshoel's *Gaa Paa/Folkets Røst,* and Waldemar Ager's *Reform,* a one-man publishing and editorial enterprise. Mathias G. Opsahl filled the editor's chair from June 1924 and until *Fremad* ceased publication a decade or so later. He noted in *Fremad* that he had earlier, for twelve years, worked with Strass "both at [editorial] desk and [typesetter] case." Opsahl, born in 1858 in Manchester, Minnesota, to Norwegian immigrant parents, attended St. Olaf College before he became active in newspaper work in his late twenties; as a second-generation Norwegian American, he earned kudos as a champion of the use of the Norwegian language, praised by no less a person than Mengshoel in *Folkets Røst.*[16]

Fremad and *Fergus Falls Ugeblad,* as evidenced in previous chapters, shared a political history as Populist organs at the time of *Fremad*'s founding, though *Fergus Falls Ugeblad* was a decade or so older; in 1909, O. P. B. Jacobson organized a stock company that purchased the newspaper from longtime publisher Anfin Solem. Jacobson, an immigrant from Sandefjord, Norway, edited *Fergus Falls Ugeblad* until 1910, when he left to accept an appointment by Swedish-born Republican governor Adolph O. Eberhart as Minnesota railroad and warehouse commissioner. He was succeeded by Nels T. Moen, born in 1866 in Freeborn County, Minnesota, to immigrants from Østerdalen, Norway; Moen was a lawyer by training and established an impressive judicial career as attorney and judge and in the political arena as a multiterm state legislator from 1916. He exemplified, as did Opsahl, a second-generation embrace of an immigrant heritage; ethnicity in this case offered a means of interacting with American politics, identified the two men with ethnic activities, and in political life made both beneficiaries of positive coverage in the Norwegian American press. Moen edited *Fergus Falls Ugeblad* until his death in 1929, though with assistance, since legislative sessions required his full attention. He reported regularly from St. Paul under the title "From the Legislature" *(Fra Legislaturen). Fergus Falls Ugeblad* declared its political affiliation on its editorial page as "an independent reform paper and the oldest Scandinavian newspaper west of the Twin Cities." Editor Moen thus professed faith in progressive Republicanism. In the 1930 U.S. Senate election, *Fergus Falls Ugeblad* gave its support to the Democratic candidate Einar Høidale, since it found the Republican candidate to be unacceptable. The newspaper defended itself against *Normanden*'s accusations of having abandoned its Republican loyalty, stating that it reserved the right to back, in its judgment, the best candidate. Høidale, a prominent Norwegian-born Minnesota newspaper publisher, attorney, and politician, lost his Senate bid in the fall election. The "censurable" Republican candidate, Thomas D. Schall, ran successfully and won the Senate seat, though with a slim margin. By the 1930s, *Fergus Falls Ugeblad,* serving mainly as a local newspaper for Otter Tail and surrounding counties, even when signaling political independence, was not likely to have exerted great influence on statewide elections.[17]

"The Big Three"

Minneapolis Tidende, Decorah-Posten, and *Skandinaven*—the so-called big three because of their national distribution—set the tone during the first two to three decades of the twentieth century, the Iowa newspaper continuing for several more decades as the last of the pioneer Norwegian-language newspapers in the Midwest.

The two major editors of *Minneapolis Tidende,* daily and weekly editions, during the three or more final decades of its existence into the 1930s were Sigvart Sørensen, editor in chief 1891–1923, and Carl G. O. Hansen, associate editor from 1897 and editor in chief after 1923. Sørensen succeeded R. S. N. Sartz, editor 1889–91, and, according to Wist, earned the honor of having edited "the one and same newspaper over a longer period of time than any other Norwegian American editor"—in all thirty-two years. He was born in Oslo in 1849; he attended the Peter Qvam private high school before his 1866 emigration to America with his parents. In America, Sørensen gained experience in banking and developed an interest in journalism; he assisted in the editorial work on *Fædrelandet og Emigranten* in La Crosse, Wisconsin, before his 1890 advance to editor of the weekly *Norden* in Chicago. Following Peer Strømme's earlier editorial tenure, *Norden* was strongly Democratic; the following year Sørensen moved to Minneapolis to assume editorial responsibility for a newspaper of the same political faith. The January 20, 1891, issue of *Minneapolis Daglig Tidende,* in the aftermath of the 1890 election, interpreted as an end to unchallenged Republican supremacy in the state, printed several congratulatory letters about the newspaper's political engagement. A letter from Duluth stated: "Welcome and interesting as *Tidende* always has been and must be for all Scandinavians who at one time had their home in Minneapolis, it has become doubly welcome and interesting for its liberal readers after last fall's election."[18]

The Democratic *Tidende* did not regularly communicate strong political partisanship; during election campaigns, however, it vigorously came to the aid of deserving Norwegian political candidates who for the most part shared its political affiliation. Nationality at times trumped politics. The newspaper defended Republican Knute Nelson—as Democratic *Budstikken* had done earlier—when the state legislature in 1895 elected him U.S. Senator. Editor Sørensen rebuked the two Minneapolis Yankee rivals, the *Journal* and the *Times,* for their "smear campaign" *(Svertekampanje)* against Nelson and all Norwegians in the state in an attempt to obstruct Nelson's election; "here in Minnesota," the editorial read, "no one has done more for the development of the state than Scandinavians, and a Scandinavian-born citizen is just as entitled to become Senator as anyone else."

As a big-city newspaper serving a large and growing Norwegian population, *Minneapolis Tidende*'s field of action was productive as well as challenging. By 1914 the weekly edition had thirty-two thousand subscribers and the daily, including the special Sunday edition, about 6,500. The daily four-page and Sunday eight- to

Minneapolis Tidende

Minneapolis, Minn., Thorsdag den 16de August 1917.

(Emigrantens 66de, Budstikkens 45de, Nordvestens 37te

Krigsmaalene.

Senator La Follette forlanger fremsat de allieredes Fredsbetingelser paa Basis af „Fred uden Seier".

Det nye Krigshospital i Bronx, New York.

Ikke til Rusland.

De fleste af Missionen aldeles imod, at amerikanske Tropper sendes til Østfronten.

Stockholmsmødet.

Britiske Arbeidere beslutter at lade sig repræsentere ved Socialistkonferensen.

Hoovers Kampagne.

Fra Fronterne.

Streik

Carl G. O. Hansen, a member of Minneapolis Tidende*'s editorial staff from 1897 to 1935 and editor in chief beginning in 1923, was a major newsman and cultural leader in Minneapolis. This issue is dated August 14, 1917.*

twelve-page *Tidende* could—as stated earlier in the text and as announced by the paper in January 1891—be delivered to residences within the city for a weekly subscription fee of six cents; in following decades competition with rivals allowed, if at all, only small price increments in single copy sales; by 1930, however, due to inflation and loss of subscribers, single copies of the daily cost two cents with an extra penny added for the larger Sunday edition.

Tidende, most directly the daily, served a diverse Norwegian urban community; in 1912, when observing *Daglig Tidende*'s silver anniversary, the newspaper estimated that first- and second-generation Norwegians were at least sixty thousand strong and there were "thousands upon thousands of the third generation"; combined they accounted for a substantial percentage of the Minneapolis citizenry of some three hundred thousand. The considerable number of Norwegians in St. Paul interacted with their compatriots to form a Twin Cities Norwegian community. Numerous Norwegian businesses and organizations served its members: congregations and educational institutions of different Lutheran synods, among these Augsburg College and Seminary of the Lutheran Free Church, formed in 1897; societies such as the Sons of Norway; and charitable institutions, hospitals, and nursing homes founded by Norwegians. Since the first arrival of Norwegian immigrants, nearly a half-century earlier, *Tidende* recounted, "there have been festivals, which they all have united around, there have been events that have created interests in wide circles, and there has been wrangling and dissensions." The editor decided to "pass over" *(forbigaa),* quoting Ibsen, "what troubles us" *(det vrange og skakke).* And, as *Tidende* reminded its readers, Minneapolis was indeed the nation's Scandinavian capital, stating, "especially the Norwegians throughout the United States regard Minneapolis as their central place."

Working in harmony with the many disparate and not infrequently opposing interests that found voice among Norwegians in the city and far beyond its boundaries might well have exacted the most imminent demand on the editor's social skills and practicality. Sørensen's strength, as set forth by Wist and evidenced on *Tidende*'s pages, was "a never failing impartiality, an admirable sober-mindedness, and a highly developed good judgment." Wist furthermore gave the newspaper credit for uniting and strengthening the many Norwegian cultural and social pursuits in the city. Sørensen, taken ill with pneumonia in February 1923, relinquished the editor's chair to Carl G. O. Hansen, who as associate editor, in addition to his special music column in the weekly *Tidende,* "rendered great service as editor of the daily edition." Hansen was born in Trondheim, Norway, in 1871; he arrived in Minneapolis from Norway with his mother and four siblings at the age of ten, his father having died when Hansen was a small child. Hansen realized an intimate sense of belonging in the new environment, expressed in his book *My Minneapolis,* written in his later years. "To me the story of Norwegian immigrants in Minnesota, especially in Minneapolis," he asserted, "is one that I intensely feel is a part of me, these developments having taken place, so to speak, before my eyes." In an extensive series of articles titled "Glimpses from Life in Norwegian America" he educated *Tidende*'s readers about their history in the New World.[19]

The common denominator for most successful Norwegian-language journals related to the business acumen and originality of the publisher. Thorvald Gulbrandsen early on made *Minneapolis Tidende* a fixed institution in the city, and once firmly established, secured its nearly unparalleled success in the Norwegian American newspaper world. *Skandinaven* in Chicago was a key rival in laying claim to even greater advances in ethnic journalism than its Minneapolis competitor; its branch office in Minneapolis secured a circulation in competition with *Tidende* in the Twin Cities. Both newspapers functioned in rapidly expanding metropolitan settings. *Skandinaven* marked its half-century anniversary in 1916; in 1914 it had a circulation of fifty-three thousand for its semiweekly edition and twenty-five thousand for its daily. The twenty-page jubilee issue paid great tribute to the newspaper's founder and longtime manager, John Anderson; *Skandinaven*'s bookstore and book-publishing department, and the large job-printing establishment that was added later, give evidence of Anderson's vision for the financial success—achieved only by degrees and great effort—of the highly regarded John Anderson Publishing Company.

John Anderson worked hard right up to his untimely death on February 24, 1910, one month short of his seventy-fourth birthday.

His business was then at the height of its prosperity; *Skandinaven* reached its full grandeur and prominence. His son, Louis M. Anderson, became president of the firm, a position he held until the John Anderson Publishing Company came to an end in 1949. In 1911, John Benson, an immigrant from Mandal, Norway, succeeded Nicolay Grevstad as editor in chief after having served as associate editor of *Skandinaven* since 1893. The newspaper's jubilee issue carried congratulatory greetings from such prominent Norwegian American politicians as senators Knute Nelson of Minnesota and Asle J. Grønna of North Dakota, congressmen Andrew J. Volstead of Minnesota and H. T. Helgeson of North Dakota, among other well-wishers. Republican candidates—conservative or progressive—for elected office eagerly sought *Skandinaven*'s endorsement.

In his greeting, second-generation Progressive Republican Congressman Helgeson made clear how Norwegian-language journals, in this instance *Skandinaven,* met the needs of the Norwegian American community. He was born in 1857 to immigrant parents from Vang in Valdres, Norway, on a farm near Decorah, Iowa, and shared his recollections:

> As a boy, living then in Winneshiek County, Ia, my first recollection of a newspaper was the "Skandinaven," which was religiously read every week by my parents. Being farmers, and newspapers not being so plentiful then as they are today and our present wonderful postal service not having been even dreamed of at that time, they did not get many newspapers, and therefore the "Skandinaven" became such a household necessity that, to use a common American expression, they "could not have kept house without it." It was therefore through the "Skandinaven" they kept in touch with the world, it was through its columns they kept track of the religious discussion that created so much interest and at times excitement among the Norwegians of the Northwest during the years following the civil war, and politically the "Skandinaven" was the guide in whose wisdom and patriotism they had so much confidence that few indeed were the Norwegians who voted contrary to its advice.

Skandinaven was the major political Norwegian-language organ for the Progressive movement in Wisconsin; Norwegian voters followed the lead of Robert M. LaFollette and showed stronger progressive loyalties there than Norwegians in Iowa or in Minnesota because of lack of leadership of equal stature, especially in the latter state, as Lowell Soike argued. Under LaFollette's leadership Wisconsin's progressives dominated the Republican Party from 1900 until 1914. During these same years of the Progressive Era, Soike stated, "hopeful reformers looked to Wisconsin—the laboratory of political progressivism." Theodore Roosevelt, in the 1912 election greedily pushing aside the presidential candidacy of his fellow Republican Progressive LaFollette, gained the backing of Norwegian American reformist journals for his own presidential candidacy for the newly formed Progressive Party. Running for president in 1924, LaFollette as a Progressive gained a respectable number of votes, indicating the movement's continued appeal. In gauging Norwegian political behavior, it is worth noting that with the exception of Knute Nelson, prominent Norwegian members of the U.S. Congress—Senate and House—cast their ballot for the great reform measures of the day. *Skandinaven* joined the chorus of politically progressive newsmen in the service of reform-minded and social-uplift Norwegian-language newspapers in the states of the Upper Midwest.

John Benson served as editor until 1930, at which time his predecessor Grevstad resumed his post as chief editor. Benson came to America in 1887 at age twenty-five; he embraced the policy of the Liberal Party *(Venstre)* under the leadership of Johan Sverdrup, and in America, to cite his obituary in 1939, "he was and remained a broadminded man of the liberal school" and "kept abreast of developments in this country, especially the 'Norwegian states' and Norwegian America."

As big-city newspapers, *Skandinaven* and *Minneapolis Tidende* both faced difficult prospects after World War I; restrictions on publishing foreign-language journals, an emphasis on American patriotism, and anti-hyphen propaganda all had an adverse effect on their circulation. Publication expenses rose due to the persistently high cost of paper. American advertisers focused more on English-language journals, realizing that Norwegian-language subscribers read these as well; American advertisers in Chicago invested advertising allotments in the journals of ethnic groups less assimilated than the Scandinavians. The newspapers had little choice but to raise the annual subscription rates. Growing overhead in their urban setting necessitated retention of the higher fee, making sales drop precipitously. These unfavorable circumstances hit *Skandinaven*'s daily edition, intended mainly for Chicago readers, especially hard, and on March 31, 1930, the loss of advertising and subscribers convinced the publishers to let it expire after nearly sixty years of publication. The *Minneapolis Tidende* daily followed suit two years later, ceasing publication on April 29, 1932. The early demise of Norwegian American journalism for many seemed certain.[20]

Decorah-Posten, although facing the same challenges as other foreign-language journals, benefited from the lower overhead of its small-town location; after raising subscription fees briefly, it lowered them to the original level, something the other two in the big three category could not afford to do. In 1910, three years before his death, *Decorah-Posten*'s founder and publisher Brynild Anundsen formed the B. Anundsen Publishing Company; it became the official publisher of the newspaper with R. B. Bergeson as business manager. The firm's operations adhered to strict commercial considerations and were characterized by a spirit of frugality. While *Skandinaven*'s semiweekly edition was reduced from a circulation of 53,000 in 1914 to 25,000 in 1925, and *Minneapolis Tidende*'s weekly suffered a decline from 32,000 to 17,000 in the same period, *Decorah-Posten*'s semiweekly circulation actually peaked, increasing from 39,000 in 1914 to 45,000 paying readers in the mid-1920s.

The success of *Decorah-Posten*—regularly claiming to be "significantly larger than any other Norwegian newspaper in America"—may partly be attributed to its imaginative use of premiums to attract new subscribers: a colorful print of the Lord's Prayer in Norwegian became one of the most treasured subscription prizes; it could be framed for hanging and found a place of honor in thousands of immigrant homes. There was as well the inherent appeal of the newspaper's diverse features. These included serialized fiction, as noted in chapter five, but also an original comic strip cartoon, the popular "Han Ola og han Per" by Peter J. Rosendahl, a Spring Grove, Minnesota, farmer; it was the single Norwegian American newspaper to entertain its readers with its own cartoon series. Rosendahl's drawings, which began appearing in 1918, became one of *Decorah-Posten*'s most talked-about features. Rosendahl, born to immigrant parents, drew more than seven hundred cartoons by the time of his death in 1942; his vivid imagination and a unique sense of humor were evidenced in the ridiculous situations in which he placed his protagonists, Ola and Per; he used mixed Norwegian vernaculars and intended ridicule of Norwegian American life. The popularity of the cartoons and their poking fun at familiar immigrant experiences show that they were enjoyed by an ethnic group with established traditions and culture. *Decorah-Posten* clearly identified with an older immigrant tradition and captured the interests of a readership in tune with its customs and practices. In addition, the newspaper's editorials offended no one. Einar Lund, associate editor from 1927 when he joined editor in chief Kristian Prestgard, explained how *Decorah-Posten* had not espoused a partisan political cause and had "always sought to inform rather than direct its readers." This journalistic policy attracted a large readership.[21]

The Fuhr Publishing Empire

Jørgen Jansen Fuhr organized the Fuhr Publishing and Printing Company in Duluth, Minnesota, in 1918; it became a force in Norwegian American newspaper publishing in the Upper Midwest. Jørgen Fuhr served as chief editor for both *Duluth Skandinav* in Minnesota and *Superior Tidende* in Wisconsin. The firm expanded its publishing empire even across the border to Canada. In 1927, Fuhr began publication of *Grand Forks Skandinav* (Grand Forks Scandinavian) in Grand Forks, North Dakota, *Dominion Skandinav* (Dominion Scandinavian) in Winnipeg, Manitoba, Canada, and later *Dansk-Skandinav* (Danish Scandinavian) in Winnipeg as well. They were all set and printed in his plant in Duluth—the largest outside Brooklyn, Chicago, and Decorah.

Jørgen Jansen Fuhr was born in 1876 at Trondenes, near Harstad, Norway; he moved to Oslo in his teens and worked in journalism for ten years. Fuhr in some respects exemplified the range of individuals serving the ethnic press and how they were recruited. An early acquaintance from his years in Oslo, Knute Haddeland, later in life described Fuhr as "a personality who would attract attention in any kind of gathering." "He was strappingly handsome," Haddeland went on, "well-proportioned with a moustache á la Kaiser Wilhelm, polished manners, cultured, amiable and consistently elegantly dressed with a silk hat." While in Oslo, he established himself as an author of popular theater revues, comedies, and light operas; he also managed an amateur theater. In 1909 he made his first trip to America as a lecturer and newspaper correspondent for Norwegian dailies; he made a second trip a few years later, but this time to stay. He visited Norwegian settlements in every state, Canada, and Alaska. When war broke out in 1914 he was in Duluth, "a city after his own heart . . . and Norwegian scenery with hills, mountains and fjord . . . with a port where ships from all parts of the world docked . . . many with the beautiful three-colored Norwegian flag high on the mast . . . bringing greetings from the fatherland." Fuhr found employment as editor of *Duluth Skandinav,* and his work in Norwegian American journalism commenced.

In 1924, Jørgen Fuhr married Anna Dahl, following a first marriage in Norway to actress Julia Johnsen. Anna Dahl Fuhr became an active participant and mainstay in her husband's complex and extensive undertakings. After his untimely death in 1930, she became a major figure in Norwegian American journalism in her own right as both publisher and editor. Anna Dahl was born in 1891 in Meløy, a coastal community in the county of Nordland; she attended a folk high school and thereafter sought education as a nurse. She traveled to America in 1918, in part for additional training, but instead of returning to Norway, which had been the original plan, she remained. She did not see the homeland until after World War II, and then only as a visitor. Through association with Nordlandslaget, the local society for people with roots in north Norway formed in 1909, she befriended such prominent cultural personalities from her own district in Norway as Ole E. Rølvaag and contributed well-written sketches and short pieces to Nordlandslaget's membership magazine *Nord-Norge* (North Norway) and other Norwegian American publications.[22]

Because they shared editorial leadership, *Duluth Skandinav* and *Superior Tidende* did not differ in political affiliation or content, save for local news items from their individual regions of distribution. Both journals held special attention for the Trøndelag counties and north Norway; *Trønder Tidende* (The Trønder Times) was a regular feature. Lars Heiberg was a popular correspondent from Balstad in the Lofoten Islands; regular letters from his district in Norway, filled with notations about fishing and extreme weather, related well to the experience of the immigrants from northern coastal communities in Norway who developed commercial fishing along the North Shore of Lake Superior. The two newspapers took care to collect money at Christmastime for Heiberg, described in 1927 as "an old man in years, physically fragile, but still quick and fiery in spirit." It was a two-way communication: the Lake Superior journals were read and commented on in the distant Lofoten, with such features as "The Week in Duluth" and "The Week in Superior," and in return Heiberg kept readers in America informed about the variability of life in his part of the world.[23]

Bridge building represented a significant province of the Norwegian American press; simultaneously it reported on changes occurring in Norway, international news, and milestones and happenings within the Norwegian subculture. Job printing allowed the Fuhr company to expand its business enterprise. In its October 14, 1927, issue it announced the launching of *Grand Forks Skandinav* that week and the following week *Dominion Skandinav*. The expansion to North Dakota was prompted by the opportunity provided when *Normanden* moved publication from Grand Forks to Fargo. Henry Holt, a respected businessman in the city, succeeded P. O. Thorson as manager of the *Normanden* Publishing Company in 1922; he left in 1925 to start his own printing business. *Normanden*'s printing office was unable to compete, and *Normanden* had to be sold. The newspaper then entered into a short politically reactionary period in its history; J. G. Halland of Fargo purchased *Normanden* with money supplied by the conservative Republican politicians Louis B. Hanna and Porter J. McCumber, with the clear purpose of working among the Norwegian electorate for Hanna's 1926 candidacy for the U.S. Senate. Hanna ran against the Nonpartisan League candidate Gerald P. Nye, who ultimately won the Senate seat. That ended conservative fiscal support, and *Normanden* moved on to new owners.

Normanden's move to Fargo left Grand Forks without a Norwegian-language newspaper. Obliging the wishes of prominent Norwegians in Grand Forks, the Fuhr Company began publication of *Grand Forks Skandinav;* under challenging circumstances and meager means it continued publication until 1941. The earlier editor of *Normanden* K. M. Nass was hired to manage the Grand Forks office and edit the local news printed on the last page; aside from local news and advertising, content was identical to that found in Fuhr's two other American journals.

The foray into Canada began with Jørgen Jansen Fuhr's attendance at the impressive convention of Canadian *bygdelag*—old home societies—July 4–6, 1926, in the small prairie town of Camrose, Alberta; it assembled thousands of Norwegian Canadians from all parts of the Dominion. He discovered opportunities for Norwegians in Canada at a time when the gates were closing for immigrants south of the border. British Columbia held the greatest promise, in his mind, and in cooperation with the Canadian government he engaged in an ambitious colonization effort. His newspaper ventures in Winnipeg became a part of the project. *Duluth Skandinav* and *Superior Tidende* were for some years, until Fuhr's death and the closing of the Winnipeg office, filled with news and promotional articles from the Canadian provinces.[24]

Rasmus B. Anderson and His Amerika

In his biographical treatment of Rasmus B. Anderson, Lloyd Hustvedt described him, until his fiftieth birthday in 1896, as the "hub" around which Norwegian cultural life in America turned. He aroused interest in the Norwegian heritage and the history of the Norwegian people on both sides of the Atlantic. The focus of this study allows for a mere sketch of the services he rendered. Anderson published the newspaper *Amerika* in Madison, Wisconsin, from 1898 until 1922. He was by all accounts a complex and controversial figure, frequently described as vain and self-preoccupied. He was born in 1846 to Norwegian immigrant parents on a farm in the pioneer Koshkonong settlement in Dane County, Wisconsin. After studies at Luther College he taught at the Seventh Day Baptist Albion Academy; he joined in *Skandinaven*'s uncompromising stand against the Norwegian Synod's educational program. His lecture series on Leif Erickson in Norwegian settlements gave him public exposure and the reputation of a scholar—a precursor to his 1874 treatise *America Not Discovered by Columbus.* In 1869, the young Anderson was appointed instructor of Scandinavian languages at the University of Wisconsin–Madison, then promoted to professor in 1875, becoming the first person to hold a professorship in Scandinavian studies in America. He was Bjørnstjerne Bjørnson's impresario on his lecture tour of America 1880–81. After Anderson left his university position, President Grover Cleveland appointed him ambassador to Denmark, 1885–89. Some nine years after his return from Denmark, he took over *Amerika.*

In 1895 he published his *The First Chapter of Norwegian Immigration (1821–1840),* making him the historian of his people, so acclaimed by Norwegian American newspapers throughout the Midwest. At this time Anderson abandoned his earlier liberalism; personal animosity made him strike many from his list of friends. He joined the conservative forces in the Republican Party and allied himself with the clergy of the Norwegian Synod. His condemnation of modern Norwegian literature rallied the Synod pastors behind his literary views. The old guard in the Republican Party helped Anderson raise the $4,000 needed to purchase the merged *Amerika og Norden;* after taking over its management in late 1898, he shortly restored the original title, *Amerika.*[25]

The first issue under Anderson's proprietorship, still titled *Amerika og Norden,* was dated October 12, 1898; it was the beginning of a stormy twenty-four year career. In the initial number Anderson explained why he left the Democratic Party and its free-silver policies during the 1896 election and joined the sound fiscal policy of the stalwart Republicans. *Amerika* remained loyal to the Republican Party. The weekly was a personal organ imbued with the spirit of the master, his virtues and faults, his vigor and whims, his ideas and passions, summarized Hustvedt. Anderson recruited subscribers by extensive lecture tours speaking on "Our Fathers' Heritage" and by purchasing other newspapers. Circulation topped at ten thousand in 1904, up from forty-five hundred in 1898; circulation after 1910 declined from year to year.

Two major evils, in Anderson's opinion, tarnished and jeopardized cultural life of Norwegians in America: first, Norwegian naturalistic literature and its outgrowths, and second, the language used in patent medicine advertisements in Norwegian American

Published and distributed under Permit No. 411, authorized by the Act of October 6th, 1917, on File at the Post Office, Madison, Wis. By order of the President,
A. S. BURLESON, Postmaster General.

Amerika.

37te aarg. | Madison, Wis., fredag den 7. jan. 1921 | No. 1

Kensington Rune a Joke, Anderson Insists; Replies to Peer Stromme

"Amerika's" Editor Likens It to Other Great Fakes; Tells of History of Stone Messages

BY RASMUS B. ANDERSON
(Editor of "America," former U. S. Minister to Denmark and former U. of W. Professor.)

Some of my readers will remember the Cardiff Giant, the supposed fossil giant which was unearthed near Cardiff, Onondago county, New York, in October, 1869, and exhibited for several months, but was finally proved to be a fraud. This giant was ten and a half feet high and made from a block of gypsum.

The Kensington Rune-stone is, in my judgment, a parallel. One is as much a fake as the other.

A week ago my friend, Peer Stromme, appeared in The Wisconsin State Journal, not exactly in defense of but as one inclined to accept the Kensington rune-stone as genuine and asking for more evidence from those who repudiate it.

My position is that this runic inscription has already been sufficiently discussed by those who reject it, and that the burden of proof of its genuineness rests wholly upon its advocates. I do not assume to be an authority on the subject of runes. Runology has never been one of my specialties. I know the runes simply as a part of my interest in northern languages, history and literature. What I have shown is that this Kensington rune-stone has been examined and definitely repudiated as a fake, a joke, a fraud, and as a monstrosity by all the most eminent historians, philologists and runologists of Scandinavia, such as Doctor J. H. E. Schueck, Doctor A. G. Noreen, and Doctor M. B. Olsen. On the basis of my interview with Andrew Anderson at Stanley, North Dakota, on the seventeenth of May, 1910, I have shown how this joke could have been made by the knowledge and skill of Mr. Fogelbad, Andrew Anderson and Olaf Ohman. While Andrew Anderson did not admit to me that these three had made the inscription, I became entirely convinced in my interviews with him that they were the perpetrators of this very clumsy fake.

IMPORTANT EVIDENCE

I know nothing about the poplar tree under whose roots the stone was found. If these roots by their flattened appearance were important as evidence, it is a great pity that they were not preserved by the State Historical Society of Minnesota, or by some similar institution. Mr. Ohman, who is so much interested in Alexander von Humboldt's Cosmos, could not have been blind to the value of this runic inscription, if he believed it to be genuine. He would have saved the roots of the poplar tree and he would not have converted the rune-stone to such sordid use, as a stepping stone to his granary.

Peer Stromme tries to make capital out of the fact that Ohman did not settle on his farm before the year 1892, but he neglects to call attention to a more important fact; viz., that Ohman came from Helsingeland in Sweden in 1875 and that he then settled near Kensington and has lived in that neighborhood continually ever since that time. That is twenty-two years before the unearthing of the rune-stone in 1897.

The runes transcribed: Shanmals auk Olauf leta Kiara Merki thausi efter Suain fathus sin. Than Kuth hialbi Salu haus.

Translation: Shanmals and Alauf (names of women) had these monuments made after Swain, their father. God help his soul.

In speaking of Professor Magnus B. Olsen, the foremost authority in Norway on runology, Peer Stromme says:

"Professor Olsen never has examined the stone. He assumed that the thing was an American joke and turned the matter over to one of his young students, who promptly declared the inscription a forgery."

To this I reply: Professor Magnus B. Olsen did make a careful examination of the inscription on the Kensington stone and decided it to be a forgery, but instead of preparing an opinion himself, he turned the matter over to one of his students in order to give him some practice along this line. The student's report was approved by Magnus Olsen. Does it not frequently happen that the famous Mayo doctors in Rochester, Minn., make a thorough diagnosis of a case and then turn it over to an assistant for operation? Thus Dr. Magnus Olsen made the diagnosis of the rune-stone and the student performed the operation.

Again, I quote Mr. Stromme:

"Then there is the famous Doctor Schueck, the president of Upsala university, quoted at some length by Prof Anderson. His opinion, is, of course of great weight, but we may have some doubt as to the care with which he went into the matter."

QUOTES PROF. SCHUECK

In reply to this, let me quote Professor Schueck himself. He says:

"They had had facsimiles of the Kensington rune-stone in Upsala and Dr. A. G. Noreen, the eminent author in Sweden on Northern languages, has studied the inscription. He, like all other historians and linguists of Sweden, was of the opinion that it is a clumsily contrived joke."

Thus, it would appear th... matter was investigated ... care.

Naturally Scandinavi... would approach the Ke... stone in a most frie... table spirit for, if i... genuine, it would ... or and glory of t... The stone, if gen... a million, nay, ... the owner wo...

portuning historical societies to purchase it for the paltry sum of five thousand dollars. I think it was in 1912 that the present owner of the stone took it with him to the Scandinavian countries and submitted it to the scholars over there, but as Stromme admits, all of them merely laughed at it. If one of these authorities had recognized the stone as genuine, the present owner would not have failed to keep megaphoning this fact throughout the length and breadth of this country. And, it may be that such endorsement, if he had secured it, might have helped him to obtain the five thousand dollars which, I understand, is the price he is asking for the Kensington rune-stone.

May I not ask the defenders of this rune fake why they prate so much about the eight Goths and 22 Norwegians coming up the Red river from Hudson Bay, while the makers of the runic joke claim they came from Vinland, which we all know was somewhere on the Atlantic coast? Why not rather argue that they came up the St. Lawrence river and the great lakes to Duluth and thence penetrated the country to the present Kensington? This would seem to be indicated by the inscription itself.

SUBJECT OF INQUIRY

While comparatively little attention has been paid to runes by American scholars, runology has long been the subject of much investigation in Europe and particularly in Denmark, Sweden and Norway. A collection of all the books, pamphlets and essays on the runes would make a formidable library. In the three northern countries, there have for several centuries been scholars who have made the study of runes their specialty. Over two thousand runic inscriptions on monuments have been found in Sweden alone, about three hundred in Denmark and not a few in Norway. A runic inscription was found in the graveyard of St. Paul's church in London; runes were also found on a grave-stone in Orleans, France; and in the Viking period, runes were carved on a marble lion in the harbor of Athens, Greece. This lion covered with runes may still be seen at the Arsenal of Venice, Italy. Above, I have given a typical specimen of a runic monument found in Sweden. I have taken it from the great history of Sweden by Oscar Montelius. It illustrates the most common use made of the runes.

And, now, for the edification of my readers, I am going to close this discussion of the Kensington rune stone with the story of an interesting runic fake in Sweden.

From pre-historic times we have a tradition of a Danish king, by name, Harald Hildetand. In his old age, his kingdom began to have bad luck. He decided to die as a hero in battle and sent a message to his nephew, King Sigurd Ring in Sweden. He challenged him to meet him in combat with as large an army as possible. For seven years the two kings prepared for war and when they finally had gathered large ... all over the north, ... kings met on ... In this ...

Rasmus B. Anderson in his highly personal newspaper Amerika, *published in Madison, voiced his combative opinions with force and became a controversial figure in the Norwegian American community. This issue is dated January 7, 1921.*

newspapers. A focus on these two issues will reveal much about the nature of the newspaper. In a January 1903 editorial, Anderson declared his preference:

> Give us back the old Romanticists! It was Romanticism that awakened in us a sense for history, in Norway for the saga literature, and gave impetus to the national spirit. . . . But during the last quarter century we have had Realism, Pessimism, Decadence. We have had winter instead of spring and summer.

Anderson's attacks called contemporary literature swinish and atheistic and created great controversy with his fellow penmen. These confrontational exchanges served only to fortify Anderson's views and rigidify his position; he denounced Norwegian literature after 1880 as anti-Christian for the most part. He now repudiated his friendship with Bjørnson and dealt harshly with him and his literary works, reminding *Amerika*'s readers that the Norwegian poet scorned God and during his visit to America, when Anderson was his promoter, had in his speeches insulted Norwegians in America. Anderson's crusade against modern literature reached new heights of contention in 1903, focused on, among Anderson's other irritants, the founding of the Norwegian Society in America. Anderson was present at the initial meeting in Minneapolis on January 28 and gave a detailed, if not uncritical, report in *Amerika.* Anderson's two motions were both rejected. He wished to add "sound" to the Norwegian literature the Society should promote and limit membership to persons who were members of a Lutheran congregation. If passed, Waldemar Ager and others Anderson disliked would have been excluded, which likely was one of Anderson's motives for making the failed motion. He never joined. By degrees, newspapers like *Reform, Skandinaven, Nordiske Blade, Minneapolis Tidende,* and in spite of an initial friendly relationship also *Decorah-Posten* were listed as his enemies. *Skandinaven* infuriated Anderson by adopting a policy of complete silence in regard to *Amerika.*

Nordiske Blade in Brooklyn reproved his "absurd opinions about Bjørnson and his relationship to the church," concluding that "Mr. Rasmus makes himself more ridiculous and unpopular in those circles where common sense prevails." Ole S. Hervin—using the nom de plume Herm. Wang—in his monthly *Smuler* (Crumbs), published

1901–12 in St. Paul, Minnesota, joined in the journalistic melee, describing Anderson's *Amerika* as stupid and reactionary. *Smuler* consisted of short satirical articles, a format well suited for critical reflection. Even earlier, in 1899, Hervin had risen up in righteous anger in St. Paul's *Nordvesten,* a journal he earlier had edited, at Anderson's description of modern Norwegian literature as depraved and blasphemous.

The November 13, 1908, number of *Amerika* contained Anderson's lamentation over "the disparaging [*nedsættende*] writings" about him in a long list of Norwegian-language newspapers. He complained that every issue of *Smuler* made him "the target for ridicule"; in addition, the malicious 1908 exposé by the scandal author Lars A. Stenholt titled *Paven i Madison* (The Pope in Madison) lambasted Anderson.[26]

In January 1909, Anderson narrated the history of *Amerika* as he saw it. He dwelled on his campaign against patent medicines; the passage of the Pure Food and Drug Act in 1906 directed attention not only to the "unclean" language, but also to the products themselves. He claimed progress in his campaign against "the filth in our Norwegian American "'large newspapers'" *(Storblade),* but at the price of making many enemies; Anderson took credit for what he considered to be a fact—namely, that "of the Scandinavian newspapers in this country the Norwegian are the cleanest." Just look at the Swedish American press, Anderson proclaimed, "where no battle has been waged, is as dirty as our Norwegian large newspapers were ten years ago."

Rasmus Anderson persisted in his personal vendettas against high and low; these included not only "unscrupulous" *(samvittighedsløse)* newspaper publishers like John Anderson and Brynild Anundsen, but also J. N. Kildahl, president of St. Olaf College, reviled for his association with these men and his writings about the Lutheran church in *Skandinaven* and for opening the door to the school for Hjalmar Rued Holand, whom he dismissed as a "freethinker"—the accepted term for an atheist—and "pioneer slanderer" *(Pionerbagvasker)* for his books on Norwegian settlement. Sons of Norway was not spared, highly criticized as a "secret society" and for naming local lodges Bjørnstjerne Bjørnson, in Chicago, and Henrik Ibsen, in Stoughton, Wisconsin, since these two authors, "in their books and other writings have acted as Christianity's bitterest enemies."

Controversies on a number of levels characterized *Amerika*'s columns from first to last. Anderson did, however, reconcile with some of his enemies. According to statements in both *Normanden* and *Amerika,* in December 1919 Peer Strømme and Rasmus Anderson "buried the hatchet" after having done battle, at times loaded with personal disparagement, in the press over differences of values and opinions all the way back to Anderson's takeover of *Amerika.* By this time they were aging men: Strømme in his mid-sixties and Anderson about ten years his senior. On July 28, 1922, Anderson announced on the front page of his newspaper, "*Amerika* passed away" *(hensovet).* He succinctly explained, "I don't have the strength to put out *Amerika* and have therefore sold the print shop to the Norwegian Synod." His reference is here to the congregations in the Synod that opted to remain outside the 1917 merger that created the Norwegian Lutheran Church of America and that the following year formed the conservative Norwegian Synod of the American Evangelical Lutheran Church.[27]

"An Objective Nordisk Tidende*"*

In 1910, *Amerika* imputed *Nordisk Tidende* for making a false claim when it advertised itself as "The only Norwegian paper published in the Eastern States," pointing out that *Den Norske Amerikaner* (The Norwegian American), edited by Hanna Astrup Larsen, was published in Brooklyn. The newspaper, a successor to *Nordiske Blade* in 1906, ceased publication that very year. *Nordisk Tidende,* in spite of *Amerika*'s reproach, might consequently be justified in its publicized assertion. The short-lived Brooklyn weekly *Norges-Posten* (The Norway Post), mentioned earlier, was discontinued in 1904 after a year's publication. Franklin Petersen—editor of *Nordisk Tidende* from November 1907 until September 1911—put out a weekly he called *Nye Norge* (The New Norway) in New York 1911–13. Petersen had strong literary interests and published fiction and nationalistic poetry; his newspaper contained aggressive reviews of local circumstances, occasionally even personal criticism of leading members of the Norwegian community. Petersen's journalistic practice was thus in the spirit of the editorial style of *Nordisk Tidende*'s founder Emil Nielsen, if not as consistent or striking.[28]

Norwegian-language newspapers in the East functioned in a much different environment from the Midwest with its large concentrations of people of Norwegian birth or descent. In the East, Norwegians constituted but a small percentage of an ethnically diverse society; ethnic enclaves of people from nearly every nation of the world competed for attention and influence. Greater New York, a consolidation of New York, Brooklyn, and smaller adjoining towns, in 1900 had a population of nearly one-and-a-half million; only thirty years later the city could boast of sheltering almost seven million residents. The 1930 census classed 38,130 Norwegian-born and 24,785 with at least one Norwegian-born parent, for a total of 62,915 Norwegian residents. Concentration in specific neighborhoods was the secret to success and progress. In 1910, of 32,013 first- and second-generation Norwegians, 26,090, or 80 percent, lived in Brooklyn, concentrating in the Bay Ridge district. "The strength of the Norwegians in Brooklyn," Andreas N. Rygg wrote, "has in no small measure rested on the fact that a large proportion of them have been living close to one another in Bay Ridge." Norwegian Americans prospered from the late 1800s and up to the time the United States entered World War I; the rapid growth in immigration augmented their power and secured their steadily growing influence and prosperity.

The large Norwegian American population in greater New York in 1910, with some five thousand or more elsewhere in the state, and smaller numbers in other regions on the eastern seaboard could certainly sustain a weekly news organ; the high percentage of Norwegian-born residents was another telling factor. They were the most loyal subscribers. Many of the Norwegian-born stayed only a few years; the steady stream of newcomers revealed an evident "bird of passage" migration. These circumstances kept the Norwegian impulse strong and vibrant. Whereas the second generation in Minnesota, according to the 1910 federal census, constituted 62 percent of the total Norwegian stock, in the state of New York this group amounted to only 33 percent of the whole. *Nordisk Tidende,* in fact, prospered during these years. A new leadership took advantage of favorable circumstances to secure the newspaper's position as an influential regional organ. Its circulation in 1910 stood at 3,500; instead of decreasing as its midwestern colleagues did, *Nordisk Tidende* increased its circulation to 7,760 by 1925. Roedder in his history of the newspaper describes the period from 1922 to 1929 as "the seven fat years."

Karsten Roedder, *Nordisk Tidende*'s editor in the 1960s, defined the years after 1911 as "the objective period"; he credits Sigurd J. Arnesen, business manager 1911–58, and Andreas N. Rygg, editor 1912–29, with the newspaper's progress. Arnesen immigrated at age seventeen with his family to Brooklyn from Stavanger, Norway, in 1904; after several meetings in 1911 with E. T. Christensen, president of the Norwegian News Company, *Nordisk Tidende*'s owner, Arnesen was hired as manager but shortly took over as both manager and interim editor. Arnesen had differences with editor Franklin Petersen, who was dismissed in August but only after editorially having described Arnesen as "a young and inexperienced man who must not be taken seriously." In January 1912 Rygg took over the editorship, which before his arrival had been held by Harald Waage. Rygg was, on his own call, granted part in the company.

Arnesen became "the young man who put things in order." Rygg was not a young man but shared Arnesen's great sense of organization. The two men complemented each other in their respective areas of responsibility. In August 1921 they announced that they jointly had assumed ownership of the Norwegian News Company. Rygg was born in Stavanger in 1867 and in 1888 immigrated to Chicago; he worked for some years as treasurer for *Skandinaven,* which apparently gave him sundry insights into the editorial process, though he had no experience in journalism. In 1905 he moved to Brooklyn; there he engaged in charitable work, especially a home for children, until he joined *Nordisk Tidende.* As editor, he moved the newspaper to "the fundament of the church and to the service of charity." Waage continued to be responsible for printing newsworthy material; Hanna Astrup Larsen became a contributing journalist.

A newspaper publisher must run the operation as a business venture; Arneson's early engagement reveals much about the Brooklyn colony and how his predecessors conducted business. A practice immediately terminated was "the well-known tradition that bar owners paid for their advertising in alcoholic beverages and the editor was the debt collector." It had, Roedder suggested, been a popular assignment for many an earlier editor, which a temperance-minded *Nordisk Tidende* disallowed. Arnesen persisted in taking strict commercial considerations as business manager; to the business community, he held out the prospect of a readership approaching thirty thousand, half of these concentrated in south Brooklyn, Bay Ridge, and Staten Island.

In January 1920, *Nordisk Tidende* proudly announced the start of its thirtieth volume; Rygg, as editor and a central figure among Norwegians in New York, left the trying years of the world war behind; Norwegians' growing numbers in New York powered greater ethnic self-confidence and visibility. Many in the Norwegian American community prospered in commercial enterprise or were leaders in establishing socially beneficial institutions. "In the Midwest," Roedder noted, "the Norwegian element has had an impact also on political life." "In this regard," he explained, "Norwegians on the East Coast have accomplished nothing." *Nordisk Tidende* thought the time was propitious to make its mark also in the political arena. It would do so as a Republican voice; save for the overwhelmingly Democratic New York City, the state electorate mostly voted Republican, as did Norwegians in Bay Ridge, where most of them resided. But there was no united Norwegian Republican front; the clergy, congregational leaders, and most church people were Republican; union people, whether church members or not, were generally Democratic. The majority of Norwegian Brooklynites were, however, politically indifferent and unchurched. A Norwegian Republican political campaign was nonetheless organized; no Norwegian candidate was elected, though one had been nominated and ran for office. *Nordisk Tidende* editorially found comfort in being able to report "an emerging political consciousness and sense of duty" in the Norwegian Brooklyn colony. In spite of having little political clout, *Nordisk Tidende* had the same function in the East as newspapers in the West, namely to facilitate a separate ethnic group existence.[29]

The Press in the Pacific Northwest

The Puget Sound region persisted as the chief Norwegian settlement in the Pacific Northwest; the 1930 census shows that better than 85 percent of first- and second-generation Norwegians in Washington resided there. There were smaller colonies in western Oregon and eastern Washington. As in New York, the immigrants outnumbered the American-born generation, but not by the same margin; the large movement of Norwegians directly from Norway after 1900 swelled the ranks of the Norwegian-born, while migration from older settlements in the Midwest continued unabated. In 1910, about 46 percent of the Norwegian stock in Washington and Oregon belonged to the second generation; in the Midwest the children of the immigrants greatly outnumbered the parent generation.

The western urban frontier attracted Norwegian migrants early on. By 1910 Portland, Oregon, with a population of 258,547, sheltered 4,838 first- and second-generation Norwegians of the state's 14,435 residents of Norwegian origin. Two weeklies, published briefly into the early 1890s, *Stillehavs-Posten* (Pacific Ocean Post) and *Vor Tid* (Our Age), were followed in October 1904 by the more successful *Pacific Skandinaven* (Pacific Scandinavian). Advertising itself as "The only Scandinavian newspaper in Oregon," it declared editorially that it would not "take up for discussion religion, politics, and the temperance question." Ludvig B. Larsen, the original editor and part owner of the Scandinavian Publishing Company—the weekly's publisher—departed abruptly in December, selling his shares back to the company's business manager and owner H. Ellingsen. Harald Lange replaced Larsen in the editorial post. In March 1905, the newspaper reported that it had been sold to "a syndicate of six gentlemen who have let the newspaper be incorporated as a stock company," which indicates further instability. It was a brief involvement. O. H. Skotheim, a Baptist pastor from Albert Lea, Minnesota, assumed ownership and editorial responsibility in November 1905. His initial editorial was titled "A New Time" for *Pacific Skandinaven,* which "has gained deserved recognition" and as the only Scandinavian newspaper in Oregon, "has the support of Norwegians and Danes, and even some Swedes on the West Coast." Perhaps reflective of existing discord among the journal's shifting personnel, Skotheim, active as an evangelist, expressed his wish to build a new Scandinavia on the Pacific Coast, "but a Scandinavia as much as possible liberated from pettiness, narrow-mindedness, national conflict, and religious sectarian strife."

Pastor Skotheim's lofty visions of what could be achieved went unrealized, at least with him at the helm; March 29, 1906, after a brief spell as assistant to Skotheim, Haakon J. Langoe took over as owner and editor of *Pacific Skandinaven.* He disassociated himself from previous editorial opinions. The untidy and clearly stressful and contentious start of the journal is here narrated in some detail to exemplify the unfortunate experience of many novice newspaper publishers. Langoe lacked experience and requested time to prune his journalistic proficiency. He published and held primary editorial leadership in *Pacific Skandinaven* until its demise in December 1919. The weekly, as it regularly posted editorially, sought to serve the Norwegian and Danish interests on the coast; it served the Danes more directly after Langoe in 1909 inherited the subscription list of the briefly published *Vestkystens Danske Ugeblad* (The West Coast's Danish Weekly). Langoe thought of his newspaper as a literary journal with brief news reports from compatriots in Oregon. Basically a local newspaper, *Pacific Skandinaven* carried news of major events in the two homelands, and on occasion from other parts of the world, and even engaged in political commentary, the latter leaning toward the progressive Republican camp. The newspaper's growth from four to eight and finally to twelve pages indicates success.

Pacific Skandinaven had voiced concern about the march toward entry into the European conflict; in July 1917 the editor objected to the discrimination directed against "the foreign editors" by Oregon's autocrats, who in that regard, Langoe wrote, "more than in other states have become 'the vanguard.'" *Pacific Skandinaven* became a victim of the English-only legislative act signed into law by Oregon's governor in January 1920 and could not continue as a Norwegian-language publication. On April 29, 1920, it reappeared under the name *The Northman,* published by the Northman Publishing Company. Haakon Langoe, no longer publisher, was listed as managing editor. The newspaper printed a letter of commendation from the American Legion—which had taken an active part in passing the restrictive legislation—to Langoe and his associates for their "stand in this matter and for the spirit which prompted it." Langoe had apparently capitulated to the biased message of the vocal apostles of Americanization.[30]

The short-lived Portland weekly *Vor Tid,* as stated in chapter four, originated as *Spokane Falls Ekko* (Spokane Falls Echo) in Spokane, Washington, in 1890; Norwegian settlers from Wisconsin, Minnesota, and Dakota Territory had come to the Spokane Falls area in the 1880s. As the wheat-growing possibilities in eastern Washington developed and Spokane became a milling center, Norwegian numbers increased, concentrating largely in Spokane County. By 1910 nearly four thousand Norwegians made Spokane, a city of some one hundred thousand, their home. Aside from *Ekko,* the first Norwegian-language newspaper in the city, a few more weeklies appeared briefly in the early 1890s, among these the temperance weekly *Hjemmets Værn* (The Home's Protector); they are, as was the case in Portland, evidence of both the zeal and the ease to start a journal and even more clearly demonstrate the daunting task of securing a long-term presence. In August 1896, the small four-page weekly *Spokane Skandinav* (Spokane Scandinavian) was launched as a local organ for Norwegians in that part of the state; it was soon expanded in size and content. Only a few copies from 1896 exist; these do not list the name of an editor. Johannes Wist identified M. Marken as publisher and editor in 1906, which most likely is correct, even though the date he gave for the newspaper's founding was wrong. Marken was an immigrant from Vestnes in Romsdal, Norway; he managed *Spokane Skandinav* until it ceased publication in 1924.

In welcoming "a new Norwegian newspaper" in 1896, a correspondent in *Pacific Herold,* organ for the Lutheran academy—Pacific Lutheran University, founded in 1890 but opened for classes in October 1894, in Parkland, Washington—found the newcomer attractive but missed church news and political point of view. In later issues the editor announced the Parkland institution's third academic year, rejected the Populist Party, and gave news coverage of Denmark, Norway, and Sweden. The newspaper appealed to all three nationalities; Swedish news was written in Swedish and everything else in traditional Dano-Norwegian. The extant copies from December 1914 record the newspaper's journey to nearly the end of the European conflict. *Spokane Skandinav* no longer used the Swedish language; as war clouds gathered, it gave much space to "News from Mother Norway. The Land we Left." Although Dano-Norwegian dominated, the weekly increasingly used English and expanded local news coverage, most directly to Idaho through an office in Coeur d'Alene. *Spokane Skandinav* made these changes to attract more subscribers.[31]

Norwegians and Danes in Everett in Snohomish County, north of Seattle, could subscribe to *Everett Ekko* (Everett Echo). On November 16, 1906, Danish publisher and editor H. S. Hagerup began the four-page weekly, "devoted to the interests of the Scandinavians of Northwestern Washington." Hagerup declared that "tolerance and independence in religious and political issues is a part of our program, but any honorable Scandinavian who seeks election to political office will have this newspaper's support." *Everett Ekko* engaged greatly in Scandinavians' campaigns to municipal and state positions; in a column titled "Plain English" it addressed political concerns in English. For the 1906 city election Hagerup supported the Democratic ticket, the only one with a Scandinavian candidate; he continued to do so in later local and national elections, taking strong issue with "the moneyed interests' policy of oppression." He spoke against "special interests and prohibition fanaticism," which led to Sunday closing of all saloons and other businesses in the city. The editor's tolerance—even to the extent of reminding readers that socialism "did not conflict with the teachings of the Bible"—became an affront to some influential people. Their angry interchange appeared in *Ekko*'s columns. In spring 1908 Hagerup's critics started a rival newspaper in Everett titled *Pacific-Posten* (The Pacific Post), edited by the Lutheran pastor Magne Schilliaas. Six months later *Everett Ekko* printed "a few commemorative words" *(Mindeord)* over the departed weekly; "Silliaas-Posten," as Hagerup dubbed his antagonist, did not, as was intended, replace *Everett Ekko*. In November 1908, the newspaper reported to have attained "a circulation that justifies us to claim a weekly readership of 2,000." Competition from larger journals published elsewhere, contentious local opposition, and lack of adequate resources caused the modest news sheet to fold the following year.[32]

Tacoma in Pierce County, with its substantial Norwegian citizenry, offered a more promising venue for Norwegian-language publications. The weekly *Tacoma Tidende,* founded in 1890, in 1910 listed a circulation of two thousand. The following year John Blaauw, publisher since 1897, sold the newspaper to Rudolf Blom Andersen, an immigrant from Larvik, Norway; his graduate degree in the humanities gave him a higher education than most Norwegian American newsmen. Before becoming publisher and editor of *Tacoma Tidende,* Blom Andersen had gained experience on *Washington Posten*'s editorial staff. Several competitive ventures in reaching a Norwegian readership were made in Tacoma. The weekly humor magazine *Braat og Brand* (Clearing and Fire), 1907–12, was described by the captious editor of *Everett Ekko* as the kind of magazine "that will not be 'appreciated,' although we absolutely prefer it ahead of the boring fare *(Tørkost)* of most other [Norwegian] weeklies here on the coast."

Vestkysten (The West Coast), founded in Tacoma in 1906 as a regular news organ, presented a potentially greater challenge to *Tidende*'s prosperity than *Braat og Brand*, yet it suffered a premature demise, the unfortunate fate of many similar ventures. The weekly *Vestkysten* declared as it entered its second year of publication that its purpose had always been "to work for the common good and stand independently and free of all petty partisan dispute." But, the editor reminded the newspaper's readers, "in order for a public newspaper to be moral and be doing good it must have support" because "a newspaper depends on the support it gets from its subscribers." The later frequently became an uncertain commodity. Einar Finsand, an immigrant from Ringerike, Norway, was co-owner and editor for a year or more until the new journal apparently went out of business in 1909. He had earlier edited *Tacoma Tidende.* The experience of *Vestkysten* as well as *Tacoma Tidende* typified the uncertainty of journalistic ventures and the interrelationship of the constituent branches of the Norwegian American press.

In 1920, John Soley purchased *Tacoma Tidende* from the then owner O. M. Overn and served as its publisher and editor. Soley, an immigrant from Bodø, Norway, in 1907, was a printer by trade, associated with several journals in Norway, and exhibited early musical talent; in Tacoma he organized and directed Soley's Orchestra.

Soley altered the name to *Vestkysten* in 1925, perhaps inspired by the earlier newspaper of that name; he published the journal as *Vestkysten (Tacoma Tidende),* retaining volume numbering of *Tacoma Tidende,* the latter placed within parenthesis on the masthead. The newspaper in general became simply known as *Vestkysten.*

Preserved copies of *Vestkysten,* beginning January 6, 1928, give evidence of an active editorial engagement. Soley allotted much space to local Norwegian organizations and events; his presence and leadership in social and cultural activities, in particular musical performances, benefited the newspaper's popularity. The strong focus on local happenings echoed the content of thousands of small-town American newspapers. Soley's was, however, not the only local news journal in the city. *Western Viking* was launched in 1929 by the Puget Sound Publishing Company; A. Bjerkeseth occupied the editor's chair. Bjerkeseth broadcast "The Scandinavian Hour," sponsored by *Western Viking* and the Swedish-language *Puget Sound Posten,* weekly over KVI in Tacoma. The program regularly featured letters of appreciation. A "Mrs. Margit Mendes and family" had the following to say to the editor:

> Dear Countryman! We listen to your Norwegian program every week, which we are most grateful for. It gives an indescribably warm feeling to hear the old familiar tunes in our fine Norwegian language, which we heard back home in our childhood.

Appeals to nostalgia and loyalty might serve a newspaper enterprise well; *Western Viking* carried serious discussions on the preservation of Norsedom, the editor insisting that "Norsedom will never die as long as there are Norwegians in this country who have been taught to honor their father and their mother." It was a concern much discussed at the time. In a regular column titled "Open Discussion" *(Ordet Fritt), Western Viking* let readers vent opinions about a large number of issues, from Norsedom, to evolution, to political chicanery; it served as an urban community medium as well as a local news sheet. Readers were involved in the newspaper's content and circulation in a variety of ways. In December 1931, Soley sold *Vestkysten* to *Western Viking*'s publishers, in order to, as he explained, "enter other business," which, given the dire economic times, likely would be a better livelihood than publishing a small Norwegian-language journal. *Western Viking,* by permission, adopted the volume numbering from the founding of *Tacoma Tidende.* Only a few volumes of *Western Viking* are preserved; the fact that the newspaper survived the Great Depression and continued publication until 1941 suggests a run of some success as a local medium of news and entertaining reading.[33]

Washington Posten *and Gunnar Lund*

Gunnar Lund became a major figure in the world of Norwegian American journalism. He had no journalistic training or experience at the time he purchased *Washington Posten.* His wife, Marie Vognild Lund, became a co-worker in the enterprise. In *Trønderlagets Aarbok* (Annual for Trønderlaget), she reminisced about her husband's entry into journalism. Gunnar Lund was born in Stavanger in 1865; he had studied law, Old Norse, and English at the University in Oslo before he immigrated in 1889. He came to the Pacific Coast where he supported himself working on railroad construction and in sawmills, much like many other young Norwegian men. In 1893, he moved to Chicago, taught English in night school classes for Norwegian newcomers, and started his own business. In 1900, while in Chicago, he and Marie Vognild married. The Lunds moved to Seattle, where Gunnar Lund continued in the business world.

When *Washington Posten,* published north of Tacoma in Seattle, was offered for sale in 1905, Marie Lund recalled, the temptation to pursue intellectual interest in journalism impelled him to purchase the newspaper, investing the family's savings in the transaction. Lund persisted to run the newspaper as publisher and editor until his death in 1940.

Washington Posten rose to the level of regional newspaper for the Pacific states, Alaska, and British Columbia, giving local news coverage from Norwegian enclaves and communities in its area of circulation. It reached a maximum circulation of fifteen thousand in the 1920s. Before Gunnar Lund's 1905 takeover, the newspaper had wandered randomly from one publisher to another since its 1889 founding. It was with the new owner that *Washington Posten* gradually attained its position of influence and power in the Pacific Northwest. In competing for the favor of the Norwegian American community Lund faced few rivals; he moved circulation from 2,900 in 1905 to eight thousand in 1915. Its urban setting allowed for handsome advertising revenue from American and Scandinavian businesses. Seattle experienced a large influx of Norwegian immigrants after 1900. By 1920, people of Norwegian birth or descent formed a vigorous urban colony of 17,628, heavily concentrated in Ballard in the northwestern part of the city, which was annexed in 1907; more than one quarter of all Norwegians in the state of Washington lived in Seattle at that time. Norwegians in Seattle lived more residentially segregated than other ethnic groups in the city.

Gunnar Lund benefited from the rapid growth in the Norwegian population on the coast and his good relations with the Scandinavian commercial community; like the successful Midwest and East Coast publishers, he also possessed business acumen. Politically,

Gunnar Lund, in Washington Posten*'s office in about 1920, had purchased the paper a decade and a half earlier. As publisher and editor, he secured its success as a major regional Norwegian periodical.*

Lund continued to associate *Washington Posten* with the Republican Party, though on its progressive wing; in 1912 the newspaper's support went to the Progressive Party. Ethnic self-assertion at times, however, trumped party loyalty. Editorially Lund reminded *Washington Posten*'s readers that the foremost concern should be to elect Scandinavians, if they were otherwise able men, because "one can safely assume that Nordic men through their upbringing are Progressive regardless of the ticket on which they appear." Arguing for greater Norwegian or Scandinavian political representation was a common feature of the Norwegian American press. *Washington Posten* went one step further and voiced support for a quota system that would assure Scandinavian input in city and county affairs. The editorial column was no less vocal in insisting greater Scandinavian political weight after the newspaper's 1914 return to the mainstream Republican camp. Throughout his editorship, Lund expressed opinions on national and international political issues, with a dominance of local concerns.

Washington Posten's audience was mainly urban Norwegian Americans with many nonchurchly interests; the community was indifferent to politics and organized religious life, arousing Lund's critical editorial response. The new arrivals after 1900 were in large part young men not ready to settle down and establish permanent commitments to church and community. Many of the newcomers intended to return to Norway. The growth of secularization further alienated them from the church. Church activity and charitable concerns were apparent in the newspaper's columns; secular interests, however, seemed to dominate, evidenced in an abundance of advertisements for ethnic organizational and social life. In keeping with the ethnic press in general, readers maintained a lively contact with *Washington Posten;* a democratic tone and closeness between reader and publisher go a long way in explaining the community-building impact of an ethnic newspaper.

The landscape and familiar modes of livelihood in fishing, shipping, and lumbering attracted many immigrants to the Pacific Coast from north Norway and the coastal districts in west Norway. *Washington Posten* carried regular features titled *Nyheder fra Kysten* (News from the Coast), *Fra Havnen* (From the Harbor), *Bynytt* (City News), and *Seattle-Nytt* (Seattle News). These told "about the launching of a new halibut schooner, the departure of the halibut fleet for the Alaskan fishing waters in spring, and individual catches upon their return." Some claim that a Norwegian coastal culture was transferred to the West Coast of America. Reading the regular local news columns and *Washington Posten*'s coverage of ethnic events, small and large, notices of personal occasions, and reports about employment possibilities mimicked life in a port city in Norway. *Washington Posten* played a significant role in Norwegians' adjustment to life in America and in transforming disparate ethnic neighborhoods into a Norwegian community.[34]

The Norse American Centennial

The Norwegian American press, like American newspapers in general in the early decades of the 1900s, did not shy away from hyperbole in reporting the achievements of their generation. It was a time of many firsts in technology and social advances. The Norwegian American community, as upheld in the Norwegian-language press, boasted significant contributions to progress and the building of America. In the 1920s, a need to defend and protect an ethnic heritage under siege aroused traditionalists to take action; prevailing super-patriotic pressures weighed heavily on the Norwegian American community and its press. Among the most alarming national initiatives, as America turned in on itself, were the new barriers to immigration under a quota system; when fully operative in 1929, the system allowed a quota of 2,377 from Norway. This allotment was generous in comparison to immigration from eastern and southern Europe, yet the Norwegian American press protested loudly; in doing so it revealed an existing and shared prejudice against immigrants from those parts. *Vestkysten* (*Tacoma Tidende*) gathered signatures for a letter of protest against the "national origins" system, which it insisted discriminated against Scandinavian immigration; it reprinted other Norwegian American newspapers' commentary in protest of the law. A 1928 editorial stated,

> This new system, if enacted, is not only unjust, but a great affront to the Scandinavian nations, which have invested so much work and helped to build this country and made it what it is today.

These sentiments were widely echoed by Norwegian American columnists. *Minneapolis Tidende* in 1929 printed a petition, intended to be signed and mailed to one's senators and congressman requesting that they vote for the repeal of the national origins provisions of the Immigration Act and revise it so that calculations of quotas were based on the national composition in 1890, as the original act had, favoring Nordics, rather than the 1920 census, which upheld an ethnic status quo.

An accelerated shift toward English and the rapidly declining Norwegian-born population made ethnic distinctiveness fade; a monolingual American-born generation was clearly emerging. Newspaper readership fell off. It must be noted, however, that Norwegian newspapermen accepted an inevitable assimilation into American society and cannot have seen the preservation of an ethnic culture as a major purpose. For them, as for the great majority of immigrants, making good in the new land seemed to have been a higher priority than perpetuating a Norwegian subculture; they looked forward to an expanding and prosperous America. In a similar vein, the Lutheran church did not see its chief role as that of defender of Norwegian ethnicity. Americanization of the Norwegian Lutheran Church of America proceeded rapidly following its formation in 1917. By 1925 congregations held more services in English than in Norwegian; only six years earlier Norwegian worship services accounted for 66 percent. Far more people attended the English services than the Norwegian services. Many still defended the Norwegian bond, however. When church leaders at the newly organized church body's first biennial convention in June 1918 resolved to drop the word "Norwegian" from the name, adverse reaction was widespread and strident. Andreas H. Lindelie, *Normanden*'s previous editor, contributed to its columns the thought that judging "by the space our newspapers allocate to the name-change question, the uproar is assuming dimensions that threaten to put both the Nonpartisan League and the war in the shade." "The end of the war, together with a backlash against the excesses of postwar nativism," wrote historian Carl Chrislock, "seems to have tipped the balance in favor of those wishing to return to the old name." The church leaders, encouraged by a combination of assimilative motives, backed down and accepted the defeat of the name-change resolution. A strong sense of Norwegian identity was clearly present among the protesters, along with a conviction that identifying symbols had their own import and persuasive influence.

May 17 observances gained renewed vigor in the postwar years; they clearly communicated a message of pride in ancestry and a rejection of the xenophobic condemnation of foreign cultural and linguistic traditions. Anti-foreign sentiment weakened by the mid-1920s. The Norwegian-language press gave the May 17 festivities much space, as well as editorial reflection. *Fremad* in Sioux Falls, founded on May 17, paid special attention to the day, praising American-born generations for "treading in their departed ancestors' path"; by observing the day, they honored their own heritage, which, the editorial held forth, would make them better Americans. It was, to be sure, ethnicity on parade: by no means an act of ethnic segregation, but rather an effort to gain visibility and respect as Americans of Norwegian ethnicity. In 1924, *Normanden* invited prominent Americans of Scandinavian descent "to estimate the value of their heritage, insofar as that might be said to have influenced their attainment of ability and success." Their responses expressed a common theme of gratitude for inherited physical and spiritual qualities. They all stressed inheritance and not environment in listing the outstanding attributes of "Scandinavians as a race." J. A. O. Preus, governor of Minnesota, in a representative answer found, in his long recital of virtues, that especially in the northwestern states, Scandinavians "were possessed of a strong desire and will to do that which they convinced was right, and the courage so to do."

October 9, 1925, marked the centennial of the epochal voyage and arrival in the port of New York of the sloop *Restauration,* carrying the first boatload of Norwegian immigrants; it offered a unique opportunity to pay tribute to the Norwegian American people and their contributions to the American nation. The Norwegian American press early on turned its attention to an appropriate observance of the event; it would be impossible to give a comprehensive report on editorial opinions and of the general press coverage of the centennial itself. From coast to coast local and regional newspapers promoted observances near their place of publication. Local festivities were arranged in places like Seattle, Chicago, and New York, but the main one, like the 1914 commemoration, was held in the Twin Cities of Minneapolis and St. Paul. Carl G. O. Hansen, *Minneapolis Tidende*'s editor, had, beginning October 1924, a weekly column titled "Norwegian America through One Hundred Years"; the May 22, 1925, article offered "The Saga of Our Press from 1847 to 1925." Filled as these contributions are with historical ken, they deserve to be assembled and published in English translation.

May 28, 1925, preceding the planned festivities June 6–9, *Minneapolis Tidende* published a sixty-four page jubilee edition; Hansen's editorial pronounced the four-day festivities the largest ever, unparalleled in Norway and America. As in 1914, the *bygdelag* took the initiative through their Council of Bygdelag formed in 1916, joined by civic groups. The festival, headquartered at the state fairgrounds between Minneapolis and St. Paul, presented a varied program, extending it back to the heroic age of the Vikings and the exploration and discovery of America by Leif Erickson around the year 1000; a centennial pageant with one thousand actors focused on the life of Colonel Hans Christian Heg of Civil War fame, described in the program as "the type of all that is best and noblest in a citizen."

President Calvin Coolidge spoke on June 8—the high point of the centennial observance; an estimated one hundred thousand persons attended the open-air meeting. He complimented his audience, exciting booming enthusiasm: "You have given your pledge to the Land of the Free. The pledge of the Norwegian people has never gone unredeemed." The president endorsed Erickson's claim as the first European discoverer of the New World; it was a major boon to the persistent cause, extending back to Rasmus Anderson and his treatise on discovery, of having an official national Leif Erickson Day. By naming Leiv Eiriksson Square in Brooklyn in the centennial year and in later years raising a number of statues of the brave Norseman, the Norwegian American historical experience in an assimilative fashion was placed within an American historical reality. *Reform*'s editor Waldemar Ager in his prizewinning essay "Why We Celebrate" viewed the festival as a major argument for a pluralistic society and rejected "The now dominant 'melting pot' idea"—invoked by Coolidge—which he insisted would only result in "vulgarization" of American culture. *Minneapolis Tidende* weighed in with an editorial of the dual role of the press, praising Anundsen in *Decorah-Posten* and Anderson in *Skandinaven* for their visions for immigrant journalism. Editor Hansen wrote,

> It is generally conceded that the Norwegian American press has been a very essential factor in the work to preserve Norsedom. This could possibly be stated even stronger by bestowing upon the press the status of being the foremost means to protect a feeling of Norwegianness while it at the same time and in addition has taught its readers about in what genuine Americanism consists. Many men in the church have surely also shown that they honor and respect Norsedom, but as an institution the church has its purpose in a different field.

The board of the Norse American Centennial mailed a thank-you letter "to our Norwegian newspapers for the great service they have given in order to make the festival the success it was." The main message of the festival for most Norwegian Americans was a defining positive ethnic image and identity and a sense of being a part of American society and history.[35]

Reflections

The present chapter covers the last great age of the Norwegian American press. Newspapers from the past are absorbing reading material; contemporary reporting about a time that was and now long gone provides modern-day readers insights on life as lived by unknown forebears. On the yellowing pages of the aging journals lies an opportunity to enter the world of past generations and learn about their agonies and hardships, as well as their successes and hopes, not much different from those of the present generation, though played out under different circumstances and opportunities.

The Norwegian American press recorded and greatly influenced the two decades or more during which a viable and forceful Norwegian subculture prospered; by the 1920s no one considered the possibility of a lasting Norwegian America as they might have in prewar years. Waldemar Ager might at that time have envisioned a Norwegian American community that would continue to use the Norwegian language indefinitely; his hopes were dashed in the years after the Great War, though he persisted in championing its cause. Ager wrote a prizewinning essay in 1925 in Norwegian: the only Norwegian-language contribution to the jubilee publication. The two centennials—one celebrating Norway's constitution of 1814 and the second a hundred years of Norwegian group immigration—were markers in a historical journey for an immigrant people.

The Norwegian American press reached its largest circulation during the prewar years, reflecting the apex of "the golden age." According to Juul Dieserud the secular daily and weekly newspapers and monthly magazines enjoyed a total distribution of nearly four hundred thousand, based on published circulation statistics and private information; "the big three" combined accounted for about 38 percent of the total. These figures, even allowing for a somewhat inflated estimate, would suggest that one or more Norwegian-language publications had entry to nearly every home where Norwegian was spoken. As the use of the mother tongue declined, circulation suffered. Another consequence of the passing of time was the loss through death of a number of prominent personalities in the Norwegian American newspaper field; among them by 1925 were Johannes Wist of *Decorah-Posten,* P. O. Thorson of *Normanden,* Johan Strass of *Fremad,* and Peer Strømme, roaming reporter and editor. Those at the helm of Norwegian American newspapers, men like Carl G. O. Hansen of *Minneapolis Tidende* and Kristian Prestgard of *Decorah-Posten,* and newcomers to the field of journalism all faced the challenges of a rapidly transforming environment, an expanding consumer society, competition from radio and the movie industry, and the life-altering impact of the automobile. The culturally homogenizing effect in speech and lifestyle of these agents of change alongside a generational shift dictated that the Norwegian-language press could never be the same. The situation placed heavy requirements on those who would carry forward the ambitions of Norwegian American journalism.[36]

NORDISK TIDENDE

NORWEGIAN NEWS NORSKE NYHETER

Torsdag den 10. April 1941

CHAPTER 7

A Changing Final Role

The Norwegian American press produced . . . an enormous number of words, which when you come right down to it, were written in the sand.

CARL SØYLAND, the philosophical editor of *Nordisk Tidende,* quoted above, might well have wondered about the significance of his own role as an immigrant newsman. Were the thousands and thousands of printed words really written in the sand only to be washed away without leaving a trace? The question was posed at a time of troubling prospects for Norwegian-language publications. Søyland lamented how "the decline of the Norwegian language in speech and print was notable from year to year." For those who could not read or comprehend the words printed in the Norwegian-language newspapers, the story past and present contained on their pages vanished and left no trace. Søyland doubted his own powers to recapture the historical evidence and human drama the Norwegian American newspapers through the decades had recorded. Søyland humbly acceded that whatever he wrote "would only be written in the sand."

The present chapter will discuss the final decades of a Norwegian-language press and its changing role as its readership shrank and it accommodated shifting contingencies. The economic downturn in the 1930s caused the demise of some of the largest news organs. World War II witnessed a revival of the remaining newspapers as the Norwegian American community rallied to come to the aid of an occupied homeland. Postwar immigration was not sufficiently large to sustain a Norwegian-language press for long. The present study's aim has been to trace the history and significance of a secular Norwegian-language press on American soil. The final chapter will complete the story.

The Norwegian-language newspapers traveled a long and arduous historical course. The year 1927 marked the eightieth anniversary of the Norwegian immigrant press. That year, though not directly related, twelve American newspapermen, six of them Norwegian American, were invited to tour Norway; the other six newsmen had had no previous contact with Norway. The prevailing motives were to promote Norway as a tourist destination. Norway's National Association of Tourism and the Norwegian America Line were both sponsors; invitations were extended by the press office of the Norwegian Foreign Ministry, the Norwegian Press Association, and Nordmanns-Forbundet. The Norwegian American editors and publishers were Gunnar Lund of *Washington Posten,* Kristian Prestgard of *Decorah-Posten,* and Andreas N. Rygg of *Nordisk Tidende;* included were Norwegian-born journalist and author H. Sundby-Hansen, who represented the *New York Herald,* and two second-generation newsmen, John A. Anderson, copublisher of *Skandinaven,* and Herman Roe, publisher of *Northfield News,* Northfield, Minnesota. The group represented the major regions of Norwegian settlement; therefore the initiative was likely to have been directed at the Norwegian American community. It became a memorable summer for the newspapermen; they were special guests of the Norwegian government and private organizations and, one can claim, of the entire Norwegian people. The Norwegian American newsmen highlighted the tour and gave full coverage in their respective newspapers. These comprehensive accounts were of obvious interest to their readers.

Norwegian Americans became directly involved in the tourism trade; many of the Norwegian American newspaper publishers had long served as agents for the Norwegian America Line and other passenger steamship lines. Visits to the ancestral turf became commonplace in the 1920s. The *bygdelag* arranged joint Norway tours in 1921 and 1926; in 1921 parties of individual *bygdelag* members arrived in two fully booked chartered ships of the Norwegian America Line. It was obviously good for the line's business. Norwegian American newspapers were involved in these and many similar tour operations; the largest and most noted homecoming tour took place in 1930 when Norwegians commemorated the nine-hundredth anniversary of the martyrdom of St. Olav on July 29 and the establishment of the Christian church on Norwegian soil. Much of the festival centered on the historic Nidaros Cathedral in Trondheim. Nordmanns-Forbundet organized a service conducted by American-born bishop J. A. Aasgaard of the Norwegian Lutheran Church of America at the cathedral on the following day. In the evening the young singers of the St. Olaf College Choir offered a concert. Norwegian American attendance at commemorative events and visits to ancestral homesteads created bonds across the Atlantic. By their promotion of homecoming tours, the Norwegian-language press in America engaged not only immigrants, but also American-born generations and inculcated in them a sense of Norwegian ancestry and heritage independent of a comprehension of the ancestral tongue. To reach out further to the American-born, some Norwegian American newspapers began to fill their newspapers partly or completely with material in English. Publishers likely thought this tactic might help newspapers better endure the test of time.[1]

The Press in the Great Depression

Norwegian immigration might have been larger in the decade of the 1920s without the restrictions imposed by the national origins act; even so, between 1920 and 1929 a total of 88,520 Norwegians emigrated. Unemployment struck Norway in 1921 and the U.S. economy improved after 1922. A large exodus from Norway in 1923 shows the interplay of such forces. The earlier youth labor migration came to an end in 1930. The Great Depression caused many more people to return to Norway than those leaving; World War II put an end to regular emigration. There was consequently a long break in the welcoming of new arrivals. The Norwegian American community was not being sufficiently replenished to maintain a viable subculture. Some more or less insular and compact Norwegian farming communities preserved the Norwegian language into the third generation; it also persisted in some urban settings beyond the immigrant generation. The Norwegian language for many continued as a basic means of communication within the family and in ethnic relations. An accent or foreign brogue might become a serious handicap, however, so many immigrant parents abandoned the idea of passing a non-English mother tongue on to their American-born children. The number of Norwegian-born residents declined from 345,522 in 1930 to 232,820 in 1940. The figures suggest a precipitous drop in the number of Norwegian language speakers in that decade. The 1940 federal census listed 344,240 second-generation individuals who claimed Norwegian as their home language from earliest childhood, down from 658,589 two decades before; only 81,160 of the third generation made a similar claim. It is revealing of the general situation that in the 1930s Lutheran congregations abandoned all attempts to give young people religious instruction in Norwegian.[2]

The Great Depression coupled with the force of assimilation and changing demographic factors deprived Norwegian American journalism of means and readers. Some optimistic publishers nevertheless initiated a few ventures. Karsten Roedder, long associated with *Nordisk Tidende,* in 1926 published initially weekly then semimonthly *Symra* (The Anemone) for those liberal in mind and spirit and of independent thought; he calculated 164,000 Norwegians nationwide "who rejected or were dissatisfied with . . . the conservative and reactionary *Skandinaven, Minneapolis Tidende,* and *Decorah-Posten.*" These were *Symra*'s potential readers, Roedder believed.

In 1929, when Andreas N. Rygg retired from the editorship of *Nordisk Tidende,* it claimed an impressive circulation of eighteen thousand. Publisher Sigurd J. Arnesen listed himself as both publisher and editor, although since Rygg's retirement Hans Olav, a notable penman, had been responsible for the daily editorial management. From September 1930 Olav assumed the editorship. In January 1933 *Nordisk Tidende*'s publisher began a local tabloid weekly edition of the paper, titled *Kolonien* (The Colony): "As *Nordisk Tidende*'s distribution over the entire country increased, a clash of interest between the local news and news of general interest increased." *Kolonien* would, as announced, be a local organ for Brooklyn and environs and "a forum for exchange of opinions about current issues." The "meager lively years," as Roedder described *Nordisk Tidende*'s situation in the 1930s, ended the local news organ's existence after less than a year and a half. During its brief life, its announcements and editorials gave evidence of how a common nationality compelled the colony to assist compatriots in need; fund-raising arrangements promoted ethnic cultural activities. "One has festivals for the needy," *Kolonien* stated, and proceeded to make a list of festive events, where the proceeds would go to *Den norske Nødhjelp* (The Norwegian Relief Fund Office).

Emergency assistance appeared more urgent among Norwegians in large urban centers than among small-town and rural Norwegian Americans; *Nordisk Tidende* printed appeals on behalf of destitute Norwegians; their need was often depicted in graphic terms. The names of eight thousand Norwegians in Brooklyn were on a list of destitute people. The following are examples of appeals received by *Nordisk Tidende:*

> The family is sitting home and starving. For several days we have had nothing but a drop of coffee and some dry bread.
>
> If we cannot manage to pay the milk bill on Monday, there will be no milk for our baby. Our son's shoes are in such bad condition that he can no longer go to school.
>
> If we cannot in some way produce some money immediately, we will be out on the street tomorrow morning with our children. We owe three months' rent.

Brooklyn missionary Karl Holm gave the name *Ørkenen Sur* (The Bitter Desert) to large vacant lots in the Red Hook district, adopting the name Moses had given one of the miserable places the Israelites had encountered in their wanderings in the desert. The residence of the downtrodden in society, among these Norwegians, *Ørkenen Sur* is suggestive of the bad times and unemployment, as well as of the drunkenness and misery that might afflict stranded seamen in a port city like New York. *Nordisk Tidende* reported the death of seven Norwegians after a party of drinking wood alcohol. "They had come from places like Fredrikstad, Bodø, Holmestrand, Stokmarknes, Eidanger, and Oslo."[3]

The radical weekly *Ny Tid* (New Age) advocated the cause of the downtrodden and unemployed and attacked capitalism and its exploits. Its history began in Chicago March 10, 1922, with the appearance of the Swedish-language *Ny Tid,* succeeding a consolidation of earlier journals on the left. Its publication began one month after a merger of the Scandinavian Socialist Federation and the Communist-inspired Workers Party at a February 1922 meeting in Chicago. The Workers Party of America, as a legal political party, functioned as a legitimate Communist organization; both the Communist Party and the Communist Labor Party had gone underground for fear of persecution by the federal government. Communists found ample opportunity during the depressed 1930s to propagate their ideas. *Ny Tid* was published in New York beginning April 4, 1931. The decision to move was political: to gain greater visibility and means and to acquaint Scandinavian workers in the East with "a Scandinavian revolutionary workers newspaper." Beginning December 8, 1932, *Ny Tid* appeared in a four-page Danish and Norwegian edition alongside the Swedish one; Swedish workers' clubs were encouraged to work among Danish and Norwegian laboring men. The workers' charge was to prevent the deportation of foreign-born seamen; *Ny Tid* recorded several instances of Norwegian merchant mariners forcefully expelled. *Ny Tid* caustically reproved *Nordisk Tidende*'s publisher for "swinging the starvation whip," when in order to avoid "lay-off of employees during the present emergency," he found it necessary "effective immediately to reduce all salaries 25%." *Ny Tid* itself felt "threatened" *(hotat)* by lack of sufficient means; appeals to "comrades" to engage in fund-raising were regular fare in its columns. It became an insurmountable challenge, and in July 1936, *Ny Tid* disappeared from the field.[4]

Moves to the political left, if not by any means as far as *Ny Tid,* might be symptomatic of difficult economic times. In Minnesota, radical movements surged forward with the Depression in 1929, stated James Youngdale. The Scandinavian connection to the Farmer-Labor Party was strong. Founded in Minnesota in 1922, it united many protest groups in a radical third-party movement; the Nonpartisan League was the springboard from which it was organized. During the interwar years, Scandinavian working-class voters clearly transitioned into the Democratic Party nationwide, following the trend of more recent immigrant groups as well as of African Americans who streamed north to America's industrial cities. As an example, *Washington Posten* changed its political allegiance: in the 1932 contest, editor Gunnar Lund gave Republican Herbert Hoover his favor while predicting victory for Franklin Delano Roosevelt, whereas in the 1936 election he editorially embraced the Democratic cause and Roosevelt's New Deal program, introduced in 1933 to counter the Depression.

In Minnesota the Farmer-Labor Party cooperated with the Democratic Party in national elections; the parties fused toward the end of World War II, creating the Democratic-Farmer-Labor Party. Signs of political liberalism in the Minnesota electorate, as Youngdale pointed out, were the elections in 1930 of Farmer-Labor candidate Floyd B. Olson to the governorship with Democratic support and in 1932 when Roosevelt became the first Democratic presidential candidate to win Minnesota; the Farmer-Labor Party viewed Roosevelt's New Deal program with favor, as did a revitalized Nonpartisan League in North Dakota. The Norwegian American press reflected these political alterations. Even as its readership and political clout diminished, subscribers eagerly read the individual journals.[5]

Minneapolis Tidende described the 1930 election results as "sensational" *(Opsigtsvækkende);* the Republicans' strength had been reduced and the Farmer-Labor candidate Olson was elected governor. Editorially *Tidende* praised the "election landslide" *(Valgskred)* two years later that secured the presidency for Roosevelt, a Democratic Congress, and Olson's re-election to the state's governorship. The financial hardship, which editor Carl G. O. Hansen competently covered, affected *Minneapolis Tidende*'s operations adversely. Circulation dwindled. The sky was furthered darkened with the death of the newspaper's founder and longtime publisher, Thorvald Guldbrandsen, October 12, 1934, a few months past his eightieth birthday. "[T]he burden of making both ends meet," Hansen wrote, "fell on the shoulders of John Bjørhus," then *Tidende*'s business manager. On March 21, 1935, on the newspaper's front page readers were informed, "with this issue *Minneapolis Tidende* bids its subscribers farewell." As melodramatic as this depiction of events may sound, there was clearly deep sadness in witnessing the departure of a cherished institution.

The earlier "People's Party Journal," *Fremad* in Sioux Falls, South Dakota, before the national election in 1932 refuted accusations by other South Dakota newspapers that it had become Democratic; editor M. G. Opsahl reiterated the weekly's political independence, stating that at least during his editorship *Fremad* "has been neither Democratic nor Republican and has not functioned as any other party's organ either." Opsahl editorialized, "We believe we have sufficient common sense to see the merits of a person regardless of party affiliation, and just as much understand who the hypocrites are." Roosevelt won *Fremad*'s confidence; at least the newspaper came to the defense of the political remedies he initiated to alleviate "the hard times." Following the Democratic advances in the 1934 election, it declared: "South Dakota decidedly for the New Deal." *Fremad*'s own prospects were, however, dimming; the small four-page publication was not turning a profit. For the publishers, the Strass Publishing Company, bilingualism appeared to be the right course; from the January 3, 1935, issue *Fremad* had an "English Editor" and a "Norwegian Editor." In May, Opsahl, the Norwegian editor, was no longer listed and *Fremad* became an English-language weekly. It proved to be a futile conversion. In August *Fremad* ceased publication.[6]

Visergutten, published in Canton since 1917, remained the sole Norwegian-language news organ in South Dakota. It encountered bumps and obstacles on the road. A conflict with the shareholders of Visergutten Publishing Company in 1927, fueled by the deep debt it had incurred, convinced Gustav Amlund, the famed publisher and editor of *Visergutten,* to seek a new field for his talents. Osmund Gunvaldsen of Fargo, newly appointed U.S. marshal for North Dakota, proposed Amlund publish and edit *Normanden,* then published in Fargo; after its brief conservative sojourn in 1926 and loss of support it was in dire straits. Amlund and his sons accepted the invitation. With great fanfare, Amlund launched the newspaper on September 22, 1927, under the presumptuous masthead *Norrøna, Visergutten og Normanden. Norrøna* (The Norse) referred to the monthly *Landsmaal* magazine published in Fargo before the United States entered the Great War. Not unexpectedly, the publishers of *Visergutten* in Canton objected strenuously.

In extensive printed communications *Visergutten* informed its subscribers about the conflict. Sigurd Knudsen, an immigrant from Hordaland, Norway, succeeded Amlund as editor; he later took over as both publisher and editor. Threat of legal action forced Amlund to drop the two first elements of the title, yet the revised masthead heralded, "*Normanden.* Published by the founders of *Visergutten.*" Amlund was unable to redeem the bank note Gunvaldsen and other prominent Fargo Norwegians had signed due to lack of profitability of publishing *Normanden,* and Gunvaldsen as a consequence found himself the owner of a newspaper. In the 1930s, the Republican *Normanden* joined in the political condemnation of Roosevelt's New Deal program; in its opinion the program was so costly that the nation could not bear it. On another count, *Normanden* saw the president flaunt one of its signature precepts, the repeal of the eighteenth amendment, ending Prohibition. Gunvaldsen published *Normanden,* he recounted, until 1940, when he sold it to Ingvald H. Ulsaker. Ulsaker, with his own printing company, great dedication to the task at hand, and newspaper experience as the publisher of *Fram,* was associated with *Normanden* from 1930 to near the newspaper's end, two decades or so later. In 1944 *Normanden* merged with *Visergutten.*[7]

The Fuhr Publishing Company in Duluth had Anna Dahl Fuhr at the helm following her husband's death in 1930; she headed the editorial board as well and in time earned the title "Paper Lady." *Superior Tidende* and *Duluth Skandinav* became the two remaining journals; the Winnipeg publications were discontinued. Anna Dahl Fuhr inherited considerable debts; in 1935 the company went into receivership. The latter development bore upon its North Dakota journal *Grand Forks Skandinav* as well. Fuhr hired Odd Charles Lunde shortly after his arrival in America in the early 1930s, to take care of the Grand Forks branch office. Lunde emigrated from Halden, Norway, and had been associated with the Oslo daily *Aftenposten.* In correspondence with the author, Lunde describes his dismay when arriving in "the God-forsaken state of North Dakota" to take on his duties, finding inadequate or no facilities in his editorial office. In June 1933, Einar E. Fekjar, a recent immigrant from Valdres, Norway, succeeded Lunde; discouraged by the lack of opportunities at home, Fekjar had sought his fortune overseas only to be swept into the despairing conditions in a depressed America. *Grand Forks Skandinav* was a poor business, but rather than let the newspaper die, Fekjar purchased it from the receiver; shortly

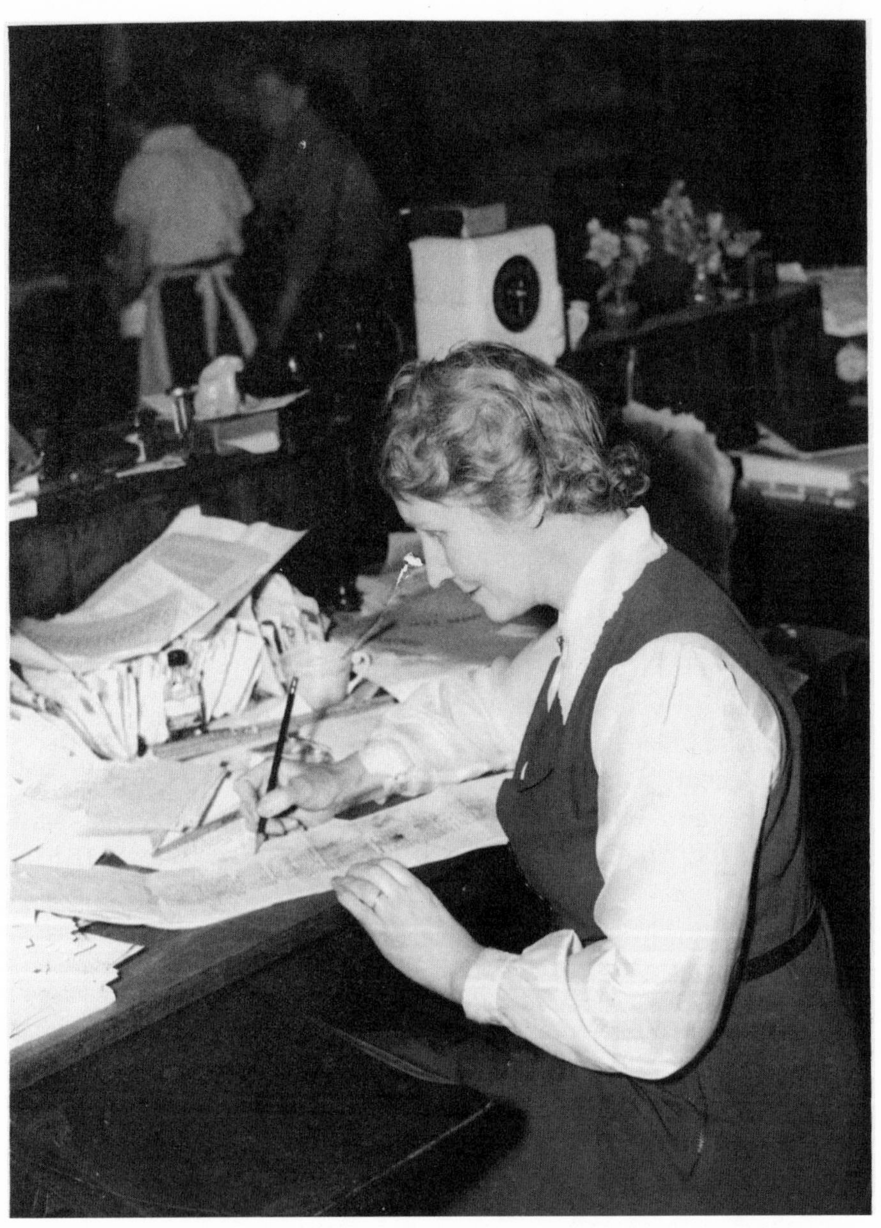

Anna Dahl Fuhr in the editorial office of Duluth Skandinav *about 1950. Following her husband's death in 1930, she directed the Fuhr Publishing Company in Duluth. She also headed the editorial board and in time earned the title "Paper Lady."*

thereafter he went into partnership with *Normanden,* which he then edited together with Ulsaker. In 1937, he recovered his list of subscribers and revived *Grand Forks Skandinav* in Grand Forks; coverage was limited to news from Norway and local items. Its survival was often in doubt, partly because, as Fekjar found, it was difficult to make subscribers realize that newspaper publishing was a business dependent on a profit and their payment of fees in order to exist. The Grand Forks journal nonetheless continued publication until May 1941.[8]

The vagaries of the small field of Norwegian American journalism placed Odd Charles Lunde in *Normanden*'s editorial chair in March 1938. Lunde introduced a personal widely read English-language column headed: "As I See It—By ODD." In May 1939, he began, "I am a proud man today. I am an American citizen. Tuesday I pledged allegiance to the American flag, the beautiful Stars and Stripes." The general move toward English, irrespective of American citizenship, was motivated by a wish to reach potential subscribers not versed in Norwegian. *Scandia* in Chicago is an example of the progression. In January 1939 it added *American Scandinavian News* to its masthead, announcing that it would expand "to cover the American Scandinavian field in the Middle West." The publisher hired separate Norwegian, Swedish, and Danish editors; one issue each month would be in English and three in Norwegian. *Scandia* became a semimonthly publication later that year with alternate languages, thereafter an English-language monthly, only to return in 1940 as a small four-page English-language weekly until it ended publication May 16, 1940. It was obviously a risky experiment initiated during changes of ownership that failed.

Skandinaven took a different linguistic course; the semiweekly harbored traditional Norwegian *Riksmål.* It, like *Scandia,* was much aware of changing political loyalties in the Norwegian electorate; they both identified themselves politically neutral or independent. Nicolay A. Grevstad, *Skandinaven*'s editor, however, in 1932, notwithstanding a personal thank-you from Roosevelt for his reporting, following Roosevelt's election editorially stated that "The nation, after *Skandinaven*'s opinion, would have been best served by [Herbert Hoover's] reelection." Editor Hans Olav in *Nordisk Tidende* in July and again in November expressed reservations about Roosevelt's candidacy, calling "the governor of New York, at least until now, a vacillating and two-faced politician"; he nonetheless encouraged *Nordisk Tidende*'s readers to vote for the Democratic Party and to consider the platforms of the two parties rather than the candidates. Olav wrote, "The succinct, straightforward, and courageous Democratic election proposal *[Valgprogram]* is more appealing than the cliché-filled 'platform' that the Republicans have adopted." *Nordisk Tidende,* as time passed, gave President Roosevelt and his New Deal legislation favorable reviews.

Skandinaven's editorial opinion became for the most part less pointed later; in January 1934, Grevstad praised Roosevelt for his "courage and resoluteness," which "the people had rewarded him for by their confidence and admiration." On the other hand, before the congressional election that year the editorial judgment expressed the idea that "it is of paramount importance for the nation that the Republicans become so strong in numbers *[mandsterk]* in the next Congress that they can obtain a real debate about leading issues at hand." Grevstad here referred to the New Deal, which won "a great victory," he reported, with the Democrats in control of both houses.

Following Roosevelt's landslide reelection in 1936, Grevstad summarized that "the President, as an individual, was stronger than his program" and cautioned that "aside from that, the election was essentially a battle between the old and the new, between the existing order in social control and economic life and something else which is advancing along more or less clear lines." Grevstad's successor, Reidar Rye Haugan, a longtime member of the editorial board, also favored the existing social order. Grevstad enjoyed a long lifework as a pressman; he served as editor in chief nearly until his death in February 1940, three months shy of his eighty-ninth birthday; "along in years *[tilaarskommen]*, but not a tired man," *Skandinaven* editorialized in Grevstad's honor. In October the following year *Skandinaven,* having passed the age of seventy-five, ended publication. Like *Minneapolis Tidende*'s subscription list, *Skandinaven*'s was taken over by *Decorah-Posten.* The Decorah journal thereafter advertised itself as "the only Norwegian American newspaper with a bona fide nation-wide distribution among the Norwegian people." Its singular position in Norwegian American journalism worked greatly to *Decorah-Posten*'s advantage.[9]

A Royal Visit Rallies the Norwegian American Community

Waldemar Ager's *Reform* ceased publication September 18, 1941, a month before *Skandinaven*'s demise; it survived Ager, who passed away August 1, by only a few weeks. The discontinuation of major Norwegian American journals, all in the course of five or six years, could surely be seen as the end of an era. The history of the Norwegian-language press might easily have been concluded at this point. A convergence of events was under way, however, that extended the story. The outbreak of World War II and the German occupation of Norway greatly stirred the emotions of Norwegians in America and called them to action; the preceding celebratory journey across the American continent by the heirs to Norway's throne, Crown Prince Olav and Crown Princess Märtha, reinforced awareness of Norwegian nationality and heritage.

Their visit and local arrangements received front-page coverage, not only in Norwegian American newspapers, but also in the press on their established route in general. On April 27, 1939, they landed in the port of New York on board the Norwegian America Line's *Oslofjord*. *Nordisk Tidende* in a long editorial welcome titled "An Immigrant People's Handshake" reminded its readers, "the Crown Prince and his entourage have now made the same journey as his countrymen had done before him." However, they stepped onto American soil "on the background of the threatening stormy skies that hang over Europe." The brewing conflict was much in evidence in the media the spring and summer of 1939; open warfare broke out that fall. Before continuing on their journey westward, Crown Prince Olav and Crown Princess Märtha paid a visit to President Roosevelt. The Crown Prince opened the Norwegian pavilion at the World's Fair in New York. The royal couple met with Norwegian Americans and their societies, churches, and educational institutions; wherever they went, at public events and receptions, they received a rousing welcome. May 2, *Skandinaven* offered a detailed account of their schedule of events in Chicago, wishing them "Welcome to the wide Norwegian *Bygder* [communities] in the Northwest!" *Skandinaven,* in a special front-page column with an everyday rural greeting as title, "Welcome to the Farm *[tilgårds],* Olav and Märtha," expressed the following hope:

> As we greet our high guests with a resounding welcome to our new Norway under the Star Spangled Banner, it is our hope that they at the end of the America journey will be able to report to Norway's people and King [Haakon VII] that we of Norwegian descent have conducted us well as citizens of our new homeland and to the honor of our common Mother: the old and the new Norway.

This sentiment was regularly expressed: a desire to earn the homeland's approbation as citizens of the United States or, perhaps, inclusion in "a greater Norway," as Nordmanns-Forbundet—which played a significant role in arranging the royal tour—might have contended. The better than two-month-long foray to regions of Norwegian settlement acquainted a large number of villages, small towns, and metropolitan areas with the trappings of a royal visit. Only a brief sampling, based on extensive news accounts, is possible. *Decorah-Posten* described the royal couple's visit to the city and Luther College May 6–7 as "a spectacular festival"; Northfield and St. Olaf College were next in line; the royal couple celebrated May 17 in San Francisco. Editor Gunnar Lund, in wishing them welcome to Seattle in late May, stated the following in *Washington Posten:* "The joy which this visit gives, is the most flaming event that has ever gripped Norwegian America."

On their return journey east, Crown Prince Olav and Crown Princess Märtha stopped in Fargo June 8–10 and, as reported in *Normanden,* received the adulation of large admiring gatherings of Norwegian Americans; across the state line in Moorhead, Minnesota, Crown Prince Olav gave the commencement address at Concordia College. In Minneapolis the royal party was paid high honors at a folk festival *(Folkefest)* Sunday, June 11, on the fairgrounds between the Twin Cities with more than twenty thousand people in attendance. Anna Dahl Fuhr, editor and publisher, offered a thirty-five-page special issue of *Duluth Skandinav* in connection with the visit of their royal highnesses to that part of the state. On the day of departure from New York, July 6, Crown Prince Olav, as fully covered in *Nordisk Tidende,* dedicated a memorial stone—a replica of a rune-stone found in Tune, Norway—to Leif Erickson on Leiv Eiriksson Square in Brooklyn; its inscription made a claim of discovery the year 1000 by the brave Norseman. It was the ultimate homemaking myth—Nordics were the first Europeans in the New World. Italian American mayor Fiorello La Guardia graciously received the monument on behalf of New York City, not only as the city's mayor, as he stated, "but as a son of Columbus greeting [Crown Prince Olav] the son of a Viking." The coast-to-coast royal visit was a historic moment with great symbolic import for Norwegians in America; commentators saw it as a reaffirmation of Norway's discovery of a Norwegian American community during the heady years following the dissolution of the Swedish-Norwegian Union.[10]

World War II and Ethnic Revival

Cataclysmic world events shortly upon Crown Prince Olav's and Crown Princess Märtha's return to Norway caused the royal couple and their three young children—the princesses Ragnhild and Astrid and prince Harald, the heir presumptive—to seek asylum in the United States. They in fact became Norwegian Americans as residents of Washington, D.C., during the years of German occupation of the homeland. War broke out in Europe with the Nazi blitzkrieg against Poland on September 1, 1939, and the Anglo-French declaration of war two days later. On April 9, 1940, German troops invaded Norway; by June 22, Norway, Denmark, the Netherlands, Belgium, and France had all capitulated to the German military machine.

Carl G. O. Hansen commented, "No single event has as the invasion of Norway by German troops on April 9, 1940, in its effects been so powerful in creating solidarity among Norwegian American groups." Patriotism toward Norway surged. The Norwegian American press and the community it served found a new cause to champion: relief and aid to Norway. Front-page headlines in large type announced the progress of the war, Norway's capitulation June 7, the departure of King Haakon VII, the crown prince, and his government to Great Britain for the duration of the war, and the worsening conditions as the war and occupation persisted. May 21, *Skandinaven* headlined how twenty-five thousand people in Chicago had convened to celebrate May 17 and consider relief efforts. Postal services were disrupted and after April 9, 1940, discontinued with nations at war with Germany, which after December 7, 1941, with the Japanese attack on Pearl Harbor, included the United States. The attack brought the United States into the global conflict; declarations of war were exchanged not only with Japan, but with the Axis powers as well.

Norwegian American newspapers relied upon news from occupied Norway. Before the entry of the United States, newspapers and letters—censored and uncensored—from different parts of Norway made it across the Atlantic; so too did private telegrams. In an agreement between the Norwegian government in exile and BBC Overseas Service, London Radio broadcast in Norwegian three times a week about the German occupation of Norway.

The challenge following the disruption of regular channels of communication called for an immediate solution. Hans Olav, *Nordisk Tidende*'s editor, had studied journalism at Columbia University School of Journalism and had established credentials as a seasoned newsman. On March 28, 1940, the Norwegian government appointed him press attaché at the Norwegian legation in Washington, D.C.; he assumed his duties there April 4, only a few days before the German attack on Norway. Olav headed the newly organized Norwegian Information Service. It worked closely with the remaining Norwegian American newspapers. In February 1942 the Norwegian American editors were invited to a two-day press conference at the Norwegian legation; seven editors attended. The chief press officer of the Norwegian press office in London informed them about the news service to and from Norway.

The embassy's press and information department provided Norwegian American newspaper publishers with news releases by airmail about the situation in Norway, transmitted telegraphically by the Norwegian London press office. This was the most important source of information about internal circumstances in an occupied homeland. Delivery could be obstructed. In January 1942, *Visergutten,* then published in Canton, South Dakota, regretfully informed its readers that, "Because of the dreadful cold and the resulting railroad and airplane delays, the Norway news from Washington, D.C. is this week missing." *Nordisk Tidende* had a great advantage because of its location and access to the Norwegian exile community with visiting or resident "Norwegian cabinet ministers and other excellencies" who established themselves in greater New York. Journalists could depend upon these expatriates for engaging newspaper interviews as well as personal opinion pieces about "the free Norway." Among the many Norwegian luminaries with frequent visits or temporary residency in greater New York or Washington, D.C., were Halvdan Koht, historian and Norway's foreign minister until November 1940; C. J. Hambro, president of the *Storting*; Trygve Lie, foreign minister in the London government, succeeding Koht, and from 1946 secretary general of the United Nations; the author Sigrid Undset; and other prominent members of Norwegian society in a variety of pursuits. A January 1944 *Washington Posten* editorial complained about its geographic disadvantage, which deprived it of interviews and an opportunity to reference speeches. Hans Olav protested most vigorously to the charge that news releases were delayed. He explained,

> The embassy's press office has in no way given preference to *Nordisk Tidende,* or to any other Norwegian newspaper. But sent all of them the same news at the same time by air mail. We have also as much as possible made an effort to prevent Norwegian officials visiting America from giving special interviews to *Nordisk Tidende,* inasmuch as we do not think that it is fair toward the collective Norwegian American press that a single newspaper should have a clear geographical advantage.[11]

Most of the Norwegian American newspapers that survived the hardships of the Depression, remarked *Nordisk Tidende* in 1941, "noticed a larger or smaller increase in their circle of readers since April last year, so at this juncture the press is stronger than in many years." *Nordisk Tidende,* in a surprisingly accurate estimate, considering later grossly overstated assessments, editorialized that "more than 300 newspaper and magazine ventures had at different times been started. Those left can now be counted on the fingers [of both hands]." The same editorial calculated a combined publication of eighty to ninety thousand copies. *Tidende* prospered and increased its number of printed copies 100 percent.

Carl Søyland, on *Nordisk Tidende*'s staff since 1926, succeeded

Hans Olav as editor in chief on April 8, 1940, the day before Norway was caught in the maelstrom of the war. He was born in Bergen, Norway, in 1894, but grew up in the coastal town of Flekkefjord. Among a series of strong editorial leaders, Søyland stands out as likely the most remarkable and influential. His sense for adventure took him on a lengthy five-year journey in the United States and Alaska; he found employment as a seaman, took on an eclectic array of other jobs, and for some months in 1924–25 edited the failing *California-Vikingen* (The California Viking), published in Los Angeles for subscribers in southern California, and contributed popular travel accounts titled "Vagabond Observations" *(Vagabondsbetraktninger)* to *Nordisk Tidende.* Søyland was musically gifted, and in Brooklyn spearheaded musical entertainment, dramatic productions, lectures, and discussions under the auspices of the society *Intime Forum,* a gathering place for expatriate Norwegians, which he led from 1935 to 1945; he enrolled in university courses in journalism and other subjects and earned a reputation as a man of rare knowledge. Søyland eventually became the Norwegian colony's grand old man. The war exacted new responsibilities; Søyland made *Nordisk Tidende* a major source of information for Norwegians in exile and American society about occupied Norway.[12]

"The Midwestern Norsedom" was the name Søyland bestowed on the Upper Midwest. In these older settlements assimilation had progressed further than in the Norwegian enclaves in the East with their geographic and other advantages. The region continued to need Norwegian-language community and national newspapers, however. *Skandinaven*'s demise October 30, 1941, was described by Reidar Rye Haugan, then its editor, and John A. Lindrup, also on its staff, as "the most searching news that ever has befallen Norwegian Chicago." The two men as early as November 6 launched the weekly *Viking,* announcing it on the masthead as "Chicago's Norwegian Newspaper." Its Viking designation encouraged the use of terminology reminiscent of the Viking Age: one lit "signal fires" *(Varder),* sent "message sticks" from neighbor to neighbor, and formed "the battle line" *(Fylking);* conditions brightened and the imminent threat dissipated with the decision by "two experienced Norwegian American pressmen" to publish *Viking.* It was consistently a safe course to fall back on the idea of descent from heroic

Viking forebears. In the second issue of the newspaper, the publishers expressed their gratitude for a rallying around the new venture beyond their most optimistic expectations. Their question in the initial issue "Do we need our own newspaper" had been answered by a resounding yes. Lindrup, an immigrant from Tromsø, Norway, in 1947, became sole owner and editor of *Viking*. As announced, it served the interests of Chicago Norwegians; its coverage was limited to local news and reports from Norway. Throughout its existence, it remained loyal to the Norwegian language, reporting all news in this medium until its demise May 17, 1958.

An important function of community journals was to serve as announcement sheets for Norwegian American organizations, events, and undertakings. Carl G. O. Hansen emphasized with some reproach the vacuum that was created with the loss of *Minneapolis Tidende* in 1935. "The Norwegians in the city began to understand what a valuable vehicle for the promotion of the work and activities of the different organizations it had been." The Norwegian National League, a cooperative union of Twin Cities societies formed in May 1920, made vain efforts to solve the problem by inducing established newspapers to locate in Minneapolis. To no avail, *Visergutten* in Canton, South Dakota, *Reform* in Eau Claire, Wisconsin, and *Normanden* in Fargo, North Dakota, were all invited to change location. A solution was not found until November 1940 when the League managed to convince Anna Dahl Fuhr to devote the fourth page of *Duluth Skandinav* to Minneapolis news and publish that edition as *Minneapolis Posten*. It was a satisfactory arrangement until 1953 when the National League decided to publish *Minneapolis Posten* itself and move publication to Minneapolis. The local organ filled a special need and grew in popularity. It thus came as a shock, Hansen writes, when the League in November 1956 announced that it had sold the subscription list to *Decorah-Posten*.[13]

The passing of several major figures in Norwegian American journalism was another sign of the times. *Decorah-Posten*'s Einar Lund, who had assisted editor in chief Kristian Prestgard since 1927, assumed full editorial responsibility upon Prestgard's death in January 1946. Prestgard's obituary noted that he had been bedridden for a year and not been to *Decorah-Posten*'s office the last two or so years of his life. The transition in the newspaper's history thus preceded Prestgard's death by many years. In the Pacific Northwest a major shift occurred with the death in November 1940 of *Washington Posten*'s decades-long publisher and editor Gunnar Lund. O. L. Ejde thereafter became the most important person in *Washington Posten,* succeeding Lund as editor, a position he had filled from the late 1930s as Lund's health gradually failed. Ejde had emigrated from Orkdal in South Trøndelag in 1910 as a young man of twenty-one. He had worked on *Washington Posten* since 1913, save for a brief absence in the 1920s; in December 1943 he purchased *Washington Posten* from the Lund family and became its sole owner.

Carl Søyland interviewed all the editors attending the press conference at the Norwegian legation in Washington in February 1942 about "the future of the press." They all agreed that they had benefited from "*Skandinaven*'s death"; local subscribers turned to a journal closer at hand. Otherwise, their responses reveal the un-

Kristian Prestgard and Einar Lund enjoy a summer's evening on Solihøgda, Lund's residence in Decorah. Prestgard served as assistant editor of Decorah-Posten *from 1898 to 1923 and then as editor in chief nearly until his death in 1946. He was succeeded by Lund, who had been Prestgard's assistant since 1927.*

certainty they faced as well as the effect of the war years. Editor Rye Haugan of *Viking* firmly believed that the interest in the press "will continue as long as the war lasts." He further optimistically wished that "When peace arrives and travel to Norway can begin, one might hope for a new golden age for the press." *Normanden*'s editor Ingvald H. Ulsaker, after forty years in the service of the press, saw the direction it was taking. He was of the opinion that "There is no long future for Norwegian newspapers in America in our days. . . . It is the interest in the war that sustains *Normanden.*" Ejde in *Washington Posten* answered that "the newspaper picked up with the outbreak of war, and the interest has for the most part been the same since." Also Ejde hoped for continued interest after the war, at least for a period, based on Norway correspondence and travel descriptions "as never before." *Visergutten*'s Sigurd Knudsen maintained, Søyland wrote, "that no one can make a living on a Norwegian American newspaper alone, if one does not also have a printing shop and other jobs." He had "fifteen years ago predicted that Norwegian newspapers could last another thirty-five years. This he still stood by, which would give a twenty-year life respite." The publisher and editor of *Duluth Skandinav* and *Superior Tidende,* Anna Dahl Fuhr, hoped "that the interest in Norsedom would persist as it has done since the invasion." Like Knudsen, she was mindful that a newspaper "could hardly exist except as a part of a profitable print shop." Editor Dahl Fuhr conceded, "the newspaper has no ambitions as a national newspaper, but the field in Duluth [and Superior] and environs is still good." Einar Lund represented *Decorah-Posten* and simply acknowledged the benefits of the "blood infusion" the newspaper got by inheriting the subscription lists of its two major competitors.[14]

The local Minnesota newspaper *Fergus Falls Ugeblad* (from January 1940 spelled *Ukeblad*) was not represented at the Washington conference. It continued to proclaim itself "An Independent Reform Newspaper." In the late 1930s Marcus J. Quarum, born in Abercrombie, North Dakota, to Norwegian immigrant parents, moved to Fergus Falls, where he purchased *Ugeblad* and its printing press; he had long been financial manager for the low-church pietistic Church of the Lutheran Brethren *(Brodersamfundet),* from the mid-1930s headquartered in Fergus Falls, and its school

Hillcrest Lutheran Academy. Quarum printed the Brethren's Norwegian-language organ *Broderbaandet* (The Brethren Bond). It was a relationship that colored *Fergus Falls Ugeblad*. Pastor Rasmus S. Gjerde of the Brethren church, an immigrant from Tysvær, Norway, served as editor of both *Broderbaandet* and *Fergus Falls Ugeblad*. The weekly regularly carried "The Week's Sermon" *(Ukens Preken)* on the front page, with such pious headings as "Does the Lord Know You as His Own?"—reflecting the Brethren's idea of not receiving the unconverted into full membership or admitting them to Communion.

After April 9, 1940, the disturbing news from Norway received front-page coverage, relegating religious reflections to a less prominent niche. Disquieting headlines—"Riots, Murder, and Arson Everywhere in Norway," "The Germans' Treatment of Norwegians Increasingly More Brutal," "Between 1,200–1,500 Students Arrested," "Eighteen More Executions," and even "Norway Faces Starvation"—caught the attention of the readers and created great sympathy for the people of Norway. Quarum published the weekly until its final issue December 18, 1946; he bid his readers farewell in recognition that "Norwegian is less and less read from year to year."[15]

The headlines cited above and others equally eye-catching appeared in Norwegian American newspapers wherever they were published. While the European theater of war was fully covered, much less attention was accorded the Pacific situation. Norway obviously was of greatest concern to the Norwegian American newspapers. Columnists reported widely on the terror unleashed in Trondheim in October 1942 to break all resistance; the extensive persecution of Norway's Jewish population that same year; and the deteriorating supply of food. By September 1, 1944, as reported in the Norwegian American press, 49 percent of Norway's free merchant fleet sailing for the Allies in foreign waters—475 vessels and a great number of lives—had been lost. Journalists gave much news about Norway's resistance. As the Norwegian home front organized and grew in force, even a publication that by German edict was illegal, such as "the free Norwegian newspaper *Krigsoversikt* [War Survey]," could be cited in the Norwegian American press; the illegal sheet in 1944 lauded the Norwegian "abroad front" as an admirable partner in the war effort. In February 1945, Norwegian American newspapers listed the names of thirty-four Norwegians executed as a reprisal for the liquidation of the Norwegian traitor Vidkun Quisling's chief of security; other instances of sabotage and civilian opposition to Nazification were described and commented on by columnists, all of it dated in Washington, D.C.

Norwegians fleeing across the North Sea to Great Britain or through neutral Sweden joined the "abroad front" against the Axis. The most celebrated military endeavor on North American soil was Camp Little Norway *(Lille Norge)* near Toronto, Canada, established by the Norwegian government in exile in November 1940 as a training camp for the Royal Norwegian Air Force; in total, when it closed in February 1945, more than twenty-five hundred Norwegian airmen of all categories had been educated in the camp. Norwegian American columnists and editors visited and regularly wrote about the activities in the camp. Members of the royal family headed by Crown Prince Olav and other prominent Norwegians in exile, political leaders like C. J. Hambro, made well-reported tours of Little Norway and spread information to Norwegian and American audiences through extensive speaking engagements.

Financial support for the training camp came from the Camp Little Norway Association, formed in October 1941; it eventually merged with American Relief for Norway, a comprehensive nationwide aid organization begun only a few days after the April 9, 1940, German invasion of Norway. Editorial appeals and active participation by Norwegian American newspaper publishers greatly aided the association's success. Carl Søyland, viewing "Norwegian America" as many concentric circles, described the war's effect on the Norwegian American community:

> In the middle was a newspaper circled by the strongest Norwegian interests, represented by individuals, churches and clubs. With the end of immigration and hard times, there had been a gliding out from the center toward a nebulous outer circle. . . . When the war reached Norway, it activated everything that was Norwegian among the emigrants. People of Norwegian descent who moved in the outermost rings, were drawn in again toward the center by this event. People popped up everywhere, identifying themselves as Norwegians and now showed their kindheartedness and willingness to help.

Syttende Mai Nummer Og Femti Aar[illegible]tgave

Washington Posten

Largest Circulation Of Any Foreign Language Paper In The Pacific Northwest

Syttende Mai

[illegible]andt Hilsener Mottatt I Anledning Jubileet:

STATSMINISTEREN:

THE WHITE HOUSE
Washington

STORTINGSPRESIDENTEN:

9. April 1940 - KRIGENS AAR I NORGE - 9. April 1941

NORDISK TIDENDE

NORWEGIAN NEWS — NORSKE NYHETER

Nr. 15 — 51. Aargang · Torsdag den 10. April 1941 · Enkelt Nummer 7 Cents

La oss nu lese Kapitlet om den 62 Dages aktive Krigsmotstand i Norge

Og i den ulike politiske Kamp staar Norges Folk nu samlet mot Nazismen

Omkring Aarsdagen:

Norges fortsatte Kamp mot Fienden

Washington Posten, *May 13, 1938, was published as a special fiftieth anniversary and May 17 issue. On the front page the newspaper printed anniversary greetings from President Roosevelt, the state's governor, Norway's prime minister, the president of the* Storting, *and other dignitaries. The newspaper did indeed connect Norway with the new land.*

Søyland went on to describe how thousands of Norwegian women's auxiliaries went to work knitting and sewing for American Relief for Norway; nearly all of the two hundred lodges of the Sons of Norway and five thousand Norwegian Lutheran congregations in the United States took up the cause to aid the homeland, Søyland reported. Social networks were created and reinforced. National holidays and symbols were prohibited in countries under German occupation; in Norway May 17 became an ordinary workday. In America, the Norwegian flag could be flown and festive pub-

Skandinaven

Minneapolis Tidende

Decorah-Posten has a larger circulation than all other U. S. Norwegian newspapers combined.

Decorah-Posten og Ved Arnen

No. 3 | General Edition | Decorah, Iowa, Fredag den 19de September 1947 | General Edition

Stormødet.

De høie Priser.

Arbeiderleiren.

Første Uge.

Forenede Nationer.

Traktater træer ikraft.

Folkemængden.

General Pershing.

Orkan.

Sidste Nyt fra Norge.

Nordisk Tidende, *April 10, 1941 (opposite page), reviews the year in Norway after the brutal German invasion on April 9, 1940. This paper played a special role as a source of information during the years of German occupation of the Norwegian homeland.*

Decorah-Posten, *September 18, 1947, having absorbed both* Skandinaven *and* Minneapolis Tidende, *as the masthead shows, was the sole survivor of "the big three." In this issue the venerable journal reports on wartime conditions and the current situation in Norway.*

lic observances of May 17 be arranged; these frequently became fund-raising events for relief for Norway. In 1943, *Superior Tidende* and *Duluth Skandinav* published an extensive "Syttende Mai" supplement with detailed information on the monetary, knitting, and sewing contributions of the Women's Committee of Norwegian Relief. Norwegian seamen outside Norway were beneficiaries of their generosity; clothing, food, and money were sent to Norway through neutral Sweden and occupied Denmark. The day's observance was subdued and reflective with speeches, presentations by male choruses, and singing of Norwegian and American patriotic songs. Norwegian centers throughout the land replicated the program; Norwegian political leaders in exile were regularly featured speakers. "We Norwegians in America," editor Dahl Fuhr wrote in 1943, "assemble around our Seventeenth of May festivals." "Let no one," she admonished, "pass an opportunity to attend at least one 'Syttende Mai' festival."

The spring of 1945 brought great hope of a complete liberation of Norway. By March, as announced in the Norwegian American press, following the Soviet attack on German military installations and invasion in north Norway the previous fall, aid could reach "the free far north" directly; early German capitulation was anticipated. The unconditional surrender of Germany May 8 received the newspapers' bold headlines; Norway, it was noted, was the last country to be liberated. "Germany Defeated. Norway Rejoicing," *Normanden* declared on its front page; *Washington Posten* echoed the sentiment, announcing, "Norway is Free—Norway Celebrates." *Decorah-Posten* took heart at the news that "Quisling and his 'Ministers'" had been arrested and jailed. The Norwegian American newspapers noted, to cite *Nordisk Tidende,* that "From all parts of America where Norwegian Americans live, reports are flowing in about divine thanksgiving services and May 17 festivals." Norwegians in New York assembled in Carnegie Hall to celebrate Norway's regained freedom.

The return to Norway of the exiled Norwegian government May 31 and of King Haakon VII on June 7—a day with profound historical significance—stood as the ultimate evidence, as expressed in Norwegian American newspapers, of "a new day" in Norway. Only by citing the visionary reporting of the Norwegian American press is it possible to convey the deep emotional attachment of Norwegians worldwide—conditioned by Norway's inequitable historical experience—to the concept of an ancestral homeland.[16]

A Final Chapter

Norwegian Americans quickly resumed normal commerce and travel contacts with Norway. *Duluth Skandinav* found evidence of peace and an enduring Norwegian Americana in the fact that after its absence for five years the ethnic dish *Lutefisk* was again offered for sale. "Eat *Lutefisk* and Help Norway," urged a December 1945 editorial. In other respects, the postwar era witnessed new challenges and sweeping winds of change that transformed familiar social, political, and cultural circumstances. The Norwegian American press as well confronted an ever-changing environment that ultimately defined a final chapter in its restless historical journey among Norwegians in America. A resumption of massive migration from Norway might have renewed and preserved a Norwegian-language press. It was not to be, even though a flow of immigration resumed after a significant breach and a loss of continuity in the Norwegian pattern of immigration. In 1946, the first full year of peace, nearly one thousand Norwegians crossed the Atlantic to the New World; some of the first to leave were people reuniting with family members separated by the war. The movement never gained a significant proportion in numerical terms; it reached its maximum for any one postwar year in 1952 with the departure of 2,958 emigrants.

Tracing the declining number of first-generation Norwegians will cast light on the perplexity faced by publishers of Norwegian-language texts. In 1970, the federal census reported 97,243 Norwegian-born residents in the United States and 517,406 with at least one Norwegian-born parent; the second generation had thus fallen off from its maximum size in 1930 with 752,236 members. The number of foreign-born was less than half of that in 1950 when they tallied 202,294. The majority of the Norwegian-born had arrived in the decades before 1930; the rapid numerical decline of the residents of Norwegian birth tells its own story: an aging generation of immigrants gradually passing away. The population could not be replaced by the limited number of postwar immigrants.

The newcomers generally selected traditional regions of Norwegian settlement, though they were influenced by the economic situation in their choice of destination. In 1970, New York State had 17,371, or 17.9 percent, of America's Norwegian-born residents. Nearly 80 percent of them lived in the Bay Ridge section of Brooklyn; 24,252 second-generation people also lived there, making the Brooklyn colony an enclave of 39,522 residents. The upper midwestern states, including Montana, had 32 percent, numbering 31,240, and the state of Washington had 11,657, or 12 percent of the Norwegian-born. Within these regions of the United States were the urban centers that supported a Norwegian American press.

Many in the American-born generation might subscribe to a Norwegian American newspaper; publishers endeavored in various ways to recruit readers from their ranks. The Seattle-Everett area and small communities in the Puget Sound country had major concentrations of first- and second-generation Norwegians; combined for the state they were 60,427 strong in 1970. The Norwegian stock in Minneapolis accounted for 40,341, the Norwegian-born numbering only 4,072. Chicago housed 5,588 persons of Norwegian birth and 22,149 individuals with immigrant parents. These figures suggest the relatively modest influx of newcomers to the older regions of settlement; the recent Norwegian impulse was more evident on either coast.

Ethnic organizations and festivals and even Norwegian-language church services persisted in the postwar decades in both traditional and newer centers for Norwegian American domicile. However, to quote this author's earlier work, "when one ignores the flurry of activity and individual efforts on special occasions, such as jubilees and prominent visits from Norway, it becomes clear that there has been an obvious decline in ethnic community life."[17]

There were Norwegian American anniversaries to observe, to be sure. The year 1947 would, as *Normanden* reported in a front-page article, mark "the centennial jubilee year of the immigrant press." By coincidence the jubilee dovetailed an invitation extended that year by the Norwegian Ministry of Foreign Affairs through the Norwegian Embassy's information service in Washington, D.C., to thirteen Norwegian American and Norwegian Canadian editors to a two-month-long visit to Norway, including a three-week joint excursion throughout the country. The main objective of the press tour was, as tendered in the letters of invitation,

> meant as a salute to the Norwegian American and the Canadian American press for their efforts on behalf of Norway during the war. This press tour will also signify a renewal of the connection and the reciprocity between the emigrant people and the old country.

This group includes ten of the thirteen Norwegian American and Norwegian Canadian editors invited by the Norwegian Ministry of Foreign Affairs to a two-month-long visit. A salute to the Norwegian press in North America for its efforts on behalf of Norway during the war, the invitation also marked the centennial jubilee of the Norwegian press in America in 1947. Pictured from left to right are: Thorvald A. Larssen, Norsk Nytt, *New Westminster B.C., Canada; Editor (?) Svendsen; Carl Søyland,* Nordisk Tidende, *Brooklyn; H. C. Caspersen,* Folkebladet, *Minneapolis; P. A. Hovland,* Minneapolis Posten, *Minneapolis; Ingvald H. Ulsaker,* Normanden, *Fargo; Sven N. Oftedal, Norwegian press attaché; Carl G. O. Hansen, Sons of Norway monthly magazine (previously editor* Minneapolis Tidende*), Minneapolis; Anna Dahl Fuhr,* Duluth Skandinav, *Duluth; Arthur A. Gomsrud,* Scandinavia in USA, *New York; E. O. Hjelmseth,* Norsk Ungdom, *Chicago; Einar Lund,* Decorah-Posten, *Decorah; O. L. Ejde,* Washington Posten, *Seattle. Not pictured are Sigurd Knudsen,* Visergutten, *Fargo; Herman E. Jørgensen,* Lutheraneren, *Minneapolis; and Magnus Talgøy,* Norrøna, *Winnipeg, Canada.*

The editors departed from New York on board the passenger ship *Stavangerfjord* on August 22, 1947. For the Norwegian American press—asserted in the *Normanden* release cited above—the invitation in a sense became Norway's recognition of the centennial jubilee, notwithstanding the fact that the embassy's records show no documentation to support that assumption. Among the invited participants were Ingvald H. Ulsaker of *Normanden* and Sigurd Knudsen of *Visergutten;* Knudsen revived his journal in time for the 1947 tour, following the May 1944 merger with *Normanden* when the two aging men had pooled their resources. Some of his contemporaries questioned his motives. "These were not young folks," Søyland writes of the thirteen pressmen, who "together reached 837 years," for an average age of sixty-four. It was more "writing on the wall" about the Norwegian American newspapers' future. In any case, the liner docked in Bergen, Norway, August 30. *Decorah-Posten* reprinted a September 1 editorial in the Oslo journal *Aftenposten* titled "The Hand across the Atlantic"; the editorial outlined how the Norwegian American press had spread knowledge about and created goodwill for Norway "during her darkest hours." The tour became a hectic adventure and a professional success. Impressions of a homeland as it engaged in reconstruction after the destructive years of occupation filled the columns of the newspapers the editors represented over many months.[18]

An assessment of the benefits to the Norwegian American newspapers of the closer contact with Norway, aside from the clear appeal to their readerships of travelogues and informative articles, is not readily made. The press responded more directly to realities in its place of operation in the United States. In January 1952, Ulsaker, then in his eighties, realized it was time to retire from the newspaper business; the new owners turned the newspaper primarily into an English-language organ and added *The Norseman* on the masthead below *Normanden.* It was a short-lived attempt, the newspaper losing subscribers steadily; in November 1954, the venture was abandoned. *Visergutten* struggled on for another half year; in April 1955, Knudsen, like *Normanden*'s publishers had done earlier, sent his list of fewer than one thousand subscribers to *Decorah-Posten.* The era of the Norwegian American press in North Dakota came to an end.

Certain characteristics identified earlier to a great extent progressively became the norm. Ethnic newspapers in general as they address a decreasing number of readers become more limited in focus, concentrating on events and personal relationships within their ethnic group. It was a reasonable adjustment as these journals increasingly functioned as supplements to other news sources. They carried news and reports not offered in the American mainstream media and appealed to an engaged ethnic readership. The postwar vestiges of a once-blossoming Norwegian American press followed the pattern of adjustment to shifting contingencies evidenced in ethnic newspapers in general.

An overview of the experience of the midwestern Norwegian-language newspapers suggests an evolving situation that does not discount the favor and enthusiasm individual newspaper ventures enjoyed and the great feeling of loss they evoked when discontinued. An appreciative readership existed, though it was eventually not sufficiently large to ensure profitability. *Minneapolis Posten* is a case in point; as indicated earlier, its loyal patrons were roused to anger and disappointment when its publisher, the Minneapolis Norwegian National League, announced in November 1956 that it had sold the subscription list to *Decorah-Posten*. The locals ridiculed the League for trying "to hand the newspaper over to an out-of-state publisher without consulting the subscribers." The subscribers were of course members of the nearly thirty Norwegian organizations associated with the League. On November 8, 1956, even before the business transaction with *Decorah-Posten* was complete, Jenny Alvilde Johnsen, *Minneapolis Posten*'s editor at that time, continued the weekly publication under the name *Minnesota Posten* (The Minnesota Post). Editor Johnsen, a second-generation Norwegian American on her mother's side and third on her father's, had earned the displeasure of the publishers by her crusading editorials, including protests against the Norwegian Lutheran church's discrimination of women. What role this displeasure might have had in the decision to sell *Minneapolis Posten* is not evident.

J. Jorgen Thompson, on the faculty of St. Olaf College and active in Norwegian American cultural affairs, even called "the people who want to discontinue *Minneapolis Posten* . . . enemies of the people

[and] traitors." Johnsen, a contributor to *Duluth Skandinav* and *Superior Tidende,* chided the League, editorializing that the board "reckoned unwisely when they thought they could sell subscribers, who for the most part paid to receive the kind of newspaper that this editor has been giving them." Referring to *Decorah-Posten* as the "morgue for Norwegian newspapers," Johnsen appealed to subscribers to stay with her. Judging from the many letters to the newspaper, the attraction for the subscribers was, to quote from one of them, the opportunity "to see what is going on among our people in the Twin Cities."

Though advertised as a "Norwegian language paper," *Minnesota Posten* was published weekly in a bilingual eight-page tabloid format. The regular feature titled "Minnesota Eyewitness" by Brenda Ueland, a well-known journalist, editor, freelance writer, and teacher of writing, created interest and evoked commentary; other columnists' contributions also added to the newspaper's appeal. Subscription support assured the solvency of the undertaking; it was in all respects a popular local organ. Special events and historical summaries relating to Norway received first-page coverage. *Minnesota Posten* exemplified developments in post–World War II Norwegian American journalism. Its final special twelve-page Syttende Mai issue, published by an elderly Jenny Alvilde Johnsen, was dated May 17, 1979.[19]

Chicago was another instance of local newspaper publishing to meet the needs of a Norwegian American urban community in transition—even as the market decreased. The untimely death of *Viking*'s publisher and editor, John A. Lindrup, at age fifty-two in June 1958, deprived the community of a devoted leader in its cultural and organizational life and the journal essential to the community's civic activities. Lindrup's friends published *Viking*'s final May 17 issue. Bertram Jensenius, a Chicago journalist and author, came to the rescue; he took over *Viking* and renamed it *Vinland.* Chicago symbolically became the new Vinland, the storied name given to the part of the North American East Coast discovered by Leif Erickson and his Norse explorers around the year 1000. Jensenius was born in February 1898 to missionary parents on Madagascar; in the late 1920s he settled permanently in Chicago. In 1948, Jensenius published a novel about his Norwegian missionary childhood on the island of Madagascar titled *Deilig er Jorden* (Beautiful Is the Earth). In an interview in *Nordmanns-Forbundet* in 1963, Jensenius expressed confidence in the prospects for "Norsedom and Norwegian language in Chicago" but noted "in my newspaper I use both English and Norwegian . . . otherwise I would not get to speak to the second generation." Jensenius published *Vinland* until his death in 1976. Under the title "I Saw a Newspaper Die," Arthur A. Gomsrud, editor of *Scandinavia in USA,* deplored *Viking*'s passing, as he mused about the continued significance of the foreign-language press in general and *Viking* in particular:

> When *Viking* died, the Chicago-Norwegians had all but concluded arrangements for the annual 17th of May celebration. In Chicago, as in New York and many large American cities, Norway's Constitution Day has always been celebrated with parades, pomp, and circumstance. When the May 1 and also May 8 editions of *Viking* failed to appear, the machinery behind all Norwegian activities in Chicago came to a sudden stop. The members of the many committees that constitute the machinery were left floundering; they had lost the one central link that bound them all together, the one joint source of information and communication which reached them all, individually and collectively, and through which they reached one another.

It would, indeed, be a challenging enterprise to continue on the course established by Jensenius without external means. In May 1976, Norwegian-born Arve O. Kilen and Jon Thallaug—both associated with the successful Scandinavian Design retail furniture company, founded by Kilen in Evanston, Illinois, in 1963—purchased *Vinland.* Its place of publication became Evanston. In the first issue, dated May 6, 1976, Thallaug responded to his own question of why they did not let *Vinland* die:

> First and foremost because there still is a Norwegian community in Chicago which looks forward to news in its own newspaper. We still have an active [Lutheran] church, many different social groups and a business circle that appreciates *Vinland.*

Vinland appeared semimonthly and was published in English save for minute notes titled "From Country and Town" *(Fra Bygd og By)*—an ethnic cue, if you will. After several years Kilen became the sole owner and publisher. The change produced a new volume numbering beginning in January 1983, which basically created a second series of the journal. An array of short-term editors and associates served *Vinland* during its lifetime. To expand its circulation, *Vinland* opened an office in Minneapolis and appointed a local editor for the Upper Midwest, and in time ventured as well into reporting on Swedish and Danish American activities. It was a losing proposition. September 1, 1987, *Vinland,* then in its fifth volume, ceased publication.[20]

The two newspapers in the Twin Ports of Duluth and Superior had a more successful run in terms of durability as local journals. They in fact continued publication for an impressive length of time: *Duluth Skandinav,* when it expired in 1965, had served the local community for nearly eighty years, and *Superior Tidende,* when it was discontinued in 1962, for close to seventy years under that masthead, with another five if its predecessor *Superior-Posten* is added to the volume tally. They then became the inevitable victims of demographic changes as a readership in tune with the Norwegian language gradually disappeared from the scene. The increasing use of English in both journals did not attract a sufficient response in American-born generations to secure solvency.

Anna Dahl Fuhr's name appeared in the editor's spot nearly to the end of her life; her struggle with Parkinson's disease, as reported in the two journals, kept her away from the editor's desk during the last weeks of 1955. Fuhr Publishing Company in addition faced financial difficulties; beginning in January 1956 *Duluth Skandinav* and *Superior Tidende* were reduced in size and published in tabloid format. In their March 9, 1956, issues, both newspapers announced, "Mrs. Anna Fuhr, widely known Norwegian leader and longtime editor and publisher of *Skandinav,* has discontinued her association with the newspaper." During the final years, with shifts in ownership and editorial leadership, the two journals continued to be printed in the Fuhr print shop nearly to the end. Editorials in the two weeklies' November 16, 1962, numbers deplored that "it is the owner's intent to bring to an end *(sette punktum)* and stop publishing *Duluth Skandinav* and *Superior Tidende.*" Though it represented the original resolve, the inclusion of *Duluth Skandinav,* that year marking its seventy-fifth anniversary, was premature. To the contrary, the newspaper gained a new publisher in Leif O. Selbak, a longtime Duluth resident from Trondheim, Norway, and a self-employed public accountant; his wife, American-born Lucile Strom Selbak, librarian at the Duluth Public Library, took over the editorship. The small four-page sheet reported enthusiastically and insightfully on local affairs, including public markings of May 17, Leif Erickson festivals by the Norse hero's statue in the park bearing his name, dockings of Norwegian ships, and prominent visitors, as well as editor Selbak's well-written account of her visit to Norway. August 6, 1965, the Selbak family team signed off with a brief note in *Duluth Skandinav,* declaring it the journal's final issue. The mailing list would be merged with *Decorah-Posten.*[21]

Decorah-Posten persisted as a national periodical for a few more years. Longtime associate editor and editor in chief Einar Lund was a mature man of nearly forty years old when he in 1919 arrived in America; he had considerable experience in editorial work from Norway and, like many successful newsmen, had learned the printing trade. His experience in journalism and printing stood him well in *Decorah-Posten*'s employ. His cultural and political convictions were much like his predecessors. Lund expressed his concern for the immigrant experience through creative writing. His novel *Solveig Murphy,* published in *Ved Arnen* in the 1930s, depicts the dilemma of adjustment facing American-born generations. Their problem, Lund asserted, was greater than for those born in Norway, because "the old had the memories and traditions from their old fatherland and family—the young remain rootless and groping."

Lund retired in his early eighties in 1962 and was succeeded by Erling Innvik, from Sunndalsøra, Norway, who had journalistic experience in the homeland. He modernized the appearance and language of *Posten* but, conscious of the preferences of an aging readership, not radically. *Decorah-Posten* continued publication a couple of years following Innvik's return to Norway in 1970. The consolidation with other Norwegian American journals gave *Decorah-Posten* a circulation of more than thirty thousand in 1950, even when taking into account that only a minority of subscribers continued with the new and unfamiliar newspaper. When it discontinued publication December 28, 1972, less than nine months from the start of its centennial year, it was still a profitable enterprise with 4,263 subscribers; future prospects, however, looked discouraging. It bid its readers "Farewell!" in Norwegian and English editorials, though Norwegian was the dominant, nearly exclusive, medium throughout *Decorah-Posten*'s existence. It succinctly traced its history "through nearly four generations" in which it "had freely entered thousands of Norwegian and Danish homes from coast to coast and made many friends." *Decorah-Posten* was likely the most distinctive and most treasured of all Norwegian American journals. Many interpreted the passing of *Decorah-Posten* as the loss of a vigorous and comforting spokesman for a cherished tradition. It by all accounts signified the closing of an era in Norwegian immigrant life that could never be retrieved.[22]

East and West Meet

The larger number of recent Norwegian immigrants on both coasts assured Norwegian American journalism greater postwar success there than in the Norwegian heartland; even so, as the years passed, publishers in these regions of Norwegian settlement faced an identical shrinking of potential subscribers. Kristine Haugen, in 1957 visiting *Washington Posten*'s publisher and editor O. L. Ejde at the newspaper's offices on the ninth floor of the Seaboard Building on Fourth and Pike in downtown Seattle, hailed him as the second savior of the journal, after Gunnar Lund. In Haugen's estimation, *Washington Posten* functioned on a solid economic foundation. Newspaper offices had the potential to become important centers for the local Norwegian community and beyond. Ejde noted nostalgically that "in and out of this office since 1917 have wandered most of the thousands of Norwegians who live in Seattle, in other towns and cities in Washington, and in neighboring states." The newspaper and its place of operation became a fixed orientation point in the lives of Norwegians on the coast, attesting to the central role a newsman like Ejde enjoyed as a social and cultural leader.

Washington Posten, in the manner of ethnic newspapers in general, was a prime mover in upholding a separate ethnic community life; it was a familiar and reassuring weekly guest in the homes of its many readers. In 1959, Ejde having turned seventy, "age of man" *(støvets år),* as he wrote editorially, decided that having been with the newspaper forty-six years, it was time to turn *Washington*

Posten over to younger and more energetic hands. Ejde sold the newspaper to Henning C. Boe, effective June 1, 1959. Born in Oslo, Norway, in 1915 and an immigrant in 1951, Boe was a trained typographer, "a trade," as Ejde correctly stated, "that through time has given the world lots of capable journalists, editors, and newspaper publishers." Ejde continued as editor until October 1967, when Boe himself took on that added responsibility.

The newspaper altered both its image and its name as it adjusted to changing circumstances by following the prevalent example of ethnic newspapers and "developed into a publication for the few." June 9, 1961, it was published under the masthead *Western Viking;* the same issue announced the opening of Trans-Globe Travel on Market Street in Ballard, owned by Boe, who editorially explained that "extra income was needed to keep the newspaper going"—a successful arrangement adopted by other newspaper publishers. The name change—again typical for ethnic journals confronted with a diminishing pool of readers—was a move intended to extend circulation nationwide. *Western Viking* adopted a twelve-page tabloid format in 1964; it was, like *Washington Posten,* basically a Norwegian-language publication. The amount of English-language items varied; Boe alternated between Norwegian and English in his well-written commentary under the heading "Publisher's Corner," where he reflected on such varied topics as the political immaturity of the young, the benefits of the Sons of Norway, and the esteemed career of Norwegian American Eric Sevareid. Boe gave front-page priority to news from Norway, focusing on political life, cultural events, and sports. Correspondents contributed news from many parts of the United States and also from Canada; Norwegian happenings, organizations, and people in Seattle received generous column space. *Western Viking* thus exhibited a familiar trend in ethnic newspaper publishing. Henning Boe announced his retirement—then in his seventy-sixth year—in a July 27, 1990, editorial. *Western Viking* was sold to a corporation formed by a group of Norwegian American business people in the greater Seattle area; this group continued its publication.[23]

On the East Coast, *Nordisk Tidende* experienced similar developments to its colleague in Seattle. In December 1959, in a published response to a questionnaire, the readers indicated "a clear tendency to a greater tolerance toward material in English." Some respondents thought that in order to reach "the younger generation . . . [and] stay alive" it would be necessary to go totally over to English. Editor Søyland expressed his opinion: "We consider it doubtful that a Norwegian American newspaper can totally go over to English—and succeed in the competition." Earlier attempts to publish purely English-language periodicals for a Norwegian American readership had not succeeded; these were journals like the early Chicago *Viking,* 1894–95, *The North* in Minneapolis, 1889–93, and the *Norwegian-American* in Northfield, Minnesota, 1908–18. The several earlier adoptions of English in order to save a failing newspaper, exemplified in *Fremad*'s and *Normanden*'s futile English-language transformation, might have provided the compelling evidence for Søyland that "going English" was not a viable course.

The historian of *Nordisk Tidende,* Karsten Roedder, took over the editorship January 1, 1963 until 1967; Søyland continued full time as "consulting editor." *Nordisk Tidende* marked its seventy-fifth year in 1966 with a series of articles written by the editor about the historical path it had traveled. The intriguing question of subventions to the Norwegian American press from Norway's tax coffers surfaced at this time, prompted by the debate in Norway over "the newspaper death" in that country and proposals for public funding; the debate was expanded to encompass the situation in Norwegian American journalism. *Dagbladet* in Oslo reminded its readers of "all the free advertising and public relation benefits Norway received in the Norwegian American press." Whereas *Nordisk Tidende,* better situated than its rivals, rejected the idea of "beggary" *(tiggergang), Decorah-Posten* saw it differently and voiced its frustration over the fact that "nothing has been done in Norwegian public quarters to preserve the Norwegian press in America." No support would be forthcoming.

In January 1971, Sigurd Daasvand assumed the position of editor in chief. Daasvand had a warm personality and created much goodwill for the newspaper; he left *Nordisk Tidende* in July 1982. Daasvand arrived with experience from the Norwegian resistance movement, from imprisonment by the Nazis, and in journalism after 1945, including in the Norwegian press service *(Norsk Telegrambyrå).* In connection with the celebration of the sesquicentennial

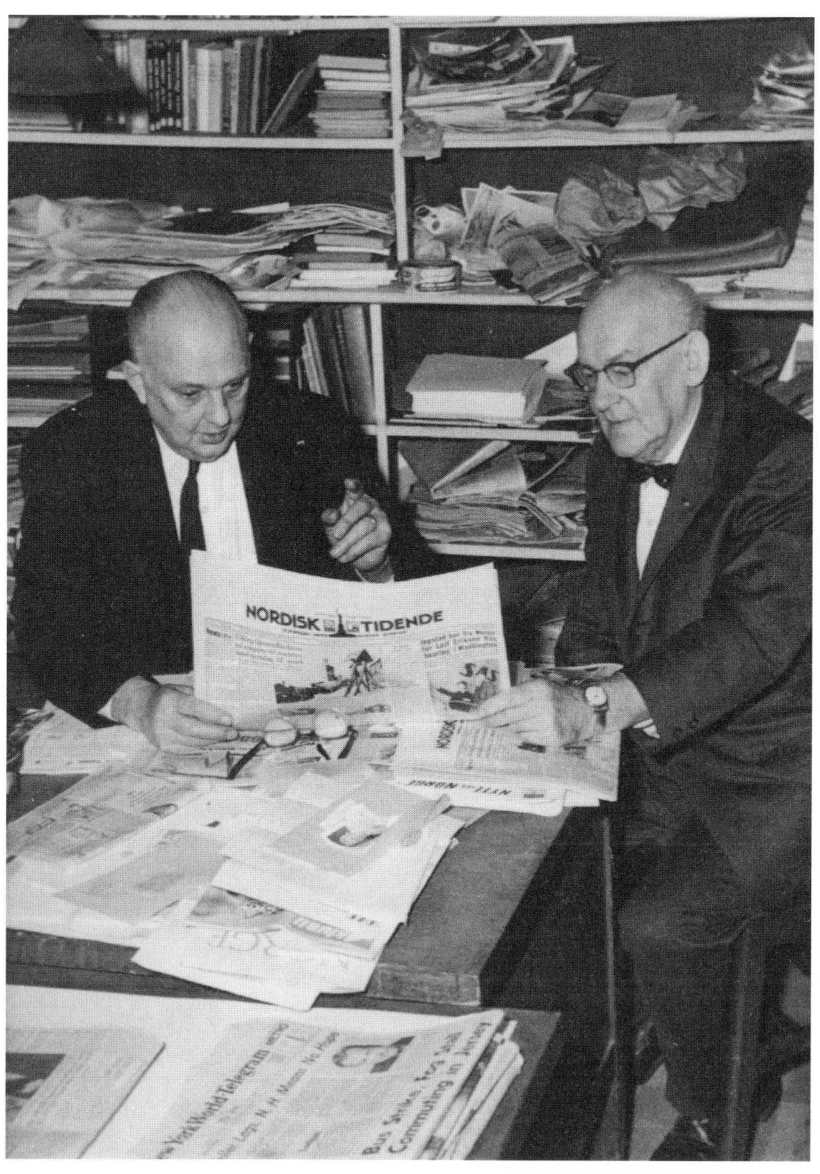

Karsten Roedder, historian of Nordisk Tidende *and its editor from 1963 to 1967, with Carl Søyland in the newspaper's Brooklyn office. Søyland, on* Nordisk Tidende*'s staff since 1926, served as editor in chief from 1940 until he was succeeded by Roedder. Among a series of strong editorial leaders, Søyland stands out as the most remarkable and influential.*

of Norwegian immigration to America and visit by King Olav V, on October 9, 1975—the date marking the 1825 arrival of the sloop *Restauration* with the first boatload of immigrants from Norway—*Nordisk Tidende* appeared in a record-setting souvenir number of one hundred pages. The special issue gave a historical overview of "why the emigration memory is celebrated" by printing "old America letters, articles, reports, and interviews." It was Leif Erickson Day as well, and in his proclamation of the day, New York Governor Hugh L. Carey praised the exploratory achievements of "seafarers of Norwegian blood" and dwelled on the debt "Our civilization owes . . . to Americans of Norwegian origin." It was a grand moment in the life of Norwegians in America observed in all centers of Norwegian settlement.

The movement toward more English and preparation for becoming primarily an English-language organ accelerated. A special English section editor was appointed early in Daasvand's tenure. At the time of Daasvand's retirement in July 1982, the publishers in a radical move appointed a new editor in chief with no Norwegian background and demoted the responsibility for the diminishing Norwegian text to an assistant editor. Gunnar Bjørkman, president of Norse News, *Nordisk Tidende*'s publisher, explained "A New *Nordisk Tidende*":

> In the near future we will publish more and more in English to interest the many second and third generations of Norwegian Americans and a new format of *Nordisk Tidende* might change to tabloid form for easier reading and handling. We also have plans to bring in sophisticated computers in Oslo and here to bring faster news and other personal information to our readers.

The decision to appoint an American editor in chief was, it seemed, premature; the newspaper's administration accepted the recommendation of its advisory board that "in this period of expansion the newspaper should be guided by someone who is both Norwegian and has long experience in newspaper management." After "reaching an agreement with the earlier intended editor," Sigmund Torvik, *Nordisk Tidende*'s editor in Norway, succeeded Daasvand as *Nordisk Tidende*'s editor in chief.[24]

Norway Times—*Nordisk Tidende*'s new masthead—was launched

January 5, 1984, in tabloid format and with a new editor. Geirr Aakhus, born and raised in Risør, Norway, "with a long experience in newspaper work with a specialty in the tabloid format," took over the editorship. Save for the last three of twenty-four pages, the initial issue of *Norway Times* was entirely in English. The transformation had taken longer than predicted earlier. The intent was not only to attract American-born generations as subscribers, but also to strengthen the weekly's national appeal. The appointment of a Midwest editor denoted an ambitious capitalization on the void created by the loss of a midwestern Norwegian American press. *Western Viking* in Seattle was the single Norwegian American newspaper competing with *Norway Times* for a national readership. Its access to the Midwest profited from its acquisition in January 1973 of *Decorah-Posten*'s subscription list when this venerable news organ went out of business; the cartoon characters "Han Ola og han Per" thereafter greeted *Western Viking*'s readers in weekly installments. In their adjustment to the shifting contingencies, both journals followed a typical course for foreign-language publication; their survival depended on reaching readers nationwide who were no longer proficient in Norwegian, as circulations inevitably would dwindle. As announced in *Norway Times,* however, circulation the first three months after the change rose about 30 percent.

Western Viking and *Norway Times* became largely English-language publications. They continued to address themselves to a Norwegian American population and thus may be considered in a history of the Norwegian American press. In 1984 *Norway Times* editor Aakhus saw the business of "ethnic newspapering" as "a duty to keep up tradition, the love of language and the feeling of community"; yet he stated regret that the newspaper reached but few of the more than 3.6 million people in America who in the 1980 census filled in the block marked "nationality" with "Norwegian." The vast majority of Americans of Norwegian ancestry would not have been aware of their existence. The reality faced by Norwegian American publishers was a loss of subscribers and advertising; newspapers' weekly appearance regularly required an inordinate effort with few monetary rewards. In the mid-1990s *Norway Times* was failing; the investment company that owned it then sold it to Marianne Onsrud Jawanda, born in Oppland, Norway, and a group of *Norway Times* employees, who, in the words of Onsrud Jawanda, "recognized it as a cultural treasure." From 1990 Alf Lunder Knudsen for a decade or so served as *Western Viking*'s editor and publisher. He was born in Brooklyn but grew up in Stavanger, Norway, and later moved to Seattle, where, at the University of Washington, he earned advanced degrees in music and the history of the Norwegian male choir movement in America. His public appearances as a male chorus director called attention to *Western Viking*.

A merger of the two remaining representatives of a Norwegian American press might seem inevitable. *Western Viking*, owned and published by Norway Posten, Inc., announced in November 2006 that it was "getting married," purchased by Norwegian American Weekly, Inc., owned by the Norwegian American Foundation, created in 2001, as explained by its executive director and chief executive officer Kim Nesselquist, "to increase the visibility and further the cooperation among Norwegian Americans for the purpose of strengthening the ties between modern Norway and people throughout the United States." The new masthead read *Norwegian American Weekly*. As of January 1, 2008, *Norway Times* was purchased and combined with the weekly, with offices in Seattle and New York, printing in Minneapolis, and correspondents in Norway and throughout the United States. At the time of purchase *Western Viking* had a weekly distribution of 2,100 and *Norway Times* 2,210. The greater resources of *Norwegian American Weekly* have benefited the marketing and also the professional look of the newspaper. In February 2008 its total distribution stood at 4,170 and growing; currently *Norwegian American Weekly* has an estimated readership of 18,000 to 20,000. Who are the subscribers and why do they subscribe might be a concluding question. Sigrid Schneider in her essay "The German-American Press Today" concluded that the German American journals complemented the functions of the American mass media, encouraged and promoted a strong relationship between reader and newspaper, and fulfilled the need for group communication and a desire for information about ethnic life and the old country. These same motives might apply equally well to a Norwegian American journal like *Norwegian American Weekly*.[25]

The Norwegian Press in America

The importance of the Norwegian American press has elicited opinions and debates throughout its history of more than a century and a half. Supporters consistently stressed its bridge-building function with the Norwegian homeland, its promotion of Norsedom in America, and its Americanizing efficacy. These separate roles did not conflict, but were played out simultaneously and may be claimed to have complemented each other. The Norwegian ethnic newspapers' presence and influences throughout these many decades is an unquestionable historical reality. The newspapers were a major force in maintaining a separate ethnic existence while the immigrants adjusted to the demands of the new society; ethnic newspapers adjusted to the shifting needs and preferences of their readers, to deviating American attitudes toward its immigrant citizens, and to changing social and political contingencies. By reporting local news from regions of Norwegian settlement throughout the land, they bound together groups of Norwegians separated by distance and thereby gave meaning to the concept of a Norwegian America.

Norwegian American journalism has a tangible significance for present generations as well. The publications it produced, in the manner of all ethnic newspapers and periodicals, constitute the major source of information on the cultural heritage and historical development of the Norwegian ethnic group in the United States.

Beginning in 1847, with the publication of the weekly *Nordlyset,* the growth and maintenance of a Norwegian-language press related to the volume of Norwegian immigration and the preservation of the mother tongue in the Norwegian American population. Nearly three hundred Norwegian-language newspapers were founded from first to last when only taking into account the number of journal titles. *Emigranten* was the only of the pre–Civil War ventures to continue publication after the end of hostilities; in the following decades as mass exodus from Norway commenced it was joined by an avalanche of journalistic enterprise. Many failed after a year or less; in fact, again only considering titles, 64 percent lasted three years or less. The figure is, however, somewhat misleading since a great number of the discontinued news sheets did not simply succumb, but rather were consolidated with another journal; in some cases and for a variety of reasons, the publishers adopted a new masthead. A precise accounting of the actual number of individual newspapers is therefore difficult to make. Their significance in the Norwegian American community is not as a consequence diminished. The great majority of the Norwegian-language news organs saw the light of day between 1877 and 1906. *Skandinaven,* founded in 1866, *Decorah-Posten* in 1874, and *Minneapolis Tidende* in 1888 were the major national journals; they were joined in the Upper Midwest by an impressive number of local journalistic ventures, with mastheads like *Normanden, Fram, Visergutten, Fremad, Fergus Falls Ugeblad, Duluth Skandinav,* and *Amerika. Washington Posten* on the West Coast and *Nordisk Tidende* on the eastern seaboard were both major players in Norwegian American journalism.

The decades following World War I witnessed a rapid decline of the number and circulation of Norwegian American newspapers; eventually bilingualism became the norm in the columns of the surviving journals. The present chapter has traced the successive discontinuation of individual newspapers warranted by the lack of resources and the diminishing support from Americans of Norwegian ancestry; only a minute number of the 4,477,725 Americans nationwide who in the 2000 federal census subjectively claimed Norwegian ethnicity would have been aware of existing Norwegian American journals. Their sense of ethnicity was not, as it might have been in earlier generations, affected by subscription to a Norwegian ethnic journal, but related to family and community ties and a recognition of heritage. A Norwegian American identity—regularly interpreted as a state of mind—manifests itself in organizational activity, festivals, and visits to the ancestral homeland.[26]

APPENDIX 1

Secular Norwegian American Publications

THE LIST OF SECULAR NEWSPAPER TITLES is based on inventories of archival collections, references in Norwegian American newspapers, and secondary sources. Johs. B. Wist, *Norsk-Amerikanernes Festskrift* (1914), gives the most complete early treatment of Norwegian American periodicals. In 1947, in connection with the centennial of the beginnings of Norwegian-language newspaper publishing in the United States, Olav Morgan Norlie assembled an impressive list of these publications, mimeographed as "Norwegian-Americana Papers, 1847–1946." It is a helpful, even essential tool in identifying publications but must be consulted critically. Norlie in his tally differentiates between secular and religious publications. His list of 569 ventures has nevertheless been cited—disregarding the fact that secular, church, and organizational periodicals are included—as the number of Norwegian-language newspapers published. It might be safely claimed that the total number—from 1847 to the present—of secular semimonthly, weekly, semiweekly, or daily newspapers never surpassed three hundred. Even that figure might be questioned since it includes all titles without taking into account shifting mastheads of single journals. Even so, it is a figure that speaks volumes about the numerical strength and impact of Norwegian American journalistic enterprise.

California

Los Angeles

California-Vikingen (The California Viking), 1924–25, weekly

San Francisco

Bien (The Bee), April 22, 1882–90, weekly (Revived in 1891 as a Danish weekly. Still published 2010)

California-Posten (The California Post), December 25, 1874–76, weekly (First Danish-Norwegian newspaper on Pacific Coast. Continued as *Valkyrien*)

Fram (Forward), 1903–4, weekly

Lanternen (The Lantern), 1892, semimonthly

Pacific Posten (Pacific Post), September 15, 1904–April 12, 1906, weekly

Pacific Posten (Pacific Post), 1907–8, weekly

Pacific Skandinav (Pacific Scandinavian), 1886–1905, weekly (Danish-Norwegian. Continuation of *Valkyrien*. Absorbed by *Pacific Posten*, November 16, 1905)

Valkyrien (The Valkyrie), 1878–86, weekly (Continuation of *California-Posten*)

TOTAL: 8 weekly and 1 semimonthly publications

Connecticut

Hartford

Connecticut Folkeblad (Connecticut People's Newspaper), 1898–1901, weekly (Absorbed by *Nordiske Blade*, NY)

TOTAL: 1 weekly publication

Illinois

Chicago

Afholdsbladet (Temperance Paper), 1880–88, monthly (Merged with *Arbeideren* in Eau Claire, WI, 1888)

Afholds-Vennen (The Friend of Temperance), 1894–96, weekly (Continued as *Illinois-Posten*)

Amerika (America), August 13–December 31, 1872, weekly and daily (Merged with *Skandinaven* as *Skandinaven og Amerika* January 3, 1873)

Amerika (America), January 7, 1885–July 28, 1922, weekly (Sample copies from October 1, 1884. Moved to Madison, WI, April 1896. Merged with *Norden* as *Amerika og Norden*, October 20, 1897. *Norden* deleted from the name October 1898)

Arbeideren (The Laborer), 1877–78, weekly (Continued as *Folkets Røst* for less than a year)

Chicago Viking, 1880–81, monthly

Daglige Skandinaven (The Daily Scandinavian), January 1, 1873–March 31, 1930, daily (Began 1870 as *Skandinaven tre ugentlig udgave*, a separate local, triweekly edition with nearly the same content as the daily. It became daily in 1871, using the weekly edition's volume numbering until January 1, 1873)

Dagslyset (The Light of Day), April 1869–February 1878, monthly (January 1877–February 1878, published in Becker, MN. Not published last six months of 1877)

Den Norsk-Amerikanske Independent (The Norwegian American Independent), January 1877–79, weekly

Den Nye Tid (The New Age), 1878–84, weekly

Det hvide Baand (White Ribbon), 1899–1915, monthly

Familie-Kredsen (The Family Circle), 1883–84, weekly

Figaro (Literary figure), 1877–80, weekly

Folkebladet (The People's Newspaper), September 22–29, 1860, weekly

Folkets Røst (The People's Voice), 1878, weekly (Continuation of *Arbeideren*)

Fremskridt (Progress), 1894–95, weekly

Frihed og Fangenskab (Freedom and Captivity), 1879–80, weekly

Friheden (The Independent), 1870–71, weekly

Fridheds-Banneret (The Banner of Freedom), October 4, 1852–May 7, 1853, weekly

Hejmdal (Norse god), 1874–78, weekly (Danish-Norwegian)

Idun (Norse goddess), 1908–10, monthly

I ledige Timer (In Idle Hours), 1895–96, monthly

Illinois-Posten (The Illinois Post), 1896–1910, weekly (Continuation of *Afholds-Vennen*. Published in Ottawa, 1899–1910. Continued as *Ottawa Tidende*)

Illustreret Familieblad (Illustrated Family Magazine), 1879–80, monthly

Illustreret Husbibliothek (Illustrated House Library), October 1873–October 1941, monthly (From 1882 a literary supplement to *Skandinaven*. Original title *Husbibliothek*)

Marcus Thrane's Norske Amerikaner (Norwegian American), May 25–September 13, 1866, weekly

Norden (The North), October 13, 1874–October 1897, weekly (From March 1892 *Norden* published *Chicago Norden* for local consumption. October 1897 it merged with *Amerika*, Madison, WI)

Norden (The North), December 1928–May 1933, monthly

Norden Dagbladet (The North Daily), 1889–91, daily

Nordisk Folkeblad (Nordic People's Newspaper), 1888–89, weekly (Absorbed by *Norden*)

Nordlyset (The Northern Lights), 1869–73, monthly

Norsk Aftenblad (Norwegian Evening Newspaper), 1870–71, weekly

Nye Tid (New Age), 1870–71, weekly

Samfundet (The Society), 1895–1901, monthly

Sang og Idræt (Song and Athletics), 1892–93, monthly

Scandia, April, 1888–May 16, 1940, weekly (Published in Duluth, MN, 1888–99. Published in English 1939–40)

Skandia (Scandia), 1884–85, weekly

Skandinaven (The Scandinavian), June 1, 1866–October 30, 1941, weekly/semiweekly (First sample number dated May 2, 1866. Volume numbering from June 1, 1866. Published as *Skandinaven og Amerika*, January 3–December 30, 1873. January 1874 a semimonthly European edition of *Skandinaven* was begun, intended mainly for subscribers in Norway and Denmark. It continued publication until September 1893)

Social-Demokraten (The Social Democrat), 1911–21, weekly

Søndag Skandinaven (Sunday Scandinavian), July 1890–30, weekly

Templarbladet (The Good Templar Magazine), 1890–1900, monthly (Published in Milwaukee, WI, 1899–1900)

Typografitidende (Typographical Times), 1889–92, monthly (Published in Minneapolis, MN, 1890–92)

Verdens Gang (The Way of the World), 1878–1919, weekly (Published by *Skandinaven* as a low-price edition)

Viking, 1894–95, weekly

Viking, November 6, 1941–May 17, 1958, weekly (Continued as *Vinland*)

Vinland, September 18, 1958–September 1, 1987, weekly, semimonthly (Continuation of *Viking*. New volume numbering from January 1983)

LELAND

Wossingen, December 1856–March 1860, monthly (irregularly) (1860 published in Milwaukee, WI. 1871 removed to Voss, Norway)

MORRIS

Vesterland (Western Land), 1915–16, monthly

OTTAWA

Ottawa Tidende, 1910–13, weekly (Continuation of *Illinois-Posten*. Merged with an English-language local newspaper)

TOTAL: 29 weekly, 18 monthly, 3 daily, 1 semimonthly publications

Iowa

CEDAR RAPIDS

Fra alle Lande (From All Nations), 1885–88, weekly (Danish-Norwegian. Continued as *Kvinden og Hjemmet*)

Kvinden og Hjemmet (The Woman and the Home), May 1888–August 1947, monthly (Published in Swedish as *Qvinnan och Hemmet*, 1893–1947)

Vort Bibliothek (Our Library), 1888–1947, monthly (A supplement to *Kvinden og Hjemmet*. Other supplements: *Nordisk Folkebibliotek* [Nordic People's Library], 1905–15. Merged with *Vort Bibliothek* 1915. *Mønstertidende* [Pattern News], 1915–47, monthly)

DECORAH

Decorah-Posten (The Decorah Post), September 5, 1874–December 28, 1972, weekly/semiweekly (1872–97, 1941–72 weekly, 1897–1941 semiweekly)

Ervingen (The Heir), 1897–1913, monthly

Familie-læsning (Family Reading), 1895–96, monthly

Fluen (The Fly), 1869–70, monthly

For Hjemmet (For the Home), 1870–88, semimonthly

Fra Fjernt og Nær (From Far and Near), 1869–70, weekly (Began as a supplement to *Ved Arnen*)

Illustreret Familieblad (Illustrated Family Magazine), 1887–88, monthly

Moderlandet (The Mother Country), 1866–67, monthly

Symra (The Anemone), 1905–14, annual, quarterly (1909–14 published quarterly)

Ved Arnen. Et Tidsskrift for Skjønliteratur (By the Fireside. A Magazine for Belles-Lettres), September 1866–70, monthly, October 1882–December 28, 1972, monthly/weekly (Published in La Crosse, WI, 1866–67. It was revived October 1882 as a literary supplement to *Decorah-Posten*, monthly until 1887 and thereafter weekly)

JOICE

Dølen. Tidsskrift paa Norsk Maal (The Dalesman. Magazine in the Norwegian language), 1903–4, monthly (Only six issues appeared, the final one in Minneapolis, MN)

LAKE MILLS

Republikaneren (The Republican), 1897–1903, weekly (Continuation of *Sioux City Tidende*)

NORTHWOOD

Index, 1885–86, weekly (Norwegian-English)

SIOUX CITY

Sioux City Tidende (Sioux City Times), 1890–97, weekly (Continued as *Republikaneren*)

Sioux City Tilskuer (Sioux City Observer), 1887–88, weekly (Continued as *Vesterheimen*)

Vesterheimen (The Western Home), 1888–89, weekly (Continuation of *Sioux City Tilskuer*)

STORY CITY

Norsk-amerikansk Musiktidende (Norwegian American Musical Times), 1890–92, monthly (Published in Minneapolis, MN, 1891–92)

Skolen og Hjemmet (The School and the Home), 1891–96, weekly

Visergutten (The Errand Boy), 1894–1955, weekly (Published in Canton, SD, 1917–44, and in Fargo, ND, 1944–55. It merged with *Normanden* in Fargo in 1944 and was revived as an independent publication in 1947)

Vor Republik (Our Republic), 1890–91, weekly

TOTAL: 10 weekly or semiweekly and 11 monthly publications, 1 quarterly

Kansas

GIRARD

Gaa Paa (Press Forward), November 29, 1903–October 26, 1918, weekly (Published in Minneapolis, MN, 1904–18. Name changed to *Folkets Røst*, December 21, 1918–October 31, 1925)

TOTAL: 1 weekly publication

Massachusetts

BOSTON

Heimskringla (Orb of the World), 1916–?, weekly

WORCESTER

Skandinaviska God Templaren (The Scandinavian Good Templar), 1901–30, monthly (Swedish-Norwegian temperance magazine)

TOTAL: 1 weekly and 1 monthly publications

Michigan

MANISTEE

Michigan Skandinav (Michigan Scandinavian), 1887–90, weekly

TOTAL: 1 weekly publication

Minnesota

ADA

Folkets Blad (The People's Newspaper), 1906–7, weekly (Merged with *Fram*, Fargo, ND, August 1907)

ALBERT LEA

Albert Lea Posten (The Albert Lea Post), July 5, 1882–March 17, 1885, weekly (Absorbed by *Nordvesten*, St. Paul, March 1885)

Albert Lea Skandinav (Albert Lea Scandinavian), 1879–80, weekly

Nordstjernen (The North Star), July 12, 1899, weekly (Only one issue published)

Samvirke (Joint Action), 1881–82, weekly

Søndre Minnesota (Southern Minnesota), April 1880–81, weekly

BAGLEY

Fremskridt (Progress), 1918–19?, weekly

BEMIDJI

Normannaheimen (The Norman Home), 1906–7, weekly

Vort nye Hjem (Our New Home), 1905–6, weekly

CANBY

Minnesota Folkeblad (Minnesota People's Newspaper), 1892–97, weekly (Absorbed by *Minnesota Tidende*, August 1897)

CROOKSTON

Folkets Tidende (The People's Times), 1891–92, weekly

Red River Dalen (The Red River Valley), 1890–96, weekly (Continued as *Fjerde Juli*)

Red River Tidende (The Red River Times), 1895–99, weekly (Published simultaneously in Fergus Falls. Merged with *Nordvesten*, St. Paul, December 1899. *Tidende*'s subscription list sold to *Amerika*, Madison, WI, August 1900)

DANE

Nordlyset (Northern Lights), 1870–73, weekly

DULUTH

Duluth Banner, 1902–3, weekly (Absorbed by *Superior Tidende*)

Duluth Skandinav (Duluth Scandinavian), December 7, 1887–August 6, 1965, weekly (Absorbed by *Decorah-Posten*, Decorah, IA)

Namdaltidende (The Namdal Times), 1920–25?, weekly

Scandia, April 1888–May 16, 1940, weekly (Published in Chicago, IL, 1899–1940)

Trønder-American, 1936–38, monthly

ELBOW LAKE

Samhold (Solidarity), 1892–94, weekly (Merged with *Rodhuggeren*, Fergus Falls, November 1894)

Tiden (The Age), ?–1891, weekly (Absorbed by *Scandia*, Duluth)

FERGUS FALLS

Fergus Falls Ugeblad (From January 1940 spelled *Ukeblad*) (Fergus Falls Weekly Magazine), January, 1883–December 18, 1946, weekly (Continuation of *Normanna Banner*)

Normanna Banner (Norman Banner), 1881–82, weekly (Continued as *Fergus Falls Ugeblad*)

Nyt Normanna Banner (New Norman Banner), 1883–84, weekly

Rodhuggeren (The Radical), November 28, 1893–May 10, 1898, weekly (Purchased *Folkets Tidende*'s printing press in Crookston. Merged with *Fjerde Juli og Dakota*. The merged newspapers continued as *Fram* in Fargo, ND)

Tiden (The Age), 1881–82, weekly

FERTILE

Arbeidsmanden (The Laborer), 1900–1905, monthly (Published in Portview 1902–4, and in Brainerd, 1904–5)

GLENWOOD

Fakkelen (The Torch), 1885–86, weekly

GRANITE FALLS

Norge (Norway), August 18, 1899–September 24, 1901, weekly (Absorbed by *Amerika*, Madison, WI, September 1901)

LANESBORO

Det udflyttede Norge (The Emigrated Norway), 1888–89, weekly (Part of 1889 published in Preston)

LITCHFIELD

Heimdal (Norse god), ?–1891, weekly (Absorbed by *Scandia*, Duluth)

MADISON

Madison Tidende (The Madison Times), 1894–August 5, 1897, weekly (Continued as *Minnesota Tidende*)

Minnesota Tidende (The Minnesota Times), August 12, 1897–August 31, 1899, weekly (Continuation of *Madison Tidende* and *Minnesota Folkeblad*)

MINNEAPOLIS

Aftenlæsning (Evening Reading), March 1895–December 7, 1905, semiweekly, weekly (Published by *Minneapolis Tidende*. Merged with *Nordvesten*, St. Paul, December 7, 1905)

Allarm (Alarm), 1915–18, monthly (Swedish-Norwegian-Danish) (First ten issues published in Seattle, WA)

Almuevennen (The Friend of the People), January 1898–December 1900, monthly (Published as a literary supplement to *Nye Normanden*, which moved from Moorhead to Minneapolis July 1895)

Arbeidets Ridder (The Knight of Labor), 1886–87, monthly

Budstikken (The Messenger), September 2, 1873–December 26, 1894, weekly (Owned by T. Gulbrandsen Publishing Company from November 1888 and published as *Minneapolis Daglig Tidende*'s weekly edition. Merged with *Minneapolis Tidende* January 4, 1895)

Familiebladet (The Family Newspaper), 1931–32, weekly

Familiens Magasin (The Family's Magazine), 1916–28, monthly (Continuation of *Ungdommens Ven*)

Familievennen (Friend of the Family), 1885–86, weekly (Continued as *Feltraabet*)

Feltraabet (The Battle Cry), 1886–89, weekly

Folkebladet (The People's Newspaper), August 1877–January 1878, September 1879–September 1880, monthly, October 6, 1880–December 29, 1915, weekly (Continued as a purely church organ January 1916–July 1952)

Folkets Røst (The Voice of the People), December 21, 1918–October 31, 1925, weekly, semimonthly (Continuation of *Gaa Paa*, published in Minneapolis from 1904)

Folkets Ven (The People's Friend), 1907–30, monthly

For Spøg og Alvor (In Jest and Gravity), October 1899–1903, monthly

Fremtiden (The Future), 1880–81, weekly

Heimskringla (Orb of the World), 1896–?, monthly

Idun (Norse goddess), 1896–1900, monthly

Krydseren (The Voyager), 1888–92, weekly

Kvartalskrift (Quarterly), 1905–22, quarterly (Published in Eau Claire, WI, 1906–22)

Kvindens Magasin (The Woman's Magazine), 1905–17, monthly

Lynilden (The Lightning), 1892–94, weekly

Minneapolis Daglig Tidende (The Minneapolis Daily Times), January 24, 1887–April 29, 1932,

Minneapolis Posten (The Minneapolis Post), November 1940–November 1956, weekly (Continued as *Minnesota Posten*)

Minneapolis Søndag Tidende (The Minneapolis Sunday Times), November 24, 1889–April 24, 1932, Sunday (Replaced the Saturday daily issue in November 1889)

Minneapolis Tidende (The Minneapolis Times), January 7, 1888–March 21, 1935, weekly (Continuation of *Grand Forks Tidende*, ND, owned by T. Gulbrandsen)

(Through merger with *Fædrelandet og Emigranten* in 1893, *Tidende* claimed *Emigranten*'s founding in 1852 as the start of its own history)

Minnesota, 1872–September 30, 1873, weekly (Absorbed by *Budstikken* October 1873)

Minnesota Posten (The Minnesota Post), November 8, 1956–May 17, 1979, weekly (Continuation of *Minneapolis Posten*)

Minnesota Skandinav (Minnesota Scandinavian), 1879–80, weekly

Normanna (The Norse), 1888–94, weekly

Norsk Maanedstidende (The Norwegian Monthly Times), 1870–71, monthly

Norsk Tidsskrift (Norwegian Magazine), January 1896, monthly

Ny Tid (New Age), November 1907–June 1909, monthly (Merged with *Smuler*, St. Paul)

Politiken (The Politics), June 26, 1904–7, weekly (Continuation of *Nye Normanden*. In 1907 became the monthly *Ny Tid*)

Saamanden (The Sower), September 1887–December 1894, monthly (January 1895 moved to Norway)

Sanger Hilsen (Singers' Greeting), 1910– , semimonthly (Current address in Decorah, IA)

Sport og Friluftsliv (Sport and Outdoor Life), January 1897–99, monthly

The North, 1889–93, weekly (English-language publication)

Ungdommens Ven (The Friend of Youth), March 1890–1916, monthly (1916 name changed to *Familiens Magasin*)

Vaart Folk (Our People), 1940–41, monthly

Vikingen (The Viking), 1893–95, monthly

Vikingen (The Viking), 1906–7, monthly

Vor Tid. Maanedsskrift for Litteratur og Samfundsspørgsmaal (Our Times. Monthly for Literature and Social Issues), 1904–8, monthly

MINNESOTA FALLS

Minnesota Falls Journal, 1870, weekly (Norwegian-English)

MOORHEAD

Dagen (The Day), 1897–98, daily

Folkets Ven (The People's Friend), 1895–97, weekly

Nye Normanden (The New Norseman), 1894–July 19, 1904, weekly (Published in Minneapolis, 1895–1904. Continued as *Politiken*)

NORTHFIELD

Nordlyset (Northern Lights), 1870–71, 1878–79, weekly

Norwegian-American, 1908–December 27, 1918, English-language weekly (March 29, 1918, changed name to *United-American*)

OSLO

Skøiergutten (The Joker), 1912–14, monthly

PORTVIEW

Familiebladet (The Family Magazine), 1905–6, weekly

RED WING

Minnesota Posten (The Minnesota Post), 1878–79, weekly

Nordstjernen (The North Star), 1895–1901, weekly

ROCHESTER

Nordisk Folkeblad (Nordic People's Newspaper), March 12, 1868–July 7, 1875, weekly (First Danish-Norwegian weekly in Minnesota. Published in Rochester March 12–May 14, 1868, in Minneapolis March 17, 1869–July 7, 1875. Absorbed by *Skandinaven*, Chicago, July 1875)

RUSHFORD

Vesterheimen (The Western Home), 1881–83, weekly

SACRED HEART

Sacred Heart Bladet (The Sacred Heart Newspaper), 1891–95, weekly

Sacred Heart Posten (The Sacred Heart Post), 1890–94, weekly

Sacred Heart Republican, 1895–96, weekly (Norwegian-English)

ST. PAUL

Folkets Røst (The Voice of the People), July 10–November 20, 1858, semimonthly (A single number published October 1, 1857. Earliest Norwegian-language newspaper in Minnesota)

Heimdal (Norse god), December 1891–1902, weekly (Norwegian-Danish) (Continued as the Danish weekly *St. Paul Tidende*, 1902–28)

Jubilate (The Jubilee), 1899–1901, monthly

Nationaltidende (The National Times), 1893–96, weekly (Published in Duluth, November 1895–November 1896. Absorbed by *Nordvesten*)

Nordvesten (The Northwest), 1881–June 27, 1907, weekly (Absorbed by *Minneapolis Tidende*)

Smuler (Crumbs), 1901–12, monthly (Additional issues came out irregularly until 1916)

Tiden (The Age), 1878–79, weekly

SPRING GROVE

Spring Grove Posten (The Spring Grove Post), April 12, 1880–81, weekly

STARBUCK

Vor Flyvende (Our Leaflet), 1917–18, weekly

WALNUT GROVE

Norrøna. Det fyrste Blad paa Norskt Maal i Vesterheimen (The Norse. The first Magazine in the Norwegian language in the Western

Home), 1900–1901, monthly (Revived and published in Fargo, ND, 1914–15)

WARREN

Red River Dalens Sol (The Red River Valley's Sun), 1886–91, weekly

WEST DULUTH

West Duluth Ekko (West Duluth Echo), 1905–6, weekly

WILLMAR

Western Minnesota Press, 1880–85, weekly (English and Norwegian. Continued as *The Atwater Press*. 1885–1900)

WINONA

Folkevennen (The People's Friend), 1868, weekly

TOTAL: 74 weekly, 3 daily, and 28 monthly or semimonthly, 1 quarterly publications

Montana

BUTTE

Montana Skandinav (Montana Scandinavian), January 1893, weekly (Merged with *Montana Tidende*)

Montana Tidende (Montana Times), 1893, weekly (Merged with *Montana Skandinav*)

Montana Tidende og Skandinav (Montana Times and Scandinavian), 1893–95, weekly

GREAT FALLS

Indlandsposten (Also titled *Indland-Posten*) (The Inland Post), 1915–17, weekly (November 1916 moved to Fairfield)

HELENA

Montana Folkeblad (Montana People's Newspaper), 1890–91, weekly (Continued as *Montana Statstidende*)

Montana Posten (The Montana Post), October 11, 1890–August 10, 1893, weekly

Montana Statstidende (The Montana State Times), 1891–92, weekly (Continuation of *Montana Folkeblad*)

Rocky Mountain Scandinavian, March 26–December 24, 1920, weekly (In English for Scandinavian Lutherans)

TOTAL: 8 weekly publications

New York

BROOKLYN

Den Norske Amerikaner (Norwegian American), 1906–10, weekly (Continuation of *Nordiske Blade*)

Kolonien. Nordisk Tidendes Lokalavis (The Colony. Nordic Times' Local Newspaper), January 6, 1933–May 18, 1934, weekly

Nordisk Tidende (The Nordic Times), January 3, 1891–December 28, 1983, weekly (Continued as *Norway Times*)

Nordiske Blade (Nordic Newspapers), 1878–1906, semimonthly, weekly (Continued as *Den Norske Amerikaner*)

Norges-Posten (The Norway Post), 1903–4, weekly

Norges-Posten (The Norway Post), May 8, 1924–February 28, 1933, weekly

Norway Times, January 5, 1984–February 4, 2008, weekly (Continuation of *Nordisk Tidende*. Merged with *Norwegian American Weekly* February 2008)

Symra (The Anemone), September 10–December 2, 1926, semimonthly

NEW YORK

Hvepsen (The Wasp), 1914–15, monthly

Klæggen (The Horsefly), 1910–11, monthly

Koloniens Argus (The Colony's Argus [Giant in Greek mythology]), 1895–96, monthly

Krydseren (The Voyager), 1884–85, monthly (Absorbed by *Nordiske Blade*)

Norge (Norway), 1912–13, monthly

Ny Tid (New Age), December 8, 1931–July 16, 1936, weekly (Norwegian edition of the Swedish *Ny Tid*, published in Chicago March 10, 1922–March 29, 1931, and in New York April 4, 1931–July 16, 1936. Continuation of *Facklan* [The Torch], Chicago, and of *Folket* [The People], Rockford, IL)

Nye Norge (The New Norway), 1911–13, weekly

Piraten (The Pirate), 1902–?, monthly (Danish-Norwegian)

Skandinavia (Scandinavia), January 1–fall 1847, semimonthly (Swedish-Danish-Norwegian) (Oldest Norwegian-American newspaper)

Skandinaven (The Scandinavian), 1851–53, weekly (Swedish-Danish-Norwegian)

Skandinavisk Post (Scandinavian Post), 1863–72, weekly (Swedish-Danish-Norwegian)

Taktstokken (The Baton), 1910–14?, monthly

TOTAL: 12 weekly and 8 monthly or semimonthly publications

North Dakota

ABERCROMBIE

Balder-Posten (The Balder Post), 1905, weekly

DEVILS LAKE

Devils Lake Tidende (The Devils Lake Times), 1884–85, weekly

Statstidende (The State Times), 1890, weekly

ENDERLIN

Enderlin Folkeblad (Enderlin People's Newspaper), 1898, weekly (Absorbed by *Fram*, November 1898)

FARGO

Amerikaneren (The American), 1884–85, weekly

Dagen (The Day), 1897–May 1898, began as a daily, soon every other day (Published in Moorhead, MN, for a while. Continued as *Det Frie Ord*, Grafton)

Dakota, 1889–March, 1897, weekly (A successor of *Fargo-Posten og Vesten*. Continued as *Fjerde Juli og Dakota*)

Den Norske Amerikaner (The Norwegian American), 1883–84, weekly

Den nye Heimen (The New Home), 1912, monthly

Eidsvold, June 1912–14, monthly, quarterly

Fargo-Posten (The Fargo Post), January 24, 1885–89, weekly (A successor to *Red River Posten* and *Amerikaneren*. Continued as *Fargo Posten og Vesten*)

Fargo-Posten (The Fargo Post), October 22, 1897–November 13, 1903, weekly

Fargo Posten og Vesten (The Fargo Post and The West), May 22–?, 1889, weekly (Continued as *Dakota*)

Fjerde Juli og Dakota (Fourth of July and Dakota), March 17, 1897–98, weekly

Folkets Ven (Friend of the People), September, 1895–97, weekly (Published in Moorhead, MN, for a time)

Fram (Forward), May 18, 1898–December 27, 1917, weekly, semiweekly (Continuation of *Rodhuggeren*, Fergus Falls, MN, and *Fjerde Juli og Dakota*. *Fram* traced its history to *Red River Posten* and through its successor newspapers to claim to be the first Norwegian-language newspaper in North Dakota)

Norrøna. Det fyrste Blad paa Norskt Maal i Vesterheimen (The Norse. The First Magazine in the Norwegian Language in the Western Home), 1914–15, monthly (Published in Walnut Grove, MN, 1901–2)

Praktisk Farming (Practical Farming), 1907–8, semimonthly

Red River Posten (The Red River Post), 1878–84, weekly (First Norwegian-language newspaper in North Dakota. 1884 absorbed by *Nordvesten* in St. Paul)

Vesten (The West), June 23, 1888–May 15, 1889, weekly (Continued as *Fargo-Posten og Vesten*)

GRAFTON

Det Frie Ord (The Free Word), May 1898–1900, weekly (Continuation of *Dagen*, Fargo. Continued as *Nord Dakota Posten*)

Grafton-Posten (The Grafton Post), February 1905–February 1909, weekly

Nord Dakota Posten (The North Dakota Post), 1889–?, weekly

Nord Dakota Posten (The North Dakota Post) 1900–1902, weekly (Continuation of *Det Frie Ord*)

Norden (The North), 1904–5, weekly

GRAND FORKS

Eidsvold, May 1909–September 1910, monthly

Fjerde Juli (Fourth of July), March, 1896–March 10, 1897, weekly (Continued as *Fjerde Juli og Dakota*, Fargo)

Grand Forks Skandinav (Grand Forks Scandinavian), October 1927–May 30, 1941, weekly

Grand Forks Tidende (The Grand Forks Times), 1880–88, weekly (Continued as *Minneapolis Daglig Tidende*)

Nord Dakota Tidende (The North Dakota Times), August 14, 1919–July 26, 1923, weekly (Sample copies from June 26, 1919. Published in Fargo, May 1922–23)

Nordlyset (Northern Lights), 1888–89, weekly

Nordstjernen (The North Star), 1879–83, weekly (Published in Fargo 1881–83. Absorbed by *Norske Amerikaner*)

Normanden (The Norseman), April 15, 1887–November 1954, weekly, semiweekly (Published in Fargo, 1925–54)

HATTON

Banneret (The Banner), 1892–94, weekly (Continued as *Vesterheimen* in 1894, moved first to Mayville then Crookston)

HILLSBORO

Afholds-Basunen (The Temperance Trumpet), 1887–96, weekly (Continuation of *Folkets Røst*)

Dakota-Bladet (The Dakota Newspaper), 1886–87, weekly

Folkets Avis (The People's Newspaper), 1898–1904, weekly (Intended as a successor to *Afholds-Basunen*. Absorbed by *Statstidende*)

Folkets Røst (The Voice of the People), 1886–87, weekly (Continued as *Afholds-Basunen*)

Fremtiden (The Future), 1901–8, weekly

Statstidende (The State Times), 1897–1909, weekly

KINDRED

Kindred-Blad (Kindred Newspaper), 1880–82, weekly

MAYVILLE

Landmanden (The Farmer), 1894–96, weekly (Published in Fargo, 1895–96)

Vesterheimen (The Western Home), 1894–1919, weekly (Published in Mayville 1894–1900 and in Crookston 1900–1919)

MINOT

Minot-Posten (The Minot Post), December, 1905–9, weekly (Continued as *Nordvesten*)

Mouse River Tidende (The Mouse River Times), 1902–3, weekly

Nordvesten (The Northwest), 1909–December 1910, weekly (Continuation of *Minot-Posten*)

Nordvesten (The Northwest), 1916–30, weekly, from August 1918 semimonthly, from December 1921 monthly (English and Norwegian. After January 1921 a part of the newspaper titled *Northwest Monitor Farm Journal*)

Verkefingeren (The Aching Finger), 1925–26, monthly

PORTLAND

Dakota-Bladet (The Dakota Newspaper), 1886–87, weekly (Continuation of *For Fattig og Rig*, Madison, SD. Published for a time in Hillsboro)

RAY

Dakota Tidende (Dakota Times), 1918–19, weekly

Williams County Skandinav (Williams County Scandinavian), 1906–9, weekly

VALLEY CITY

Den Frie Presse (*Valley City Posten*) (The Free Press), 1895–96, weekly

WAHPETON

A weekly, name unknown, was published in the early 1890s.

TOTAL: 45 weekly and 7 monthly or semimonthly publications

Oklahoma

GUYMON

Oslo Posten (The Oslo Post), May 20, 1910–May 15, 1913, weekly/monthly (Norwegian-English)

TOTAL: 1 weekly and monthly publication

Oregon

PORTLAND

Pacific Skandinaven (Pacific Scandinavian), October 1904–December 12, 1919, weekly (Continued in 1920 as the English-language *The Northman*)

Stillehavs-Posten (Pacific Ocean Post), 1889–91, weekly

Vor Tid (Our Age), April 1891–?, weekly (Successor to *Spokane Falls Ekko*, Spokane, WA)

TOTAL: 3 weekly publications

South Dakota

BROOKINGS

Syd Dakota Ekko (South Dakota Echo), 1889–1906, weekly (Continuation of *Vesterheimen*)

FLANDREAU

Vesterheimen (The Western Home), 1884–89, weekly/semiweekly (Published in Sioux Falls 1885–89. Continued as *Syd Dakota Ekko*)

MADISON

For Fattig og Rig (For Poor and Rich), 1885–86, weekly (Continued as *Dakota-Bladet*, Portland, ND)

PIERRE

Almuevennen (The Friend of the People), 1890, weekly (Listed also as *Almueven*. Published in 12 issues)

SIOUX FALLS

Folketidende (The People's Times), 1879–80, weekly

Fremad (Forward), May 17, 1894–1935, weekly

Sioux Falls-Posten (The Sioux Falls Post), November 1907–16, weekly

SISSETON

Sisseton-Posten (The Sisseton Post), 1902–June 1912, weekly

TOTAL: 7 weekly publications

Utah

SALT LAKE CITY

Bikuben (The Beehive), August 1, 1876–1935, semimonthly, weekly (Danish-Norwegian)

Utah Posten (The Utah Post), December 20, 1873–September 5, 1874, weekly (Danish-Norwegian)

Utah Posten (The Utah Post), January 1–April 8, 1885, weekly (Danish-Norwegian. Absorbed by *Bikuben*)

Utah Skandinav (Utah Scandinavian), October 22, 1874–77, weekly (Anti-Mormon organ)

Varden (The Beacon), January 1910–December 1911, monthly

TOTAL: 4 weekly and 1 monthly publications

Washington

EVERETT

Everett Ekko (Everett Echo), November 16, 1906–9, weekly

Pacific-Posten (The Pacific Post), 1908, weekly

SEATTLE

Folketidende (People's Times), 1895, weekly

Fram (Forward), 1895–97, weekly (Absorbed by *Washington Posten*)

Hammerslag (Hammer Blow), 1911–12, monthly

Normanna (The Norse), 1907–9, weekly

Norsk-Amerikaneren, Illustreret Kvartalmagasin af historisk Art (Norwegian American, Illustrated Historical Quarterly Magazine), 1916–25, quarterly

Norwegian American Weekly, December 22, 2006– , weekly (Continuation of *Western Viking* and *Norway Times*)

Pacific Posten (The Pacific Post), 1891–92, weekly

Papegøien (The Parrot), 1895, weekly

Sambaandet (The Common Bond), 1923–28, weekly

Seattle Tidende (The Seattle Times), 1895–96, weekly

Washington Posten (The Washington Post), May 17, 1889–May 26, 1961, weekly (Continued as *Western Viking*)

Western Viking, June 9, 1961–December 22, 2006, weekly (Continued as *Norwegian-American Weekly*)

SPOKANE

Hjemmets Værn (The Home's Protector), 1891–92, weekly

Spokane Falls Ekko (Spokane Falls Echo), 1890–91, weekly (Continued as *Vor Tid*, Portland, OR)

Spokane Skandinav (Spokane Scandinavian), August 1896–1924, weekly

Spokane Tidende (The Spokane Times), 1893–94, weekly

Vestens Skandinav (The West's Scandinavian), 1892–95, weekly

TACOMA

Braat og Brand (Clearing and Fire), 1907–12, weekly

Norsk Magasin (Norwegian Magazine), 1905–6, monthly

Skirnir ("The Light," figure from the Elder Edda), 1895–97, monthly

Tacoma Budstikke (Tacoma Messenger), December 1889–90, weekly

Tacoma Folkeblad (Tacoma People's Newspaper), 1890, weekly
Tacoma Tidende (The Tacoma Times), July 4, 1890–1925, weekly (Continued as *Vestkysten* [*Tacoma Tidende*])
Vestkysten (The West Coast), 1906–9, weekly
Vestkysten (*Tacoma Tidende*), 1925–December 1931 (The West Coast and Tacoma Times), weekly (Absorbed by *Western Viking*)
Washington Tidende (The Washington Times), 1889–February 1890, weekly (Moved to Seattle February 1890. Merged with *Washington Posten*)
Western Viking, 1929–41, weekly (Adopted volume numbering from the founding of *Tacoma Tidende* in 1890)

TOTAL: 24 weekly, 3 monthly, and 1 quarterly publications

Wisconsin

EAU CLAIRE

Arbeideren (The Laborer), February 9, 1886–88, weekly (Continued as *Reform*)
Eau Claire Tidende (The Eau Claire Times), 1884–85, weekly
Lyngblomsten (The Heather Flower), 1908–15, monthly
Maanedlig ISWA *Journal* (Monthly Independent Scandinavian Workers Association Journal), 1907–14, monthly
Reform, 1889–September 18, 1941, weekly (Continuation of *Arbeideren*)

INMANSVILLE

Emigranten (The Emigrant). January 23, 1852–August 24, 1868, weekly (Published in Madison, 1856–68. Merged with *Fædrelandet* as *Fædrelandet og Emigranten*)

LA CROSSE

Amerika (America), August 1868–December 30, 1872, weekly (Continuation of *Skandinaviske Demokrat*. Continued its numbering. Published in Rochester, MN, December 23, 1868–January 21, 1869, Winona, MN, May 11, 1869–December 30, 1872)
Fædrelandet (The Fatherland), January 14, 1864–August 27, 1868, weekly (Merged with *Emigranten* September 3, 1868, as *Fædrelandet og Emigranten*)
Fædrelandet og Emigranten (The Fatherland and the Emigrant), September 3, 1868–October 7, 1893, weekly (Published in Minneapolis, MN, July 13, 1886–October 1893. Merged with *Minneapolis Tidende* October 7, 1893)
Folkevennen (The People's Friend), 1893–December 1895, weekly (Absorbed by *Norden*, Chicago)

Husvennen (The Friend of the Home), ?–?, monthly

La Crosse-Posten (The La Crosse Post), 1897–98, weekly

La Crosse Tidende (The La Crosse Times), September 1895–September 1897, semiweekly (Merged with *Fram* as *La Crosse Tidende og Milwaukee Fram*)

La Crosse Tidende og Milwaukee Fram (The La Crosse Times and Milwaukee Forward), September–October, 1897, semiweekly

Norsk Maanedskrift (Norwegian Monthly), October 1874–75, monthly

Skandinaviske Demokrat (Scandinavian Democrat), June 18–August 1868, weekly (Continued as *Amerika*, La Crosse)

Udflyttede Norge (The Emigrated Norway), ?, weekly

Varden (The Beacon), 1881–April 1883, weekly

Varden (The Beacon), 1890–July 1894, weekly (Absorbed by *Norden*, Chicago, IL)

Ved Arnen (By the Hearth), 1866–68, monthly (Published in Decorah, IA, 1868–70, 1884–1972 weekly)

MADISON

Billed-Magazin (Picture Magazine), October 3, 1868–September 17, 1870, weekly

De Norskes Ven (The Norwegians' Friend), 1850–51, weekly (Published for about six months)

Den Norske Amerikaner (The Norwegian American), January 1, 1855–May 27, 1857, weekly (Continued as *Nordstjernen*)

Den Norske Immigrant (The Norwegian Immigrant), 1871, weekly

Liberal Demokrat (Liberal Democrat), 1874–75?, weekly

Madison Tidende (Madison Times), 1894–97, weekly

Nordstjernen (The North Star), June 10, 1857–October 10, 1860, weekly (Absorbed by *Emigranten*)

Nordvesten (The Northwest), 1875–77, weekly

Organ (Organ), 1856–61, monthly

Skandinavisk Billed-Magazin (Scandinavian Picture Magazine), 1868–70, monthly

Skandinavisk Tribune (Scandinavian Tribune), 1887–July, 1888, weekly (Absorbed by *Skandinaven*)

Vikingen (The Viking), 1888–89, weekly

Wisconsin Banner (Wisconsin Banner), September–November 1875, weekly

Wisconsin Nordmanden (The Wisconsin Norseman), 1895–96, weekly (Absorbed by *Amerika*, Chicago, IL)

MARINETTE

Marienette Fremad (Forward), 1890–1904, weekly (Danish-Norwegian)

Nordmannen (The Norseman), 1887–89?, weekly

MILWAUKEE

Folkebladet (The People's Newspaper), 1878–83, weekly

Fram (Forward), 1894–97, weekly

Fremad (Forward), April 1868–October 1871, weekly (Danish-Norwegian) (Published in Chicago, IL, 1869–71)

MOUNT HOREB

Dagen (The Day), 1891–92?, weekly

MUSKEGO

Democraten (The Democrat), spring–fall 1848, weekly

Nordlyset (Northern Lights), July 29, 1847–May 18, 1850, weekly (Its address was Norway Post Office. Published in Racine, 1850. Oldest Norwegian-American newspaper in the Midwest. Continued as *Democraten*)

NORTHLAND

Busletts (Buslett's), 1922–23, monthly

RACINE

Democraten (The Democrat), June 8, 1850–October 29, 1851, weekly (Published in Janesville June–October 1851. Continuation of *Nordlyset*)

RHINELANDER

Rhinelander Tidende (The Rhinelander Times), 1896–98, weekly

SHEBOYGAN

Fra Land og Hav (From Land and Sea), 1873, monthly (Only nine issues published)

STOUGHTON

Aaret Rundt (The Year Around), 1885–86, quarterly

Alvor og Skjæmt (Gravity and Jest), 1905–6, weekly

Gauken (The Joker), 1887–90, weekly (Continued as *Normannen*)

Norge (Norway), 1904–5, weekly

Normannen (The Norseman), 1890–94, weekly (Continued as *Wisconsin Normannen*)

Wisconsin Normannen (The Wisconsin Norseman), 1894–95, weekly (Continued as *Wisconsin Nordmanden,* Madison)

SUPERIOR

Superior-Posten (The Superior Post), January 1888–93, weekly (Continued as *Superior Tidende*)

Superior Tidende (The Superior Times), 1893–November 16, 1962, weekly (Continued volume numbering from *Superior-Posten*. Absorbed by *Duluth Skandinav*, Duluth, MN)

WHITEHALL

Nordstjernen (The North Star), 1879, weekly

TOTAL: 49 weekly or semiweekly, 10 monthly or semimonthly, and 1 quarterly publications

Wyoming

LARAMIE

Patronen (The Patron), 1888–90, weekly

Vor Talsmand (Our Spokesman), 1888–89, weekly

TOTAL: 2 weekly publications

Total Secular Periodicals

277	weekly and semiweekly newspaper titles
6	daily newspaper titles
283	weekly, semiweekly, and daily newspaper titles coast to coast, 1847–2010
89	monthly and semimonthly publications/magazines/newspapers
4	quarterly publications

Organizational Periodicals

Organizational periodicals of many kinds are not included in the count of secular publications. The *bygdelag* publications are left out as well. These were annual, quarterly, and occasionally monthly publications.

Religious Periodicals

Religious publications of many kinds numbered about 190. The figure does not include congregational newsletters and other published material distributed by individual congregations.

APPENDIX 2

Time of Founding

Founding by decades of 283 weekly, semiweekly, and daily secular periodicals listed by titles to conform to the listing in Appendix 1.

1847–50:	2
1851–60:	9
1861–70:	18
1871–80:	39
1881–90	82
1891–1900:	70
1901–10:	35
1911–20:	12
1921–30:	6
1931–40:	4
1941–50:	1
1951–60:	2
1961–70:	1
1971–80:	0
1981–90:	1
1991–2000:	0
2001–10:	1

APPENDIX 3

Length of Publication

Length of publication of 282* weekly, semiweekly, and daily secular periodicals listed by titles.

Less than 3 years:	181
4–9 years	49
10–20 years	20
21–30 years	10
31–40 years	3
41–50 years	5
51–60 years	5
61–70 years	4
71–80 years	3
81–90 years	0
91–100 years	2

**Norwegian American Weekly* not included in count.

For consistency, the length of publication is by title and does not consider shifting mastheads or consolidations. Appendix 1 traces the continuation of all the listed newspapers under new mastheads or consolidated with other periodicals.

The following examples should be noted:

Washington Posten/Western Viking/Norwegian American Weekly, Seattle, Washington, when successive changes in masthead are taken into account, in 2009 reached its 120 anniversary and is currently published as the single Norwegian American secular newspaper.

Nordisk Tidende/Norway Times, Brooklyn, New York, had a combined 117 years of publication when it merged with *Norwegian American Weekly* in 2008.

Minneapolis Tidende, Minneapolis, Minnesota, founded 1888, through consolidations extended its volume numbering back to the founding of *Emigranten*, Inmansville, Wisconsin, in 1852.

Fram, Fargo, North Dakota, founded in 1898, traced its history to *Red River Posten*, founded in 1878, and held itself to be the first Norwegian-language newspaper in the state.

The Socialist *Gaa Paa*, founded in 1903, published in Minneapolis from 1904, in 1918 changed its masthead to *Folkets Røst* so that it could continue publication.

Notes

Notes to Chapter 1

1. *Skandinaven,* Jan. 4, 1888; Bernard A. Weisburger, *The American Newspaperman* (Chicago: The University of Chicago Press, 1961), 3, 204: Knud Langeland, *Nordmœndene i Amerika. Nogle Optegnelser om de Norskes Udvandring til Amerika* (Chicago: John Anderson & Co., 1889), 94.

2. Robert E. Park, *The Immigrant Press and Its Control* (New York: Harper & Brothers Publishers, 1922), 3, 7; Carl Wittke, *The German-language Press in America* (Lexington: University of Kentucky Press, 1957), 1, 14–15, 36–37, 75.

3. Park, *The Immigrant Press,* 5; Benedict Anderson, *Imagined Communities: Reflections on the Origin and Spread of Nationalism,* rev. ed. (London: Verso, 1991), see ch. 2 and 3; *Skandinaven,* June 1, 1866.

4. Park, *The Immigrant Press,* 442–47; Marion Tuttle Marzolf, *The Danish-Language Press in America* (New York: Arno Press, 1979), 3–19; Odd S. Lovoll, "*Washington Posten:* A Window on a Norwegian-American Community," *Norwegian-American Studies* 31 (1986): 174; Theodore C. Blegen, *Norwegian Migration to America: The American Transition* (Northfield, MN: Norwegian American Historical Association [hereafter, NAHA], 1940), 285.

5. Odd S. Lovoll, *The Promise of America: A History of the Norwegian-American People,* rev. ed. (Minneapolis: University of Minnesota Press, 1999), 10–13, 44–58; E. Clifford Nelson and Eugene L. Fevold, *The Lutheran Church Among Norwegian-Americans: A History of the Evangelical Lutheran Church* (Minneapolis, MN: Augsburg Publishing House, 1960), I:13–23; Carlton C. Qualey, *Norwegian Settlement in the United States* (Northfield, MN; NAHA, 1938), 40, 52–55, 69, 218, 221, 222; C. A. Clausen, trans. and intro., *A Chronicler of Immigrant Life: Svein Nilsson's Articles in* Billed-Magazin, *1868–1870* (Northfield, MN: NAHA, 1982), 9, 54, 113. Christiana is a misspelling of the name of Norway's capital Christiania, now Oslo.

6. Langeland, *Nordmœndene i Amerika,* 94; *Nordlyset,* July 29, 1847; Lovoll, *The Promise of America, 55–58,* 102–3; Gunnar T. Malmin, trans. and ed., *America in the Forties: The Letters of Ole Munch Ræder* (Northfield, MN: NAHA, 1929), 179; Clarence A. Clausen and Andreas Elviken, trans. and ed., *A Chronicle of Old Muskego: The Diary of Søren Bache, 1839–1847* (Northfield, MN: NAHA, 1951). The diary is preserved in the archives of NAHA at St. Olaf College.

7. Juul Dieserud, "'Skandinavia' ikke 'Nordlyset,' var det første norsk-danske blad i Amerika," *Nordmands-Forbundet* 22 (Jan. 1929): 14–17, quote 15. Dieserud, a librarian in the Library of Congress, was encouraged by Gunnar J. Malmin, professor at Drake University, Des Moines, Iowa, to investigate the newspaper's existence. Malmin had discovered references to *Skandinavia* when doing research in the University of Oslo Library in 1923–24. He relates his discovery in his historical introduction to *America in the Forties,* xx-xxi; Marzolf, *The Danish Language Press,* 29–30; Blegen, *Norwegian Migration to America,* 287–89.

8. Blegen, *Norwegian Migration to America,* 289–90; Clausen and Elviken, *A Chronicle of Old Muskego,* 211–21, quote 217; Odd S. Lovoll, *A Century of Urban Life: The Norwegians in Chicago before 1930* (Northfield, MN: NAHA, 1988), 11–12.

9. *Nordlyset,* May 11, 1848, Feb. 1, 1849, May 18, 1850; Langeland, *Nordmœndene i Amerika,* 96–97, 99–107; *Democraten,* June 8, 1850, Oct. 29, 1851; Arlow W. Andersen, "The Norwegian American Press," in Sally M. Miller, ed., *The Ethnic Press in the United States: A Historical Analysis and Handbook* (New York: Greenwood Press, 1987), 262; Merle Curti, *The Making of an American Community: A Case Study of Democracy in a Frontier Community* (Stanford, CA: Stanford University Press, 1959), 390, 398; Hjalmar Rued Holand, *De Norske Settlementers Historie,* 3rd rev. ed. (Ephraim, WI: Trykt paa Forfatterens Forlag, 1909), 121–22; Wilhelm Keilhau, *Det Norske Folks Liv og Historie gjennem Tidene,* vol. 9 (Oslo: H. Aschehoug & Co., 1931), 259–67; Arne Bergsgård, *Norsk historie 1814–1880* (Oslo: Det norske samlaget, 1964), 212–13. For a more recent study of literacy in Norway, see Jostein Fet, *Lesande bønder. Litterœr kultur i norske allmugesamfunn før 1840* (Oslo: Universitetsforlaget, 1995), esp. 274–94, which treat the history of the first rural newspaper in Norway, *Norsk Landboeblad* (Norwegian Newspaper for Country Dwellers), 1810–16. Only six newspapers existed in Norway in 1810.

10. *Nordlyset,* July 29, 1847, Feb. 3, 24, Nov. 16, 1848, June 7, 28, 1849; *Democraten,* July 13, Oct. 12, 1850. *Democraten* subscribed to *Morgenbladet* and informed its readers (July 13, 1850) that it had paid for the order and "waited daily to hear from Norway." See John Steele Gordon, *A Thread Across the Ocean: The Heroic Story of the Transatlantic Cable* (New York: Walker & Company, 2002).

11. *Nordlyset,* Nov. 4, 26, 1847, May 17, June 7, Oct. 11, 1849; Holand, *Norske Settlementers,* 187; Terje Mikael Hasle Joranger, "The Migration of Tradition. A Study on the Transfer of Traditions Tied to Intergenerational Land Transfers among Emigrants from the Valdres Region, Norway, to the Upper Midwest and their Descendants for Three Generations, 1850–1980" (Dr. Art. diss., Department of Archaeology, Conservation, and History, University of Oslo, 2008), 188; Malmin, *America in the Forties,* 177–78.

12. *Nordlyset,* July 29, 1847, Feb. 24, Sept. 7, Nov. 3, 1848; Roy F. Nichols and Eugene H. Berwanger, *The Stakes of Power, 1845–1877,* rev. ed. (New York: Hill and Wang, 1982), 24, 43, 61; Malmin, *America in the Forties,* 18n. Blegen, *Norwegian Migration to America,* 294,

lists the only surviving number of *Democraten* as dated Apr. 27, 1848.

13. Arlow W. Andersen, "Knud Langeland: Pioneer Editor," *Norwegian-American Studies and Records* 14 (1944): 122–38; Langeland, *Nordmœndene i Amerika,* 96–97, 119–24; Johs. B. Wist, ed., *Norsk-Amerikanernes Festskrift 1914* (Decorah, IA: The Symra Company, 1914), 17–18; Knud Langeland obituary, *Skandinaven,* Feb. 14, 1888; *Democraten,* Mar. 9, Aug. 10, Nov. 9, 1850.

14. Andersen, "Knud Langeland," 123; *Democraten,* Nov. 9, 1850; "Den Skandinaviske Presse i Amerika," in *Emigranten,* May 20, 1853; *Amerika,* Jan. 4, 1899; see Sigrid Schneider, "The German-American Press Today: Patterns of Communication in an Ethnic Group," in Henry Geitz, ed., *The German-American Press* (Madison, WI: Max Kade Institute, 1992), 257–70.

15. Blegen, *Norwegian Migration to America,* 304–5; Olaf Morgan Norlie, *History of the Norwegian People in America* (Minneapolis, MN: Augsburg Publishing House, 1925), 226; Oliver A. Linder, "Newspapers," in Adolph B. Benson and Naboth Hedin, eds., *Swedes in America, 1638–1938* (New Haven, CT: Yale University Press, 1938), 181–90, quote 185–86; *Friheds-Banneret,* Oct. 4, 1852; *Emigranten,* May 20, 1853; Wist, *Norsk-Amerikanernes Festskrift,* 23. Only a single copy of *Skandinaven,* June 19, 1852, appears to have survived.

16. *Friheds-Banneret,* Oct. 4. Nov. 27, Dec. 4, 1852, Jan. 8, Apr. 9, 23, May 7, 1853; Nichols and Berwanger, *The Stakes of Power,* 43.

17. Clausen and Elviken, *A Chronicle of Old Muskego,* 120–21, 149–52; J. Magnus Rohne, *Norwegian American Lutheranism up to 1872* (New York: The Macmillan Company, 1926), 57–61, 64–67; *Nordlyset,* Mar. 15, 1849.

18. Nelson and Fevold, *The Lutheran Church Among Norwegian-Americans,* I:41, 61, 70, 71–81, 95, 117–19, 123, 126–27, 151–53, 154, quote 80; Blegen, *Norwegian Migration to America,* 302–3, quote 303; Langeland, *Nordmœndene i Amerika,* 98. In *Nordlyset,* Jan. 27, 1848, C. L. Clausen announced the intent to start a Lutheran monthly. Under changing names and mergers, *Maanedstidende* (*Kirkelig Maanedstidende, Evangelisk Luthersk Kirketidende, Lutheraneren*) continued until 1956. Information on Norwegian Lutheran pastors in Rasmus Malmin, O. M. Norlie, and O. A. Tingelstad, *Who's Who Among Pastors in all the Norwegian Lutheran Synods in America, 1843–1927* (Minneapolis, MN: Augsburg Publishing House, 1928).

19. *Friheds-Banneret,* Nov. 27, 1852; *Minneapolis Tidende,* Nov. 17, 1927; *Emigranten,* Apr. 16, Dec. 26, 1852; *Den Norske Amerikaner,* Jan. 1, 1855, Dec. 27, 1856; Wist, *Norsk-Amerikanernes Festskrift,* 25–28; Blegen, *Norwegian Migration to America,* 304, 339–41; Rohne, *Norwegian American Lutheranism,*152.

20. *Emigranten,* Aug. 24, 1855, Oct. 3, Nov. 7, 21, 1856; *Den Norske Amerikaner,* Sept. 29, 1855, Aug. 16, Nov. 1, 15, Dec. 27, 1856, Mar. 14, Apr. 4, 18, May 27, 1857. In its Jan. 8, 1857, number *Emigranten* stated editorially: "Our opponents have used as criticism against us that we in 1854 left the 'democratic' party and later have worked in union with the Republicans."

21. *Nordstjernen,* June 10, July 22, Aug. 12, Oct. 7, Dec. 19, 1857, Mar. 20, May 27, Sept. 7, Nov. 9, 1858, Nov. 22, 1859, Jan. 28, Oct. 10, 1860; circular distributed by *Emigranten* dated Jan.

1861; Theodore C. Blegen, "The Early Norwegian Press in America," *Minnesota History Bulletin* 3 (1920): 514; Carl N. Degler, *Out of Our Past: The Forces that Shaped Modern America,* rev. ed. (New York: Harper and Row, 1970), 202–5; Wist, *Norsk-Amerikanernes Festskrift,* 28.

22. Qualey, *Norwegian Settlement,* 97, 103; Blegen, *Norwegian Migration to America,* 321–22; Theodore C. Blegen, *Minnesota: A History of the State,* second ed. (Minneapolis, MN: University of Minnesota Press, 1997), 217; *Emigranten,* Nov. 27, 1857; *Folkets Røst,* July 10, Nov. 20, 1858. (Blegen incorrectly dates the first issue of *Folkets Røst* July 24, 1858.)

23. Circular distributed by *Emigranten* dated Jan. 1861; *Emigranten,* Jan. 23, 30, 1852; *Democraten,* June 18, Oct. 29, 1851; Albert O. Barton, "The Beginnings of the Norwegian Press in America," *State Historical Society of Wisconsin. Separate No. 174. From the Proceedings of the Society for 1916* (1916): 200, 201, 205, 210–11; Blegen, *Norwegian Migration to America,* 305–12; Langeland, *Nordmœndene i Amerika,* 109–10.

24. *Emigranten,* Jan. 23, Feb. 20, July 30, 1852, May 27, June 10, 17, July 1, 1853, Jan. 6, 13, 27, 1854, Jan. 8, Apr. 3, 20, 25, 1857, Feb. 22, Mar. 17, 22, 27, May 19, 1858, Apr. 18, 1859; Harold M. Tolo "The Political Position of *Emigranten* in the Election of 1852: A Documentary Article," *Norwegian-American Studies and Records* 8 (1934): 92–111; Wist, *Norsk-Amerikanernes Festskrift,* 21–22, 27; "Til Skandinaverne i de Forenede Stater!," appeal from the Scandinavian Press Association, dated July 26, 1854, signed by G. F. Dietrichson, J. Ingebrethsen, and K. J. Fleischer; Barton, "Beginnings of the Norwegian Press," 201–2. Barton lists an incorrect date for the cyclone.

25. Carl Fredrik Solberg, "Reminiscences of a Pioneer Editor," Albert O. Barton, ed., *Norwegian-American Studies and Records* 1 (1926): 134–44, quotes 136, 140; *Emigranten,* Nov. 21, 1856, Apr. 3, 20, 25, 1857, Mar. 3, May 26, June 30, July 7, 1858, Jan. 7, 12, Feb. 8, Apr. 18, 1859, Jan. 21, 1861; *Minneapolis Tidende,* Nov. 10, 1927; Ottar Dahl, *Norsk historieforskning i 19. og 20. århundre* (Oslo: Universitetsforlaget, 1970), 37; Carl G. O. Hansen, *My Minneapolis: A Chronicle of What Has Been Learned and Observed About the Norwegians in Minneapolis Through One Hundred Years* (Minneapolis: privately printed, 1956), 159–65, quote 164.

26. *Folkebladet,* Sep. 22–29, 1860; *Emigranten,* Mar. 27, 1858, first installment published the Norwegian poet Henrik Wergeland's memoirs "Hasslenødder" (Hazelnuts); Marcus L. Hansen, "Immigration and Puritanism," *Norwegian-American Studies and Records* 9 (1936): 18–19, 20; Solberg, "Reminiscences of a Pioneer Editor," 142; Lovoll, *A Century of Urban Life,* 53–54; *Emigranten,* July 22, 1957, Jan. 20, 27, 1858, Sept. 12, Oct. 3, 24, Nov. 14, 21, 1859; Jan. 2, 9, 23, May 21, June 11, Sept. 3, Nov. 5, 12, Dec. 3, 1860.

Notes to Chapter 2

1. Proclamation to "Our Countrymen," *Emigranten,* Sept. 30, 1861.

2. Blegen, *Norwegian Migration to America,* ch. titled "The Era of the Civil War," 383–417, quote 389; *Emigranten,* Dec. 26, 1860, Jan. 7, 14, Feb. 4, 18, 25, Mar. 11, Apr. 14, 22, Sept. 30, 1861.

3. *Emigranten* Apr. 22, 29, May 13, Sept. 16, 30, Oct. 7, 14, Nov. 11, 18, 1861, Mar. 14, 21, 1862; T. J. Widvey obituary, *Minneapolis Tidende,* Oct. 1, 1914; Solberg, "Reminiscences of a Pioneer Editor," 142; Blegen, *Norwegian Migration to America,* 390–92; see William L. Burton, *Melting Pot Soldiers: The Union's Ethnic Regiments* (Ames: Iowa State University Press, 1988), 166–69, treating the Fifteenth Wisconsin Regiment.

4. *Emigranten,* Jan. 13, June 23, Sept. 8, 1862, June 8, Sept. 14, 28, Oct. 5, 12, 19, 1863; Waldemar Ager, *Colonel Heg and His Boys: A Norwegian Regiment in the American Civil War,* tr. by Della Kittleson Catuna and Clarence A. Clausen, intro. by Harry T. Cleven (Northfield, MN: NAHA, 2000), 6, 54–62, quotes 164, 179–83.

5. *Emigranten,* Aug. 12, Oct. 7, 1861; Wist, *Norsk-Amerikanernes Festskrift,* 145; Ager, *Colonel Heg and His Boys,* 180. *Emigranten* printed the names of Norwegians in the regiment at the Battle of Bull Run.

6. *Emigranten,* Feb. 3, May 19, 26, July 28, 1862; Jerry Rosholt, *Ole Goes to War: Men from Norway Who Fought in America's Civil War* (Decorah, IA: Vesterheim Norwegian-American Museum, 2003), 20; Ager, *Colonel Heg and His Boys,* 66; *Fædrelandet,* Aug. 11, 1864.

7. *Emigranten,* Apr. 14. May 19, 1862, Mar. 14, 1864, Apr. 10, 17, 30, May 8, 1865; Solberg, "Reminiscences of a Pioneer Editor," 143; Rosholt, *Ole Goes to War,* 41.

8. Blegen, *Norwegian Migration to America,* quote 402; 309n26 cautions against making *Emigranten* a "pastors' organ." Wist, *Norsk-Amerikanernes Festskrift,* 41–43; *Fædrelandet og Emigranten,* Nov. 20, 1878, carried several obituaries of Frederick Fleischer; *Fædrelandet,* Jan. 14, 1864. Johan Schrøder in 1867 published *Skandinaverne i de Forenede Stater og Canada* (The Scandinavians in the United States and Canada) in La Crosse. The Canadian chapters are published in English translation in Orm Øverland, ed., tr., intro., *Johan Schrøder's Travels in Canada, 1863* (Montreal: McGill-Queens University Press, 1989).

9. Blegen, *Norwegian Migration to America,* ch. 14, 418–53, deals with the slavery controversy, quotes 163, 427; see also Arlow W. Andersen, *The Immigrant Takes His Stand: The Norwegian-American Press and Public Affairs, 1847–1872* (Northfield, MN: NAHA, 1953), 58–76, quote 71; *Emigranten,* May 6, June 3, 17, 24, July 8, 15, 1861; Nelson and Fevold, *The Lutheran Church Among Norwegian-Americans,* 169, 173–74, 175; Rohne, *Norwegian American Lutheranism,* 206, has the pastors' statement in translation. The declaration was reprinted from *Kirkelig Maanedstidende* in *Emigranten,* Feb. 17, 1862.

10. *Emigranten,* Oct. 7, 1861, carried Knud Langeland's front-page article on slavery; *Emigranten,* Dec. 2, 1861, July 8, 1868; *Fædrelandet,* Feb. 14, 1867; *Fædrelandet og Emiganten* carried exchanges between A. C. Preus and C. L. Clausen in issues dated Feb. 11, 18, Mar. 18, Apr. 15, 1869; Blegen, *Norwegian Migration to America,* 435–37, quotes 437, 447; Andersen, *The Immigrant Takes His Stand,* 72–76, quote 75; see also Laur. Larsen, *Historisk Fremstilling af den Strid, som i Aarene 1861 til 1868 indenfor den norske Synode i Amerika har været ført i Anledning af Skriftens Lære om Slaveri* (Madison, WI: Norwegian

Synod, 1868), and C. L. Clausen, *Gjenmæle mod Kirkeraadet for Den Norske Synode i Anledning af dets Skrift kaldet "Historisk Fremstilling af den Strid, som i Aarene 1861 til 1868 indenfor den norske Synode i Amerika har været ført i Anledning af Skriftens Lære om Slaveri"* (Chicago: "Skandinavens" Trykkeri, 1869); Joseph M. Shaw, *Bernt Julius Muus: Founder of St. Olaf College* (Northfield, MN: NAHA, 1999), 198–99.

11. Qualey, *Norwegian Settlement*, 217–51; Julie E. Backer, *Ekteskap, fødsler og vandringer i Norge 1856–1960* (Oslo: Statistisk Sentralbyrå, 1965), 158; Solberg, "Reminiscences of a Pioneer Editor," 144; *Emigranten*, Jan. 6, 1868; *Fædrelandet og Emigranten*, Sept. 3, Oct. 1, 1868.

12. *Emigranten*, Feb. 18, 1861, Sept. 8, 1862, Aug. 10, 22, 1863; *Fædrelandet*, Jan. 14, June 16, Aug. 4, Oct. 6, 1864, July 27, 1865; *Fædrelandet og Emigranten*, Oct. 12, 1871.

13. *Emigranten*, Apr. 8, 1867; *Fædrelandet*, Aug. 6, 20, 1868; *Fædrelandet og Emigranten*, Sept. 17, 1868, Jan. 28, 1869, Feb. 24, May 20, Oct. 20, 1870, Jan. 4, 1872; Odd S. Lovoll, "'For People Who Are Not in a Hurry': The Danish Thingvalla Line and the Transportation of Scandinavian Emigrants," *Journal of American Ethnic History* 13.1 (Fall 1993): 48–67.

14. For an excellent discussion of the role of ethnic newspapers, see Matthew Lindaman, "*Heimat* in the Heartland: The Significance of an Ethnic Newspaper," *Journal of American Ethnic History* 23.3 (Spring 2004): 78–98; Odd S. Lovoll, "The Changing Role of May 17 as a Norwegian-American 'Key Symbol,'" in Brit Marie Hovland and Olaf Aagedal, eds., *Nasjonaldagsfeiring i fleirkulturelle demokrati* (Copenhagen, Denmark: Nordisk Ministerråd, 2001), 65–78; *Emigranten*, June 26, 1865.

15. *Emigranten*, June 15, 1868; *Skandinaven*, May 14, 21, June 28, 1866; *Fædrelandet*, Apr. 19, 1866, May 21, 1868; John R. Jenswold, "The Rise and Fall of Pan-Scandinavianism in Urban America," in Odd S. Lovoll, ed., *Scandinavians and Other Immigrants in Urban America: The Proceedings of a Research Conference Oct. 26–27, 1984* (Northfield, MN: St. Olaf College Press, 1985), 159–70.

16. *Emigranten*, June 22, 1868; Hildegunn Bjørgen and Brit Marie Hovland, "I takt med nasjonen—Den nasjonale 17. Mai-paraden gjennom historia," in Hovland and Aagedal, *Nasjonaldagsfeiring i fleirkulturelle demokrati*, 29–31. The Swedish king Carl 13 (Carl 2 in Norway in 1814) had no children; Jean Baptiste Bernadotte was chosen crown prince in 1810, becoming Carl 14 Johan in 1818 (Carl 3 Johan of Norway). See Rolf Danielsen et al., *Norway: A History from the Vikings to Our Own Times*, Michael Drake, tr. (Oslo: Scandinavian University Press [Universitetsforlaget], 1995), 30–32, 206–14.

17. *Emigranten*, Apr. 11, July 18, 25, 1864, Aug. 7, Oct. 30, 1865, Oct. 1, Dec. 17, 1866, Mar. 11, 1867, Oct. 16, 1868; *Fædrelandet*, Jan. 10, Mar. 21, 1867; *Fædrelandet og Emigranten*, Sept. 10, 1868; Anne Helene Høyland Mork, *Unionen i historieundervisningen. Synet på den svenske og norske union (1814–1905) i svenske og norske lærebøker for folkeskolen i perioden 1860–1920* (Oslo: Prosjekt 1905—skriftserie nr. 5, 2005), 56–58, 105.

18. Lovoll, *A Century of Urban Life*, 77–83, 96, 100–4, 195; Wist, *Norsk-Amerikanernes Festskrift*, 61, 81; *Emi-*

granten, April 6, 29, June 8, 1860; *Nordisk Folkeblad,* April 21, 1869.

19. Lovoll, *A Century of Urban Life,* 11–12, 131–32; Wist, *Norsk-Amerikanernes Festskrift,* 47–48, 81–82; Marzolf, *The Danish-language Press,* 35–36; A. E. Strand, comp. and ed., *A History of the Norwegians in Illinois* (Chicago: John Anderson Publishing Co., 1905), 87.

20. *Skandinaven,* June 1, 1866; Lovoll, *A Century of Urban Life,* 20–21, 49–50, 101–2; Langeland, *Nordmændene i Amerika,* 220–21; Wist, *Norsk-Amerikanernes Festskrift,* 45; Blegen, *Norwegian Migration to America,* 328–29. *Wossingen* removed to Voss, Norway, in 1871.

21. Lovoll, *A Century of Urban Life,* 57, 63–65, 102–4; *Emigranten,* July 16, 1866; *Fædrelandet,* Feb. 22, Mar. 14, Aug. 29, 1866; *Fædrelandet og Emigranten,* Jan. 5, 1871; *Skandinaven,* June 28, July 26, Aug. 2, 9, 1866, Apr. 18, May 23, 1867, Dec. 29, 1869, Feb. 10, Oct. 5, Dec. 28, 1870. *Skandinaven*'s Jan. 3, 1872, issue reported that the church conflict was more peaceful. The Archives Collection in the Preus Library at Luther College, Decorah, Iowa, has extensive files on the controversy, illustrating the exclusion of members and the resignations of others during Pastor Petersen's ministry.

22. Lovoll, *A Century of Urban Life,* 102–3; Langeland, *Nordmændene i Amerika,* quotes 221–22; Blegen, *Norwegian Migration to America,* ch. titled "The Common School," 241–76, is a standard treatment of the controversy. See also Lovoll, *The Promise of America,* 98–102, and Arthur C. Paulson and Kenneth O. Bjørk, tr. and ed., "A School Controversy in 1858: A Documentary Study," *Norwegian-American Studies and Records* 10 (1938): 76–106; Wist, *Norsk-Amerikanernes Festskrift,* 50. For samples of the newspaper polemics, see *Skandinaven,* Sept. 6, 27, 1866.

23. Lovoll, *A Century of Urban Life,* 105–8, quote 107; *Skandinaven,* Oct. 14, 19, 1871; *Skandinaven* (triweekly), Oct. 18, 1871.

24. *Amerika,* Aug. 13, Oct. 4, 7, 23, Dec. 14, 30, 1872; Wist, *Norsk-Amerikanernes Festskrift,* 17, 46; Agnes M. Larson, *John A. Johnson: An Uncommon American* (Northfield, MN: NAHA, 1969), 5, 12–15, 73–87, 89; Jean Skogerboe Hansen, "History of the John Anderson Publishing Company of Chicago, Illinois" (master's thesis, University of Chicago, 1972), 21–24, 25–26, 27–28.

25. Wist, *Norsk-Amerikanernes Festskrift,* 51–52, quote 52; "Introduction" in Clausen, *A Chronicler of Immigrant Life,* 1–8; D. G. Ristad, "Svein Nilsson, Pioneer Norwegian-American Historian," *Norwegian-American Studies and Records* 9 (1936): 29–37; Skogerboe Hansen, "History of the John Anderson Publishing Company," 38; *N. W. Ayer & Son's American Newspaper Annual* (Philadelphia: N. W. Ayer & Son, 1880), 173; Lovoll, *A Century of Urban Life,* quote 104.

26. Lovoll, *A Century of Urban Life,* 101; Ulf A. Beijbom, "The Swedish Press," in Sally M. Miller, ed., *The Ethnic Press in the United States: A Historical Analysis and Handbook* (New York: Greenwood Press, 1987), 369–92.

27. Terje I. Leiren, *Marcus Thrane: A Norwegian Radical in America* (Northfield, MN: NAHA, 1987), 3, 6–16, 21–22, 29–30; Oddvar Bjørklund, *Marcus Thrane. En stridsmann for menneskerett og fri tanke* (Oslo: Tiden Norsk Forlag, 1951), 332–33; Lovoll, *The Promise of*

America, 195–96; Danielsen, *Norway,* 256–57; *Emigranten,* Aug. 20, 1866; Supplement to *Fædrelandet,* June 28, 1866; *Fædrelandet,* Sept. 5, Oct. 4, 1866; *Skandinaven,* Sept. 13, 1866.

28. *Skandinaven,* May 5, 1869; *Dagslyset,* Nov. 1869, June 1875; Lovoll, *A Century of Urban Life,* 168–69, 333n44; Leiren, *Marcus Thrane,* 79, 88, 89–92, 103–4, 114–17; Wist, *Norsk-Amerikanernes Festskrift,* 93.

29. Lovoll, *A Century of Urban Life,* 103, 137, 169–72; Leiren, *Marcus Thrane,* 119–21; Marzolf, *The Danish-Language Press,* quotes 42, 43–44; Wist, *Norsk-Amerikanernes Festskrift,* 93, incorrectly states that Marcus Thrane edited *Den Nye Tid.*

30. Arlow W. Andersen, *Rough Road to Glory: The Norwegian-America Press Speaks Out on Public Affairs, 1875 to 1925* (Philadelphia: The Balch Institute Press, 1990), ch. titled "Women's Rights: The Struggle for Equal Suffrage," 90–101; Andersen, *The Immigrant Takes His Stand,* 122–24, quotes 123; C. A. Clausen, ed. and intro., *The Lady with the Pen: Elise Wærenskjold in Texas* (Northfield, MN: NAHA, 1961), 3–24, quote 6; *Fremad,* Nov. 16, 1868; *Fædrelandet og Emigranten,* June 3, 1869, May 19, 1870; *Billed-Magazin,* Feb. 19, 1869; *Norden,* Jan. 8, 1879.

31. Karen Larsen, *Laur. Larsen: Pioneer College President* (Northfield, MN: NAHA, 1936), 127; Beijbom, "The Swedish Press," 386, 388; Andersen, "The Norwegian American Press," 261–62; Park, *The Immigrant Press,* 135; Dirk Hoerder, ed., *The Immigrant Labor Press in North America, 1840s–1970s: An Annotated Bibliography,* vol. 1 (Westport, CT: Greenwood Press, 1987), 23; Marzolf, *The Danish-Language Press,* 9.

Notes to Chapter 3

1. Johan Schrøder in *Amerika,* Dec. 23, 1868, after moving publication from La Crosse, Wisconsin, to Rochester, Minnesota.

2. Lovoll, *The Promise of America,* 31–36; Odd S. Lovoll, "Norwegians on the Land: Address for the Society for the Study of Local and Regional History" (Department of History, Southwest State University, Marshall, MN, 1992), 1–16; *Morgenbladet,* Dec. 14, 1879; Olaf Morgan Norlie, "Norwegian-Americana Papers, 1847–1946" (Northfield, MN: mimeographed, 1946), 30, 33. Norlie lists 570 titles, including church and organizational publications. Citing Norlie's statistics, though these are not limited to secular news organs, gives an indication of publishing activity in general. In the decade 1877–86, about 100 new titles appeared; in 1887–96 about 142; in 1897–1906 about 104. See list of secular newspapers in the appendix.

3. *Morgenbladet,* Sept. 27, 1880; Lovoll, *A Century of Urban Life,* 151–52; Lovoll, *The Promise of America,* 126–28, 231–32; Backer, *Ekteskap, fødsler og vandringer i Norge,* 163–73, 174; see Odd S. Lovoll, *Norwegians on the Prairie: Ethnicity and the Development of the Country Town* (St. Paul: Minnesota Historical Society Press, 2006), 3–12, 127–29; U.S. Bureau of the Census, *Twelfth Census of the United States, 1900.*

4. *Nordisk Folkeblad,* Mar. 12, 1868; *Amerika* (La Crosse), Sept. 10, 17, Oct. 8, 22, 29, Dec. 23, 1868, Jan. 21, May 11, July 22, Sept. 28, 1869; John A. Fagereng, "Norwegian Social and Cultural Life in Minnesota, 1868–1891: An Analysis of Typical Norwegian Newspapers" (master's thesis, University of Minnesota, 1932), 4–7.

5. Qualey, *Norwegian Settlement,* 232; Odd S. Lovoll, "Paul Hjelm-Hansen: Norwegian 'Discoverer' of the Red River Valley and Settlement Promoter," in Vidar Pedersen and Zeljka Svrljuga, eds., *Performances in American Literature and Culture: Essays in Honor of Professor Orm Øverland on His 60th Birthday* (Bergen, Norway: University of Bergen, 1995), 161–78, quote 171–72; Fagereng, "Norwegian Social and Cultural Life in Minnesota," 4–6; Wist, *Norsk-Amerikanernes Festskrift,* 57–69, 100–101; Søren Listoe, *Staten Minnesota i Nordamerika. Dens Fordele for den Skandinaviske Indvandrer med særligt Hensyn til Jordbrugeren* (Minneapolis: Trykt i "Nordisk folkeblads" Trykkeri, 1869–70); *Nordisk Folkeblad,* Mar. 12, 1868, July 14, 21, Aug. 11, Sept. 22, 1869, Feb. 2, 1870; *Minneapolis Tidende,* Nov. 10, 1927.

6. *Budstikken,* Sept. 2, 16, Dec. 9, 1873, Nov. 13, 1878; *Fædrelandet og Emigranten,* Nov. 20, 1878, Mar. 12, 1879; Wist, *Norsk-Amerikanernes Festskrift,* 43–45, 62–63; *Skandinaven,* Feb. 21, 1894; Blegen, *Minnesota,* 291–92; Norman K. Risjord, *A Popular History of Minnesota* (St. Paul: Minnesota Historical Society Press, 2005), 145–48.

7. Biographical sketch of Luth Jæger by Johannes J. Skørdalsvold in Knut Gjerset's biographical listings of Norwegian American editors and publishers in NAHA Archives; Wist, *Norsk-Amerikanernes Festskrift,* 62, 63, 66–68, 94–96; biographical information on Marcus Mills Pomeroy at http://www.wisconsinhistory.org/dictionary/; *Minneapolis Tidende,* Jan. 17, 1932; *Budstikken,* Oct. 10, 17, 1877.

8. Luth Jaeger, "Norskarbeidet og ungdommen," *Symra* (1913): 171–73; Wist, *Norsk-Amerikanernes Festskrift,* 66–67; *Budstikken,* May 14, 1879, Jan. 13, Apr. 20, 1880, Aug. 16, 1881, Jan. 10, 1883; *N. W. Ayer & Son's American Newspaper Annual* (Philadelphia: N. W. Ayer & Son, 1890), 366; *Minneapolis Daglig Tidende,* Nov. 3, 1887, in announcing his self-inflicted death, praises Erik L. Petersen as one of "the brightest minds among our people in this country" and traces his "tangled life course" from his birth in Oslo in 1844, his pursuits as an actor at age sixteen, then as a poet, then as a monk at a monastery in Italy, later sent to St. Paul, Minnesota, by the Catholic church, his conversion to the Episcopalian church, and his contribution to Norwegian American newspapers.

9. *Budstikken,* Jan, 10, Mar. 18, 30, Apr. 6, May 18, 25, Dec. 28, 1880, Jan. 4, Mar. 29, Apr. 12, Aug. 16, 1882; Lovoll, *The Promise of America,* 156–57, quote 156; Nina Draxten, *Kristofer Janson in America* (Northfield, MN: NAHA, 1976), 52–57, 189–90; Kristofer Janson, *Amerikanske Forholde. Fem Foredrag* (Copenhagen: Gyldendal, 1881). For a detailed account of the Muus conflict, see Shaw, *Bernt Julius Muus,* 258–78. *Saamanden* continued publication in Norway until 1900.

10. *Budstikken,* Apr. 18, Oct. 11, Nov. 15, 1882, Oct. 27, Nov. 5, 12, 1886; Odd S. Lovoll, "History of the Norwegian-language Press in North Dakota" (master's thesis, University of North Dakota, 1969), 49–52, 70–71; Wist, *Norsk-Amerikanernes Festskrift,* 69, 70, 116; Blegen, *Minnesota,* 387–88.

11. *Fædrelandet og Emigranten,* July 6, 13, 1886, Jan. 18, 1887, July 10, 17, 24, 1889, Jan. 30, Mar. 12, Aug. 20, Sept. 10, 1890, Dec. 28, 1892; Wist, *Norsk-Amerikanernes Festskrift,* 43, 116.

12. *Decorah-Posten,* Oct. 16, 1934; *Minneapolis Tidende,* Oct. 18, 1934; Wist, *Norsk-Amerikanernes Festskrift,* 102–5, 105–7, quote 102; Laurence M. Larson, "Tellef Grundysen and the Beginnings of Norwegian-American Fiction," *Norwegian-American Studies and Records* 8 (1934): 1–17. *Minneapolis Tidende,* Jan. 28, 1932, under the title "*Minneapolis Tidende* 80 Aar, *Daglig Tidende* 45 Aar," traces the newspaper's history back to *Emigranten*'s founding in 1852. Quote from the article.

13. Wist, *Norsk-Amerikanernes Festskrif,* 103, 104; *Budstikken,* June 29, July 20, 1886, July 3, Dec. 12, 1888, Nov. 14, Dec. 26, 1894; *Minneapolis Søndag Tidende,* Nov. 24, 1889; *Minneapolis Daglig Tidende,* Nov. 12, 1891, Jan. 4, 1895; *Minneapolis Tidende,* May 20, 27, 1898, Nov. 30, 1900; *Ayer & Son's American Newspaper Annual* (1890), 367. Tom Overland, *Minneapolis Daglig Tidende*'s first editor, changed his name from Orm Øverland after coming to America in 1881. By the end of the decade, he was editing an English-language labor newspaper in Duluth. See Orm Øverland, *The Western Home: A Literary History of Norwegian America* (Northfield, MN: NAHA, 1996), 10.

14. Qualey, *Norwegian Settlement,* 114–15, 116–17, 234; Holand, *Norske Settlementer,* 430–31; Wist, *Norsk-Amerikanernes Festskrift,* 72, 78–79, 144–45, 145–46, 167; *Albert Lea Posten,* Mar. 16, Apr. 6, May 4, 17, 25, 1883, Oct. 23, Nov. 20, 1884, Mar. 17, 1885; *Budstikken,* Oct. 13, 20, 1874; *Minneapolis Tidende,* Feb. 24, 1927; O. S. Johnson, "Lidt nybyggerhistorie fra Spring Grove og omegn," *Samband* (Oct. 1915), 700–701; Malmin, Norlie, and Tingelstad, *Who's Who Among Pastors,* 592–93.

15. Wist, *Norsk-Amerikanernes Festskrift,* 59, 69, 96–100; *Nordvesten,* Feb. 16, 1882; *Budstikken,* Jan. 26, Feb. 2, 1887; *Decorah-Posten,* Jan. 30, 1934.

16. Wist, *Norsk-Amerikanernes Festskrift,* 99, 120, 175–77; *Heimdal,* Jan. 17, Nov. 6, 1892, Aug. 27, Oct. 22, 1893, July 19, 1896, May 16, 25, 1897, Jan. 24, Feb. 21, 1902; *Nordvesten,* Dec. 3, 1896; *Scandia,* Feb. 4, 1897.

17. Blegen, *Minnesota,* 433; Wist, *Norsk-Amerikanernes Festskrift,* 172, 191–92; *Minneapolis Tidende,* Jan. 6, 1899; *Nordvesten,* Dec. 28, 1899, Jan. 4, 1900, Dec. 7, 1905, June 27, 1907; *Amerika,* Sept. 5, 1900; *Norge* (Granite Falls, MN), Aug. 17, 1900. The full name of the weekly *Kirketidende*—from 1874 a successor to the monthly *Maanedstidende*—was *Evangelisk-Luthersk Kirketidende,* published by Lutheran Publishing House, Decorah, Iowa.

18. Wist, *Norsk-Amerikanernes Festskrift,* 116–17; Lowell J. Soike, *Norwegians and the Politics of Dissent, 1880–1924* (Northfield, MN: NAHA, 1991), 77, 84–88, 94–95, 102; *Fergus Falls Ugeblad,* Jan. 6, 1886, Nov. 5, Dec. 24, 31, 1890, Jan. 7, May 20, 1891. *Normanna Banner* continued for about a year as *Nyt Normanna Banner,* published by I. F. Strass, who in 1894 established the Populist *Fremad* (Forward) in Sioux Falls, South Dakota.

19. Soike, *Norwegians and the Politics of Dissent,* 96, 103, 114; Blegen, *Minnesota,* 388–89; Wist, *Norsk-Amerikanernes Festskrift,* 128; Risjord, *A Popular History of Minnesota,* 148–52, 156–61; *Rodhuggeren,* Nov. 28, 1893, Nov. 12, 1895, Apr. 14, May 10, Aug. 4, Nov. 3, 10, 1896; *Fergus Falls Ugeblad,* Nov. 8, 1893, Jan. 7, 1904. In 1895 *Samhold* (Solidarity), started in Elbow Lake,

Minnesota, by G. T. Hagen, merged with *Rodhuggeren.* The original name of *Normanden* was the correct *Nordmanden;* it was altered to ease pronunciation for those who did not know Norwegian.

20. Lovoll, "History of Norwegian-language Publications in North Dakota," 14–19; Lovoll, *Norwegians on the Prairie,* 157; Wist, *Norsk-Amerikanernes Festskrift,* 124–27, 170–71; *Rodhuggeren,* Dec. 19, 1893, Jan. 2, 1894; *Nye Normanden,* Sept. 20, Dec. 24, 1895, May 28, 1901; *Madison Tidende,* Apr. 18, 1895, June 25, 1896; *Minnesota Tidende,* Aug. 12, 1897.

21. Wist, *Norsk-Amerikanernes Festskrift,* 125; *Nye Normanden,* Jan. 7, Apr. 14, Oct. 20, 27, Nov. 10, Dec. 29, 1896, Jan. 2, Oct. 30, Nov. 8, 1900, May 7, 1901; *Politiken,* June 26, 1904, Sept. 5, 12, 1905, Mar. 6, May 15, Oct. 30, 1906, Jan. 8, 1907. Laurits Larsen Stavnheim (his first name given as Laurence) obituary in *Sønner af Norge,* Feb. 1940; Laurits Stavnheim to Knut Gjerset, Mar. 17, 1936, Gjerset Collection, NAHA Archives.

22. Blegen, *Minnesota,* 452; Jon Gjerde and Carlton C. Qualey, *Norwegians in Minnesota* (St. Paul: Minnesota Historical Society Press, 2002), 23–24; Wist, *Norsk-Amerikanernes Festskrift,* 149–50; U.S. Bureau of the Census, *Twelfth Census,* 1900; *Duluth Skandinav,* Oct. 31, 1919.

23. *Superior Tidende,* Dec. 20, 1935; special golden jubilee supplement of *Superior Tidende* and *Duluth Skandinav* dated Nov. 1937; *Duluth Skandinav,* June 16, 1916, Nov. 23, 1917, Feb. 1, 1918; Wist, *Norsk-Amerikanernes Festskrift,* 149. The jubilee issue in 1937 and *Superior Tidende,* Dec. 20, 1935, are at odds with dates of purchase and creation of the Fuhr Publishing & Printing Company found in contemporary newspaper data in 1917 and 1918.

24. *Superior Tidende,* Sept. 24, Oct. 28, Nov. 4, 1896, Mar. 4, 1897, Sept. 20, Nov. 29, 1900, Jan. 10, Feb. 7, Mar. 7, 14, July 18, Oct. 3, 31, 1901; Lovoll, *A Century of Urban Life,* 166, 208, 209; Jørn Brøndal, *Ethnic Leadership and Midwestern Politics: Scandinavian Americans and the Progressive Movement in Wisconsin* (Northfield, MN: NAHA, 2004), 58–65; Wist, *Norsk-Amerikanernes Festskrift,* 284.

The Independent Scandinavian Workers Association (ISWA) was founded in early 1893 when the Norden branch of the Scandinavian Workers Association (SWA) in Chicago, due to inner dissent and bad management during hard times, withdrew from the mother organization and formed an independent mutual insurance company.

ISWA began as a truly pan-Scandinavian venture and promoted a secular Scandinavian American identity. In reality, however, it had a majority of Norwegian members and moved toward becoming less pan-Scandinavian and more Norwegian. As a secret order, its relationship with the Lutheran church was distant and frosty, as was generally the case for Scandinavian American fraternities. As a mutual aid society ISWA at its regular meetings and celebrations offered members alternative social activities and a secular leadership; Lutheran churches might thus view such organizations as a threat. Practical working relationships with secret societies were, however, after 1900 sought by some church leaders. ISWA grew to become Wisconsin's largest Scandinavian American insurance fraternity; by

1912 it boasted 4,826 members in ninety-six lodges; there were sixty lodges in Wisconsin, twenty-nine in Minnesota, and seven in North Dakota.

25. Wist, *Norsk-Amerikanernes Festskrift,* 120, has incorrect date of *Scandia*'s founding; "*Scandia* gjennem 50 år," *Scandia,* Apr. 7, 1938; Peer Strømme, *Erindringer. Efter hans død utgit av en komite* (Minneapolis, MN: Augsburg Publishing House Trykkeri, 1923), 313, 353; *Scandia,* Oct. 9, Nov. 27, 1891, Feb. 5, Mar. 4, 1892, Feb. 16, 1894, Dec. 10, 1895, Feb. 11, 1896, June 3, 1897, Dec. 8, 1900, Sept. 28, 1901; L. H. Lund obituary, *Scandia,* Nov. 28, 1935; H. Sundby-Hansen obituary, *Minneapolis Tidende,* Feb. 17, 1927.

26. *Scandia,* Jan. 8, 1921; Lovoll, *A Century of Urban Life,* 165–66.

27. Nelson and Fevold, *The Lutheran Church Among Norwegian-Americans,* 124, 147, 203–6; Rohne, *Norwegian American Lutheranism,* 190, 233–37. There were in the late 1870s no fewer than five Norwegian American Lutheran ecclesiastical bodies: the Eielsen Synod, the Norwegian Synod, the Norwegian Augustana Synod, the Conference, and Hauge's Synod.

28. Nelson and Fevold, *The Lutheran Church Among Norwegian-Americans,* 253–70, quote 254.

29. Wist, *Norsk-Amerikanernes Festskrift,* 112–14; *Ayer & Son's American Newspaper Annual* (1890), 121; *Amerika,* Oct. 1, 15, Dec. 9, 1884 , Jan. 7, 1885, Jan. 6, Oct. 20, 1886, Jan. 5, 1887, Jan. 4, 1888; *Norden,* Feb. 1, 1887. O. M. Kalheim obituary, *Amerika,* Oct. 9, 1895; David T. Nelson, *Luther College, 1861-1961* (Decorah, IA: Luther College Press, 1961), 109, 137. Two earlier journals titled *Amerika* were published in La Crosse, Wisconsin, 1868–72, and in Chicago, 1872.

30. *Ayer & Son's American Newspaper Annual* (1890), 127; Wist, *Norsk-Amerikanernes Festskrift,* 84, 86, 89; *Norden,* Oct. 13, 1874, May 31, July 19, 1877, Jan. 4, Apr. 12, 1882; *Skandinaven,* June 5, 1877.

31. Wist, *Norsk-Amerikanernes Festskrift,* 84, 87–88, quote 88; *Norden,* Jan. 4, Apr. 12, July 4, 12, 1882, Sept. 2, 9, 1884, Aug. 26, 1885; Nelson and Fevold, *The Lutheran Church Among Norwegian-Americans,* 250–51. *Decorah-Posten,* Feb. 11, 1891, and *Norden,* Feb. 10, 1891, have biographies of I. T. Relling. His death by suicide Feb. 5, 1891, was "an absorbing event in the Scandinavian world in [Chicago]."

32. *Norden,* Nov 5, 1885, Oct. 19, Nov. 18, 1886, Jan. 21, 1888; Wist, *Norsk-Amerikanernes Festskrift,* 137–38; Strømme, *Erindringer,* 20, 136, 221–22, 234–35. Peer O. Strømme obituary, *Amerika,* Sept. 16, 1921.

33. Wist, *Norsk-Amerikanernes Festskrift,* 88–89. Wist does not mention Andrew Jensen's ownership of *Norden. Norden,* June 24, 1890, Mar. 8, June 21, 28, July 5, 1892, Dec. 14, 1895; *Chicago Norden,* May 13, 1893, July 21, 1894; *Amerika,* Oct. 13, 1897; *Amerika og Norden,* Oct. 20, 1897, Oct. 12, 1898; Strømme, *Erindringer,* 339–41, 348, 356–57.

34. *Skandinaven,* May 28, 1878, Apr. 3, 10, 1883, Dec. 23, 1884, Mar. 17, Sept. 15, 1886, Mar. 9, 1887, Mar. 14, July 11, 1888, Apr. 29, 1891, Nov. 2, 1892; *Verdens Gang,* Jan. 4, 1895, Aug. 16, 1918; *Folkebladet* (Minneapolis), Oct. 7, 1880, Jan. 5, 1882, Jan. 20, 1886. *Folkebladet* became the organ of the Lutheran Free Church when organized in the

mid-1890s. Peter Hendrickson obituary, *Normanden,* Dec. 21, 1917; Nicolay Grevstad obituary, *Skandinaven,* Feb. 23, 1940; Wist, *Norsk-Amerikanernes Festskrift,* 52–55; Andersen, "The Norwegian American Press," 266–67; Agnes M. Larson, "The Editorial Policy of *Skandinaven,* 1900–1903," *Norwegian-American Studies and Records* 8 (1934): 112–35, quote 135.

35. Marcus Lee Hansen, *The Immigrant in American History* (New York: Harper & Row Publishers, 1940), 137; Wist, *Norsk-Amerikanernes Festskrift,* 86; Laurence M. Larson, *The Changing West and Other Essays* (Northfield, MN: NAHA, 1937), 16–38, quote 19; Blegen, *Norwegian Migration to America,* 545–47, quote 546.

Notes to Chapter 4

1. Lee Hansen, *The Immigrant in American History,* 138.

2. Lee Hansen, *The Immigrant in American History,* 137–38; Wist, *Norsk-Amerikanernes Festskrift,* 188–89; Alfred Söderström, *Minneapolis-Minnen. Kulturhistorisk Axplockning från Qvarnstaden vid Mississippi* (Minneapolis: Svenska Folkets Tidnings Forlag, 1899), 265; *Budstikken,* Dec. 18, 1883.

3. Wist, *Norsk-Amerikanernes Festskrift,* 189–91; Hansen, *My Minneapolis,* 35–36, 241–43; Blegen, *Norwegian Migration to America,* 284; *Norden,* Oct. 6, 1894, Mar. 16, June 22, 1895; *Amerika,* Sept. 27, 1899; *Nordvesten,* July 4, 1895; *Minneapolis Tidende,* Sept. 2, 1898, Sept. 21, 1900, Oct. 16, 1924.

4. *Decorah-Posten,* Sept. 5, 1874; *Kirkelig Maanedstidende,* Jan. 1, 1868; Odd S. Lovoll, "*Decorah-Posten:* The Story of an Immigrant Newspaper," *Norwegian-American Studies* 27 (1977): 77–81, 82, 88; Wist, *Norsk-Amerikanernes Festskrift,* 72, 73–76; Anundsen obituary, *Amerika,* Mar. 28, 1913.

5. Lovoll, "*Decorah-Posten,*" 81, 84, 87–88, 89, 93–94; Wist, *Norsk-Amerikanernes Festskrift,* 71, 72, 76, 77–80, 175–77; *Decorah-Posten,* Oct. 18, 1882, Dec. 4, 1894; *Norge,* Aug. 18, 1899, Aug. 24, Sept. 21, 1900, Sept. 24, 1901; biographical information on Kristian Prestgard, Knut Gjerset Collection, NAHA Archives. For an evaluation of the men who served *Decorah-Posten,* see the article by Kristian Prestgard titled "De som faldt langs veien," *Decorah-Posten,* Sept. 7, 1934. On Grundtvig, see A. M. Allchin, *N. F. S. Grundtvig. An Introduction to His Life and Work* (London: Darton, Longman and Todd, 1998), and Gerald M. Haslam, *N. F. S Grundtvig's Fædrenearv (1783–1815)* (Aarhus, Denmark: Faculty of Theology University of Aarhus, 1998).

6. *Twelfth Census,* 1900; Wist, *Norsk-Amerikanernes Festskrift,* 148; Leland L. Sage, *A History of Iowa* (Ames: The Iowa State University Press, 1974), 219–20; *Sioux City Tidende,* Nov. 1, 1890 (identified as 1.37), Nov. 15, Dec. 27, 1890, Jan. 3, 1891, Nov. 5, 1892, Mar. 13, 1897; *Republikaneren,* Apr. 3, 17, 1897.

7. *Republikaneren,* May 7, July 8, 1897, Mar. 1, May 10, 24, 31, June 21, 1901, Mar. 7, 21, June 6, Sept. 5, 1902.

8. Wist, *Norsk-Amerikanernes Festskrift,* 169; Qualey, *Norwegian Settlement,* 93–94; Lovoll, *The Promise of America,* 116–17; *Visergutten,* Feb. 28, 1896, the earliest preserved copy, is 2.9, suggesting that 1894 is the correct year of the weekly's founding; Norlie, "Norwegian-American Papers," has 1893 as the year it started. *Visergutten,* Feb. 28,

Mar. 6, Apr. 17, Oct. 9, 1896, Sept. 31, Oct. 15, 1897, Jan. 25, 1900.

9. *Visergutten,* June 27, 1901, Jan. 5, Feb. 9, Mar. 9, Dec. 28, 1905; Wist, *Norsk-Amerikanernes Festskrift,* 129–30, 172; *N. W. Ayer & Son's American Newspaper Annual and Directory* (Philadelphia: N. W. Ayer & Son, 1910), 281. Gustav Amlund obituary, *Decorah-Posten,* July 20, 1944.

10. Qualey, *Norwegian Settlement,* 130–48; Wist, *Norsk-Amerikanernes Festskrift,* 146–47; S. O. Nordvold obituary, *Reform,* Jan. 17, 1929, and *Minneapolis Tidende,* Feb. 7, 1929; *Vesterheimen,* May 17, 1887, May 23, Nov. 28, 1888, May 1, July 15, 1889; *Almuevennen,* Aug. 5, 19, Sept. 2, Oct. 7, 14, 21, 1890.

11. *Syd Dakota Ekko,* Nov. 13, Dec. 18, 1889, Dec. 29, 1898, Aug. 30, 1906; Wist, *Norsk-Amerikanernes Festskrift,* 139, 146–47.

12. *Fremad,* Sept. 24, 1896, Nov. 23, 1916; *Sioux Falls-Posten,* Nov. 19, Dec. 31, 1908, Jan. 7, 1909, June 13, 1912; *Sisseton Posten,* Nov. 11, 1902, June 6, 1912; Wist, *Norsk-Amerikanernes Festskrift,* 147, 173; *Ayer & Son's American Newspaper Annual* (1910), 834; John Milton, *South Dakota: A Bicentennial History* (New York: W. W. Norton & Company, Inc., 1977), 122–24. Biographical information from the South Dakota State Archives, Pierre, SD.

13. *Fremad,* Sept. 24, Nov. 5, 19, 1896, May 13, 1897, Nov. 10, 1898, Aug. 16, Oct. 18, Nov. 8, 1900; Milton, *South Dakota,* 124; Wist, *Norsk-Amerikanernes Festskrift,* 147. See John D. Hicks, *The Populist Revolt: A History of the Farmers' Alliance and the People's Party* (Minneapolis: University of Minnesota Press, 1931). Biographical information from the South Dakota State Archives.

14. Elwyn B. Robinson, *History of North Dakota* (Lincoln: University of Nebraska Press, 1966), quote 288; Lovoll, "Norwegian-language Press in North Dakota," 59–63; *Normanden,* Apr. 8, 1908; *Dakota,* Sept. 16, 23, 1896; *Den Fjerde Juli,* Aug. 19, 1896, Mar. 10, 1897; *Fjerde Juli og Dakota,* Mar. 17, 1897; *Fram,* Apr. 17, 1903; *Skandinaven,* "Minnesota og Dakota," July 20, 1887.

15. Robinson, *History of North Dakota,* 282–84; Qualey, *Norwegian Settlement,* 160–61, 163, 168–70; Lovoll, *The Promise of America,* 123–26; *Budstikken,* Nov. 10, 1874; *Norden,* Apr. 19, 1877; *Amerika,* July 29, 1885; *Nordvesten,* May 12, 1887; *Decorah-Posten,* Feb. 29, 1888. Newspaper publishers took part in colonization projects. Helge Opland, publisher of *Sioux Falls-Posten,* promoted the Oslo settlement on the high plains of the Texas panhandle, founded in 1908 by Anders L. Mordt, son-in-law of Nicolay Grevstad, *Skandinaven*'s longtime editor. Mordt published a propaganda newspaper titled *Oslo Posten* in Guymon, Oklahoma, from May 20, 1910, until May 15, 1913. St. Olaf College possesses a complete run of the publication. See also Peter L. Petersen, "Oslo on the Texas High Plains," *Norwegian-American Studies* 28 (1979): 138–56.

16. *Normanden,* May 1, 1917; Wist, *Norsk-Amerikanernes Festskrift,* 68–69, 135; Robinson, *History of North Dakota,* 200–201; Lovoll, "Norwegian-language Press in North Dakota," 19–22, 39, 79–80.

17. *Normanden,* Feb. 1, 1911; *Fram,* May 18, 1898, Feb. 15, 1901, June 9, 1905; *Fargo-Posten,* Jan. 24, Mar. 14, 1885, Mar. 8, Nov. 4, 1886, Apr. 14, Nov. 3, Dec. 15, 1887; *Vesten,* June 23,

July 3, Sept. 28, Oct. 30, 1888, Nov. 9, 1889; *Fargo-Posten og Vesten,* May 22, 1889; *Fram,* Apr. 17, July 3, 1903, Nov. 11, 1911; Lovoll, "Norwegian-language Press in North Dakota," 49–59, 62–63; Robinson, *History of North Dakota,* 199–203; *Ayer & Son's American Newspaper Annual* (Philadelphia: N. W. Ayer & Son, 1904), 646; *Ayer & Son's American Newspaper Annual* (1910), 661, 662. A second *Fargo-Posten* was published by T. S. Nordgaard and H. J. Kopperdahl, 1897–1903. Kopperdahl also published *Landmanden* (The Farmer) in Mayville, North Dakota, 1894–96, and together with Nordgaard in 1890–92 published *Montana Folkeblad,* Helena, Montana, the name soon changed to *Montana Statstidende.*

18. Qualey, *Norwegian Settlement,* 170–71, 193–96; *Nordvesten,* July 18–Sept. 19, 1889; *Montana Posten,* Oct. 11, 18, 1890, Aug. 15, 1891, Mar. 23, Aug. 10, 1893.

19. Darrrell J. Christofferson, e-mail to author, Feb. 28, 1995, cited in Odd S. Lovoll, *The Promise Fulfilled: A Portrait of Norwegian Americans Today* (1998; reprint, Minneapolis: University of Minnesota Press, 2007), 50.

20. *Montana Folkeblad,* Oct. 28, 1891; Wist, *Norsk-Amerikanernes Festskrift,* 169–70; Qualey, *Norwegian Settlement,* 151n; *Montana Skandinav,* Jan. 26, 1893; *Montana Tidende og Skandinav,* Feb. 9, 1894; *Indlandsposten* (The Inland Post), Nov. 26, 1915, Nov. 15, 1916, Mar. 14, 28, Apr. 4, 11, 1917.

21. William Mulder, *Homeward to Zion: The Mormon Migration from Scandinavia* (Minneapolis: University of Minnesota Press, 1957), vii, 107; William Mulder, "Norwegian Forerunners among the Early Mormons," *Norwegian-American Studies and Records* 19 (1956): 46–61; Helge Seljaas, "Norwegians in 'Zion' Teach Themselves English," *Norwegian-American Studies* 26 (1974): 220–28.

22. Qualey, *Norwegian Settlement,* 196–98; *Decorah-Posten,* Feb. 28, 1983, cited on 198; Mulder, *Homeward to Zion,* 110–11, 214, 306.

23. Mulder, *Homeward to Zion,* 258–59, 260, 261–63, 264; *Bikuben,* Aug. 1, 1876, Aug. 2, 1877, Mar. 6, 14, 1884; *Salt Lake Herald,* Oct. 23, 1874; J. C. Alter, *Early Utah Journalism* (Salt Lake City: Utah State Historical Society, 1938); Kenneth O. Bjork, *West of the Great Divide: Norwegian Migration to the Pacific Coast, 1847–1893* (Northfield, MN: NAHA, 1958), 259; Kenneth O. Bjork, "A Covenant Folk, with Scandinavian Colorings," *Norwegian-American Studies* 21 (1962): 215–20. The number of Scandinavians who abandoned the Mormon Church and their reasons for doing so after arriving in Utah as converts is not a topic of this study. Apostate Scandinavian Mormons returned to the Lutheran Church or other Christian faiths or simply departed from any religious affiliation. Mainstream churches sent missionaries and established congregations in Utah to attract Scandinavian Mormons to their particular faith. Departures of the disillusioned from Zion were common occurrences; some moved to California or other points west or even returned to the homeland. See Mulder, *Homeward to Zion,* 182–83.

24. *Bikuben,* Aug. 1, 1876, Jan. 22, Apr. 16, 1885, June 4, 1891, Nov. 23, 1893, May 24, 1894; *Utah Posten,* Jan. 1, Feb. 11, Apr. 8, 1885; Wist, *Norsk-Amerikanernes Festskrift,* 154; Mulder, *Homeward to Zion,* 261–64. A provi-

sional State of Deseret was established in the Salt Lake Valley Mar. 5, 1849; as a part of a compromise in Sept. 1850 the State of Deseret was made Utah Territory and Brigham Young was appointed governor.

25. Jan Shipps, *Mormonism: The Story of a New Religious Tradition* (Urbana: University of Illinois Press, 1985), 125–26, 145, 163, 167, 168; Bjork, *West of the Great Divide,* 266; Mulder, *Homeward to Zion,* 239, 241; Marzolf, *The Danish Language Press,* 115; *Bikuben,* Aug. 1, 1876, Jan. 15, Aug. 30, Sept. 13, 1877, June 5, 1884, Apr. 21, Dec. 1, 1886, Mar. 2, Sept. 8, Oct. 26, 1887, Apr. 10, Oct. 16, 23, Nov. 20, 1890, May 14, 1891; *Emigranten,* June 8, 1855, May 30, 1856. "Mormons" by Jessie L. Embry and "The Discontinuation of Polygamy," no author given, online article.

26. Bjork, *West of the Great Divide,* 22, 135, 151, 160, 163, 164–65, 166, 178–81, 300–303; Lovoll, *The Promise of America,* 232–35; "First Transcontinental Railroad," online article; *Twelfth Census,* 1900.

27. *Skandinaven,* Dec. 11, 1883, Jan. 8, 1884; *Norden,* Jan. 28, Feb. 25, Apr. 29, 1875; Bjork, *West of the Great Divide,* 167, 168, 169.

28. Bjork, *West of the Great Divide,* 170, 171, 175–76; *Skandinaven,* Jan. 15, 1884; Wist, *Norsk-Amerikanernes Festskrift,* 153; Marzolf, *The Danish Language Press,* 91–95; Sophus Hartwick, *Danske i California. Beretninger om de Danskes Liv og Virke fra de tidligste Pioner Dage* (San Francisco, CA: Sophus Bugge, 1939), 8, 150–62, 164–75, 444–52.

29. *Pacific Skandinav,* Sept. 11, Oct. 30, Nov. 6, Dec. 18, 1896, Mar. 26, Apr. 9, May 14, Aug. 20, 1897, Jan. 7, Mar. 11, 1898, Jan. 6, May 26, 1899, Jan. 5, Sept. 29, 1900. A separate Scandinavian Department came into being in Berkeley only in the post–World War II years. The first appointment to a full professorship in Scandinavian languages and literature was made in 1949.

30. *Pacific Posten,* Sept. 15, Oct. 6, 27, Nov. 3, 17, 24, Dec. 1, 1904, May 11, Nov. 30, 1905, Feb. 1, 8, Apr. 12, 1906; Lloyd Hustvedt, "O. A. Tveitmoe: Labor Leader," *Norwegian-American Studies* 30 (1985): 3–54; Wist, *Norsk-Amerikanernes Festskrift,* 155–56; Bjork, *West of the Great Divide,* 289, 586–87; "1906 San Francisco Earthquake," online article.

31. Wist, *Norsk-Amerikanernes Festskrift,* 156–57; Lovoll, *The Promise of America,* 232–38; Bjork, *West of the Great Divide,* 596, 612. *Tacoma Budstikke,* dated July 3, 1890, appears to be the only extant copy. It is preserved in the library of Washington State University, Pullman.

32. *Washington Posten,* May 17, 1889, Sept. 24, Oct. 8, Nov. 5, 12, 1896, May 13, 1938; Bjork, *West of the Great Divide,* 601–21; Lovoll, "*Washington Posten,*" 163, 165, 167–68, 181–82; Patsy Adams Hegstad, "Scandinavian Settlement in Seattle, 'Queen City of the Puget Sound,'" *Norwegian-American Studies* 30 (1985): 55, 57.

33. *Tacoma-Tidende,* Oct. 20, 1894, Mar. 14, Apr. 25, 1896, Apr. 3, July 24, Sept. 11, 1897, Jan. 23, 1898, Aug. 18, 1900; Wist, *Norsk-Amerikanernes Festskrift,* 152–53; Bjork, *West of the Great Divide,* 614; Lovoll, *The Promise of America,* 242–43, quote from *Washington Posten,* 242.

34. *Tacoma-Tidende,* Sept. 11, 1897, Dec. 23, 1899, Jan. 20, July 7, Aug.

11, Nov. 10, 1900, June 15, 22, July 20, Sept. 28, 1901, May 8, 1903, July 15, 1904; Wist, *Norsk-Amerikanernes Festskrift,* 152.

35. A. N. Rygg, *Norwegians in New York, 1825–1925* (Brooklyn, NY: The Norwegian News Company, 1941), 64–71, 103–15; Karsten Roedder, *Av en Utvandreravis' Saga.* Nordisk Tidende *i New York gjennem 75 År* (Brooklyn, NY: Norwegian News—Northway Printers, Inc., 1966), 14–35, quote 15–16; David C. Mauk, *The Colony that Rose from the Sea: Norwegian Maritime Migration and Community in Brooklyn, 1850–1910* (Northfield, MN: NAHA, 1997), 28–40; David C. Mauk, "Maritime Migration and the Norwegian Communities in New York City," in Odd S. Lovoll, ed., *Migrasjon og tilpasning. Ingrid Semmingsen, Et minneseminar* (Oslo: Historisk institutt, Universitetet i Oslo, 1998), 95–109; Lovoll, *The Promise of America,* 267–71.

36. Rygg, *Norwegians in New York,* 133–36, 140–41; Mauk, *The Colony that Rose from the Sea,* 65–66, 151–52, 196–99; Roedder, *Av en Utvandreravis' Saga,* 14–35, quotes 19, 25, 29; P. S. Christensen, "Lidt aviskrønike. Skandinaviske blade i Østen," in *Symra. Et Skrift for Norske paa begge Sider av Havet* (Decorah, IA: The Symra Company, 1914), 261–70, quotes 264, 265; *Everett Ekko,* Apr. 5, 1907; U.S. Bureau of the Census, *Thirteenth Census,* 1910.

37. Bjork, *West of the Great Divide,* 614.

Notes to Chapter 5

1. Wist, *Norsk-Amerikanernes Festskrift,* 39.

2. Andersen, *Rough Road to Glory,* 13–15, quote 13; Miller, *The Ethnic Press in the United States,* xi-xxii; *Skandinaven,* Mar. 27, 1895, in commenting on the union crisis is quoted; *Decorah-Posten,* Nov. 26, 1901; *Minneapolis Tidende,* Mar. 30, 1916, Dec. 13, 1928.

3. Lovoll, *The Promise of America, Decorah-Posten* quoted 201, 202; Odd S. Lovoll, "Unionsoppløsningen og det norske Amerika," in Øystein Rian, Harriet Rudd, and Håvard Tangen, eds., *100 år var det alt?* (Oslo: Nei til EU, 2005), 92–99; Odd S. Lovoll, "The Dissolution of the Swedish-Norwegian Union and Norwegian America," *The Norseman* 1 (2005): 21–32; Olav Tysdal, "The Dissolution of the Union between Norway and Sweden and the Scandinavian Americans," in *Scandinavian Studies* (Summer 2007): 167–96; *Norden,* Dec. 11, 1883, July 8, 1884, Mar. 24, 1891, Jan. 3, Mar. 7, 1893; *Verdens Gang,* Apr. 26, 1895; *Chicago Norden,* Aug. 5, 12, 1893; *Budstikken,* Feb. 12, Apr. 15, 1884; *Skandinaven,* Feb. 26, Mar. 11, 1884, Apr. 18, July 6, 18, 20, 27, Aug. 17, 1892, Jan. 28, Feb. 22, Mar. 27, Apr. 24, May 22, June 12, 19, July 8, 10, 24, 31, Sept. 4, Oct. 28, Nov. 13, 1895, May 3, 17, 24, June 9, 14, 16, 21, 23, Aug. 18, 1905, June 22, 27, 1906; *Washington Posten,* Sept. 29, 1905. The Swedish flag featured the union insignia until the union officially ended in 1905.

4. Didrik Arup Seip, "Utflytterdagen," *Nordmanns-Forbundet,* Nov. 1948, 277–79, quote 278; Lovoll, *The Promise of America,* 201; *Nye Normanden,* May 4, 1897; Odd S. Lovoll, "*Gaa Paa:* A Scandinavian Voice of Dissent," *Minnesota History* (Fall 1990): 86–99. The Norwegian American Collection at the National Library of Norway in Oslo, housing Norwegian American newspapers, books, and studies, was formally

opened only in 1958 and is thus of recent vintage; newspapers on microfilm were duplicated from the large collection at Luther College, Decorah, Iowa, listed in a compilation by Oivind M. Hovde and Martha E. Henzler, *Norwegian-American Newspapers in Luther College Library* (Decorah, IA: Luther College Press, 1975).

5. *Emigranten,* Sept. 9, 1853, Nov. 21, 1856; *Fædrelandet,* Nov. 24, 1864; *Budstikken,* Dec. 25, 1883; *Minneapolis Tidende,* Aug. 23, 1934; *Skandinaven,* Jan. 7, Feb. 28, 1867, Jan. 6, Oct. 27, 1874, Nov. 30, 1875, Dec. 23, 1884, May 20, 1891, Sept. 27, 1893; *Nye Normanden,* Dec. 24, 1895. Postage to Norway was lowered in 1867.

6. *Folkebladet,* Dec. 2, 1880; *Visergutten,* Oct. 10, 17, 31, Nov. 14, 1912; *Decorah-Posten,* Jan. 14, 1885, Oct. 30, 1900, Jan. 1, 8, Nov. 5, 15, 26, Dec. 10, 1901, Sept. 5, 1924; *The Artist Printer: A Journal for the Progressive,* Dec. 1891, 228; Ola Kvisle, *I ring om Fjøslia. Slektshistorie fra Numedal, Sigdal og U.S.A.* (Drammen, Norway: Eget Forlag, 1950). Ola Kvisle's daughter Sigrid Kvisle provided the information about her father's work, for which I thank her most sincerely. Martin Nag, *Amerikabrev frå Moster* (Mosterhamn, Norway: Moster Sogelag, 2001), 3, 8, 10, 13, 15, 40–41; Martin Nag, *Amerikabrev frå Moster II* (Mosterhamn, Norway: Moster Sogelag, 2004). I am most grateful to Martin Nag for the gift of these two anthologies of "America letters from Moster." Else Braut and Randi Hoff, *Brev hjemmefra. Brev fra Borge til utvandrere 1840–1960* (Oslo: Solum Forlag, 1997), 230. The book is a gift from Knut Sprauten, director, Norwegian Local History Institute. See also Ivar Kleiven, *Brev til* Decorah-Posten, Gudmund Harildstad, ed. (Otta, Norway: Dølaringen Boklag, 1994), and Øyvind T. Gulliksen, ed., *Torbjørg Lie. Brev til* Decorah-Posten *1890–1922* (Bø, Norway: Fyresdal Sogelag, 1996).

7. Einar Haugen, *The Norwegian Language in America: A Study in Bilingual Behavior* (Bloomington: Indiana University Press, 1969), esp. chs. 7 and 8; Botolv Helleland, ed., *Norsk språk i Amerika* (Oslo: Novus forlag, 1991), contains twelve essays by as many students of the Norwegian language in America, all consulted. See also two booklets: Didrik Arup Seip, *En liten norsk språkhistorie* (Oslo: H. Aschehoug & Co. [W. Nygaard], 1954), and Gustav Indrebø, *Norsk målsoge* (Bergen, Norway: A. S. Lunde & Co's Forlag, 1947). Nag, *Amerikabrev frå Moster,* 17. Since 1929 the two competing official written forms have been titled *Bokmål* (Book Language) and *Nynorsk* (New Norwegian); both have been subjected to a series of linguistic reforms. *Bokmål* is by far the dominant Norwegian written idiom.

8. Arne Sunde, "A Minority within a Minority: The Promotion of *Nynorsk* in the United States, 1900–1920," *Norwegian-American Studies* 34 (1995): 171–99; Gudmund Harildstad, ed., Kristian Prestgard, *Fra Heidal til Decorah. Veien jeg gikk* (Oslo: Snøhetta Forlag, 1996), 158–59; Lovoll, "History of Norwegian-language Publications in North Dakota," 111–14; Lovoll, *"Decorah-Posten,"* 98; *Decorah-Posten,* Jan. 5, 1926; *Fram,* Aug. 1, 8, 15, 1912; *Sioux Falls Posten,* Jan. 13, 1910; *Nye Normanden,* Sept. 14, 1897; Erling Innvik to author, Feb. 6, 1976; Haugen, *The Norwegian Language in America,* 124–37.

9. For a comprehensive history, see Odd S. Lovoll, *A Folk Epic: The*

Bygdelag *in America* (Northfield, MN: NAHA, 1975), 229; Odd S. Lovoll, "The Norwegian-American Old-Home Societies Viewed as a Mediating Culture Between 'Consent' and 'Descent,'" in Lars Olsson and Sune Åkerman, eds., *Hembygden och världen. Festskrift till Ulf Beijbom* (Gothenburg, Sweden: Svenska Emigrantinstitutet, 2002), 117–33, quote 119; Lovoll, *Norwegians on the Prairie,* 186–87.

10. *Visergutten,* Sept. 11, 1911, May 9, 1912, July 3, 1913; *Duluth Skandinav,* Mar. 16, 1917, Dec. 18, 1925; *Superior Tidende,* Dec. 18, 1925; Lovoll, *A Folk Epic,* 224–29.

11. Odd S. Lovoll, "A Greater Norway," *The Norseman* (Jan. 2007): 6–31, quotes 6–7, 13; Odd S. Lovoll, "Common Historical Memory," *The Norseman* 2 (Mar. 2007): 5–36; Birger Osland, *A Long Pull from Stavanger: The Reminiscences of a Norwegian Immigrant* (Northfield, MN: NAHA, 1945), 70–85, 86–96; *Pacific Skandinaven,* June 30, 1911; *Sioux Falls Posten,* Oct. 13, 1910; *Vestkysten,* Oct. 25, 1929; *Duluth Skandinav,* July 8, Nov. 18, 1938. The original name was Nordmands-Forbundet; in the 1930s the organization's name and that of its journal were modernized to Nordmanns-Forbundet. For the sake of consistency, the latter form is used throughout the text.

12. Andersen, *Rough Road to Glory,* ch. 7, titled "Women's Rights: The Struggle for Equal Suffrage," 90–101; Lovoll, *A Century of Urban Life,* 223–24, 258, 260; Ingrid Semmingsen, "A Pioneer: Agnes Mathilde Wergeland, 1857–1914," in Odd S. Lovoll, ed., *Makers of an American Immigrant Legacy: Essays in Honor of Kenneth O. Bjork* (Northfield, MN: NAHA, 1980), 111–30, quote 117; Draxten, *Kristofer Janson in America,* 194–96; *Kvartalskrift,* Jan. 1915, 12–17; *Budstikken,* May 28, Aug. 20, 1890; *Normanden,* Oct. 22, 1920, Feb. 2, 1923; *Almuevennen,* Aug. 19, 1890; *Reform,* Jan. 26, 1909; *Decorah-Posten,* Mar. 30, 1915, June 26, 1917.

13. Åse Elin Langeland, "Adjusting to America. A Study in *Kvinden og Hjemmet:* A Monthly Journal for the Scandinavian Women in America, 1888–1947" (master's thesis, University of Bergen, May 2001), 13–28, 84, 98, quote 99–100; Sigrid Brevik Wangsnes, "*Kvinden og Hjemmet:* A Magazine for Scandinavian Immigrant Women, 1901–1910," *Norse Heritage 1989 Yearbook* (Stavanger, Norway: The Norwegian Emigration Center, 1989), 105–16; Wist, *Norsk-Amerikanernes Festskrift,* 161; Andersen, "Women's Rights," 94; Martin Ulvestad, *Norge i Amerika med Kart,* rev. ed. (Minneapolis, MN: Privately printed, 1902), 54. If subscribers to the Swedish-language *Quinnan och Hemmet,* begun by Ida Hansen in 1893, are added, the total circulation in 1924 stood at 60,000. For an insightful treatment of "rural reading societies," see Steven J. Keillor, "Rural Norwegian-American Reading Societies in the Late Nineteenth Century," *Norwegian-American Studies* 33 (1992), 139–63.

14. Wist, *Norsk-Amerikanernes Festskrift,* 181–85, quote 182; Orm Øverland, "*Skandinaven* and the Beginnings of Professional Publishing," *Norwegian-American Studies* 31 (1986): 187–214; Skogerboe Hansen, "History of the John Anderson Publishing Company," 39–40, 57–68, quote 40; Jean Skogerboe Hansen, "*Skandinaven* and the John Anderson Publishing Company," *Norwegian-American Studies* 28 (1979),

35–68; Haldor L. Hove, "Five Norwegian Newspapers, 1870–1890: Purveyors of Literary Taste and Culture" (PhD dissertation, University of Chicago, 1962), 358–67; *Skandinaven*, Aug. 31, Dec. 28, 1892, May 2, 1916; *Skandinaven og Amerika*, Sept. 16, 1873; *Decorah-Posten*, Sept. 5, 1924, Lovoll, "*Decorah-Posten*," 83, 84–87. The novel by H. A. Foss ran as a serial in *Decorah-Posten* from Dec. 3, 1884, to Apr. 22, 1885.

15. *Nye Normanden*, July 2, 1901; *Budstikken*, Jan. 10, 1877, July 4, Nov. 7, 1883; Hans A. Foss, *Trediveaarskrigen mod Drikkeondet* (Minot, ND: Nord Dakota Totalavholdsselskab, 1922), 19, 46; Andersen, *Rough Road to Glory*, ch. 12, titled "America Tries Prohibition," 162–73; Lovoll, *Norwegians on the Prairie*, 200, 219; J. L. Nydahl, *Afholdssagens Historie* (Minneapolis, MN: Forfatterens Forlag, 1896), 304, 314; Lovoll, *A Century of Urban Life*, quote 121. Carrie Amelia Moore Nation (1846–1911) as a reformer devoted her life to fighting liquor, the saloon, tobacco, and fraternal orders. She began her career in legally "dry" Kansas in 1900. Armed with a hatchet, she entered illegal saloons and smashed windows, mirrors, pictures, bottles of liquor, and kegs of beer.

16. Lovoll, *Norwegians on the Prairie*, 219, 220, 222; Soike, *Norwegian Americans and the Politics of Dissent*, 45–46, 62–68; Lovoll, *A Century of Urban Life*, 120–26; Wist, *Norsk-Amerikanernes Festskrift*, 118; *Verdens Gang*, Feb. 17, 1881.

17. Robinson, *History of North Dakota*, 258–59; Foss, *Trediveaarskrigen mod Drikkeondet*, 18, 24–25, 26–28, 30, 31–34, 37–39; Simon Johnson, "Oplevd," typescript, NAHA Archives, Northfield, MN, 71–74; Wist, *Norsk-Amerikanernes Festskrift*, 142–43.

18. *Normanden*, June 8, 1939; *Fram*, Nov. 11, 1911; *Minneapolis Tidende*, Oct. 15, 1908, Oct. 14, 1909; *Decorah-Posten*, Mar. 19, 1915; *Gaa Paa*, Feb. 23, 1918; *Folkets Røst*, Mar. 1, 1919, Dec. 27, 1923, Jan. 25, 1925; Andersen, "America Tries Prohibition," 168–69, 171–72; Waldemar Ager, ed., *Afholdsfolkets Festskrift 1914:* Reform'*s Jubilæumshefte* (Eau Claire, WI: Reform Publishing Co., 1914), 5; Ernest H. Cherington, comp. and ed., *The Anti-Saloon League Yearbook* 1919 (Westerville, OH: Anti-Saloon League of America, 1919), 123.

19. *Everett Ekko*, Feb. 22, 1908; *Arbeideren*, Feb. 9, 1886; Einar Haugen, *Immigrant Idealist: A Literary Biography of Waldemar Ager, Norwegian American* (Northfield, MN: NAHA, 1989), 7–11, 16–22, 25, quote from *Reform*, Aug. 1, 1941, 154; Clarence Kilde, "Dark Decade: The Declining Years of Waldemar Ager," *Norwegian-American Studies* 28 (1979): 157–92; Wist, *Norsk-Amerikanernes Festskrift*, 117–20; Andersen, "America Tries Prohibition," 171; Genevieve Hagen and Alf Hjemboe, *A* Reform *Sampler: Selections from a Norwegian Language Newspaper 1898–1941* (Eau Claire, WI: Waldemar Ager Association, 1998), 106 pages of valuable selections, *Reform*, Mar. 2, 1927, cited 92.

20. *Nordvesten*, June 3, 1897, June 15, July 15, 1905.

Notes to Chapter 6

1. *Decorah-Posten*, Sept. 5, 1924; *Nordmands-Forbundet*, Aug. 1924, 370.

2. *Thirteenth Census of the United States, 1910: Population*, I, 781, 804, 875, 893–95, 918–24.

3. Lovoll, *Norwegians on the Prairie,* 6–7; Lovoll, *The Promise of America,* 33–34, 36–37, 38; Jenswold, "The Rise and Fall of Pan-Scandinavianism," 159–70; Lovoll, "The Changing Role of May 17," quote 70.

4. Nelson and Fevold, *The Lutheran Church Among Norwegian-Americans,* II:183–225; *Budstikken,* July 29, 1891; *Minneapolis Tidende,* June 3, 1904; *Pacific-Posten* Apr. 20, May 4, June 8, 1905; *Skandinaven,* May 24, 1905; *Normanden,* July 13, 1904; Hansen, *My Minneapolis,* 74–76, 196–97, 247. For a detailed accounting, see Alf Lunder Knudsen, "The Norwegian Male Chorus Movement in America: A Study" (PhD dissertation, University of Washington, 1989), founding of associations on 365–69. The NSAA Sangerfest 2010 will be held in Madison, Wisconsin, June 2010.

5. *Nordvesten,* Apr. 26, 1906; *Everett Ekko,* Dec. 7, 1906, Feb. 22, 1907; *Sioux Falls-Posten,* May 25, 1911.

6. Haugen, *Immigrant Idealist,* 51, 63, quote 51; Wist, *Norsk-Amerikanernes Festskrift,* 185–87; Einar Haugen, "*Symra:* A Memoir," *Norwegian-American Studies* 27 (1977): 101–10. The name *symra* is a dialect word, popularized by the linguist and creator of *Landsmaal/Nynorsk,* Ivar Aasen. Essays translated from *Kvartalskrift* were published in 1977 by NAHA, titled *Cultural Pluralism versus Assimilation,* edited by Odd S. Lovoll. The author cannot refrain from stating that he served as the last president of the Norwegian Society of America. Its only members at the time comprised its executive board. In 1976 it was dissolved and its remaining funds transferred to the Norwegian-American Historical Association.

7. Lovoll, "History of Norwegian-language Publications in North Dakota," 107–11; Wist, *Norsk-Amerikanernes Festskrift,* 136–37, 186.

8. Lovoll, *A Folk Epic,* 99–103, 113–14, 117–23; Lovoll, "The Changing Role of May 17," 72–73; *Aftenposten* (Oslo), July 4, 1914; *Nordmands-Forbundet,* Aug. 1915, 178–79; *The Norseman* (Mar. 2007): 17–20; *Minneapolis Tidende,* Nov. 4, 1909, May 18, 21, 1914; *Scandia,* Nov. 9, 1912; *Decorah-Posten,* May 22, 1914; *Reform,* May 19, 26, 1914. On Jan. 1, 2002, the 1914 memorial gift was liquidated by the *Storting,* the remaining funds transferred to the Norwegian Emigrant Museum, Hamar, Norway.

9. Carl H. Chrislock, *Ethnicity Challenged: The Upper Midwest Norwegian-American Experience in World War I* (Northfield, MN: NAHA, 1981), 13, 30–31, 33–34, 53, quote 214; Elsebeth Hansen, "*Washington Posten:* A Fixed Point of Orientation in the Lives of Norwegians in the Pacific Northwest" (master's thesis, University of Oslo, 2001), 114–20; Lovoll, *Norwegians on the Prairie,* 214–15; John Higham, *Strangers in the Land: Patterns of American Nativism 1860–1925* (New York: Atheneum, 1977), 198, 248, quote 195; *Amerika,* Feb. 19, June 25, 1915; *Pacific Skandinav,* July 3, Aug. 7, Sept. 4, 1914, Mar. 9, Apr. 6, May 11, 1917.

10. Higham, *Strangers in the Land,* 196; *Fremad,* Jan. 4, Apr. 12, May 17, June 21, July 12, Nov. 1, 1917, Jan. 3, 1918; *Sioux Falls Posten,* Mar. 16, 1916; *Skandinaven,* Mar. 21, 1914; Einar Hilsen to Knut Gjerset, undated, Gjerset Collection, NAHA Archives.

11. *Fremad,* May 17, 1917; *Skandinaven,* Oct. 3, 1917; *Reform,* June 18, 1918; Chrislock, *Ethnicity Challenged,*

65–76, 81–82; Hansen, "*Washington Posten,*" 115–16; Lovoll, *A Folk Epic,* 139–40. See also Carl H. Chrislock, "Name Change and the Church, 1918–1920," *Norwegian-American Studies* 27 (1977): 202–5.

12. *Folkets Røst,* Apr. 12, 1919; *Normanden,* Feb. 9, 1923; *Superior Tidende,* July 24, 1953; Simon Johnson to the author, Mar. 11, 1968; Chrislock, *Ethnicity Challenged,* 125. Scott Daniels of the Oregon Historical Society furnished relevant copies of State of Oregon, *The General Laws* (Salem, Oregon, 1920), and State of Oregon, *Journals of the Senate and the House* (Salem, Oregon, 1920), for which I am most grateful.

13. Lovoll, *A Century of Urban Life,* 268–72; Lovoll, "*Gaa Paa,*" 87–99; Odd-Stein Granhus, "Socialist Dissent among Norwegian Americans: Emil Mengshoel, Newspaper Publisher and Author," *Norwegian-American Studies* 33 (1992): 27–71; Henry Bengtson, *On the Left in America: Memoirs of the Scandinavian-American Labor Movement,* Kermit B. Westerberg, trans., Michael Brook, ed. and intro. (Carbondale: Southern Illinois University Press, 1999), 21–26, 65–67, 84, 85, quote 85; *Folket Røst,* Dec. 21, 1918, Jan. 18, 1919, Jan. 13, 1923, Dec. 29, 1923, Oct. 31, 1925.

14. *Folkets Røst,* Mar. 15, 1919, Sept. 26, 1925; Carl H. Chrislock, "The Norwegian-American Impact on Minnesota Politics: How Far 'Left-of-Center'?" in Harald S. Naess, ed., *Norwegian Influence on the Upper Midwest* (Duluth: University of Minnesota, 1975), 106–16; Wist, *Norsk-Amerikanernes Festskrift,* 129, 170; Robinson, *History of North Dakota,* 330–34; Lovoll, *Norwegians on the Prairie,* 214–15; Lovoll, "History of Norwegian-language Publications in North Dakota," 24–25; *Fram,* Jan. 27, Mar. 16, Apr. 6, Aug. 10, 1916, Jan. 4, 25, Dec. 6, 27, 1917; *Decorah-Posten,* July 20, 1944; *Normanden,* Mar. 3, Apr. 21, Sept. 8, 1916, Feb. 6, July 6, 1917. See also "Economic History of the United States," online article.

15. Lovoll, "History of Norwegian-language Publications in North Dakota," 97–100; *Nord Dakota Tidende,* June 26, Aug. 14, 28, Oct. 2, 9, 1919, May 18, 1922; *Normanden,* Nov. 12, 19, 1920.

16. *Fremad,* Aug. 19, Nov. 7, 11, 1915, June 7, Dec. 20, 1917, Apr. 4, May 30, July 25, Nov. 14, 1918, Oct. 26, 1922, June 5, 19, 1924, May 14, 1925, Aug. 11, 1927; *Decorah-Posten,* June 13, 1924; *Garretson News,* Dec. 8, 1945; *Folkets Røst,* Sept. 26, 1925.

17. *Fergus Falls Ugeblad,* June 18, Oct. 29, 1924, Jan. 21, Mar. 11, Nov. 5, 1925, Aug. 31, 1929, Aug. 20, Sept. 10, Nov. 12, 1930, June 26, 1946; *Minneapolis Tidende,* Aug. 29, 1929.

18. *Minneapolis Tidende,* Nov. 29, 1929, Jan. 28, 1932; *Minneapolis Daglig Tidende,* Jan. 20, 1891; Wist, *Norsk-Amerikanernes Festskrift,* 104, 107–10; Blegen, *Minnesota,* 388–89.

19. Wist, *Norsk-Amerikanernes Festskrift,* 105, 109–10, quotes 108–9; *Minneapolis Tidende,* Feb. 1, 1895, Jan. 25, 1912; *Minneapolis Daglig Tidende,* Jan. 26, 1891, Feb. 2, 1932; Carl G. O. Hansen to Knut Gjerset, Nov. 1, 1934, Gjerset Collection, NAHA Archives; *Symra,* 1908, Gjerset Collection, NAHA Archives; N. W. Ayer & Son, *American Newspaper Annual Directory* (Philadelphia: N. W. Ayer & Son, 1914), 469; Hansen, *My Minneapolis,* 11.

20. *Skandinaven,* May 2, 1916, Dec. 30, 1939; *Decorah-Posten,* Dec. 30,

1939; Ayer & Son, *American Newspaper Annual and Directory* (1914), 187, 276; Hansen, "*Skandinaven* and the John Anderson Publishing Company," 63, 65; on 63–64, M. C. Henningsen in an interview suggested some of the causes of publishing decline. Soike, *Norwegian Americans and the Politics of Dissent,* 119–21, quote 21.

21. Lovoll, "*Decorah-Posten,*" 83, 93–94, 96–97, 99; *Decorah-Posten,* Apr. 1, 1913, Feb. 10, 1915, Sept. 7, 1934; Anna T. Rosendahl, Paul E. Rosendahl, and Georgia Rosendahl interviews, June 13, 1975; N. W. Ayer & Son, *American Newspaper Annual Directory* (Philadelphia: N. W. Ayer & Son, 1925), 247, 533.

22. Einar Niemi, "Anna Dahl Fuhr—meløyjenta som ble avisdronning i Amerika," in *Meløy. Den stille fjerding. Årbok for Meløy Historielag* (Bodø, Norway: Meløy Historielag, 1994), 12–25; "Jørgen Edvart Jansen Fuhr," biographical sketch by Anna Teodora Dahl Fuhr, Gjerset Collection, NAHA Archives; *Fergus Falls Ugeblad,* Feb. 26, 1930; *Minneapolis Tidende,* Feb. 26, 1930; *Duluth Skandinav,* Feb. 1, 1918, Oct. 14, 1927; *Superior Tidende,* Dec. 20, 1935.

23. *50 Years of Progress, 1887–1937, Superior Tidende and the Duluth Skandinav,* Nov. 1937; *Duluth Skandinav,* Dec. 18, 1925, May 21, Dec. 31, 1926; *Superior Tidende,* Feb. 4, Nov. 4, 1927; Matti Kaups, "Norwegian Immigrants and the Development of Commercial Fisheries along the North Shore of Lake Superior: 1870–1895," in Naess, *Norwegian Influence on the Upper Midwest,* 21–34.

24. *Duluth Skandinav,* Oct. 14, 21, 1927, Jan. 4, Sept. 27, 1929; Lovoll, "History of Norwegian-language Publications in North Dakota," 26, 29–31, 100–104; Einar E. Fekjar to author, June 18, 1968; Lovoll, *A Folk Epic,* 178–79.

25. Lloyd Hustvedt, *Rasmus Bjørn Anderson: Pioneer Scholar* (Northfield, MN: NAHA, 1966), 3–4, 12–13, 57, 89, 93, 168–71, 201, 228–29, 230–34; Wist, *Norsk-Amerikanernes Festskrift,* 114–16.

26. Hustvedt, *Rasmus Bjørn Anderson,* 235, 236–37, 249–50, 256; *Amerika og Norden,* Oct. 12, 1898; *Amerika,* June 5, 1901, Oct. 17, 1902, Jan. 3, Feb. 6, Mar. 6, 1903, Jan. 1, Sept. 30, 1904, Nov. 13, 1908; Ingrid Semmingsen, "Who Was Herm. Wang?" *Norwegian-American Studies* 31 (1986): 215–43. Ole S. Hervin obituary, *Minneapolis Tidende,* Nov. 4, 1920.

27. *Amerika,* Dec. 13, 1907, Mar. 20, Nov. 13, 1908, Jan. 1, June 4, 1909, Apr. 22, 1910, Aug. 14, Sept. 15, 1911, June 2, Aug. 18, 1916, Apr. 6, 1917, June 28, Sept. 20, 1918, Dec. 19, 1919, Jan. 9, 1920, July 28, 1922.

28. *Amerika,* Nov. 18, 1910; Wist, *Norsk-Amerikanernes Festskrift,* 157–60; Øverland, *The Western Home,* 226; Karsten Roedder, *Av en Utvandreravis' Saga,* vol. II (New York: Norsemen's Federation, New York Chapter, 1966), 27–28, 35.

29. Roedder, *Av en Utvandreravis' Saga,* II:39–41, 42–44, 78–81, 94, 101, 102–3, 223, quotes 35, 40, 81; Rygg, *Norwegians in New York,* 140–41; *Thirteenth Census,* 1910; *Ayer & Son's American Newspaper Annual Directory* (1910), 576; Ayer & Son, *American Newspaper Annual Directory* (1925), 689; *Nordisk Tidende,* July 8, 1920, Aug. 25, 1921; *Norway Times,* Sept. 12, 1991. *Nordisk Tidende* expressed some concern about a competitor, a second *Norges-Posten,* launched in Brooklyn by Harald Wold

in May 1924, but after examining the first issue did not consider it a serious threat. The new weekly continued publication until Feb. 1933.

30. Qualey, *Norwegian Settlement,* 190–91; *Thirteenth Census,* 1910; *Pacific Skandinaven,* Nov. 10, Dec. 22, 29, 1904, Nov. 9, 16, 29, 1905, Mar. 29, Nov. 29, 1906, June 20, 1907, Jan. 2, 1908, Jan. 29, 1909, Sept. 30, Oct. 28, 1910, Oct. 25, 1912, July 20, 1917, Dec. 12, 1919; *The Northman,* Apr. 29, 1920.

31. Qualey, *Norwegian Settlement,* 193; *Thirteenth Census,* 1910; Wist, *Norsk-Amerikanernes Festskrift,* 153–54, 157. Wist incorrectly gives 1906 as the time of founding of *Spokane Skandinav.* He has the added information that Marken for a few months in 1904–5 published the weekly *Norge* (Norway) in Stoughton, Wisconsin. *Spokane Skandinav,* Sept. 19, 26, Oct. 10, 1896, Dec. 4, 1914, Jan. 8, 1915, June 2, 1916, Mar. 23, Apr. 27, 1917, Jan. 25, 1918; Dieserud, "Den norske presse i Amerika," 179.

32. *Everett Ekko,* Nov. 16, 30, Dec. 7, 1906, Jan. 11, July 26, Aug. 30, Sept. 13, 1907, Oct. 24, Nov. 7, 21, 1908.

33. *Ayer & Son's American Newspaper Annual Directory* (1910), 931; Wist, *Norsk-Amerikanernes Festskrift,* 152–53, 166; *Everett Ekko,* Apr. 12, 1907, Sept. 11, Nov. 21, 1908; *Vestkysten,* July 12, 1929; *Western Viking,* Dec. 18, 25, 1931, Jan. 1, 8, 15, 1932; *Vestkysten,* Mar. 22, 1928, printed Einar Finsand's obituary.

34. Ayer & Son, *American Newspaper Annual Directory* (Philadelphia: N. W. Ayer & Son, 1929), 1131; Lovoll, "*Washington Posten,*" 168–69, 171, 173–74, 182, quote 171–72; Hansen, "*Washington Posten,*" 32–34; *Trønderlagets Aarbok, 1940—1941,* 59; *Washington Posten,* Sept. 17, 1905, Sept. 30, Nov. 1, 1912, May 13, 1938; *Nordisk Tidende,* July 30, 1925; biographical sketch of Gunnar Lund, Gjerset Collection, NAHA Archives.

35. Andersen, "The Centennial of 1925," *Rough Road to Glory,* 203–13; *Vestkysten* (*Tacoma Tidende*), Jan. 20, 27, 1928; *Minneapolis Tidende,* Oct. 2, 1924, May 28, June 11, July 2, 16, 30, 1925, Apr. 11, 1929; *Normanden,* Sept. 12, 1918, Sept. 26, 1924; *Fremad,* May 10, 1923, May 19, 1927; Chrislock, "Name Change and the Church," quote 194; Lovoll, *A Folk Epic,* 148–73.

36. Dieserud, "Den norske presse i Amerika," 154; Andersen, "The Norwegian American Press," 270–71.

Notes to Chapter 7

1. Carl Søyland, "Reflections: Reviving the Norwegian American Press," in Rigmor K. Swensen, tr., *Written in the Sand* (Minneapolis: Western Home Books, 2005), 234, 298; *Nordmands-Forbundet,* Aug. 1927, 328–30; Terje I. Leiren, "Pilgrimage and Propaganda: The American Newspapermen's Tour of Norway in 1927," *Norwegian-American Studies* 35 (2000): 197–216; Lovoll, "Common Historical Memory"; *Minneapolis Tidende,* Aug. 14, 1930. John Arthur Anderson obituary, *Skandinaven,* Sept. 6, 1940. He was the son of John Anderson, the newspaper's founder.

2. Lovoll, *The Promise of America,* 37–38; U.S. Bureau of the Census, *Sixteenth Census, 1940. Population. Mother Tongue* (Washington, D.C.: GPO, 1943); Joshua A. Fishman, *Language Loyalty in the United States* (The Hague: Mouton & Co., 1966), 3–39, 41–42; Backer, *Ekteskap, fødsler og vandringer i Norge,* 158, 184, statistically shows that in the period 1931–40, 5,008 Norwegians emigrated overseas and estimates that

32,000 earlier emigrants returned during these same years.

3. Rygg, *Norwegians in New York,* 126; Roedder, *Av en Utvandreravis' Saga,* I:173–79, 190–91; *Kolonien,* Jan. 6, 12, 1934; Carl Søyland, *Written in the Sand,* 67–77, 78, quotes 67, 78–79; *Symra,* Sept. 10, 1926.

4. *Ny Tid,* Mar. 10, 1922, Jan. 23, 1926, Apr. 26, Sept. 27, Oct. 4, 1930, Apr. 4, 1931, Oct. 6, 1932, Sept. 29, Dec. 1, 8, 1933, Jan. 12, Apr. 6, 20, 27, 1933; Bengston, *On the Left in America,* 139, 140–150.

5. James M. Youngdale, *Third Party Footprint: An Anthology from Writings and Speeches of Midwest Radicals* (Minneapolis, MN: Ross & Haines, Inc., 1966), 54–59: Lovoll, *The Promise of America,* 196–97; Thomas C. Cochran, *The Great Depression and World War II, 1929–1945* (Glenview, IL: Scott, Foresman and Company, 1968), 14–27, 53; *Washington Posten,* Nov. 4, 1932, Oct. 30, 1936.

6. *Minneapolis Tidende,* Nov. 6, 13, 1930, Jan. 1, 1931, Nov. 10, 1932, May 3, Oct. 18, 1934, Mar. 21, 1935; *Fremad,* Oct. 27, Nov. 10, 17, 1932, May 4, 1933, Nov. 8, 1934, Jan. 3, May 9, 16, June 20, Aug. 15, 1935; Hansen, *My Minneapolis,* 247–48.

7. Osmund Gunvaldsen, interview, Fargo, ND, Mar. 16, 1968; *Visergutten,* Sept. 1, 15, 22, 29, Oct. 20, 29, 1927; *Normanden,* Sept. 16, 22, Oct. 6, 13, 1927, May 17, 24, 1928, Aug. 13, 1936, Jan. 7, 1937, Apr. 17, 1941.

8. *Duluth News Tribune,* Oct. 11, 1953, Sept. 4, 1955; *Grand Forks Skandinav,* July 2, Dec. 24, 1937, June 2, Dec. 22, 1939, May 31, Dec. 20, 1940, May 30, 1941; *Normanden,* Aug. 20, 1931, Dec. 5, 12, 1935; Odd Charles Lunde to author, Mar. 8, 16, 1968; Einar E. Fekjar to author, May 2, June 18, 23, 1968; Peder H. Nelson to author, Mar. 10, 1968; O. L. Svidal, interview, Grand Forks, ND, July 25, 1968; Niemi, "Anna Dahl Fuhr," 22–23.

9. *Normanden,* May 18, 1939; *Scandia,* Oct. 25, 1934, Nov. 28, Dec. 19, 1935, Jan. 26, May 25, June 8, 1939, Feb. 8, Apr. 11, May 16, 1940; *Skandinaven,* Nov. 11, 1932, Jan. 2, Nov. 2, 9, 1934, Nov. 6, 1936, Jan. 9, Feb. 23, 1940; *Nordisk Tidende,* July 7, Nov. 3, 1932, July 25, 1933; Roedder, *Av en Utvandreravis' Saga,* I:215–16, 224–25; *Decorah-Posten,* Nov. 4, 1941.

10. *Reform,* Sept. 18, 1941; Roedder, *Av en Utvandreravis' Saga,* I:268–79, quote 272; *Skandinaven,* May 2, 1939; *Decorah-Posten,* May 9, 1939; *Washington Posten,* May 26, 1939, quoted in Hansen; *Washington Posten,* 134–35; *Normanden,* June 8, 15, 1939; Hansen, *My Minneapolis,* 335–45; *Duluth Skandinav,* June 16, 1939. See also Hans Olav and Jen Schive, *Med kronprinsparet—for Norge! 70 dagers ferd gjennem Stjernebannerets land* (Oslo: H. Aschehoug & Co. [W. Nygaard], 1939).

11. Cochran, *The Great Depression and World War II,* 146–58; Hansen, *My Minneapolis,* 345–61, quotes 345; Roedder, *Av en Utvandreravis' Saga,* I:190–91, 300, II:18, 29, 71, 133 cites *Washington Posten,* Jan. 21, 1944; *Visergutten,* Jan. 8, Feb. 26, Mar. 12, 1942; Søyland, *Written in the Sand,* 173–76. In correspondence with the current press and cultural division at the Royal Norwegian Embassy in Washington, D.C., regarding distribution of news releases during World War II, I was informed that the embassy has no relevant information about press activities at that

time. I was left with the following discouraging notice: "In case we in the unlikely event (*mot formodning*) find something, you will hear from us." My information is thus based on the Norwegian American newspapers themselves and secondary sources.

12. Roedder, *Av en Utvandreravis' Saga,* I:129, II:62–64, 77–78, quotes 62, 63, 77; Odd S. Lovoll, "Preface," in Søyland, *Written in the Sand,* xiii-xviii; Jørn-Kr. Jørgensen, "Carl Søyland: Norwegian-American Editor," *The Norseman* 1 (2009): 28–32; Carl Søyland, *Langs Landeveien* (Oslo: Gyldendal Norsk Forlag, 1929), 130–38. Søyland notes, 137, that 280 newspaper ventures had been started in "Norwegian America." This figure conforms well to the present study's findings.

13. *Viking,* Nov. 6, 1941, Jan. 6, 1955, Dec. 19, 1957; *Sanger-Hilsen,* Aug. 1954; *Decorah-Posten,* June 19, 1958; *Nordisk Tidende,* June 19, 1958; Hansen, *My Minneapolis,* 247–48, 282.

14. *Decorah-Posten,* Jan. 31, 1946; Roald G. Lund, *Our Enduring Heritage: The Life of a Norwegian-American Family* (n.p.: Roald G. Lund, 2000), 141–60; Lovoll, *"Washington Posten,"* 169: *Sønner af Norge,* Jan. 1941; *Washington Posten,* Dec. 24, 1943, Mar. 26, 1959; Roedder, *Av en Utvandreravis' Saga,* II:79–80.

15. *Fergus Falls Ugeblad* becoming *Ukeblad* in Jan. 1940 was a consequence of adopting the Norwegian literary forms of 1917. *Fergus Falls Ugeblad,* Jan. 3, 10, Feb. 14, Apr. 10, 1940, Jan. 8, Oct. 22, 1941, Apr. 15, 1942, Dec. 15, 29, 1943, May 24, Nov. 1, 1944, Dec. 18, 1946; *Nordmanns-Forbundet,* Feb. 1965; *Decorah-Posten,* Feb. 18, 1965; Marcus J. Quarum to author, Apr. 20, May 10, July 1968.

16. *Fergus Falls Ugeblad,* Aug. 12, Nov. 11, 1942, Dec. 23, 1943; *Normanden,* Feb. 15, May 10, 1945; *Duluth Skandinav,* Dec. 5, 1941, May 22, 1942, Oct. 13, Nov. 24, 1944; *Visergutten,* Oct. 1, Nov. 26, 1942; *Superior Tidende,* May 7, 14, 1943, Mar. 30, May 11, 18, June 8, 1945; *Washington Posten,* May 11, 1945; *Nordisk Tidende,* Oct. 26, Nov. 16; *Decorah-Posten,* May 10, 1945; Søyland, *Written in the Sand,* 177–78, quote 177; Roedder, *Av en Utvandreravis' Saga,* II:144–46, 158–59, quote 158.

17. *Duluth Skandinav,* Dec. 7, 1945; Odd S. Lovoll, "From Norway to America: A Tradition of Immigration Fades," in Dennis Laurence Eddy, ed., *Contemporary American Immigration* (Boston: Twayne Publishers, 1982), 86–107, quote 100–101; Lovoll, *The Promise of America,* 231–32.

18. *Normanden,* May 18, 1944, July 10, Oct. 23, 30, Nov. 6, 13, 20, Dec. 6, 1947; *Decorah-Posten,* Aug. 21, Sept. 11, 18, 25, Oct. 2, 1947: *Nordmanns-Forbundet,* Sept. 1947, 281; *Visergutten,* Dec. 30, 1943; Søyland, *Written in the Sand,* 232–36; Georg Krane, Counselor Press and Cultural Affairs, Norwegian Embassy, to author, Oct. 18, 1968; Einar E. Fekjar to author, June 18, 1968. Editors participating in the press tour: Carl Søyland, *Nordisk Tidende;* Anna Dahl Fuhr, *Duluth Skandinav;* Einar Lund, *Decorah-Posten;* I. H. Ulsaker, *Normanden;* Sigurd Knudsen, *Visergutten;* O. L. Ejde, *Washington Posten;* Magnus Taløy, *Norrøna* (Canada); Thv. A. Larssen, *Norsk Nytt* (Canada); Carl G. O. Hansen, *Sønner av Norge;* Eilert Hjelmseth, *Norsk Ungdom;* H. C. Caspersen, *Folkebladet;* A. P. Hovland, *Minneapolis Posten;* Herman Jorgensen, *Lutheraneren.*

19. *Minnesota Posten,* Nov. 8, 15, 1956, Oct. 17, 1957, Aug. 28, Dec. 18, 1958, Jan. 9, 1976, June 22, 1978, May 17, 1979; *Northfield News,* Sept. 5, 1963; *Normanden,* Jan. 31, Feb. 7, Mar. 6, 27, 1952; Lovoll, "History of Norwegian-language Publications in North Dakota," 36–37, 105. Debbie Miller, Reference Specialist, Minnesota Historical Society, located "Certificate of Death" for Jenny Alvilde Johnsen, who died in 1982 at the age of eighty-nine, and a brief obituary in *Minneapolis Tribune,* Oct. 17, 1982.

20. *Nordisk Tidende,* Mar. 4, 1948, June 19, 1958, May 10, 1973; *Nordmanns-Forbundet,* Apr., Dec., 1963, May 1976; Lawrence Milton Nelson, ed., *From Fjord to Prairie* (Chicago: Norwegian American Immigration Anniversary Commission, 1976), 18, 21; *Vinland,* Sept. 28, 1978, July 23, 1981, June 27, 1985, May 1, May 29, 1986, Sept. 1, 1987; *Wilmette Life,* Nov. 3, 2005, carries Arve Kilen's obituary. The title "Deilig er Jorden" is the beginning of the hymn "Beautiful Savior." Arthur Gomsrud quoted in *Duluth Skandinav,* July 18, 1958. John A. Lindrup's friends joined forces to publish a final issue of *Viking,* May 17, 1958.

21. *Duluth Skandinav,* Sept. 9, Dec. 23, 1955, Mar. 9, 1956; *Superior Tidende,* Jan. 14, Dec. 23, 1955, Jan. 6, Mar. 9, 1957, Oct. 12, Nov. 16, Dec. 14, 21, 1962, Jan. 4, 11, 1963, May 21, Oct. 9, Nov. 6, Dec. 11, 18, 1964, Aug. 6, 1965; *Duluth Herald,* Mar. 21, 1978; *Duluth News Tribune and Herald,* Oct. 10, 1982.

22. *Decorah-Posten,* Sept. 19, 1963, Dec. 28, 1972; Lovoll, "*Decorah-Posten,*" 91–92, 100; Erling Innvik to author, dated Feb. 6, 1976.

23. *Washington Posten,* Mar. 26, May 22, June 5, 1959, May 26, 1961; Lovoll, "*Washington Posten,*" 170; Hansen, "*Washington Posten,*" quote 145; *Western Viking,* June 9, 1961, Jan. 8, 1964, Oct. 6, 1967, Jan. 16, Aug. 14, 1970, Mar. 12, 1971, Feb. 27, 1976, July 27, Sept. 7, 1990; *Western Viking,* May 6, 2005.

24. *Nordisk Tidende,* Dec. 10, 1959, Jan. 4, 1973, Oct. 9, 16, 1975, June 24, July 1, 29, Aug. 19, 26, 1982; Roedder, *Av en Utvandreravis' Saga,* II: 307–8, 327–29, 335–37; biographical information on Sigurd Daasvand supplied by Harald Daasvand, May 14, 2009.

25. *Nordisk Tidende,* Dec. 28, 1983; *Norway Times,* Jan. 5, June 21, 1984; *Decorah-Posten,* Dec. 28, 1972; *Western Viking,* Sept. 7, 1990, Oct., 20, 27, Nov. 17, Dec. 8, 2006; *Norwegian American Weekly,* Dec. 15, 2006, Jan. 26, 2007; *The Norseman* (Nov. 1990): 39; *News of Norway,* Jan. 19, 2001; Schneider, "German-American Press Today," 257–70; Kathleen Hjørdis Knudsen served as *Western Viking*'s last editor and publisher. Information on newspaper circulation from Kim Nesselquist, Apr. 23, 2009. Jake Moe is editor-in-chief of *Norwegian American Weekly;* Tiffanie Davis serves as managing editor in Washington and Berit Hessen as managing editor in New York. In 2005, in connection with the centennial anniversary of the dissolution of the Swedish-Norwegian Union in 1905, "The Friends of Norway" in Congress secured the Norwegian American Foundation an "earmark" appropriation of $1 million.

26. See Lovoll, *The Promise Fulfilled;* Bureau of the Census, *Twenty-second Census 2000.* See appendices 1, 2, and 3.

Index

Page numbers in *italic* refer to illustrations

Illustration Credits

Images of newspapers on pages 11, 30, 104, 156, 161, 165, 209, 244, 274, 330, 331 courtesy St. Olaf College

Images on pages 8 (masthead), 26, 39, 75, 209 (photo), 244 (photo), 285 (portrait) courtesy the Norwegian-American Historical Association

page 4: reprinted from Johan Hambro, ed., *De tok et Norge med seg* (Oslo: Nordmanns-Forbundet, 1957)

page 8: portrait from Wisconsin Historical Society, WHi-72533

page 13: portrait reprinted from Knud Langeland, *Nordmændene i Amerika* (Chicago: J. Anderson, 1888), provided by the National Library of Norway, Norwegian-American Collection

page 46: Vesterheim Norwegian-American Museum, Decorah, IA

page 54: Norwegian-American Collection, National Library of Norway, Oslo

page 59: courtesy of Luther College Archives, Decorah, IA

page 67: photo by Andrew Dahl. Wisconsin Historical Society, WHi-4243

pages 85, 228, 264, 285: images of newspapers in author's collection

pages 104, 149: portraits from Johannes B. Wist, ed., *Norsk-Amerikanernes Fesskrift* (Decorah, IA: The Symra Company, 1914), courtesy Nordmanns-Forbundet, Oslo, Norway

page 109: Minnesota Historical Society collections

pages 120 and 121: Otter Tail County Historical Society, Fergus Falls, MN

page 134: from Jon Thallaug and Rolf H. Erickson, *Our Norwegian Immigrants* (Oslo: Dreyer, 1978)

page 165: portrait from the Norwegian-American Collection, National Library of Norway, Oslo

page 193: University of Washington Libraries, Special Collections, UW457

page 215: Norwegian-American Collection, National Library of Norway, Oslo, courtesy Nordmanns-Forbundet

page 255: from Peer Strømme, *Erindringer* (Minneapolis: Augsburg Publishing House, 1923)

page 274: portrait from the Norwegian-American Collection, National Library of Norway, Oslo, courtesy Nordmanns-Forbundet

page 299: from the Collection of the Nordic Heritage Museum, Seattle, WA, 1997.048.003

page 316: courtesy Fuhr family via Professor Einar Niemi, University of Tromsø, Norway

page 326: courtesy J. R. Christianson, Decorah, IA

page 335: courtesy Nordmanns-Forbundet, Oslo, Norway

page 345: courtesy *Norway Times*, New York

Norwegian Newspapers in America was designed and set in Escrow
by Judy Gilats at Peregrine Graphics Services, St. Paul, Minnesota.
Printed by Sheridan Books, Inc., Chelsea, Michigan.